WINCHELL EXCLUSIVE

"Things That Happened to Me—and Me to Them"

by

Walter Winchell

Introduction by ERNEST CUNEO

PRENTICE-HALL, INC.
Englewood Cliffs, New Jersey

Dedicated
to all the
skeletons
in your
closets and mine

---

10 9 8 7 6 5 4 3 2 1

Library of Congress Cataloging in Publication Data
Winchell, Walter.
    Winchell exclusive.
    Autobiography.
    Includes index.
    1. Winchell, Walter, 1897-1972. I. Title.
PN4874.W67A38   1975   070'.92'4 [B]   75-16316
ISBN 0-13-960286-0

CONTENTS

★

INTRODUCTION

by Ernest Cuneo

Nine out of ten American adults heard or read Walter Winchell between his 9:00 P.M. Sunday night broadcast and his famed Monday Morning Column. His readers per day averaged 50,000,000, a column-reading total of 300,000,000 per week. By comparison the major political parties each totaled 5 million pieces of literature in a two-month campaign, much of which weren't read. Thus, in one week, Winchell could fire a broadside thirty times heavier than both political parties combined in the two-month Presidential Campaign. His almost daily broadsides for President Roosevelt for two years were a major factor in blasting FDR into a Third Term.

His radio greeting, "Good Evening, Mr. and Mrs. America—from border to border and coast to coast, and all the ships at sea" was literally true. From cowboys on the range to Maine lobster fishermen, the nation stopped what it was doing to listen to him. After his alliance with FDR's Palace Guard, the nation's capital held its breath while he dictated American public opinion, a matter of life and death to political Washington. Every focal point of decision—foreign governments, ally and foe alike; Wall Street financiers, Pittsburgh steel barons, Detroit auto magnates, AFL/CIO headquarters—monitored him. They had to: his broadcast contained the next week's headlines—among other things, the White House agenda for the next week. Also, to their fury, he was covered most fully by the vast news services, AP, UP, and INS, because he announced the headlines of the news stories they'd have to carry.

He was scarcely conscious of this. He was not interested in the story, only the headline. He didn't give a damn about anything else. Political consequences and reverberations he left behind in his wake like an ocean liner. He was not many different persons, as most of us are. Body and soul, he was one thing: Walter Winchell, Headline Hunter.

An editor is to a writer what a jockey is to a horse. Tam Mossman, who edited this book, asks his authors to do the impossible. He asked me to race through Winchell's life and times in less than 5,000 words. Impossible, but I'll try.

☆

World War I generated a terrific patriotic ecstacy approaching religious hysteria. The War passed, but the frenzy didn't. In the 20's, Americans sought to continue the ecstacy of mass hysteria through mass hypnosis, and at a high pitch. Hysteria is fun, hypnosis an addiction. Put them together and you have, to coin a phrase, the Mazeppa Complex.

Byron immortalized Ivan Mazeppa, a young Polish nobleman whom a Count caught in bed with his Countess. (In those days, this was a serious matter.) The Count ordered Mazeppa tied naked to a wild horse. The horse galloped all the way from Poland down to the Ukraine. There, it dropped dead. The World War put a similar, galloping wild horse rhythm into many American hearts.

I remember the day I picked up the Mazeppa Complex—March of 1918, when I was twelve. The Great Spring Drive of the German Armies was driving back the Allies. Field Marshal Haig declared, "My back is to the wall." If the Yanks were coming, it was clear they'd have to come fast. High on the ridge of our New Jersey town we could see it all: over at the foot of the Great Notch, hundreds of Lackawanna troop trains streaked for the Hoboken piers. Huge Pennsylvania locomotives tore up from the South. The Erie thundered in the valley.

Suddenly the railroad crossing bells started ringing in mad alarm. The gates hurried down. Tearing down the Erie Mainline came bellowing breakneck trains, with all tracks cleared to the Jersey City piers. There was a gold and blood-red flag on the first engine, stiff and taut in the wind—the United States Marines of the Second Division, United States Army. I stood rooted, transfixed. The battle rhythm hypnotized me, and millions of others, too. It was a craving, a drive. I never got over it.

In the 20's, similarly, New York City's basic rhythm was like the driving pistons of those high speed locomotives. The pile drivers ramming down steel girders; the chatter of the riveters; the triphammers battering out a skyline. Above them, the sullen roar of newspaper presses, the bark of gangsters' Tommy guns, the moan of ambulances, wails of police sirens; below street level, the crash and trembling of the subways.

Walter Winchell captured that rhythm and raised it by inventing a new style—sharp staccato. For example, when other newspapers wrote columns on the elaborate funeral of Champion Fight Promoter Tex Rickard at the Frank Campbell Funeral Home, Winchell simply rapped out: "Frank Campbell boxed Tex Rickard at the Garden for ten grand."

Walter created New Yorkese by recording it. The words of New Yorkese are hard and clipped. Like machine gun bullets, they're fired in short, sharp bursts. New Yorkers are terse because they're tense, and they like to be. Sharp and terse himself, Winchell strove to be sharper and terser, because he feared losing his lead to someone sharper and terser than he. So he was tense all the time, fearing he wasn't tense enough.

He said tenseness was the difference between a racehorse and a cow. He acted like a racehorse, trembling to get to the post and break a record every time out. He was not a gentle spirit. He was more war-horse than thoroughbred. When he was running, which was practically always, he was the most savage of gut fighters. But if Winchell was pitiless in his drive after the headlines, he was pitiless upon no man more than himself. He was out to win.

Nine newspapers and three major networks were then fighting for the headlines. It was a journalistic free-for-all. There was no second money; winner take all. No one had to tell Winchell not to be a gallant horse fallen: the way not to get trampled by the onrush was to take the lead and keep it. So he lashed himself from dusk to dawn.

It would be a gross understatement to say he was dedicated to his work. It was a driving, demoniac obsession. It grabbed Winchell from the time he opened his eyes in mid-afternoon till he closed them in the mists of dawn. This has a price. The penalty of concentration-in-depth is narrow side vision. By analogy, an R.A.F. pilot in a dogfight over France didn't get much of a glimpse of the beauty of Chartres Cathedral. There was no method to Winchell's madness; there was madness to his method. He knew what he was doing. He was what he was, and he didn't want to be anything else. On the contrary, he strove to be more of what he was, the world's greatest reporter.

I sought out Winchell for FDR. This explains much of his life there-after. Therefore, it's a necessary part of Winchell's own story.

Politically, Roosevelt and the New Deal were in desperate plight as 1937 neared its end. The President turned to the Palace Guard, com-posed of a half dozen Harvard men and a few Columbians. In the New Deal's great crusade (God must have been astonished at times), we were FDR's Right Honorable Company of Gentlemen Expendables. Be-lieve it or not, any one of us would have laid down his life for FDR and the Cause.

The Palace Guard was headed by Thomas Gardiner Corcoran, famed as "Tommy the Cork," ex-law Secretary to Mr. Justice Holmes, and a whiz's whiz of a Wall Street financial lawyer. At thirty-two, President Hoover had appointed him counsel to the Reconstruction Finance Corporation. Under FDR "R.F.C." blossomed into the world's greatest bank. FDR yanked Tom out to team him up with Ben Cohen, whose legal mind was as hard as a diamond and twice as brilliant. Ben also had the gentlest of hearts.

Tom and Ben drafted the basic New Deal legislation: Securities and Exchange Act, Public Utilities Holding Act, Social Security Act, et cetera. Speaker Sam Rayburn considered them the best single legal mind in history. The New Deal legislation rewrote the Constitution, saving not only the country, but capitalism, according to such widely different experts as Professor Eliot Morrison, Arthur Krock, and Bernard Baruch.

This is relevant to Winchell's power. Following their legal victories, FDR drafted Tom for White House service. From mid-1937 to mid-1941, Tommy the Cork, for all practical purposes, was Chief Engineer of the United States. He reversed the President's court defeat. Tom sent Black, Frankfurter, Douglas, Murphy, and Jackson up to the court. (They had hardly settled in their chairs before they started to feud to the death among themselves.) His bare two-room office, Room 1017 in the grim, grimy R.F.C. Building at Pennsylvania and H Street, was the center of power in Washington. The contents of Room 1017 were some bare tables, a few ordinary chairs, no rugs, but more telephones than a Wall Street brokerage: a Boiler Room. The key telephone ran through the White House switchboard. "Operator 306, White House Calling" carries great authority. We used it a lot. FDR knew it.

Room 1017's switchboard was the center of a vast intelligence system. Into this, we plugged Winchell's line. We didn't like to do it, but we had to. The President precipitated the necessity.

Roosevelt, a great champion who should have known better, was suffering from victory intoxication brought on by carrying 46 of the 48 states in the 1936 election. Out of a clear sky, he launched an all-out fight against the Supreme Court. He not only blew his smashing victory, he blew the country apart, and with it, the Democratic Party.

Tom and I came to know each other during the Court Fight. Chairman James Farley had appointed me Associate Counsel of the Democratic National Committee. Since I was an experienced New York reporter, Charley Michelson (the National Committee press chief) and I did a lot of ghosting for the Senators supporting the President. Ghosting is the reverse of playwriting; a ghost must fit the play to the actor. Tom Corcoran and I wrote a lot of scripts together.

At first I couldn't figure Tom out. He looked and acted like the great middlewight Mickey Walker, the Toy Bulldog—Irish, boyish. Bursting with exuberance, Tom had a political knockout punch in either mitt and could hit from any angle. It never occurred to him we could lose. The political pros first thought of him as Little Lord Fauntleroy, because he had a baby face. In no time at all, they came to think of him as Baby Face Nelson.

The worst of the Court Fight was that the Democratic Party was nearing revolt. Farley had lined up the Democratic regulars behind the President, but like Alexander the Great's army, they didn't want any more conquests. They wanted the rewards of the 1936 victory and had had enough of the New Deal Crusade. From their standpoint, they were right; from ours, so were we. (President Lincoln and General Lee were convinced they were absolutely right. They were equally honorable, equally consecrated. Result: 600,000 dead.) I saw Civil War was coming and strung along with the President. But time was on the side of the Democratic regulars. Two short years were all they had to wait; FDR's second term would expire. We had to attack.

Tom got the President to name his successor: Robert H. Jackson of Jamestown, N. Y., an excellent lawyer in the Justice Department. At year's end, Tom and FDR decided the best way to carry the White House was for Bob to capture the Governorship of New York State. This meant forcing Jackson on the New York Democrats.

The President forced the Democratic Party to accept Bob as speaker at their annual banquet. FDR knew they didn't want him. All the better, because it was an order: "Growl you may, but go you must." I was put in charge of the Jackson campaign. I went to see Adolph A. Berle, New Yorker, great mind, close friend, and my professor at Columbia. "Adolph," I said, "it's going to be rough. The Koran or the sword."

Adolph said, "You mean it's the Cor-Koran or the sword." We both laughed like hell. Adolph was right.

I went back to New York with no illusions. FDR and Farley together couldn't carry the Tammany fortress back in '32. I told Tom that unless Jackson had the President's artillery and Farley's infantry, we didn't have a prayer. Even then it would be tough, very. Tom said he'd talk to the President.

FDR said he'd pass the word to Farley, but The Word didn't come. The silence in New York City was deafening. We were in an ambush.

Two days before the banquet I called Tom, told him Farley hadn't passed The Word, that it was annihilation unless Farley did. FDR asked Farley to the White House the next day. The New York silence deepened.

The banquet was at the Commodore. I spotted Farley in the Rotunda and laid it on the line: "Jim, you were at the White House yesterday, and the President talked to you about Jackson."

Farley, characteristically, also laid it on the line: "Yes, he did. He asked me what I thought of it." (Some Presidential bombardment, I thought to myself. Away all boats.) "I told the President Bob hasn't a chance," Farley continued. "The reason is that Bob could walk from the Battery to Buffalo, and no one would recognize him." Farley was right. But the fact was, Tammany was silent because the President was.

The Tammany chiefs stalked by me. I felt like going down to Bellevue to be examined for leprosy. Bob was a political corpse before he started talking. (Parenthetically, I mutinied later that spring, for good reason: Harry Hopkins decided he wanted to be President. The President agreed to the Hopkins experiment. Harry Hopkins had become the Little Brother of the Rich. By posing as the Big Brother of the Poor. Historians to the contrary notwithstanding, Harry Hopkins groveled his way to power. By himself, he couldn't have gotten out of a greenhouse with a sledgehammer.)

I went to Washington to tell Tom we couldn't name a successor to FDR unless he was known to the American people. There was only one person who could give instant recognition to a dark horse candidate: Walter Winchell. I didn't know him personally at the time.

Tom bitched a bit about this. He said Winchell was notches below the dignity of the White House. I said, "There are vast numbers of citizens below the dignity of the White House. But the bozos vote. They hear Winchell and they buy the product he advertises." I quoted the Ancient Greek, "Necessity is above the gods themselves." That's how I got the O.K.

I called Lenny Lyons at the New York *Post* and asked him to bring Winchell over to "21." Winchell's Throne Room was at the Stork, but I didn't want to meet him there. It would be noticed, and I always liked to keep out of sight: anonymity is freedom.

Winchell came to "21." I opened with an amenity: "Georgie Jessel was reminiscing about your days in vaudeville together the other night."

"The hell with that." Winchell snorted. "That son of a bitch started to reminisce when he was eight years old. What's going to happen tomorrow?"

I slammed it on the barrel head. "Would you be willing to help President Roosevelt?"

Winchell's eyes went ice-blue cold. "Goddamn it," he said, "I thought I had. What's going to happen tomorrow?"

I am a guy who will take "yes" for an answer. I looked around the room and spotted the Marquis of Lothian, British Ambassador at Washington. Strikingly handsome, Lothian was regarded in the British Foreign

Service as a crown jewel: polished and hard. I knew Lothian; I presented Winchell.

Winchell came to a point at once. "Lord Lothian, what is Great Britain going to do about Hitler?" A duel was on.

"Mr. Winchell, we shall try to fatten the tiger without strengthening him."

Winchell replied, "I've seen some big tigers and some little tigers. I've never seen a fat one."

Lothian's eyes widened ever so little. So did mine. I came to a conclusion which I never altered: I believe Winchell had an I.Q. of brilliant proportions, nearly the equal of an Einstein. Actually, a formal education might have ruined Winchell's razor-sharp mind. Learning, said Ambrose Bierce, is that type of ignorance which distinguishes the educated. This mishap avoided Walter. He never saw things as Shakespeare or Keats, he saw them as Winchell saw them. And he saw a lot.

"Mind if I report British policy?" Winchell asked. Lothian agreed, of course. We withdrew. I ordered an orange juice with a jigger of cognac. Walter asked why. I answered that the cognac would keep me awake, and the orange juice would replace the vitamins the alcohol consumed.

Winchell's column covered British policy in one sentence. His lead was, "Britain will marry Hitler in the fall. The marriage will blow up in a World War." Then turning to more important news, he notified Broadway that the new drink was "Orange juice and cognac. Sockoes in the vitamins the alcohol K.O.'s."

Thousands ordered the drink. I asked Columbia's leading nutritionist; he said the theory was sheer rot, the worst nonsense he ever heard. But people guzzled it for months.

After the meeting at "21," I saw Walter for hours daily. He talked incessantly, always about himself. "For God's sake, Walter," I finally exploded, "don't you ever talk about anything but yourself?"

Winchell: "Name a more interesting subject."

Newswise, I was complementary to both Walter and the Palace Guard. I ran to the fires with the older leaders of the Avant-Garde Bar: Civil Liberties Giant Morris Ernst, Jerome Frank, Randolph Paul, Judge Ferdinand Pecora and I met for sundown martinis almost daily at the Lafayette Bar in the Village. Practically every prominent author and practically all labor leaders sought their advice. (Parenthetically, my own obsession was to stop child labor, to get the little boys out of the coal breakers and the little girls out of the cotton mills. Tom and Ben accomplished this by brilliantly using the Interstate Commerce Clause to break the Tenth Amendment.)

Drew Pearson was extremely close to all of this group. Oddly, I knew Drew longer than any other. He had been my instructor at Columbia. He was a war-horse, not a racehorse like Walter. Winchell got his fair share of the news from this group.

Winchell developed a blind adoration for FDR. I think I understood the President better than most. The New York chorus girls had a wise saying: "If you've been loved forever—for three months—it's a good deal." When Stage-Door Johnnies tell a girl they'll love her forever, they really think they will. FDR loved his favorites forever—for about six months. Men who believed him swore he had deceived them. This wasn't true: FDR was the greatest political Stage-Door Johnnie of them all. When he was conning them, he was conning himself more. Politicians don't understand this. This is why there are more broken hearts in politics than in chorus lines.

National and international news poured into Winchell. Within weeks, his rating soared to 150 percent, more on one network than the President himself got on all three, and Walter broadcast far more often. There was recriprocal leverage: his broadcast advertised the columns, and vice versa.

August came. The calendar was killing us. Incredibly, the President decided on the Purge, asking regular Democrats to defeat the Democratic Senators and Congressmen who had opposed him in the primaries. I knew Roosevelt couldn't possibly incite the ranks to revolt; they'd be politically slaughtered when his term ended. But the orders came down, and everything was thrown into the assault. We got killed.

The midnight the Purge failed, Tom and I met alone in 1017. Tom said, "We've got to run the President in 1940. He has only one real opponent, the Third Term Tradition. We've got to get the people used to the idea, and get the Tradition talked to death by 1940." We agreed Winchell was the guy to do it. That weekend I wrote a speech for Governor Frank Murphy of Michigan calling for a Third Term. Winchell blasted the "Draft Roosevelt" trumpet from "Border to border and coast to coast. . . ." Winchell's broadcast was the last shot of the Palace Guard. We were lost unless the Winchell blast developed a counterattack.

We didn't have long to wait. Outside, the network phone board was jammed, lit up like the proverbial Christmas tree. The President's opposition within and without the Party went absolutely berserk. A firestorm of protest developed. We nearly collapsed with relief. The enemy cannot be destroyed unless he is developed. In one week, Winchell had developed every last ounce of resistance to FDR in the country. We had nearly two full years to destroy it. We did.

It amazes me that the historians have missed this. Practically all of them say the President hadn't made up his mind. They miss the point: the great debate on the Third Term which Winchell detonated *was* the Third Term campaign itself. The President didn't have to lift a finger. Winchell would proclaim and proclaim, FDR would deny and deny, then Winchell would proclaim again. The President also knew that no other Democrat's hat could go into the ring while there was doubt about the presence of his. Winchell kept throwing his in for him. Of course the President denied it: it kept the ring clear.

A vast comedy developed. Despite my repeated assurances, Roosevelt's denials began to shake Walter's confidence. "Ernie," he anxiously said to me several times, "do you know how far out on the limb I am?"

"Hell, yes. I put you there. Cheer up, it's going to get longer."

His anxiety turned to desperation. "Are you sure?" he'd ask. "Well, when's he gonna announce that he'll run?"

"Look, Walter," I wanted to say, "you *are* the Third Term campaign." But for once in his life, he underestimated his own importance; the guy was far more powerful than he knew.

The cleared ring left a wide opening. We exploited it. We made coagulation of resistance impossible by having Winchell nominate Favorite Sons. We must have nominated a couple of dozen. It was vast fun.

Winchell, after intoning that the President would run, would pause and archly add, "But if he doesn't—watch Governor Stark of Missouri." To be mentioned for President is a big honor and big news out in the sticks. The "nominee" would be swamped with telephone calls. I can't remember how many were "nominated" by broadcast and column: Byrd of Virginia, Wheeler of Montana, Earle of Pennsylvania, Bankhead of Alabama, Bailey of North Carolina, Barkley of Kentucky. It got so ridiculous that *The New Yorker* commented, "Nominate your friends for the Presidency. It makes a harmless, inexpensive and delightful little Christmas present."

Walter was never fully aware of this tremendous political wallop. Two incidents in Tam Mossman's edited manuscript prove, I think, that I was right.

Walter mentions that Joe Kennedy gave him the scoop that Lindbergh's report on Nazi air superiority went to Prime Minister Chamberlain just before Munich. Actually, Kennedy was proud of his part in it.

To be blunt, I wasn't proud of the Ambassador's part in it. I cross-examined him: "Joe, you are sure Lindbergh's memo was the decisive factor?"

His answer was, "Yes."

"Then Chamberlain compromised because he thought Hitler was Great Britain's military superior?"

He said, "Yes, of course. Why not?"

"What of the Royal Navy?"

He answered, "Capable of defending only one of three strategic areas. Home Waters, the Mediterranean, or the Far East."

I asked, "Had decision been made?"

"Yes."

"Which area?"

He answered, "Home waters, of course."

He seemed puzzled by the question. I asked, "What about Australia?"

"Vulnerable to any two capital ships of the Japanese Navy."

"Very interesting. Thanks." I turned to Walter and said, "Walter, you've got a hell of a story."

Walter asked, "Joe, can I use it?"

Joe said, "Sure, why not?"

I couldn't believe my ears. It was diplomatic dynamite. Joe left, and Walter tapped out the story. I insisted it be held until Joe got back to Palm Beach and that it be read to him.

Joe okayed it and Walter instantly sent it out as a special headline story. Joe looked deflated when he came down a couple of days later. Walter asked, "How did you like the story, Joe?"

Joe said, "I liked it. But London didn't, and Australia is raging."

I wanted to ask Joe his question, "Why not?" In my opinion, that unforgivable indiscretion marked the end of Joe Kennedy's usefulness as American Ambassador. Never liked much, he became the bane of Churchill. FDR dumped him later, but he was by-passed long before.

Walter merely mentions that Adolph Berle said he was responsible for re-arming the nation. The fact is that Assistant Secretary of State Berle called me, urgently, to request Walter's assistance. He told me that he, Secretary Hull, and Assistant Secretary of War Johnson were called to secret conference at the White House. The President said we desperately needed a two-ocean Navy. We had no Atlantic Fleet. Congress was balking about providing one. Fifty billions were needed. Berle asked me to ask Walter's assistance. Walter needed no urging. By air and by ink, he demanded that all of his followers sit down and write their Congressmen and Senators "without fail. Now. When I stop talking." In the first week, 300,000 letters hit the Hill. Later, 400,000 followed. I was told that the congressional post office was swamped with 1,200,000 letters, not only beating down the opposition, but moving the President's candidacy over his collapsed opposition.

As France fell, Walter got his Navy: 35 new battleships, 20 carriers, 88 cruisers, 378 destroyers, 180 submarines, and 15,000 planes. Unequivocally, both State and the White House credited Walter with the victory.

Walter went out on the U.S.S. *North Carolina* on her trial run. He was deeply impressed by her broadside. With his childlike wonder he said, "Ernie, you have no idea of the noise. And the belt! It knocked the ship ten feet sidewise." He never mentioned that if it hadn't been for him, there wouldn't have been a U.S.S. *North Carolina* at all. I don't think he'd have given a damn. The White House could have the Navy. All he wanted was the headline, not the story. Actually, that compounded his power. After he skimmed the White House cream, the rest of the scooped newsmen had to deliver the milk. They didn't like it. But Winchell also got his President, too—FDR was swept back into the White House in the 1940 election. It was a smashing victory. The President even carried the coal states not only against the Republicans, but against John L. Lewis, revered leader of the United Mine Workers.

It took longer, but he blasted Senator Bert Wheeler out of Montana. The Winchell vs. Wheeler fight was the worst political Pier Sixer I ever witnessed. Wheeler accused Walter of being in the pay of the British. Winchell bellowed that like Wheeler, he was in their debt. The savagery of their exchanges was transferred to their followers. Tempers became ugly.

An angry mob attacked Wheeler, pelting him with garbage. Walter was delighted. I demanded that he denounce the mob: "If Wheeler gets killed, you'll be held responsible for his death. Call up your boss, Hearst, and ask him. He was blamed for inciting the murder of President McKinley. Ask him how he liked it."

Walter denounced the mob. If he had used as much fervor in demanding a two-ocean Navy, he'd have ended up with a couple of tugboats.

Wheeler declared Walter was in the pay of the New Deal. Livid, Walter, terribly agitated, rushed down to the White House, "Imagine it, Mr. President! Imagine! He says I'm on the payroll of the New Deal."

The President airily asked, "How much income tax did you pay last year, Walter?"

Winchell, puzzled, answered, "$294,000."

xiv

The President said, "Sit down, Walter, you're a partner."

The difference between Winchell and me was that I knew I had the Mazeppa Complex. He didn't; he thought it was the rhythm of the Universe. An immersed fish is not conscious of the sea. However, Walter knew I was in a state of tension approximating his. On broadcast nights, lots of times, he'd cheerfully call out, "Hey Ernie! Those six guys with the white coats who came for me—they want you instead."

He was a perfectionist about words. With Mark Twain, he believed the difference between the right word and the not-quite-right word is the difference between the lightning and the lightning-bug. I looked for a different kind of perfection: the difference between the right and not-quite-right word is a libel suit.

The two objectives conflict, as did we. At first I turned the other cheek, and got slugged. So I punched back, but soon relaxed, because on the hundreds of our bitter exchanges, when he reached the peak of his berserk rage, he caused me riotous laughter. I had noted that he never reached for his gun. Oddly, I don't remember our thousands of quarrels, but I do recall the thousands of laughs.

Walter would rush to his typewriter and furiously pound out a Declaration of Independence addressed TO ALL CONCERNED (which meant me—everyone knew it). He would state his grievance, adding that NO ONE—NO ONE was to interfere with his copy. This he would hand to Tom Velotta, the hapless V.P., who would solemnly pass it on to his crew, who would solemnly read it and hand it to me. I would write some appropriate comment such as "Balls!" and pass it back, where Tom would ponder its great depth and see to it that it got lost.

Walter and I fought so savagely over the years that network president

t by some visiting Hollywood magnates.
fight, that's a production." But for the
.d a single personal quarrel. We fought
it was a bloody draw; neither of us bent

' War, and I would have had a hell of an
le to confine it to this. But rightly or
: tension of believing he was carrying the
:ry time he went to the post. He was the
ously elevate FDR back into the White
er's propaganda chief, down in the gutter
the mud.
:e the Man o' War analogy. He parleyed
1½ minutes of his Sunday Broadcast. He

xv

received $1,500 a minute, $16,500 a broadcast. (No one in FDR's Palace Guard gave a damn about money. As Randolph Paul whimsied, "We never play for such picayune stakes.") Like all great champions, Winchell became increasingly tense as the adrenaline poured into his bloodstream. Man o' War Walter started kicking his stall late Thursday night. He became cantankerous, testy. By Friday night, he had to be held in; he had to be "rated." When he'd read Friday night copy, even if it was good, I learned not to approve. If I did, he'd drive both of us up the wall for the next forty-eight hours, improving the improvements.

But exchanges were sharp. Each of us frequently expressed his opinions of the other's legitimacy. I knew the symptoms, knew them myself: the adrenaline in his pulse was throbbing him up to his "edge" twenty-four hours too early.

Saturday night he was ungovernable. Nothing was good enough. A great deal of the time, we were apart, using long distance. It takes a hell of a whirlwind to throw a five-hour tantrum 1,500 miles from Florida or the 3,000 from Hollywood, but Walter accomplished it. I counter-blasted as best I could, but it was as difficult and impractical as throwing a righthander at a hurricane bombarding you with coconuts. Actually he wasn't raging at me, he was raging to get to the wire. Our Saturday encounter often went to early morning; we'd each limp off, limp, around 3 A.M.

There would be calmer exchanges during Sunday afternoon. He was gathering himself, calmed by the imminence of the contest. We'd meet about seven.

Exactly at 8:58, Walter would enter the broadcasting studio, open his shirt, loosen his belt, open the waistband of his pants and tap on his sound-effects key. I was thrilled. I knew he was going to make another great run. It was like Man o' War bursting out of the chute. Walter went to the whip as he broke from the gate.

Exactly at nine, Ben Grauer, the announcer, would give the one-minute commercial. "The Jergen's Journal, and Walter Winchell of the New York *Daily News,* columnist for the *Mirror* and other newspapers, America's one-man newspaper." While Ben gave the commercial, all studio eyes were riveted on Winchell. The second hand, as it reached the 60 mark, was the starting bell, and Winchell was off—three full minutes with not more than one breath every twenty seconds. He had a 237-word-a-minute pace, and a fighting heart as big as an ale keg.

Ben Grauer broke in for another minute. Winchell, filling his lungs with deep breaths, completely centered on the script, quivered for the takeoff. Again he sprang from the gate. He was superhumanly alert, his gray-blue eyes scanning the words and his sharp, clear pronunciation of each word barking like a Browning.

My desk was opposite his: we faced each other. Libel was small change; I dreaded, needlessly, that he might blunder himself off the air by departing from the precise script. He did go off occasionally, sometimes, I think, for the pure sadistic joy of forcing me to turn on my supercharger. When he did swerve, he'd pause to sneer through the glass as I leaped into action. Clearer than words, his face indicated, *"You* try it for a while, you bastard."

Then the commercial, and back to the home stretch. This was Winchell flailing Winchell, calling on every last raw nerve as he tore down toward the wire. "And that, ladies and gentleman, until next week at the same time, is your New York correspondent, Walter Winchell, who thinks three innings and three terms are not enough for a Babe Ruth or a Franklin D. Roosevelt."

It was over. Winchell would sink back, utterly spent—for a minute or two. But he was not exhausted. In a few minutes, he would be entirely normal, bouncing around again like a rubber ball.

Immediately after the broadcast. he would go to the Stork, whose Cub Room was the jewelcase of international brilliance and accomplishment. Actually, the public was not admitted to this inner sanctum. The important publishers, newspaper and book, the broadcasting tycoons, the bankers' bankers, the Hollywood magnates, all made it a first port of call. ("The people may be terrible," Winchell quipped at Hollywood, "but you meet some wonderful money.")

So did the Hollywood and international talents, particularly in the performing arts. Especially on Sunday nights, after his broadcast, when Emperor Winchell held court from his throne, Table 50. The international *Who's Who* stopped by: everyone from Noel Coward and Maurice Chevalier to Herbert Bayard Swope and Bernie Gimbel; from Sonja Henie and Edith Piaf to Gypsy Rose Lee (a brilliant girl) and Tallulah Bankhead. The aura of "The Cub" was like the paddock at Saratoga or Belmont. In fact, the Cub resembled a Dufy painting of Longchamps on Grand Prix Day—terrific form, terrific grace, and terrific color.

One night, Peggy Hopkins Joyce came in. She had been married six times, and was pondering trying again. One of the New York women said to her, "Hear you're getting married again, Peggy. What's new?"

Peggy blew up, turned to Walter, and said, "Can you imagine those bitches criticizing me for marrying the guys I sleep with?"

"Sure I can," Walter said. "You're giving adultery a bad name."

Walter not only rushed in where angels feared to tread, but knocked

xvii

over the furniture in doing so. But many times he was utterly innocent of any intent to damage people. On one occasion, Hemingway—apparently also a victim of the Mazeppa Complex—was out to break the world's record in deep-sea fishing. He caught several huge ones, all of which trivial news was rocketed around the world. Winchell, honestly believing the story was true, noted, "The secret of Ernest Hemingway's big sea catches is that he reels the fish to within twenty yards of his boat, and then machine-guns them."

Shortly thereafter, Hemingway tore into the Stork wearing, as they used to say there, a toupee on his chest, and offered to take Walter outside. Which invitation Walter coolly declined.

He was ridiculously proud of his gun permit as a mark of special trust, wisely restricted to the few. One night we happened into a gunfight. He had two pistols on him, but wouldn't lend me one. (Damn near got me killed, too, but that's another story.) "Some friend," I railed. "Two-gun Winchell wouldn't lend one to a pal in a crossfire!"

"Not," airily declared the Winch, "if the pal doesn't have a gun permit."

Another night a prominent newsgal came in crying, and sat right alongside us in the Stork. She had had a long affair with an oil magnate who married another girl. He was in the Waldorf Towers with his new wife. After three martinis, she said she was going to kill him. She reached down and opened her pocketbook for another handkerchief. I couldn't help noticing she had a pearl-handled .32.

She excused herself—to the powder room, we thought. After five minutes, I said, "Walter, she had a gun." The cigarette girl checked the powder room. The doorman confirmed that she had rushed out.

We got her address from the Stork's phone operator. Then we tore around to her Park Avenue apartment. Walter rang the bell. She opened the door. Assuming his Mrs.-Winchell's-Little-Boy-Walter approach, Walter eased us in. He could be as soothing as a willowed brook with women, and he often was. He really felt sorry for her. While he was comforting her, I went over, took the revolver from her purse and put it in my pocket. He made her promise she wouldn't do anything rash.

As we went to the door, he asked her to give him the gun. I told him I already had it. We stepped out into the hall. He quietly closed the door. Then he wheeled on me in blazing rage. "Give me that gun," he stormed.

"Here it is, big boy," I said, "What the hell's hit you?"

"Where's your pistol permit, mister?" he rasped. "That's the trouble with you goddamned lawyers. You've just got no respect for the law."

His concern of having brownie points scored on him by "the opposition" was delightful to behold. At the first United Nations Conference at San Francisco, he got up early, around 10:30 A.M., the middle of the night for him. He got his shave and his usual sunlamp, but the barber kept it on too long. He got a slight burn. Not much. He told me about it when we met in the Mark Hopkins lobby. He said it was a natural consequence of being 2,500 miles from Broadway.

When we went outside, a wonderful little Chinese newsboy about eight or nine years old was hawking his papers in perfect English—and selling them hand over fist. Walter waxed sentimental. He said to the lad, "I was a newsboy myself once."

The busy kid said, "What's your paper, mister?"

"And it was a great experience, too," Winchell said.

The kid, working at top speed, said, "What's your paper, mister?"

"And later on, you'll look back on these days as your happiest."

The kid stopped and looked at Winchell. "Mister, is your face hurting you?"

Winchell, astonished, said, "No, why?"

The kid snapped, "Because it's killing me."

I laughed like hell. The kid had "topped" the great Winchell. "Come on," said Winchell. He was in a state.

"What's the hurry?" I said.

"I've got to get this story on the wires right away. I gotta break it myself. Else you'll tell Pearson, and he will." An even darker thought raced through his mind. "Ed Sullivan might get it. C'mon."

I said, "Just a minute, Walter. Mind if I give the kid ten bucks?"

"Make it twenty," Winchell snapped, "It's your dough, you son of a bitch."

One of his newspapers ran a beauty contest. First prize was Winchell showing the winners around New York. They arrived, with a number of chaperones, one of whom reported that one of the girls was ducking out. Walter became taut as a piano wire. He sought the help of Runyon, me, Sherman Billingsley, the Stork doorman and the hat-check girl, and other deep thinkers in solving the mystery. What he didn't tell me was that he had also asked his detective pals to lend a hand.

They located the culprit whom she was seeing. As it happened, it was I. Walter went livid. He asked me if it were true.

I said, "What do you want me to do, plead the Fifth? Of course I'm not going to admit anything. Look, Walter, butt out. Nobody damaged her reputation."

Walter said, "I'm not thinking about her reputation. I'm thinking about *mine*. Suppose the opposition got the story. Wouldn't they love to say 'Winchell's attorney hides romance from Winchell?' " The thought was more than he could bear. But he snapped off and out of it. "Now that I know," he said grandly, "go ahead."

He was deeply moved by his own generosity.

When Walter began attacking Cissy Patterson, I said, "Walter, that's something a gentleman doesn't do."

He took his Little-Boy-Walter insouciant stance: "I'm not a gentleman, and the bastard doesn't live who dares call me that to my face."

One night at Table 50 we were discussing the difference between El Morocco and the Stork. We agreed El Morocco was the base of the idle, untalented rich. The Stork was the racetrack and showplace of the Meritocracy, the winners, the career people of both sexes. I said, "Women are the profession of idle men, and the relaxation of warriors."

"That's a good line," Walter said.

"It's not mine. It's George Bernard Shaw's."

"Well," he said, scribbling it down, "I'll give it some circulation."

Walter is buried in Arizona.

There seems to be a slight confusion about the last days of his journalistic career. I haven't any objection to people saying harsh words about Walter. He deserved many. But for the record, Walter Winchell did not quit. The New York *Daily Mirror* quit, not Walter. As with Mazeppa, it was the carrier, not the man, who failed. For the record, Walter never missed a deadline, and when he was a staffer covering a story, he never left his post until released.

Also for the record, Walter admittedly was not a Great Man. He wasn't a Great Guy, either. But that didn't particularly interest him. What did was that he wanted to be a Great Newsman. That was his driving obsession. He drove himself night and day without mercy to reach that pinnacle, and he did. He became the Greatest of the Great Reporters.

Perhaps God in His infinite mercy will show Mrs. Winchell's Little Boy Walter some of the mercy Little Walter never showed himself.

Walter had a love of jargon, and for none more than Journalese. In Journalese, "30" means "end of copy" and "GOODNIGHT" means your shift is over and you can go home. And so:

"30, GOODNIGHT . . . Walter . . . 30, GOODNIGHT"

and Good Luck

FOREWORD

"THAT'S HOW YOU WRITE YOUR BOOK!"

The late William Bolitho (his best seller was *Twelve Against the Gods*) was a charming chap, the darling of the Glitterature set in the late 1920's when New York *Herald Tribune* drama critic Percy Hammond introduced me to him between the acts of a new Broadway play. Mr. Hammond suggested that the three of us do the town together after Mr. Hammond had struggled writing his opinions on the play (he'd inspect the dictionary for just the right word or synonym).

"Rube" Goldberg, veteran cartoonist, forsook his home town, San Francisco, for New York many decades ago. Stan Delaplane, an SF man, asked "Rube" if he ever missed San Francisco. "No," was Rube's snapper, "New York is ringside."

☆

Bolitho, born in Cape Town, British by education and training, was fascinated by the passing parade of Broadway—the theater's leading men and women, the Ziegfeld Beauts (Keptives) and their current meal tickets, the socialites exploring a wilder world than their own, the known racketeers, the newspaper columnists on their offbeat beats. There were twenty-two night spots and speakeasies between Forty-fourth and Fifty-eighth streets at the time. It was the Prohibition Era, which ended in 1933. The landlords of nearly all twenty-two joynts were gangsters Owney Madden, "Big Frenchy" (George de la Mange), and Public Enemy Number Three—Larry Fay. They headed the Hudson-Duster

1

gang from Manhattan's Hell's Kitchen on the midtown West Side. The first stop for Hammond, Bolitho, and me was the Hotsy-Totsy, where Jack "Legs" Diamond later shot a foe dead and then murdered "Hymie," the bartender, a fellow Legs liked very much. When Diamond was asked by a newsman, "Why Hymie?" he shrugged and said that his mouthpiece, a former (and famous) federal magistrate, had counseled: "Never have witnesses—that goes for your mother!" Legs was never punished for the double homicide.

From the Hotsy we went to Texas Guinan's, the most popular and prosperous sip-and-sup spot along The Big Apple. It was my fort between 1:00 and 6:00 A.M. every night in the week.

Bolitho, Hammond, and I then made Club Durant, where Clayton, Jackson and Durant starred. (If you are wondering why the "Durant" is spelled thusly, where Jimmy Durante was the Big Ticket-Seller, relax. When the name of the Number One act in the Broadway nightclubs went up in lights, the electrician forgot to add the *e*.) Bolitho had never seen New York nightlife so thoroughly. He was enchanted. It was also the first time Mr. Hammond had stayed up until dawn making that scene. He was new to New York, having just come from the Chicago *Tribune*. It was early morning before I took them to Reuben's, then the most popular all-night restaurant, where "everybody" wound up—show people, politicians, gang chiefs, and newspaper people. We relaxed and ordered eggs Benedict.

Between the eggs Benedict and cigarettes, Mr. Bolitho said, "I understand that you and I have the same publisher. Simon and Schuster told me you signed a contract in 1927 to do your life story for them. That was two years ago but you haven't written it. Why not?"

Only a few years before—in 1924—I had landed my first "big" newspaper job with the New York *Evening Graphic*. I was also covering the First Nights, and was the drama editor, too. "I think I ought to live a little longer before I write a 'life' story," I said. "Anyway, I don't know how to write a book. I wouldn't know where to start."

"Which of your columns do you most dislike doing?" Bolitho asked.

"The one for the Saturday paper," I told him. "It is titled 'Things I Never Knew Till Now (But Which You Knew All Along!).' "

"Why do you dislike doing it?"

"Oh, it's a bunch of trivia. It's made up of fillers I discover in papers, books, and mags—almanacs as a rule. I kid them a lot. Like when I run a highbrow item, I add in parenthesis, 'He musta read a book!' It runs on Saturdays, the day the paper is thinnest—few pages, fewer ads. I feel too few people see the damb'd thing, so I don't put my top stuff in it. Now and then I neglect it entirely—and you'd be amazed at the great number of readers who write in and complain. I was touched one night at Sardi's when a waiter asked me why that column hadn't appeared.

" 'Do you really care that much about it?' I asked.

" 'For me,' he said wistfully, 'it's better'n goin' to night school.' I revived that feature the following Satdee. But I save the good stuff for the Monday morning column.

"It's the one I'm best known for—titled 'Man About Town.' But it's also the hardest to do. It's crowded with trivia, nonsense, three periods to divorce one item from the other. Gossip about show people, newspaper and magazine people, eccentrics, the rich and poor, society folks—Cafooey-Souseity, Cafake Society, etcetera. The girls in the show and their sweedees, people who elope—Lizzie Tish and Schmo McCarthy look like an Elopemental case—and anybody and their half-wittiest sayings. Political boners and political coups, anything, everything, so long as it will be talked about and fill a col'm of about nine hundred to a thousand words daily.

"My first paragraph, however, is the one that drives me daffy. It has to have a one- or two-liner that catches and holds the eye; an item that lifts an eyebrow—so that readers will say to friends, 'Did you see that awful thing he had this morning? Jeezuzz!' It's where I put items that may become front-page stories. I stay up until the final editions of the other papers come out on the midtown stands and I have to read almost everything in them to make sure I haven't been scooped."

"Okay," said Mr. Bolitho, "that's the column you find hardest. What column do you find easiest?"

"The one I usually do on Wednesdays: 'Portrait of a Man Talking to Himself.' Sometimes I name it 'The Private Papers of a Cub Reporter.' "

"Why is that one easy to prepare?"

"Because," I explained, "I don't have to worry about having an eye-catcher or breath-taker to lead off the gahdamb'd thing. I start with ramblings. Musings. Anything that comes to mind or from some memo scribbled on my yesterday's proof. It could be an item such as 'The prettiest gal on Broadway is not in any show or nightclub. She's the ticket peddler in the Paramount boxoffice!' An observation like that often makes people check up on me. They congest the sidewalk near that boxoffice, praps take a look at the girl, and then say, 'He's right! She's gorgeous.'

"Or, I'll jot down something like 'Hoagy Carmichael's and Mitchell

3

Parish's "Stardust" is my idea of a love song. It's the Second National Anthem over at these ears.' Or 'Texas Guinan squelched a heckler in her joynt at three thirty-eight ante-meridian with "Go right ahead, Sucker—keep it up. It'll all be on your check!"' I can put anything in that column. Opinions on new plays, movies, plugs for talented people —especially newcomers to show business. A slap at an imitator who echoes a first without credit: 'Stop Thief Dept.: That one was just as funny when it ran here a thousand years ago!' Then I put three dots after the line, meaning that's the end of that one . . . and so on. Before I know it—the column is done."

"Fine," said Mr. Bolitho the word magician, smiling like a patient parent as Mr. Hammond nodded in agreement. Then, raising his tones in capital letters, Bolitho boomed: *"THAT'S THE WAY TO START YOUR BOOK!"*

So—more than thirty-five years later—Let's Start It! Letzgotopress!

I was born in New York City (Harlem) on April 7, 1897.

I died on October 16, 1963—the day the New York *Daily Mirror* (the second largest circulation in the nation) was "assassinated."

Now, in 1966, I am sixty-nine. Is that too old? *My Life and Times* by Shirley Temple appeared in *Pictorial Review* in 1935, when Shirley was seven. Was that too young?

Will Rogers said people, like cats, have at least nine lives. They pick out the one to write about that they think will look the best. If this is going to be a book about me, it can't all be nice, because nobody would believe it. On the other hand, it can't be all bad, though a lot of people would believe *that*.

The newspaper business—the parts of it that I have been in—is rough. Also, it's hard work. One thing I can say about myself that I think nobody will dispute is that I have worked hard.

Several of my journalistic superiors have written that I popularized the "three-dot" formula. Some wrote that I invented it. I think the latter were trying to say I was to "blame" for it. No great invention, if anybody insists, but I never claimed to be Edison. At any rate, newspapers and magazines almost everywhere feature the three-dot style—on the amusement-theater-movie pages, sports sections, and the financial pages.

My competitors belatedly announced, "He is the granddaddy of us all!" In clawing their way to the top they tried to kill me.

I think I wrote more than gossip columns, but let's stay with just them

4

for a minute. That kind of newspapering means getting under people's skins, revealing things most people would prefer not be made public. It means taking a lot of risks and chances, getting to know big and minor thugs, gamblers, gangsters who live by no civilized rules, politicians, little crooks and big double-crossers. I've known many of them and made "friends" with some. If I wanted to "know" them, I had to associate with them. If I wanted them to trust me, as often as not I had to play their game their way. But winning their trust and confidence paid off big for me. I had newsbreaks about the underworld many times, and several gang chiefs surrendered to me.

I never took a bribe. Nobody ever paid me a penny, a nickel, or a dollar, or anything else, in cash or goods, to change my opinion or to say anything I wasn't going to report anyway.

My kind of reporting makes more enemies than friends. Sometimes they change: Best friends often turn into worst enemies.

Worst enemies stay worst enemies.

I never had a dull day.

★

THE MEN AND WOMEN IN MY LIFE

Winchell (with two *l*'s) is not my "real" name.

All the Winchels with one *l* in the New York City phone directory were members of my family. My handsome father once called himself Jack de Winchel (trim figger, spats, cane, little mustache). My beautiful mother married him when she was sixteen. He was twenty-two, a traveling salesman. He had been in the silk business with a partner, who allegedly backed up a small truck one middle-of-the-night and removed everything in the place to another state. My father was too poor to fight back, but he said something I say whenever somebody I trusted turns out to be No Good: "No partners!"

George Winchel, one of the founders of The American Stock Exchange, was the wealthiest Winchel. A generous man, he often staked my father (his brother) and my mother to the rent. His wife, Rae, was a Doll. A dear aunt. Uncle George named his sons Rudyard Kipling Winchel and Malcolm. He named his kid brother (three years my junior) Algernon. He named me Walter.

My folks were very unrich. My father's salary as a salesman was thirty-five dollars a week. We lived in a walkup at 125 West 116th Street,

5

on a fifth floor walkup—a "railroad flat," with rooms like train cars, all in a row. Harlem was then tenanted by middle-class families, Christians, Jews, Germans, Swedes, Poles, Irish—all Americans—respectable, hardworking men and women whose incomes were also about thirty-five dollars a week. An undertaker in the next building often left coffins in front of his place. Sometimes they were stacked against my stoop. I was so afraid of ghosts that I ran up five flights, terrified, and banged on the door until my mother let me in. I was eleven years old.

There's the one about the child who was asked if he said his prayers at night. He nodded. "And did you also say them in the morning, too?" "No," was the reply. "I'm not scared in the daytime."

My father was a Republican. The straight ticket. At supper almost every evening he would read the editorial page of the New York *Sun*. I was about twelve at the time.

Now and then he would fold the paper, mark some editorial, and pass it to me. "Read that," he said, "read it out loud."

Which I did, reluctantly. I preferred to read the sports pages. After I read an editorial (audibly), Papa would ask, "Do you know what that means?"

I shrugged and replied, "No, I don't, Dad."

"Then ask questions and learn," he counseled.

"When you ask people questions about things," I remember saying, "they think you are ignorant."

"Keep asking questions," he advised. "People who laugh at people who want to learn are the ones who are ignorant."

My father was always attractive to women—a real lady killer. And that's why my mother told him to get out of her life. When my parents separated, my beautiful mother went to Danville, Virginia, with my brother, Al, where they lived with her sister, my aunt Rose. I loved her very much, too, because she baked such delicious chawklitt and coconut cakes and gave me a nickel every day. I stayed in New York, where my Grandma, eighty years old, took care of me.

The teen-urgers today are not much different from the ones I grew up with in Harlem in 1910. If you weren't a Sissy, Queer, Minty, Petunia, Pansy, or Flaming Fhagott, you dated girls. When you were eleven, twelve, and thirteen; when you got your first "longies" and were done with short pants, you were a Man and you adored anything in skirts.

There has been more than one "love" in my life.

My first sweetheart was Margie Stewart, the prettiest kid on that Harlem block. She was eleven. I was twelve.

Margie and I went to P.S. 184 together. One winter day I was belly-whopping down a hill near the park on West 110th Street near Manhattan Avenue. A drunk suddenly staggered out of an exit. To avoid knocking him down, I steered the sled sharply to the right—skidding into the gutter. My left leg was run over by a horse-drawn wagon. No break, but a deep gash about three inches long.

My pal, Raymond Ferguson, eleven, who was on the sled with me, was so scared he got lost in the crowd that just stood there and stared and stared at me, then shrugged and walked on—the way so many people have been doing in the 1960's.

A very frightened little boy ran six blocks before he could find anybody to "Please help me, mister! Please save me!"

I was chased from the stoops of several brownstones along Manhattan Avenue by medics and their nurses who said: "Go to a drugstore!" and slammed the door.

I ran to 106th Street before I could find a drugstore. It had a very large entrance. I kept shaking the knob on the door, frantically trying to open it. In my excitement and anguish—fearing I was going to die any second—I didn't see the other half of the door. A passerby pointed and said: "Young man, that door is open!"

A policeman came in. He was gray-haired, a man of about fifty-two maybe. "Well, well, well," he said softly, "what happened, young man?"

"I got run over," I reported hysterically, breathlessly, tearfully, "on a hundred and tenth Street. Am I going to die?"

"How many of these accidents have you had?" he asked, patting my hand.

"This is my first one!" I wept at the top of my voice. "My very first one!"

"Solly," he golly'd, "you have to have one hundred accidents before you can die."

I was relieved to learn that "fact" for the first time.

He must have had children of his own. Maybe grandchildren. He knew what to say to a frightened kid. Talk about child psychology!

I have never forgotten that wonderful policeman. I can still see his face and uniform as I type this now in my usual two-finger style. I guess that's why I've been "for" all cops ever since. I mean respectful, never fearful of them. They are the Good Guys who punish the Bad Guys who hurt and rob people. Policemen, it always seemed to me when I was a kid, saved your life. The way that policeman saved mine.

The drugstore man gave first aid—stopped the bleeding. A crowd collected on the sidewalk. The ambulance from J. Hood Wright Hospital (now the Suydenham) took hours to arrive. The ambulance doctor and his helper brought in a stretcher.

They put me in the horse-drawn ambulance and told me to stay still, that everything would be all right at the hospital and I could call Grandma.

I couldn't stay still in the ambulance. I kept sitting up to look at my audience.

Margie Stewart was part of it, and she was biting her lower lip and crying.

"I love you, Walter!" she hollered as the ambulance clip-clopped off.

"I love you, too, Margie!" I called back, blowing kisses at my very first love.

At the hospital I suffered great torture—

Not from the accident, but from having to remove my short pants and drawers in front of all those nurses! There were four of them. If I wasn't going to die, why were there so many nurses? ? ?

They put me on the operating table and started unbuttoning me. I thought I'd die from the embarrassment. "We have to take off your clothes and underwear," one nurse said. "We have to make you better, don't you see?" I covered my eyes with my arms, I was so ashamed.

Each nurse held me down tight—at the ankles and shoulders. Oh, gee, it hurt when the doctor mended the gash with three stitches. They used no ether or any painkiller because it cost money. And no member of my family was present to pledge payment.

They phoned my grandmother to come for me. She came in wringing her hands and weeping.

"My darling Waltala!" Grandma said as she hugged me tight. "We will go home now and I will make you tea with hot milk and you will be fine again."

She always gave me the same "medicine" when I had a bellyache or a toothache. Hot tea and milk. Better than any aspirin or sleeping pill.

Poor thing, she spent three dollars for a crutch which I didn't need, because I kept saying I had to have one to help me limp about. That was a big fib. I wanted that crutch so I could sit on her stoop at 55 West 116th Street (same block as P.S. 184) and put the crutch across my lap so all the kids coming to and from school would feel sorry for me.

Margie was always the first to arrive at 7:45 and sit with me, hold my hand, and say dear things to me—before rushing down the street to make the 8:00 A.M. school bell.

We exchanged signet rings. We were betrothed.

After a while, her family moved away to another state. We never saw each other again.

After Margie Stewart, Eva Wolf was my favorite girl. Eva was going-on-thirteen. We'd pay a nickel each to see the movie at the nearby movie theaters. We always sat in the last row of the balcony, where it was cozier and more romantic. Last spring at a Fifth Avenue parade, a chap on the staff of the NBC newsroom, said, "Does the name Eva Wolf ring a bell in you?"

"It rings a bell in my heart. We went to school together. Do you know Eva?"

"She's my mother!"

It made my day.

George Jessel was one of my schoolmates at Prison 184. He sang bass at eleven and never quit twitting me about Eva. At the inns I later dwelt in, he would leave phone messages: "Eva Wolf called." I always knew it was Jessel—another girl-mad guy.

O. Roy Chalk, later a newspaper publisher, also went to P.S. 184. So did five-foot Harry Horowitz, who owned more pimples and acne than any of us. The ugliest guy I ever saw, with sneaky little orbs, later on, Harry was known as "Gyp The Blood." He became a front-page headliner when he was about twenty. Harry died in the electric chair at Sing Sing Prison as "Gyp," one of the four gangsters electrocuted for the murder of Herman Rosenthal, a gentleman-gambler. The other guns-for-hire were Whitey Lewis, Dago Frank, and Lefty Louie.

A police lieutenant named Becker also cooked in the same chair. "Mr." Becker, stool pigeons testified, got them to slay Rosenthal (who was to appear before the district attorney the next morning to charge that "Lt." Becker of the Broadway Squad had shaken him down for large sums too often).

The murder scene was the Metropole, a rendezvous for sports and their ladies on West Forty-third Street—not far from The Grandest Canyon—where the Broadway lights were brightest. It was later a popular foodery. Lieutenant Becker's wife ordered a headstone for her husband that hysteric'd, "Murdered By District Attorney Whitman!" Following his crime busting, Mr. Whitman was elected governor and she had to replace it with another stone.

My parents were healthy people. That's why I was rarely ill (colds now and then) but never a patient in a hospital (except for that accident) until I was sixty-eight years old. But that's another paragraph.

Later, my father and I moved into a German lady's Harlem flat. I had my own room. The lady was Mrs. Haas, a widow. She nursed my black eyes after a fight and comforted me when I had the downs.

The "women" in my teen years were many. No lady killer or any of that stuff; I just liked girls. Ruthie Rosenberg, another schoolmate, twelve and a half, was my next Big Crush. We dated in Mount Morris Park at 120th Street between Madison and Fifth. It had a "Lookout" on top of its tallest hill, built when New York City was very young. The kids always referred to it as "Lookout Mountain," triffic for Puppy-Lovers.

Ruthie and I exchanged signet rings and class pins. After I got the vaudeville bug, I did not meet Ruthie again until both of us had matured, married, and prospered. That was about twenty years ago. The scene was the lobby of the Roney Plaza Hotel in Miami Beach. She came out of the elevator with her husband—and was covered with mink and gems. "Ruthie!" I exclaimed, hugging her and kissing her cheek. "I knew this girl," I told her husband, "long before you did!"

She embraced me and sighed, "Oh, Walter! I have never forgotten you. We had such a happy childhood."

It's a woman's privilege to remember, and the duty of a gentleman to forget.

★

COAST TO COAST

In 1910 one of the first nickelodeons in the land was the Imperial Theater, across the way from P.S. 184. Jessel and a schoolmate named Jack Weiner and I got in to see the movies for nothing after the 3 o'clock school bell. We doubled as ushers and as "The Imperial Trio"—at nothing per week. While the projectionist changed reels, we harmonized the songs of the day accompanied by "illustrated" slides and the lady piano player who also played "Hearts and Flowers" when the movie villain threatened Mary Pickford. Jessel's mother was the ticket seller and Harry Horowitz was once the bouncer.

Our stage names were "Stanley, McKinley and Lawrence." I was Stanley (until I found out that it was short for Stanislaus). Jessel was

McKinley (the name of the slain President), and Weiner was Lawrence.

One matinee a song plugger named Leo Edwards came to hear us sing. His brother was Gus Edwards, the composer (lyrics by Will D. Cobb), whose lovely melodies included "School Days," "Sunbonnet Sue," and "If I Was A Millionaire," still rendered by Bing Crosby and other song stars. Edwards and Cobb never wrote a double entendre song in their long and great careers. They were the Rodgers and Hart of 1910. Leo told Gus about us.

When Gus readied his first big flash vaudeville act (thirty in the cast—mainly lovely girls), The Imperial Trio was hired as part of the act. I ran away from home and P.S. 184 (at thirteen) to go on tour with Gus Edwards' *Song Revue of 1910.*

We were members of the curtain raiser—"The Newsboys Sextet." I was the one Lou Silvers said couldn't carry a melody—and I thought I was the tenor. Jessel was singing bass even then. Jack Weiner sang the "lead."

When George and I became personalities in show biz, the interviewers for decades invariably omitted Weiner's name and called him Eddie Cantor—a real wrongo. They were misled by some journalist who had heard that Cantor had also begun his career at Gus Edwards University. Cantor (his real name) was never in the *Song Revue* or in *Gus Edwards' School Days* vaudeville acts. He was already a star at sixteen in Mr. Edwards' *Kid Kabaret.* A darling named Rita Green was also in that act, which opened across the Hudson River at the Hudson Theater in Union Hill, New Jersey. (That town has long since become Union City.) The act played only the Big-Time circuits . . . the Palace Theater on Broadway ("You Haven't Arrived Until You've Played The Palace"); the Alhambra (in Harlem at 126th Street and Seventh Avenue); the Riverside Theater (where dwelled the swells, people who made at least a hundred dollars weekly); the Colonial on Broadway near Sixty-second Street, on whose stage my TVariety program (for Old Gold) originated over forty years later.

Jack Weiner, Jessel, and I joined in the chorus when Gus sang his own song hits. I can still see Gus Edwards out there in center stage—singing it with Lillian Boardman. I was one of the kids who helped decorate the stage with the bales of cotton and all those beautiful girls. Every time I hear some actor say: "I'm the guy who *wasn't* with Gus Edwards!" I feel like saying: "That's your misfortune, mister, because many a kid who didn't get a start with Gus Edwards never got started at all!"

11

I have never met a girl I ever regretted knowing. I can't think of one who ever regretted knowing me.

Irene Martin, for example.

In 1910 she was eighteen and I was thirteen when a camaraderie began I will never forget. I was playing tag with another kid in the "Newsboys Sextet" act (before the night performance) at Proctor's Warburton Theater (Yonkers, New York). He knocked over a cheap vase that was standing on a pedestal in a living room set for the third act on the bill. He told the stage manager: "Walter did it!" I was dismissed without the usual two weeks' notice.

It was approaching show time. My only clothing was what I wore. The trousers had two holes in the derriere department. The salary had been fifteen dollars a week. (I sent my mother five dollars of it.)

I was sitting on the gutter-curb outside the stage door with my head buried in my arms so passersby wouldn't see me weep.

Along came Irene Martin, the prettiest girl in the cast of thirty. "Whatsamatta with you?" she asked.

"I just got fired."

"Why?"

"I didn't do nothing. I got blamed for breaking a vase playing tag with Georgie. He said I did it, but I didden!"

"Go right inside and put on your makeup," she ordered. And it was an Order.

I never spoke to that other ratter again. He became a vaudeville star and then a prosperous Wall Streeter. But his childish fib that I broke the vase almost cost me my job.

Mrs. Edwards mother'd us all. When Irene told her that I was dismissed, she gave her husband the Old What For, as the Runyonesque kerrickters say at "Mindy's" or in Damon's epic, *Guys and Dolls*.

Irene Martin was Mr. Edwards' favorite. She was also the favorite girl of Mrs. Edwards, a former actress, whose maiden name was Lillian Lee. That's how darling baby girl Gussie Apfel, two and a half (the daughter of a Union Hill, New Jersey, saloon keeper), got the name of Lila Lee.

Mr. and Mrs. Edwards and a few of us kids were motoring to the Hudson Theater in that town from dinner one evening when we saw this cute baby girl sitting on the curbstone dipping her naked feet into the rainwater. "Isn't she the cutest thing?" exclaimed Mrs. Edwards. She told her husband to wait while she got out of the car and learned from neighbors where to find the tot's parents. They agreed to permit the Edwardses to put Gussie (nicknamed Cuddles) in the act.

12

When Mr. Edwards was at the piano singing "Look Out For Jimmy Valentine," Lila was the tiniest thing on the piano—on the far right.

Irene was a beautiful thing, and when she turned on her infectious smile the whole world lighted up. I guess I fell in love with her—Puppy, or whatever. All I knew was that I was determined to be her protector, her bodyguard, her Number One Pest.

I carried one of her valises. I ran errands for her. She never told me to run errands or be her slave—I just was. I worried so much that someone might molest or bother her that I became her self-appointed G-man. I always got a furnished room in whatever boardinghouse she dwelled in. I slept outside her door, guarding her from all Enemies.

The flash act was booked fifty-two weeks that year—coast to coast on the Orpheum Circuit (Chicago to California and back to Chi). After the season ended I was promoted to assistant manager of Mr. Edwards' *School Boys & Girls*. The *School Days* manager was Roy Mack, a good man who treated me like one of his children. He never had any.

I wept when Irene Martin and I had to part. My age was then en route to fifteen.

When I returned and was happy to again feast on a home-cooked meal, I asked my father: "Pop, will you please lend me a dollar?"

He was still getting thirty-five dollars per week as a salesman. He reached into his pocket, handed me a dollar and asked, "How long have you been away, son?"

"One whole year," I proudly told him. "Worked steady for fifty-two weeks!"

"How much were you paid a week?"

"Fifteen dollars."

"If you had saved one dollar a week," he educated, "you now would have fifty-two dollars!" My first lesson in economics.

One day I picked up a copy of *Variety,* and read that Irene Martin had married an actor named Pat Somerset. I hated him! I never met Mr. Somerset (a British actor in Hollywood) but I was jealous of any man who loved her—let alone married her.

Then I read in the papers that Irene and her husband had divorced. I was sorry her marriage was destroyed, but inside me I felt sort of glad that no other love was in her life. She could always depend on me, I said to myself, if she would only wait until I was old enough to be a husband! My age was now sixteen and a half.

Then I lost track of her.

Decades later, I was strolling through the putting green of the Hotel Ambassador in Los Angeles, where I lived in a bungalow. As I strolled with putter in my hand, a woman (about fifty or older) approached and asked: "Do you remember Irene Martin?"

"Ohmigahd!" I exclaimed joyously. "Where is she?"

"She's living at the Hollywood Plaza Hotel near Hollywood and Vine. She'd love hearing from you. Why don't you call her?"

I raced back to the bungalow, phoned that hotel, and asked the operator for Miss Irene Martin. After a long pause, a voice answered.

"Irene?" I said, "this is Walter Winchell! Remember?"

Another long pause.

"No, sorry, she is shopping."

"Will you please tell Irene I called? I am living at the Ambassador. Tell her to call me any time—any hour of the day or night. I must see Irene, please?"

"I will tell her," was the reply. Click.

I must have phoned the Hollywood Plaza fifty times in the next two weeks. When I told the operator my name, it was always: "She's out of town. Any message?"

I had to return to Broadway. When I got back to Hollywood a few months later, I was strolling through the Ambassador's beautiful grounds (a miniature park) when who should approach me again but the same woman who had told me to call Irene.

"I called her day and night almost every hour for weeks," I reported. "Why has she never returned my call? Is she sick—something wrong?"

"No," the stranger informed me. "Irene decided not to call or see you. She wants you to remember her as she was—when you last saw her. When you both were so very young."

Another darling in my life was Nellie Cliff. Nellie was about twenty-two, maybe twenty-three. Her hair was light red-gold. I was seventeen. I was with Gus Edwards' *School Boys*. It was during a performance one humid, hot and sultry day in Lowell, Massachusetts. Nellie Cliff, sister of the star, hit me in the eye, flinging a prop. "Ofercrissakes!" I grumbled.

I overheard her say to her sixteen-year-old kid sister Dolly (the leading lady): "That Walter Winchell is a nasty little thing. If he uses such language at me again, we'll quit!"

Jeezuzz! There I go again. Losing my job!

14

Everyone in the cast laundered their own linen, but local soap was often none too good. So when Nellie told Dolly: "Oh, I'd give anything for a box of Lux," I sped to the nearest grocery store and rushed back to give it to her.

"I'm very sorry for what I said, Nellie," I apologized. "Look what I brought you."

Nellie smiled, said thanks, and I knew I had been reprieved. She invited me to sit with her in the railway coach along the New England vaudeville circuit.

"You have nice features," Nellie said one day. "You should do something about all those blemishes."

I told her I didn't know what to do about them. She suggested I buy a much-advertised pimple remedy. (I tried them all for years. No luck.)

I always carried her valise from the train to the boardinghouse or inexpensive hotel where she would stay. Dave Seed, my roommate, was courting Dolly, and before I knew what was happening to me, I was in love with Nellie.

In every town we played, the four of us were inseparable.

Breakfast at the nearby Greek's (always a Greek-owned spot—why, I dunno). Breakfast was never before noon—most of the time just before the matinee performance, which began at two-thirty. The night show started at eight-thirty. We dined at the Greek's again, or at the hotel, or at the boardinghouse, where they served home cooking, like your mother cooked. You got three meals a day—if you wanted all three—and a clean room, all for one dollar per day.

The sisters were paid a hundred dollars a week for the team. Nellie was the banker. (Her bank was what vaudevillians called "the grouch bag," pinned to her chemise.)

I got considerable "education" by reading the newspapers between performances in vaudeville. I remember how embarrassed I was one day when I tried to use a word I didn't know how to pronounce. The word was "façade." I said, "fac-a-dee."

Between shows some of us would see as much of America as we could. In the Far West burgs, the girls often rented horses and rode closer to the Rockies or the Mojave Desert. I saw America from dusty train windows. While the others had fun, I remained in the theater dressing room two-fingering a portable typewriter. That's how I created *The Daily Newsense*—a neatly typed newspaper (on one page) which I thumbtacked onto the bulletin board next to the mailbox where the performers read my "newspaper" before they looked into the mailbox.

A later columnist once complained that I "bragged" of having played the Palace—when I hadn't. Well, I hadn't, but I didn't brag, either. This is part of a "pome" I doggereled in the *Newsense*:

> *I would rather be a smallie*
> *Doing 4-a-day in Dallas*
> *Than be playing at the Palace*
> *On a Monday matinee.*

The Monday matinee at the Palace, the most important two-a-day theater in the land, was when the best talent got very nervous that they would fail.

I finally played the Palace in 1931 as a fluke headliner because of my radio renown.

In a later "exposé" series in *The New Yorker* magazine, another author noted: "We have researched everything he [thaz me!] has written and believe his first coined word was in the name of his little paper: 'Newsense'—news and sense.

"Winchell," continued the profiler, "probably didn't realize he had coined a word." But I did.

The romance with Nellie was a beautiful time in my young life. We prob'bly would have married, but along came World War I in 1914, and Nellie and sister Dolly decided to return to England where they were born . . . in Oldham, Lancashire. A grown brother was their nearest kin. "I think we should be with my brother with a war on," Nellie told me, fingering my face tenderly, her eyes filling with tears.

"Will we ever meet again?" I asked, suffering my first grown-up heartache. Now she was going away—far, far away.

One day in Baltimore between shows—between the matinee and supper show (the second performance)—Nellie asked me to "help her" while she shopped for things to bring back to her big brother. "You are about his size and weight," she said.

We went to a leading store called The Hub. She selected a suit for her brother; three shirts; boxer shorts; three solid blue neckties; half a dozen kerchiefs; a pair of black shoes, size 9A; and six pairs of navy blue sox.

After the final show (the last time Nellie and Dolly would be part of the act) we had a backstage party to bid them Bon Voyage.

The big surprise was a huge thing covered with brown paper. It was for me—a miniature wardrobe trunk containing all the things she had purchased for her brother!

"Wear these," Nellie said, choking a little, "they will keep you remembering me." It was the first new suit I had worn in years. And my own trunk—with my name on it in large letters.

Next day she came to see us all off at Grand Central Station. The act was bound for Boston. We stood on the platform alongside the train—talking, talking, and talking about our years together, and how much we would miss each other—and pledged that there would never be any other person in our hearts. That the war would be over one day. . . .

The conductor called "All aboard," and I kissed her once more as the train started moving. I never saw her again.

Definition of Carrying-the-torch: Trying to forget a pain that remembers.

In the 1960's a letter came from Sally Dawson, the loyal, longtime Girl Friday for Stork Club owner Sherman Billingsley. It revealed that Nellie had told Sally "please don't tell him about me working for you as housekeeper. He has become such a busy man and he probably has forgotten me, anyway." Sally also said that Nellie had never before mentioned my name in all the years Sally employed her. There she was all the time, living less than a mile from me! And she had never written or phoned to let me know.

Months later Sally called long distance to report that Nellie had been stricken with cancer. Sister Dolly had died in England. She had no kin or a friend other than Sally. Could I recommend a cancer specialist?

I wrote Nellie (via Sally) and told her how much a part of her remained in my heart—and that I wanted Sally to get her into the best hospital in New York, and not to worry about anything.

Sally had difficulty getting a hospital to take her in, because they first wanted to know if Nellie could afford the tariff. And if she couldn't, who would pay the bills? Nellie told Sally not to make a thing of it—she simply would *not* have my name mentioned and she was ready to suffer in any hospital ward rather than make my name known.

Nellie, however, had nothing to say about that. Sally was told to arrange everything and after several weeks, Nellie was home again "on the mend."

There were two grateful letters from her—thanking me "so very much." Then the letters stopped coming.

Sally, who suffered many operations herself, was now back in Texas, her home state. I-reported her marriage to a lad out there. Did Nellie survive? How will I ever know? I have no idea where Sally lives in Texas. Sherman Billingsley is gone. He would have told me where to find Sally.

If Nellie is alive, where is she? In some nursing home, with her memories of when we both were so very young and so much in love with each other?

☆

The *School Boys & Girls* act played New England's Poli Circuit and the small-time Keith Theater houses in the likes of New Bedford, Hartford, New Haven, Providence, and North Adams, Massachusetts—"where they sit down front and devour their young!" as the flops alibi'd.

When the season ended, Mr. Edwards gave me a job at 1531 Broadway in his music publishing office. Harry Rapf (he became a mighty man in Hollywood) was manager of it. He was always warm to me.

At night I was a song plugger. The accompanist was a lovable fellow named Harry Ruby, a frustrated ball player and later a hit songwriter. His best known click ditty: "Three Little Words."

Harry played the "88" while I tenor'd the tunes Mr. Edwards wrote with word magician Will D. Cobb. Their "If I Was A Millionaire" was my favorite.

> *I'd buy up ev'ry schoolhouse in the nation,*
> *I'd write upon the blackboard big and clear,*
> *Instead of one there will be two vacations,*
> *Each vacation six months twice a year.*
> *There wouldn't be no school when it was raining,*
> *I'd let you stay at home when all was fair,*
> *If Rocka-fella was me tenant*
> *I'd buy the Giants the pennant!*
> *If I was a mil-lion-aire.*

In the sheet music stores at Atlantic City and in New York, Harry played the pianner while I sang whatever song a customer requested. I was also a "stamp collector" in the summer when I worked as office boy for the American Felt Company on East Thirteenth Street—and for a few weeks at the Remington Typewriter Company away downtown. But those jobs bored the hell out of me, and I resigned before I got caught stamp collecting.

I never swiped more than a few at a time. I don't know why I swiped them. I guess, as the saying goes about the highest mountains, "because they were there!" When you make fifteen dollars per and you give your mother a five spot from that wage, you pilfer stamps. (You mean you never did that when you were an office boy?)

When the show biz "season" started in the fall I teamed with the girl

18

who had taken Nellie's place in the *School* act. She was Rita Green, a very pretty girl, about seventeen.

We were backed by a wonderful fellow—an agent named Samuel Baerwitz. He bought a Big-Time team's "old" act: special songs plus a "drop"—a curtain showing a pastoral scene. This was the standard equipment for most "Man and Woman Teams" that always were spotted second on the bill—second on the bill chiefly to permit the curtain to fall and allow the stage hands to set the next act, usually a sketch lasting twenty minutes or less.

Mr. Sam is still around (or was). It made me feel good when he approached one day between races at Hollywood Park Racetrack in 1967 and said: "Remember me?" I responded: "Sam!" It must have made him feel good, too, that I remembered his name. I hadn't seen him since 1918, when he put up the money for our act.

Many years later, When I was newspapering and on the air, some jurq did a knock-article that said: "As a vaudeville song and danceman, Winchell was no great shakes." He carelessly added that "Variety's file proved Winchell was not very good."

I reprinted Variety's notice of March 8, 1918:

> WINCHELL AND GREEN, SPOONEYVILLE (SKIT), 12 MINUTES, AMERICAN ROOF, N. Y.
> In forming a likable act for the no. 2 position Walter Winchell and Rita Green have made a promising start. Theirs is a sort of bench turn, but it has dialogue, songs and dances. For an opening the girl is perched on a bit of brick wall, and there is a duet, the lyric of which is rather bright. They wander to a bench for a spoony bit, followed by a song. . . . While Miss Green is making a costume change, Winchell handles a War Song, and he gives way for the girl's eccentric solo, and some stepping takes them off. The first two numbers appear to be written, and were helped by the naive manner of Miss Green.

The act rarely got more than one bow, unless we thefted the Second Bend. Most vaudeville acts did that, in a vain attempt to fool the theater manager.

We layed off more than we were booked. Most "Two-Acts" on the Small-Time suffered the same agony and humiliation.

On July 22, 1918, when I was nineteen and a half, I enrolled as an apprentice seaman in the U.S. Naval Reserve Force at New York City and served for the duration. After the Armistice I was released from active duty with proficiency marks of 4.0 (the highest record a man can get in the Navy). I came out of the war promoted to yeoman, 3rd class. After the war we resumed the act.

One day an act was too ill to show up. Our backer-agent, Mr. Baerwitz, phoned: "Get packed! You're a Disappointment!"—meaning that the scheduled act couldn't make it.

The booking was for Loew's, New Orleans—quite a costly jump from Broadway. The Loew's Circuit paid the one-way fares. The same "sick" act had been booked for Chicago, with a one-night stand in Fulton, Kentucky, to "break-the-jump."

In Kentucky I bought a week-old copy of *Variety*.

Jack Lait (years later he was my managing editor at the New York *Mirror*) was *Variety*'s Number One critic in Chi. All of us feared his fierce opinions. He rapped hard. His review of another Two-Act like ours was pure homicide.

Lait said in part: "The male member was the steenth ham to sing 'Friends,' the lyric of which has a patriotic punch line. If you don't applaud this flag-waving finish, you might be charged with treason!" I was singing the same song.

In the train that night to Chicago (no sleepers—couldn't afford luxury) I got busy revising the words of the second chorus to "Friends." De Valera, Ireland's head of state, had been in Chicago two weeks before we opened there. The revised lyric went like this:

"And so I say—from Broadway to Long Island . . . From lowland up to highland—*if we free Ireland*—we'll be *the best friends* the Irish ever had!"

Welll, lemme telll you! There must've been nothing but Irish in the packed theater that opening matinee at McVicker's in August 1919.

On January 15, 1962, the late Mike Connolly's column in *The Hollywood Reporter* first-paragraphed this: "Ed Sullivan . . . was particularly delighted when Lou Clayton told him Winchell was a small-timer [in vaudeville] and . . . waved an American flag to get applause. Sullivan says, 'As in vaudeville, he always was one to wave an American flag.' "

The editors and staffers of *Variety* know otherwise. I once waved the Irish flag in a song—when Eire was born. Clayton of Clayton, Jackson and Durante often thanked me later for the many orchids I flung at the act. So I don't believe Mr. Clayton ever said it. I believe that when an enemy constantly repeats fibs about a foe, he gets to believe them.

The Irish punch line got three encores. Jack Lait could deadrop that day so far as I was concerned. I mean that morning.

The first act went on at noon. We went on at 12:10. Can you imagine an actor having to get up before noon? The house was capacity with servicemen—many back from the front lines. Our "flag finish" got us a two-year booking on the Western Vaudeville Managers Association Circuit in the Midwest and along the Pan-Time (Pantages Circuit).

The "flag-waving finish" came from a show-stopping two-man team called Craft and Haley. The latter was Jack Haley. Years later he co-starred with Ben Bernie and WW in two films for D. F. Zanuck at Twentieth Century-Fox.

In Philly, I told Craft and Haley I was worried about clicking in New Orleans and Chicago, and they gave me two of their best quips: "You may use any gag we have," Jack said. "We're not going West—we're booked solid back here in the East."

I said thank you very much. Haley and I still talk happy-talk about how his gags saved our act from splitting.

Woodrow Wilson was President. He was on the front pages for months with his Fourteen Points to the League of Nations. He went on Henry Ford's Peace Ship. Mr. Wilson sailed back and forth on that "Peace Ship" until the editorial writers and other comedians kidded it. So Haley's topical gag went over peachy with the Chicago audience of men in uniform.

Rita and I soft-shoed the final number, which was punctuated with quips. Frinstance:

"You are away off someplace," I said to Rita. "What are you thinking about?"

"I was just thinking," she said (as she did a high kick to display her pretty gams), "that the man I marry must be capable of being President of the United States!"

"Oh," I intoned with a Pained Expression, "then I won't do!"

"Why not?" Rita straight-man'd, executing another high kick.

"Because," I groaned, winking at the audience, "I get seasick—so easily!"

This was another jab at Woodrow Wilson's attempt to keep Europeans peaceful—with his numerous appeals to the League of Nations, a famous flop show. But it was the next gag that Really Did It.

Remember now, the theater was populated to capacity with men in uniform. Mostly buck privates, sergeants, corporals, "the Little Man." As we went into the last eight bars of our finale, Rita asked: "What is your idea of a very good time?"

To which I deadpanned, "Watching a boatload of second lieutenants sinking!"

21

You never heard such applause and laughter. I mean I had never. The roof went off the theater, as show folks used to exaggerate. We got six bows.

"Swing's" review in *Variety* said: "Winchell & Green won many a hand on clean-cut performance and attractive appearance. The boy is slim, good-looking and possessor of a good voice. His partner is a cute little girl with the heels of a frisky filly. Together they blend and fill their fifteen minutes most creditably."

We were "in." We were so happy. We had planned to fold the act and resign from show biz. We figured we'd have twelve dollars each left after paying the fare via the Baltimore and Ohio back to New York, the 5 percent commission to our agent, Mr. Baerwitz, another 5 percent to the booking office (wotta racket that was) and buying a box lunch on the long ride back. All day and night—about twenty-one hours—in a coach.

But Santa Claus (make that Clauses) waited in the theater alley. About 15 or 20 "flesh-peddlers" (agents)—a phrase I coined as a columnist years later—were all anxious to sign us on the dotted line and hitchhike on our Gravy Train. I told them all thanks, but that I was going across the street to the Woods Building where the top agents in Chicago officed; that Beehler and Jacobs (the most reputable agents in Chi) had been recommended to us by other acts. Sam Baerwitz phoned B and J from New York and persuaded them to handle us.

The Beehler and Jacobs stenog staff were working swiftly, preparing our contract for a two-year booking—three days here, three days there, and some nearby burg to play on Sundays, where they permitted shows on the Sabbath. The Beehler-Jacobs stenogs had seen our names in the McVicker's lights through their office windows—and followed copy.

Looking at the theater's big sign in lights that advertised the names of every act on the bill, I saw ours: WINCHELL AND GREEN. But Winchell (with two *l*'s) is not my "real" name.

Why did the theater electrician misspell my last name? It was a goof. But very lucky for Winchell and Green.

So, because the electrician gooft, the girls at the agency spelled Winchel with two *l*'s and I had to sign my name with two *l*'s for hours.

A stupid shyster once sarcastically asked in court: "Why do you spell it with two *l*'s when your REAL name is with one *l*?"

"What the l?" I wisecracked, and lost my first libel case.

Then there was *Newsweek*'s April 11, 1936, issue. Page ads in the papers shouted in huge type: "WINCHELL'S REAL NAME! SEE *NEWSWEEK,* OUT TOMORROW!"

Text in other ads announced its "Periscope" feature—gossip and low-down about statesmen, the famed, coming events, etc. "PERISCOPE WILL OUT-WINCHELL WINCHELL!"

"Winchell's real name," *Newsweek* gleefully reported, "is Bakst."

Three days later I phoned the mag and asked to speak to the editor, the late Samuel T. Williamson. "Walter Winchell calling, Mr. Williamson . . . "

"Welllll, we wondered when you'd call. What's your problem?"

"I just read your last issue. It's a corker. But don't any of you over there know how to read *Who's Who?*"

There was a long pause—followed by a long moan—and a yelp. *"Oh, My God!"*

I hung up. My next column carried his quote.

Bakst was my mother's maiden name.

BACK ON BROADWAY WITH *THE VAUDEVILLE NEWS*

I married Rita in 1919. For an act to be booked on "The Pan Time" meant status in small-time show biz—and prosperity. Until then, our salary had been one hundred and twenty-five dollars a week. Now it was two hundred seventy-five—with no taxes (then)! Winchell and Green saved fifteen hundred dollars in the months away from New York. But with several months to go to fulfill contracts with the Pantages Circuit, Rita's state of mind was low. She was depressed day and night. She was homesick, never having been away from her family that long before.

I kept telling her, "We have only a few more months," but that didn't help at all. Her feeling for the act was gone. She really missed her folks and her beautiful sisters. Rita begged me to let her go home to her family.

I promised Rita I would get in touch with Alexander Pantages, the boss of the theater chain. I told him in a wire that my partner was ill. I promised him that "when we return to vaudeville, we will fulfill the time we owe you. Will be glad to pay transportation for act that replaces us."

Mr. Pantages responded immediately to my telegram asking for release. But our act never resumed. Mr. Pantages did not charge me for the other act's fare.

Back on Broadway, I lost no time calling on Glenn Condon, the editor of a new show biz sheet, *The Vaudeville News.*

A while back, the manager of the Pantages Theater in Tacoma, Washington, had mailed my *Newsense* newspaper to Mr. Condon in New York. Editor Condon had reproduced a facsimile of it on page two of his June 11, 1920, edition: " 'The Evening Newsense,' gotten up by Walter Winchell and issued for the members of Pantages Road Show, No. 151, is one of the cleverest things of the kind that has ever come to our notice. The miniature reproduction of a recent issue of the unique publication, shown above, gives some idea of its cleverness. It is done entirely on a typewriter."

This is what comes from being a dropout and leaving school in 6B. The dictionary, of course, explained "unique" and I was on the Cloud 9's.

The Vaudeville News, a house organ for E. F. Albee, chief of the Big-time Keith Circuit (his flagship was the Palace on Broadway), was located in the Little Palace Building adjacent to the famed Two-a-Day theater. The office itself was a tiny 2-room setup on the fifth floor—windows facing Broadway, my first box seat on The Grandest Canyon.

I asked editor Condon for a job.

"I have fifteen hundred dollars saved up," I prefaced. "Salary doesn't matter. I want to learn how to be a reporter."

Condon said he got the small paper out by himself. He didn't need an assistant. If I wished, I could come in and make myself useful—perhaps pick up some pointers. But no wages. Sorry. Mr. Albee wouldn't go for any more expenses on this little sheet.

That was okay with me. I just wanted to be around a newspaperman and a publication. So *The Vaudeville News* then had a staff of two— editor Glenn Condon, and WW, office-boy.

Glenn Condon was formerly managing editor of the Tulsa *World.* Later he became a popular news commentator in Oklahoma. He educated me on how to read proof, make up a dummy, talk printer talk at C. J. O'Brien's plant (far downtown) and when to write "who" instead of "whom." Three months later Mr. Condon got Mr. Albee (adopted granddad of the famed playwright, Edward Albee) to pay me twenty-five dollars per.

My chores included dusting the three desks—Condon's, mine, and the desk of his Girl Friday, Rose Germiese (same first name as Rose Bigman, who has been my prisoner since December 4, 1932). My other duties included putting the mail for performers in alphabetical order and

24

into boxes on the wall—labeled *A, B, C,* among others. I also dug up items about the National Vaudeville Artists Club, a gimmick dreamed up by Mr. Albee's staffers to keep them from joining The White Rats of America, a new union. The NVA was where "Variety Artists—mainly vaudeville performers—could dine and dwell." "Room and Bath for Two-and-a-Half!" Dollars, that is.

The Vaudeville News, in short, was a "company" sheet, four pages most of the time. (But *The Hollywood Reporter* format is an exact copy of *The Vaudeville News.* Publisher Billy Wilkerson admitted that to me years later in Girltown.)

I was office boy, errand boy, and Star Reporter.

My cards read: *THE VAUDEVILLE NEWS*—Ass't Editor, W. Winchell."

Condon never knew I had done that. It gave me status, I thawt. And it did get me my first interview—with George M. Cohan, then the biggest name on Broadway, starring in *The Tavern.* I sent in my "card" to Mr. Cohan via the man guarding the stage door and I was invited in. Mr. Cohan was putting on his makeup. I was shaking so nervously that I couldn't put pencil to paper. Mr. Cohan must have conducted that "interview," and he taught me a lesson I have never forgotten. When a youngster or a student requests an interview, I always oblige.

Not long after I started my apprenticeship with Mr. Condon, he suggested I do a column. I called it "Broadway Hearsay"—later on, "Your Broadway and Mine."

"The files of *The Vaudeville News"* (wrote one of my early profilers) "contained considerable paragraphs that could be printed today—so fresh are they—amusing jokes and other trivia."

Overheard somewhere or otherwise:

"What kind of a job did you say he has?"

"He's a columnist."

"I don't geddit."

"A columnist, a columnist! You know, a guy on a newspaper who thinks that his stuff is the first thing the readers turn to."

Rita, back with her devoted clan, regained her health and was very happy—so I believed. But on *The Vaudeville News,* I neglected her, not intentionally. I was a newspaperman, and I gave the job almost twenty hours a day.

After a few years of that, Rita had Haddit. There was a minor quarrel, and one day Rita left a bundle for me at the NVA club. It was my few belongings: my laundry, toothbrush, mouthwash, etc. (I was wearing my only suit.)

There was no note in the bundle. I took the hint.

Later, I heard she was planning to do another act with a new partner —a girl. The divorce was amicable. Mark Hellinger, my only real pal, testified for her that I was unfaithful, and so forth, since adultery was the only grounds for divorce in New York State.

Our lawyers arranged an out-of-court settlement—a weekly thirty-five dollars. When the cost of living went up, Rita requested that I increase the alimony, which I did. But following the abrogation, Rita Green never hurt me in any way. She could have given newspaper and magazine enemies a "story" about me. But I had never hurt Rita, except by being too busy to be a husband in my day-and-night climb up the Broadway Alps.

My column often led off with a verse, Torch-Song stuff, usually auth'd by me. I was always carrying the torch for some gal who had kicked me in the heart and behind. Anon: "A man doesn't look for a happy ending to a love affair, merely one without hysterics."

Among the very first were this one, and a sequel. (Talk about Amachoorish!)

Lines to an Old Flame

You passed me by and didn't stop to speak,
    I'm certain that you saw me standing there,
I felt the blood creep slowly to each cheek—
    And realized I hadn't ceased to care.
It seems that it was only Yesterday . . .
    My thoughts were all of you and yours of me;
We never dreamed our love could so decay
    But what will be—will be—will be—will be.
I don't suppose you'll ever see this here,
    But if you do—perhaps you'll have some laughs . . .
To think that you could make me shed a tear—
    But you've helped me to fill three paragraphs!

Pret-tee Badddd, wot? Well, I was too busy learning how to be a newspaperman to carry a *real* torch.

The actors, actresses, stagehands, agents, managers, *et al.,* who read *The Vaudeville News* (free distribution at the NVA Club on West 46th

Street opposite Dinty Moore's famed restaurant, and in undressing-rooms on all vaudeville circuits . . . and the bookers in the Palace and Little Palace Buildings) all made me feel good by saying how much they liked my doggerel.

It didn't dawn on me at the time that they were giving me "a line" because they wanted a plug. It wasn't until one lunchtime in Wolpin's, a popular foodery on the Palace Theater corner, that I had my feelings wounded.

A vaudeville team (man and woman) sat at the next table. She started reading our weekly, making fun of my love laments.

I overheard her say, "That Winchell guy is crying in the paper again!"

I felt the blood creep slowly to each cheek. Again the bitch devastated me. I worked hard and long over that poem. No matter had badly you write, no writing comes easy, pal.

The best authors will tell you that a lot of the time they stare at the floor or ceiling or out the window—waiting for the ideas and "right" words to come. As one author said, "A writer's wife is a person who thinks that her husband is not working because he keeps looking out the window instead of at the blank paper in his typewriter." Red Smith, the brilliant sports-page essayist and reporter, said it best when he ad-libbed, in a speech before a group of advertising men: "They say newspapering is a hard job, but it isn't. You just take a razor blade and cut your brow and sweat beads of blood!"

Anyway, the lady's criticism about my verse made it difficult to jot down another. I kept throwing my attempts on the floor. Then, the idea came for a sequel. I knew it was good enough to print. And, honest, I had never read or heard of Dorothy Parker's gems. I mean—the use of the acid last line. Looka:

Lines From an Old Flame

I saw your contribution in last week's
In which you state I saw and passed you by—
And that the blood crept slowly to your cheeks . . .
It made me laugh to know I made you cry.
You said you thawt that I would have some laughs—
But that I helped you fill 3 paragraphs?
Well, lemme tell you this—straight to your face,
I've answered just to help you fill more space.

☆

The slogan "You Haven't Arrived Until You've Played the Palace!" was created by a great guy and star press agent named Walter J. Kingsley. Kingsley was one of my first contributors.

His show-biz and other anecdotes made my column in *The Vaudeville News* look good. He also wrote many "specials" for the col'm (always about his clients, of course—the Palace and some of the stars who played there).

He was so knowledgeable about the theater and many other subjects that newspapers (the best and the worst) leaned on him for assistance. And Kingsley was so reliable every editor in New York (and many from coast to coast) invariably contacted him when they wanted a piece about Broadway or show folks. There was the time the drama-page editor for the New York *Sun* phoned him and requested little-known facts about Broadway, or the Met Opera House, or the origin of the word "vaudeville."

Kingsley came through every time. "Most editors, especially drama critics, are the laziest people on a paper," he once told me. "They could have done what I did for them. A copyboy could have done it."

"What did you have to do to get what they wanted?" we asked.

"I went over to the Public Library on Forty-second Street and Fifth Avenue and looked up what they wanted. It's all there—in books!"

Nennycase, I never knew Walter Kingsley to "double-plant" a news scoop or item or anecdote. And it all paid off.

When he wanted a "break" on page one (or the theater section) they paid him back. Simple as that. If you are in the press agent racket (public relations, I Begya Pod'n), you make yourself available and helpful to newspaper people and you've got to come out ahead. The army of Broadway and Hollywood "Public Relations Counselors" can take a lesson from Kingsleyana.

One day my column had a quip about Kingsley. He chuckled over it, but said: "Promise you'll tell me before you tell one on me again. Everybody on Broadway is reading your stuff, and you know how they are on Broadway. One gag that makes you look silly or a "patsy" sweeps all over the Street, and I couldn't take the ribbing."

I never again ran a gag with Kingsley as the butt. He returned the compliment by jotting down devastating quips about almost every star and nonstar in show biz. Later, as Flo Ziegfeld's pufflicist, Kingsley gave me triffic gags, wisecracks, and stories about the girls in Ziegfeld's *Follies*. He was one of my most valuable sources until he died many years later.

Milton Berle is notorious in show business and now admits that he just took everybody's best material—and that's how he made the big money and the Big Time. I gotta correct that—he was on the Big Time as a kid when he was thirteen. I took his picture when I was on *The Vaudville News* in 1920. He then played the Palace with a girl named Kennedy. I was against anybody who stole anybody else's material—a brain-picker. He almost got his old nose bent in half by Ted Healy, who really belted him out for taking his stuff.

I gave Milton the name The Thief of Bad Gags. I can't recall that I coined it, but at least I popularized it—by using it a lot. I refused to go see him anyplace because it used to make me sizzle when I saw him take somebody's best material. How I knew about it? As a kid I was a vaudeville performer and knew the acts. Even Olson and Johnson in *Hellzapoppin'* (that's another chapter) did it. Their show was funny to me because I recognized a lot of the gags—they took everybody's best act and twenty years later made a show out of it. Every critic except me panned it. They made seven million dollars in five years.

I finally went to see Milton at a place called the Carnival. It was the first time anybody ever got ten thousand dollars a week in a nightclub. And he got it. The Carnival was a little like the Persian Room, except not as classy, in the Capital Hotel on Eighth Avenue near the Garden. A cheap neighborhood and all that, but he packed them in.

Nightclub and other comedians enjoy being heckled by drunks and other pests out front. M. Berle's ace retort is: "Look, pal, I do a single!"

But Jack Waldron's squelch is a corker. "Please," he told one ringsider-oaf, "for all you know you might be heckling your own father!"

John Barrymore, one of the top drawing cards the legit theater ever had, made a bit of showbiz history before a packed house with this unexpected sizzler.

A renowned actress, seated down front, annoyed Barrymore almost all evening with her audible chatter. She acted out some of her lines by waving her arms. At curtain-time Barrymore evened matters.

In a brief talk the star reported that a famed actress had honored him by attending the performance and wanted her to take a bow. Which she did. Then he fang'd, "I want to thank you for co-starring with me this evening."

☆

Several times, when Condon was indisposed, I got out *The Vaudeville News* alone. This so impressed him that he won me a twenty-five dollar raise. My wage was now fifty dollars per. My "poems" improved somewhat months later. One of the favorites was this triple rhymer:

Broadway bred me—Broadway fed me—
  Broadway led me to a goal . . .
Broadway booed me, then it shoo'd me;
  It pooh-pooh'd me in the role.
Broadway dared me, Broadway scared me,
  Broadway spared me to earn food;
Broadway nursed me and it cursed me,
  It rehearsed me How-to-Brood.
Broadway canned me and it banned me . . .
  How it panned me and my muse!
Broadway slammed me—rammed and damn'd me.
  Broadway taught me How-To-Lose.
Broadway ruled me, Broadway fooled me,
  Broadway schooled me How-To-Cry;
Though it trumped me, bumped and dumped me
  Broadway's where I want to die.

★

LOVE'S LABOR . . .

There has been more than one woman in my life, but there is only one who mattered.

June Aster, seventeen, was part of the team of Hill and Aster, one of the most beautiful girls in the world. Her act with Olive Hill (high-kick dancing specialists) never played the Small-Time, it was always the Big-Time—the Palace on Broadway, B. F. Keith theaters in various leading cities, high-class two-a-day temples.

The first time I saw June (Elizabeth June Magee of Brookhaven, Mississippi—her grandpa founded Wentworth College in that state) the ignition switch in me turned on. Ohmigahd! She was so very beautiful. Still is.

Her figure and her legs intoxicated me, a nondrinker then. I'm a one-drink-drunk now.

My *Vaudeville News* "beat" included the NVA Club, the center for many entertainers who appeared on the two- and three-a-day circuits. Everybody gave me news about themselves—where they would play "next week" or "next month," the latest romance, an anecdote, a gag,

30

a wisecrack. I always credited them with the offering—it was pluglicity for them. Everybody, that is, but June Aster.

Her respectability was Topic A around the NVA Club, where she lived when in New York. Her beauty and grace drove all the guys nuts. They all hoped to date her. She avoided me like a plague.

One 2:00 A.M. a tipster told me: "Walter, there is a darling story about a very young girl who lives here. She is June Aster of Hill and Aster. She can't be more than seventeen or eighteen—just a kid. She has adopted a baby! Imagine that, such a very young girl herself adopting an infant. Her room is on the third floor. Why don't you do a piece about her?"

Broadway chorus and show girls then had a neat trick to keep certain people from getting their phone number. Men they didn't want to date were told the number to call was BU8-9970.

This number was a special number used by the phone company to test its busy signal. So I checked with the desk clerk and got the number of her room. It didn't dawn on me that I would be disturbing her sleep or that of the baby. People in show business usually slept until noon. So Mr. Boy Reporter stupidly knocked on the door until she asked (without opening it): "Who izzit? What *doooo* you want?"

"My name is Walter Winchell, Miss Aster. I'm a reporter for *The Vaudeville News*. I'd like to interview you about the baby."

"Oh, go 'way!" she grumbled. "You woke us up. It's after two in the morning. Go away or I will call the manager."

I felt pretty sappy. I returned to the lobby and wrote her an apology, adding: "May I please meet you in the daytime and interview you?" I got what Damon Runyon called The Old Ignore.

About two weeks passed when June was pointed out to me on her way to Broadway. I blocked her way, and cooed: "Hello, I'm that awful person who woke you and the child that two A.M. Have you forgiven me?"

She gave me a "don't-bother-me" glare and walked on. My second defeat in my encounter with June Aster.

As the old line goes: "Man is the hunter, woman the hunted." I decided to trap her.

One of my chores at *The Vaudeville News* was arranging the mail for performers—mail forwarded from the theater at which they had last appeared. Actors and actresses always left a forwarding address—usually the NVA Club, where they held the mail for two weeks—and if not picked up, it was relayed to *The Vaudeville News* for publication.

The plot thickens. I included under A the name, "Aster, June."

She took the bait. June came to the office and asked for her mail.

I kept looking through all the mail under A. No got. But I didn't tell her that—I wanted to keep here there . . . to look at her. I said: "Maybe it got mixed up with mail in the other pigeonholes." She tapped her foot impatiently as I went through them from *A* to *Z*.

Thirty minutes later she left. I had lost her again.

I read Variety's "Next Week" department. This feature listed where every act was playing. I kept looking for Hill and Aster. When I found it, I took the next train to whatever city their act was playing—Washington, Baltimore, Philly, Boston, New Haven, Hartford, Albany, Troy, Cohoes, Newark, Atlantic City, and so on. Like the lovesick jurq I was, I found myself playing the role of Stage Door Johnny. I sent her flowers, candy, presents—all out of my fifty dollars per on *The Vaudeville News*.

But La Belle Aster couldn't be bribed, bought, or nuttin'. She was civil, polite and all that, but she always "had a date" or "my mother is waiting for me!" The Old Brush-off.

Then a friend of hers told me to forget-the-whole-thing . . . that she had a favorite feller.

Overheard: "Here she comes with the busy signal I've been getting."

Then I saw them strolling along Forty-sixth Street . . . or in Child's Restaurant on the corner. He was one of those gahdamb'd good-looking guys—about six feet three. No man to duel. I saw them together in my nightmares . . . I hated him! He was dating the one girl I wanted to be mine. If he would only drop dead or something! How could she do that to me?

I learned long ago that if you want to keep all your teeth, never fool around the Other Feller's Girl. I gave up.

I couldn't eat, sleep, or laugh at the funniest comedians in show biz . . . I couldn't do a column in less than four or five hours. (It takes only two hours at the most—often an hour and a half.) I was mizzable.

★

GUYS AND DOLLS

When I was starting as a cub, Damon Runyon was a star newspaperman. We had a nodding acquaintanceship for over thirty years.

Runyon's sports page reports still are borrowed by historians. His accounts of the most sensational murder cases are studied in schools of journalism and newspaper city rooms.

One night when he went to his typewriter (to prepare a column for the papers) nothing came out of his fingers. This continued for three months. He wasn't sure why. "Have I run dry?" he mused.

To intimates he confided that he feared he was washed up; that some of the new breed of writers were so good they made his word magic look old hat, etc.

One 3:00 A.M. he decided to try writing fiction for magazines. He had never done that before. *Cosmopolitan* paid fifteen hundred dollars for that first story and invited him to write one a month.

Damon had discovered a new career! *The Saturday Evening Post, Collier's,* and other magazines outbid one another for his pieces. He continued the daily newspaper column, which was brighter than ever.

One article was christened "Romance in the Roaring Forties." The central character was a Broadway columnist named Waldo Winchester, who bore a distinct and not altogether flattering resemblance to me.

H. L. Mencken and other reputable writers hailed him as one of the innovators in the use of American slang. Hollywood paid him fancy fees to prepare the screen versions of many of his magazine articles for Shirley Temple and other movie favorites. *Little Miss Marker* and *Lady For A Day* were among the first.

Your folks and grandkin will certify how entertaining those films were —as was nearly everything else Runyon wrote.

He made several million dollars from his new career. But he saved no money for the sunset years. When one of his pals suggested he bank some of it, he asked, "What good would it do me in a bank?"

"Give you a sense of security," was the reply.

"Not me," said Damon. "I only feel secure when I am spending money. That's the only way I can tell I have it."

One of Damon Runyon's best stories became a smash Broadway musical and movie—*Guys and Dolls.* All concerned got wealthy with that show. It was credited to adapters Abe Burrows and Jo Swerling. But they did not create the story.

Runyon wrote it for the *Collier's* January 28, 1933, issue and called it "The Idyll of Miss Sarah Brown." In the fiction article the heroine was a mission girl (Salvation Army). The "villain" was a handsome gambler. But it was based on a true story.

The Salvation Army lassie was one of the loveliest girls I ever knew.

33

I met her (she was seventeen) when she captivated, hypnotized, and mesmerized her "congregation," of which I was one almost nightly, as she preached the gospel from the Gayety Theater steps near the Broadway and Forty-sixth Street corner. Down the same street a bit was the NVA Club.

I named her The Angel of Broadway in my articles about her for *The Vaudeville News* in the early 1920's.

She was Captain Rheba Crawford, daughter of a captain in the Salvation Army. She had the girliest, trimmest figure you ever saw. No lipstick, no makeup, just a few freckles and the babiest stare.

The pieces I wrote about Rheba attracted the attention of the New York newspapers. She became famous.

E. F. Albee, the owner of the Palace Theater and other Big-Time amusement temples, was fascinated with the yarns I wrote about Rheba. He suggested that all show people thank her (for bringing religion to sinful Broadway) with a testimonial dinner in her honor at the NVA Club.

Rheba told me she could not accept. "We are not permitted to frequent places where drink is served." But several top Broadway showmen and others persuaded the Salvation Army to allow us all to honor dear Captain Crawford.

It was a thrilling evening. The biggest stars from the legit and allied branches of show biz were out front or on the dais.

Rheba loved it all. No hooch was permitted throughout the event. But the cigar smoke and cigarette stink made her slightly ill. She so informed me as we left the place looking for a cab.

"Oh, Walter," she said, "I must walk. I need fresh air. I feel like I'm going to choke."

And so we walked to Broadway and then south on it—Rheba in her blue bonnet (with bow under her chin) and Salvation Army uniform and cape.

I felt, as we strolled along The Bright Lights, that pedestrians, cops, cabdrivers, motorists, and so on were glaring at me in my tux, "dating" a Messenger of God; that they saw me as a Broadway Roué—which is only partly troo. I was self-conscious about it. I told Rheba so.

We had been walking slowly for a long time. Now we were at Thirty-fourth Street—over half a mile from Forty-sixth Street. "Can't I get you a cab now?" I asked her.

"No, thanks. I want to keep walking. I don't feel too peppy. This is way past my bedtime."

"Where do you live?"

"On Bank Street in the Village."

"Oh, sister," I sighed, "that's away downtown!"

"You take a cab home," she suggested politely. "I'll walk it."

Of course I didn't leave her. With all those drunks and panhandlers and scum that stink up midtown Manhattan after midnight? No, sir. So we walked and walked and walked and talked and talked and talked.

"Walter," she said, "do you know why you came back every night to hear me preach—even when it was so bitter cold?"

"No, why?"

"It's a trick. I use it on a few people nightly. Don't you remember how often I would pause—after a piece in the Bible—and aim a finger at you? Didn't you feel that I was sermonizing especially for you?"

"Well, yes, I did. But I noticed you did that to others, too."

"That's what I mean," she giggled. "You all thought I was talking only to those I looked at for longer than a moment. You didn't walk out on me because you didn't want to hurt my feelings."

Sure enough! In vaudeville many of us did the same thing, appearing to sing or tell a gag to a person in the front row. This young lady of only seventeen was a Real Pro.

Now Rheba and This Sinner are approaching Greenwich Village where the gay places are in bunches on almost every block. "That's the famous Village Nut Club over there," I said, pointing to it.

"Where people stay up very late?"

"Yes, they do. But before going to bed, many of them stay up until early Mass or until their church opens."

Rheba was impressed. "Really? You mean they do go to church?"

"Oh, I know many people who do—even when they are a little spifflicated!" We had to cross the avenue to get to her street. I held her by the arm as we got to the Nut Club. "Don't you want to take a look —not go in, just take a look in the doorway?"

"No, it's not allowed."

"Oh, Rheba, I often see Salvation Army girls go in these places with tambourines for coins and folding money."

She didn't budge. I mean, she didn't keep walking on.

The manager, seated at a table near the entrance, recognized me. He came out and invited us in.

"No can do," I told him. "We all may get struck by lightning. Thanks."

Rheba looked in.

"Look," I urged, "can't we just sit at this table near the door, and rest our feet? I'm hungry, anyway. How about a sandwich and a Coke?"

I moved her inside. We sat at the manager's table for two. He left. I ordered a glass of Bristol Cream—a mild sherry.

The waiter assumed I had ordered a double. "Take a sip," I said, handing it to Rheba. "Makes you sleepy, really." Dat Old Debbil was at work. Satan himself. In person. Me!

She took a sip. Then another. She finished it.

I ordered another sherry to quench my own thirst. Rheba drank half of it, then fell sound asleep—head on the table.

"Jesus Christ!" I shuddered. "What'll I do now?"

I tried to wake her, but she slept like a Salvation Army Girl who had never had a drink or a sleeping pill in her life!

Maybe she's dead! I panicked. People will say I doped her.

I asked the manager to get the ladies' room attendant to help Rheba. As they tried to bring her out of it, I frantically phoned June Aster (also seventeen), at the NVA club.

"I'm in terrible trouble!" I almost kept into the phone. "Please hurry down to the Village Nut Club. That Salvation Army girl we gave that big dinner for this evening is very sick. I don't know where she lives— somewhere in the Village. Junie, please hop in a cab and take her to your room until she snaps out of it."

June dressed hurriedly and came to my rescue.

She took Rheba to her hotel club and tucked her in.

Rheba slept it off. Nine hours in dreamland—more from exhaustion than from the wine.

"What happened?" she asked June. "Why am I here?"

They became gal-pals. Rheba told her superiors that the excitement of the affair at the club—and the heavy cigar smoke, etcetera—had wearied her; and so she'd been invited to share a room with a nice girl in show biz. Her reputation was intact.

We both laughed about it for decades. Rheba, when she was a little older, married a devoted man in California. She left New York and her Blue Bonnet and uniform and became chief assistant to West Coast evangelist Aimee Semple McPherson.

One night-to-dawn in my car, I tried to keep Damon Runyon from getting bored. I told him the above saga about how I almost went to purgatory (before I was ready) doing what I didn't mean to do to a Messenger of God.

Damon was amused. He jotted down notes. I thought he planned on using them for his daily newspaper column.

But it never appeared in the paper. He sold it to a magazine, changing the character from a newspaper columnist to a gambler-lothario.

The plot of the Broadway musical came from Runyon's story, "The Idyll of Miss Sarah Brown." Its title came from a collection of Runyon's stories published in 1931 by Frederick A. Stokes Company, *Guys and Dolls*.

It was and still is a champion show. Stock companies play it every summer. Revivals of it play the sticks. The songs by Frank Loesser are still hits.

Abe Burrows and Jo Swerling and the producers still enjoy royalties.

Months later as I walked from the NVA Club to Broadway, who should ankle along (and oh, man, what ankles!) but Miss Uppitty Aster, the Gal of My Dreams, who would have no part of me.

I blocked her path, jumping from side to side so she couldn't pass. She put her beautiful hands on her beautiful hips and groaned: "What *doooo* you want?"

"I want you!" I gushed.

"Please leave me alone," she said. "Leeeeve meeee alone!"

"You are driving me crazy," I told her. "Why won't you be a regular guy and treat me like a friend? I'd love to be your friend."

We were married a week later.

Ten years later, along Hollywood Boulevard in Movietown—when I was a syndicated paragrapher in the forty-eight states and a dramatic critic and Big-Head—who should come along but June's onetime Big Date. Once upon a time in New York this bloke had kept my heart in tears dating the Girl I Wished Were Mine—and now in Hollywood, I couldn't remember his name, and I never asked June, either. It might have started her wondering whether she married the wrong man.

GLORIA

I didn't tell June that I was making only fifty dollars a week. I kept flashing a bankroll—money paid by show people for ads in the paper. June thawt I was "in the chips."

We lived beyond my means. Then she found a lovely apartment in the swanky Seventies.

As the saying went, "We have a small apartment. Nothing elaborate, except the rent." I couldn't afford it, but I didn't tell her that. I kept using some of the money the actors paid for the ads, and marked down what I "owed" to Mr. Condon for the adverts—plus the names of the advertisers. I was always in hock, pawning this and that for small sums. Condon never got wise to what I was doing. Nor did my wife.

One day I asked her whatever became of the child she'd "adopted" when I'd first heard of her.

The child was about six, of Italian-American parentage. Her name was Angelina. June had borrowed her from her mother, a stranger, when she saw Angelina sitting on a stoop where her mama was busy attending to her several other kids.

"I love children," June told the mother. "I live right next door at the NVA Club. I'm a dancer. Please let me help you care for this one," looking at Angelina. "Only for a few days. I leave town then. My act is booked upstate."

Angelina was the first of dozens of tots June took care of—as a helper for a foster child agency. The head lady of that wonderful organization was the wife of Charles Dana Gibson, a famous illustrator for the top magazines.

Whenever these ladies were short of assistants and foster mothers they phoned June and said: "We do not want to impose on you, June, but we need your help again." And so saying, agency women brought in three infants. They were given TLC (Tender Loving Care) until "placed" in other homes.

One morning my wife introduced me to a baby six weeks young.

June had been walking along West Forty-ninth Street (near the Hotel Markwell) that morn shopping. She saw a tall, thin, sickly-looking mother sweeping the sidewalk. She had several tots with her: broom in one hand, a baby cradled in her left arm, two others holding onto mama's dress, as they sucked their thumbs.

"Can't I help you with one of your babies?" June asked.

"Oh, I wish you would," said the overburdened mother. "You must love children to want to do that."

"I do, I do!" exclaimed my wife. "I'm in show business and I live not far away. Hy husband is a newspaperman." She gave the lady a five spot and her address and phone number—also my office phone number and address. "I will bring her to see you every day, I promise," June told the mother and she did so.

"Her name is Gloria," June told me, "the poor little thing, so thin and emaciated." Gloria was our "first baby," such a darling! Pablum and the other baby food that you feed infants with a spoon—and so much Love. That's what did it—Love. Gloria grew up strong and healthy. I don't recall her ever crying the way most babies cry. She never screamed or shrieked, never disturbed my sleep. I often washed and changed her diapers, took the chill off her bottle, and shoved the nipple into her rose-bud mouth around 6:00 A.M. when I came in from doing the Broadway night places just as Gloria was about to wake up—so that June could slumber a little longer.

I knew she had been up hours before, feeding Gloria. I was a Very Good Daddy. Ask Junie.

Our next address was closer to my *Vaudeville News* office in the Little Palace Building. June found an apartment above Billy LaHiff's Tavern, one of the more popular feasting places in New York. The address: 154 West 48th Street. It was later Zucca's and the owner's daughter was Axis Sally, Mussolini's "Tokyo Rose." The Tavern is gone now, but Jack Dempsey lived there, as did his manager, Jack Kearns, and Bugs Baer, the great Hearst humorist, whose stuff was swiped by more brain-pickers than anyone in the newspaper profesh. Other tenants were Damon Runyon and his new wife, Patrice, and show biz stars. Ed Sullivan and his wife, Sylvia, once dwelled there.

At a very late party (where it invariably takes everyone an hour to say ta-ta) a bore mumbled, "Hope I haven't kept you up too late."

"Oh, no," sarcasm'd the host. "We would have been getting up now anyway."

Making the nightlife rounds with my best pal, Mark Hellinger, and coming home around 6:00 A.M., I often fell asleep before June and Gloria awakened.

I hadn't seen my wife for two weeks after moving into the Tavern. She was asleep or out shopping for groceries when I left for the barber-shop or whatever I had to do in a hurry. Then one night I came in as she was feeding Gloria and I asked: "How much rent we paying in this fancy joint?"

"Only a hundred and fifty dollars a month, honey."

"*Only* a hundred and fifty a month?" I groaned. "Who's got a hundred and fifty dollars? We gotta get outta here—but right away. It's almost the first of the month!"

"All right, all right, don't get excited. I didn't know it was too much. It's a furnished apartment. It's a real bargain."

"I know that, but it's away over my head. I'll tell the landlord right away."

Downstairs (we were one flight up) I went into the Tavern and asked a man I thought was the manager of the restaurant, "Who's the landlord around here?"

"I am," said Mr. LaHiff, a gentle man. "May I help you?"

"I'm Walter Winchell," I said with a pained expression. "My wife just told me the rent is a hundred and fifty dollars and, Mr. LaHiff, I make only fifty dollars a week. I can't afford a hundred and fifty. We are moving this week."

"Justaminit," said Mr. LaHiff. "How about making it one twenty-five?"

"Oh, thanks," I told him, "but I can't make that, either."

"Hmmm," he hmmmmd. "Can you afford a hundred?"

"Yes, thanks. That'll be fine, Mr. LaHiff, thanks very much."

"Okay then," he punch-lined. "It's a hundred a month. Just promise me you won't take that baby's carriage from in front of this building—it's the only sign of respectability it has!"

That novella has been printed a lot by columnists—Runyon, Bill Corum (another sports-page star), and other colleagues. It was always my favorite story whenever I was "On," reminiscing at the now-gone Stork Club's Table 50, at El Morocco, Lindy's, and all the other favorite midnight-to-sunup places.

A onetime longtime friend of mine (I'll spare his name) wrote a book about me many years ago. He heard me relate that baby-carriage piece at least a million times. To my amazement, his ghostwriter—or the "author"—screwed it up so inaccurately that I stopped speaking to him for about twenty years. I never told him the reason. I just felt that I couldn't speak freely in front of him again. Not only because he got it so wrong, but because most of his "book" was crowded with material from my newspaper and radio-TV files, all lifted without my Go-Light. Many of the pepigrams I've published since 1920 he and his spook brazenly "borrowed." They also took (word for word) scads of my "Mr. and Mrs. United States!" radiotorials, plus my combats with numerous U. S. senators and some traitorous congressmen who were pro-Commy or pro-Nazi.

His book was a Big Phlop (financially) for the would-be fast-buc brain-pickers. And while I've forgotten it and them—I can't get myself to trust my old false friend anymore. "No partners!"

LAUNCHING THE NEW YORK *EVENING GRAPHIC*

Mr. Condon's patience with me for four years, and my determination to be a newspaperman, started a career on September 15, 1924, that brought me Fame and Riches, as they say in the Horatio Alger books.

Norman Frescott, one of the finest men I ever knew, tipped me off that Fulton Oursler was organizing a staff for the New York *Evening Graphic.* I got the job—five actually—drama critic, drama editor, Broadway columnist, and Broadway reporter for the city desk. When I ran into a hot one, it invariably was played big up front. My fifth "job" was visiting the J. P. Mueller ad agency on Forty-second Street to pick up the theater adverts for the weekend edition. No commissions—at a hundred dollars per week. Because I was well apprenticed.

After I had the job, Mr. Oursler told an interviewer why he picked me: when I was on *The Vaudeville News,* Oursler sent me quips, gags, etc., which I threw in the wastebasket. He decided that if I knew his offerings were no good, I'd make a good editor!

Bernarr Macfadden's New York *Evening Graphic* invaded Manhattan on September 15, 1924. Journalistic historians recorded the fact that "it was one of the worst newspapers in history."

Ed Sullivan and I met at the *Graphic* in 1924. It was my first big-city paper, but his first bib-burg blatt had been the New York *Mail,* years earlier. When that paper sank, he came to the *Graphic* as a sports editor —later (in 1927) a sports columnist as well. No matter how hard we dueled, I always liked him. I always liked anybody who read my column.

A few weeks after the *Graphic* signed me, a staffer I hadn't met before came to my desk and said, "Will you please loan me two bux until payday?"

"Sure," (handing him the dollars) "but whom have I the pleasure of not knowing who I'm talking to?"

"I'm," was his glum retort, "the financial editor."

But people who invest in the stock market should be reminded of this fact: over a hundred reporters are assigned to the Wall Street beat. Not one of them is rich.

Wilson Mizner's capsule critique of people who never pay back what they borrow: "No is a beautiful word. Look at all the money you save." Or as the oldie goes: "The difference between a reporter and a journalist is that the journalist is the one who borrows two dollars from a reporter."

The managing editor was Emile Gauvreau, a cripple, who had resigned editorship of the *Hartford* (Connecticut) *Courant.* Some of us wondered how an editor who worked for such a reputable newspaper could demean himself on the *Graphic,* a scandal sheet. Gauvreau stopped at nothing to win circulation, faking a lot of the sensational "news."

Imagine, then, my astonishment when he blue-pencil'd my items about married people having a baby! "This is a family newspaper," he thundered (reading proof of the column). "You cannot say people are having babies!"

To get around his edict, I reported: "Soandso and his wife anticipate a Blessed Event."

In 1925 the New York *Daily News* headlined a "scoop" on page one: "Mrs. Coolidge [President Calvin's wife] To Have Baby!"

That "scoop" lasted two editions. The White House vigorously denied it.

Time magazine featured the boner under "Press" and tittered: "We suggest the New York *Daily News* study the new columnist named Walter Winchell and get some education on the accuracy of people having a baby."

Later, one of President Calvin Coolidge's cronies brought him Rupert Hughes' devastating revelations about the Father of Our Country. "Have you read this awful stuff about George Washington?" the President was asked. "It doesn't stop at anything. It is amazing what these writers will do."

Coolidge kept looking out the window and then indifferently said, "I notice the Washington Monument is still standing."

Decades ago the leading columnists included BLT (Bert Leston Taylor), FPA (Franklin Pierce Adams), Eugene Field, Heywood Broun, Russel Crouse, Don Marquis, and Ring Lardner. Newspaper veterans say these popular paragraphers were harder workers than the current crop. They labored without the help of press agents.

Mr. Taylor came to work every morning at nine-thirty and rarely left his desk until the paper came out late at night. He didn't trust the proof-readers to catch and correct all the errata.

Lardner was so shy, they say, he sent his copy to the office via messenger, because he feared criticism and the kidding of colleagues.

FPA timidly submitted his column to the m. e. hoping for a chuckle or laugh rather than a raise in wages.

Crouse deserted the craft to be a prosperous playwright. Topnotcher Marquis gave up his column because, he said, it made him feel that he was digging a daily twenty-three-inch grave.

It was pundit Walter Lippmann who pointed out that "the reader expects the fountain of truth to bubble, but he enters into no contract, legal or moral, involving any risk, cost or trouble to himself. He will pay a nominal price when it suits him, will stop paying whenever it suits him, will turn to another paper when that suits him. Somebody has said quite aptly that the newspaper editor has to be re-elected every day."

So the newspaper—and newspapermen—feuds were fearsome. *Mirror* exec Arthur Brisbane, a hefty-sized fellow, once slugged it out with star newsman Richard Harding Davis near the old *World* building on Park Row.

The incident recalled the feud between the publishers of the old New York *Evening Post* and the New York *Sun*. An editorial in the *Post* called the *Sun* "a yellow dog." To which the *Sun* replied: "The *Post* calls the *Sun* a yellow dog. The attitude of the *Sun* will continue to be that of any dog toward any post."

During the "speakeasy" era after the Volstead Act became law—Prohibition—(no Laughing Soup), the glitterati found a refuge in the Furnace, a hot-spot owned by Broadway mobsters. You could always count on hearing gossip and guessip—or a printable anecdote about show folks, chorines' latest dates, and writers.

One 3:00 A.M., after making some of the midnight-to-dawning rounds, I wound up at the Furnace. There was one of my early boosters, the New York *World*'s Heywood Broun, a giant at word juggling. Broun, who left his mark on the craft, once told me: "Never go to the typewriter to do an editorial unless you are angry about something."

His wife, Ruth Hale, a novelist, was with him. At their table was a show-oaf named Arthur Caesar. His caustic cracks were echo'd along Broadway with the speed of an ugly rumor.

He probably was telling them a gag when Mr. Broun invited me—a newcomer nobody—to join the table. Mr. Caesar's punch line, I suppose, was ruined. He gave me a glare and said, "Go away, you gag-mendicant!"

Mrs. Broun (I mean Miss Hale) was a founder of the Lucy Stone League, which campaigned for women's rights to retain their maiden names.

Miss Hale held my arm and said, "You sit right here. Pay no attention to this fellow." She then squelched him when she consoled me with: "Mr. Winchell, Arthur is one of those bores who gate-crashes other people's heaven—and then resents it when others are invited in!"

Caesar never again cut me down or dead.

In fact, when the banks closed (in 1933) and depositors couldn't cash a check, Arthur Caesar borrowed a hundred dollars in cash. He told FPA and other top columnists and editors that he did so.

I had never met FPA, who wrote me requesting the same favor "until the banks open—here's my check."

These men ("journalism is the most underpaid of the professions," FPA once colyum'd) apparently never stashed cash in a safety deposit box. They all paid the "debt" and I made new friends.

Cast your bread upon the waters, I once read, and sometimes you get back angel food cake. All of them helped fill my column with quips and advance news about their intimates—which newspaper exec was on the Way Up or Out and so on.

The scene was Jack Dempsey's famed place, one of Broadway's bestaurants. The occasion was a beefsteak affair in a private dining room. The guest of honor was London drama critic St. John Irvine, who was guest critic for the New York *World* for seven months. He was departing for Britain the next day. His colleagues on the First Night aisles and other admirers populated the place.

Why I was invited I never found out—since we had clashed from the day his initial play reviews appeared. The windiest, dullest, and most repetitious I ever groaned about—chiefly because I had difficulty trying to find out if he had voted for the show or blackballed it.

Anyway the other critics said it would be rude if I was the only reviewer who didn't show up. So I did. I was seated between critic George Jean Nathan and novelist Jim Tully. Never met Mr. Tully until that night. Only via the mails.

Dig up his books. Tully was a writer. Not, as Truman Capote has said of others, "a typist!" Particularly eye-arresting is his tome about men he met—capsule blasts at contemporaries in the book-writing biz, the "Seven Lively Arts," journalism, stage, screen, radio, etc. His murderous essay on Charlie Chaplin (then the top film star all over the globe) is a classic. Every word of it knocks you over. The author evened matters with Chaplin, a former friend.

I was answering questions put to me by Tully—and when I "get on" (as intimates will certify)—I "stay on."

Mr. Nathan was trying to get my attention. I kept gabbing.

"I don't know how in hell you get all that news and gossip," he taunted, "when you never listen!"

Minutes later, as Mr. Tully was telling me how he started as a hobo and made the heights as a novelist, I interrupted him with, "Didja hear that funny crack Nathan just pulled?"

"George!" called Tully, "I just found out that Winchell does listen. He listens with both ears!"

Tully used that line in a book.

The New York *World* was the newspaper most New Yorkers read first in the 1920's. It created the opposite-editorial page on which columns by brilliant journalists were starred—Walter Lippmann, Heywood Broun, F.P.A., Laurence Stallings, and Alexander Woollcott.

Bob Davis, a long-ago newspaper great, was credited with helping to discover O. Henry. Davis was on the staff of the New York *Morning World,* to which O. Henry contributed a weekly story for the mag section. One day the mag editor ordered that O. Henry be dropped, saying "his stories are not good."

Davis turned a shocked stare on the editor and intoned: "God heard you when you said that."

World executive editor Herbert Bayard Swope was another memorable gent. His wife was expert at pulverizing people who said the wrong thing. One of the weekend guests at her Sands Point (Long Island) estate kept complaining about this&that. "And the flies in the sun room!" exclaimed the heckler. "I don't know how they get in a nice house like this."

As polite as all getout, Mrs. Swope said, "They come in on the guests."

But Mr. Swope and Heywood Broun clashed bitterly one day, and Broun was fired.

Mr. Swope sent for me and invited me to take over Broun's old space. He offered four hundred dollars per week.

The New York *Graphic* paid me a hundred. When I informed my editor of the *World*'s offer, he got the publisher to raise my wage to three hundred per. Friends and family shook their heads. "You had a chance to escape from the filthiest rag in town to land among the stars on the city's most readable paper and you turned it down!"

Good thing I did. The New York *World* died six months later.

★

MY GIRL FRIDAY

My first Girl Friday, Ruth Cambridge, an unemployed Broadway show girl, appointed herself my secretary.

I used to arrive at my chair-and-desk "office" in the *Graphic*'s editorial department at about three in the afternoon. I usually left around six for the barber's, a hurried snack, then to a First Night. I returned to the paper, located far downtown, to make sure my review got in and to finish the column I had begun the previous morning at one or two o'clock. I needed a secretary like Ladybird needed Eartha Kitt.

Besides, I could not afford one. A finance firm got twenty dollars from me every week, and I had my family and mother to support.

"My name is Ruth Cambridge," prefaced the tall beaut, as I two-finger pecked at the typewriter. "I understand you have no secretary, and I need a job." She explained that mutual friends (drama reporter and critic Ward Morehouse; Mark Barron, drama man for the Associated Press; and Willard Keefe, press agent for legit theater productions) had told her I had no sec.

"Sorry," I said, "I cannot afford a secretary. I cannot have anyone looking at the mail. If that got around—people might stop sending me stuff."

The phone rang. She picked it up and cooed, "Walter Winchell's office."

Oh boy! That was the first time I ever heard that one! It made me feel like a Big Shot. It intoxicated me.

She covered the phone as she relayed the name of the caller, and I signaled "not in." Ruth, who had a flirtatious way of getting rid of a pest, had her shapely leg in my door already.

The phone ding-dinged again. She picked it up and said, "Winchell's office. Miss Cambridge speaking."

The caller was an "item" in that morning's column, and he was scream-ing: "Tell that boss of yours if he doesn't retract it tomorrow—"

46

"Oh," Ruth romanced the caller, "please don't be so upset. I am sure Mr. Winchell will correct. Tell me why it was inaccurate and how you'd like it said."

Ruth got the job—because of the way she handled Mr. Threatener.

"Look," I told Ruth, "there's really very little for you to do for me except jot down phone numbers of people who call. Or an item a trusted source submits. But do not open the mail, please. Come in about two P.M. and leave at five. I'll start you at fifteen dollars per. Okay?"

Next day I found out that Ruth not only could not take dictation, but she couldn't type! When the word got around Broadway that my secretary was a Doll, the press agents and other wolf packs came all the way downtown (near Park Row) to flirt with her and hope for a date.

One of the girls I met on the Midnight Beat had had a five-year romance with a walking bank. It abruptly ended. Unlike the average Broadway Babe, she refused to take her heartache to a court and blackmail him for jilting her.

Her Romeo lost no time marrying another doll. One night the newlyweds were dining at a fashionable spot and were seated at a table next to one occupied by the heroine of this novella. The orchestra innocently added to her agony by playing five torch tunes in a row: "Can't We Be Friends?", "True Blue Lou," "Moanin' Low," "The Man I Love," and "What Is This Thing Called Love?"

The unwanted one told us the tale of the jilt in whispers. "What is his name?" I asked her. "I've forgotten it."

"Please don't ask me for it. I do not want to hurt him or his bride."

"Well, then," we persisted, "who's the gal he married?"

"A dear friend of mine," was the reply. "She was always so lonesome that whenever he took me out, I always insisted she come along."

When my column featured "Confucius Say" one-liners (in The Very Long Ago) this one was my pet: Beware of Cutie With Baby Stare. Safer To Sit In Electric Chair.

Dorothy Parker's wonderful wit has been recorded perhaps more than any other laugh-getter's and spellbinder's in *Bartlett's Quotations* and elsewhere.

I overheard this dialogue in the Stork Club Cub Room one midnight.

Miss Parker, en route to the powder room, was stopped by actress Luella Gear of the Ligit Thittr.

"Dorothy," said Luella, "I wish you would stop roasting my friend [naming another actress]—she is really a very dear person. She wouldn't harm a fly!"

"Not," needled Parker, "unless it were open."

☆

Beatrice Lillie, whose capsule comments about people invariably made the rounds from London to Hollywood, was introduced to my eyes and ears in 1924—the season that *Charlot's Revue* was imported from Piccadilly to Broadway.

Gertrude Lawrence and Jack Buchanan also starred. One of the most delightful revusicals in show biz history, few revues matched its talent and class.

Miss Lillie, alias Lady Peel (having Committed Merger with Lord Peel of Britain), never took her "Ladyship" seriously. She kidded it.

One 4:00 A.M. the Stork Club was emptying. Bea and friends were at the far end of the Cub Room. Owner Sherman Billingsley and I were at Table 50 at the other end.

Our hairlines were swiftly receding.

Sherm and I once pledged that we would never wear toupees the way star vaudevillian Phil Baker did, the way Bing does, and so many other well-knowns. Mainly because "Little Farvel" (little Phil, one of the "Boys") grabbed Baker's wig off his conk at Jack White's hilarious Club 18 on Swifty-Second Street and flung it at the comics onstage. Jackie Gleason was one of them.

"Nobody's ever gonna do that to me!" I told Billingsley.

"Me, too," he agreed.

(Billingsley broke the pledge when he invaded television. He wore a "rug" or "lace," as it is called in show biz.)

Anyway, there we were at Table 50 when along came Lady Peel.

"Oh-oh," I oh-oh-d, "here she comes more than slightly woofled, wot?"

Her Ladyship paused at our table. In all her swaying elegance. Studying our balding pates—first Mr. B's, then mine—she deadpanned, "You know why most men lose their hair?"

"No, why?"

"That's what comes from fighting your way under tight nightgowns!"

48

★

TEXAS GUINAN

Texas Guinan, a devout Catholic, reared in a convent, sold more booze during Prohibition in the 1920's and early 1930's than anyone. But she never touched it. Her top vice, she said, was chain-smoking cigarettes. You couldn't put one between your lips and light it without Tex taking it.

She hostessed the most prosperous nightclub in New York at the time. The $ocially Regi$tered were her Second-Best spenders and tippers. The Number One spenders and tippers, of course, were the Mobsters.

The Hudson-Duster gang chiefs (Madden and Big Frenchy) were her bosses—in the dark background.

Long before Murder, Inc. made the headlines, Owney Madden was Manhattan's Number One tough guy. He led "The Irish Mafia" long before newspaper people pinned that label on President J. F. Kennedy's inner circle: The Palace Guard.

Mr. Madden came from Liverpool, England. He began his underworld career as a chicken thief on the midtown West Side near the Hudson River. His partner in the Hudson-Duster gang was a character called Big Frenchy, whose square monicker was George de la Mange. His parents came from France. The Irishers in the mob included "Johnny Irish" Costello, formerly of Boston, and one of the gang's marksmen—named Sullivan.

He prospered along with Big Frenchy and others during the Prohibition era peddling booze—mainly lager beer.

They rented a large brewery near the Hudson River in the lower Forties. The law made a few "token" raids. But the mob had the City Fathers in their hip pockets.

They soon owned twenty-two night spots on Broadway and side streets between Forty-fourth and Fifty-eighth streets. They also were the proprietors of The Cotton Club in Harlem when Lena Horne was a chorus girl in the line there. Their gold mine was Texas Guinan's. This was where the rich-raff of the town, along with playboys (Tommy Manville, Harry Kendall Thaw, *et al.*), hookers, and columnists (such as Mark Hellinger and this reporter) gathered almost nightly from 11'ish until 6 A.M. French and Little Gus; Big Gus; Honest Joe, the Goniff; Feets Edson; Tommy Guinan, Miss Guinan's brother; and city and state officials, judges, lawyers, and respectable citizens alcoholidayed there nearly every midnight.

Tex was the only ally of the gangster night spot-speakeasy-owners I ever knew who bulldozed them. They didn't dare raise their voices to her. She was their Big Front. And she hated them all.

Texas was a very attractive woman (in her fifties—I was twenty-seven) when we first met. She "invented" the modern gossip column. I mean the one for which I am best known.

The column I did when I started contained no chitchat or gossip. It dealt mainly with theater-people quips, anecdotes, and human-interest stories and gags told by people in show biz—folks with whom I'd soft-shoe'd on the vaudeville bills coast to coast.

After a long night from about nine till sunup, perched on a bar stool a bit to the right of the podium where her lovely chorus girls hoofed (Ruby Keeler started with Texas when she was sixteen), Miss Guinan then relaxed for an hour or two with the newspaper people who covered her place nightly. Like Mark Hellinger and Walter. In those days, when I was on the *Graphic,* Mark was at the *Daily News* at 25 Park Place, not far from the *Graphic* on Varrick Street—both in lower Manhattan.

When I got through with another column, I was ready to phone Hellinger: "You done? I'm done! Meetcha at Spinrad's." That was a barbershop in the Forty-seventh Street subway where you could get a shave, a hair trim, and a manicure up to midnight. You saw all the gang chiefs and their stooges there. Lucky Luciano, Bugsy Siegel, Owney Madden, Big Frenchy, Little Gus, and other Underworld Phaggitz. Mark was doing one column a week, and also did the up-front, city-side stuff so far as Broadway was concerned. One of his big stories was about Tot Quarters, the Winter Garden's number one show girl, who eloped with a rabbi's son. That was the kind of stuff they were featuring. Mark was a specialist at that. He started on *Zits Weekly,* which was really a scandal sheet, very much like the *National Inquirer* and all those other things.

We covered Broadway from midnight to sunup seven nights a week. "If Hellinger comes," the saying went, "can Winchell be far behind?" The gintellectuals nicknamed us the Damon and Pythias of Broadway. The population Hellinger and I wrote about were mainly illiterates . . . gangsters, playbores, chorines, show gels, Prohibition Agents and society youths. The latter moonlighted as tipsters to the Feds, on where the lawmen could make a raid . . . Charming stool pigeons. One two-legged rodent wound up losing all of his teeth when the proprietors of the twenty-two joynts found out about him.

I often escorted Texas Guinan back to her Greenwich Village address about seven o'clock in the yawning. But between five o'clock and ta-ta-time, Texas drank as many cups of java as she smoked cigarettes. And she kept up a running commentary about the people who jammed her night club.

"Oh, Brutha!" she said one 6:00 A.M., "could I tell you one!"

"Frinstance?"

"Mrs. Vanderbilt is going to have twins!"

"Who?"

"Mrs. Vanderbilt! One of the most famous society ladies in the world!"

"Oh." My world then was populated with show folks. Vanderbilt? So wot?

"I just gave you a heckuva scoop," said Texas. "Why don't you make a note of it for the column, you fool!"

"How does anyone know," I asked, "if a woman is going to have twins?"

"Doctors can tell. They listen for two heartbeats. Don't you read the papers?"

The next column included that item. Weeks later, Mrs. Vanderbilt had twinfants.

Readers began taking my column "seriously" because it contained tidbits like that item. Someone once said, "Gossip is what everybody enjoys when it's about the other fellow." Here is a paragraph from the works of Matthewman that should be thumbtacked on the walls of every newspaper office: "Even those who do not repeat scandal are generally willing to listen to it. Talk of virtue and your readers will become bored. Hint of gossip and you will secure perfect attention." A country weekly offered the best observation, to wit: "If you get born, marry, have a baby, die or some other accident happens to you, please let us know. Not that we give a darn, but most of our readers have a lot of curiosity."

Texas was a mine of anecdotes, too, and wisecracks. I quoted her almost daily. "Texas Guinan tells the one about the fellow, who . . ." Dorothy Parker, s'helpme, never was quoted so often.

Texas went into the books with her affectionate greetings to male patrons: "Hello, Sucker!" and "Why, if it isn't my old friend, Fred, the Butter-and-Egg man!"

She gave me more "big" column-scoops than any contributor.

When Gloria was six weeks young, Texas went to Macy's Thirty-fourth Street department store at nine in the morning and almost bought out the doll and toy department. A mountain of playthings for an infant! They were delivered in the largest box I ever saw. We didn't have to buy our children a doll or toy for years.

Miss Guinan, who seemed to stay healthy on only black coffee and cigarettes, rarely had time to feast. I do not recall seeing her finish a steak or a real meal. Club sandwiches often sufficed. Perhaps she didn't enjoy food.

And that's the Irony-Of-It. Food killed her. She died in a San Francisco hotel—from food poisoning.

I still can't believe she isn't around. She was so much a part of my heart.

I have never really felt she has Gone. She was so alive!

In show business, people go on tour for months, sometimes for a year, and your act is booked miles from where people you like a lot are performing. You become accustomed to "not seeing each other" for long spells. That's how I've always felt about Tex.

I just haven't seen her lately. We'll be seeing each other again one day. Maybe next year . . . next month . . . next week?

When other echoes pirated word weddings, style, and stuff for which I was credited (by some of the fiercest foes) as "The Daddy Of Them All" and "the creator of the modern gossip column," many of them said in person, and in print, "Stop complaining. Imitation is the sincerest form of flattery!"

The Hell It Is! Robert Ripley's "Believe It Or Not" was perhaps the most widely syndicated feature of its kind and one of the tallest paid in the United States. Many of the big-city papers paid as much as two hundred and fifty per week for it.

Ripley, riding on the highest cloud, decided to relax. He taught one of his staff how to do his trick. He revealed the secret for making countless pinpoint ink dots—Ripley's remarkable "magic" was embossed paper. Running a thick black crayon over it made all those mini-dots, like periods.

The staffer (went the legend in the craft) was paid fifty dollars per week. He was so good at copying Ripley's style, you couldn't detect the difference between his skill and Ripley's.

One day he resigned and went into business for himself. He offered many of Ripley's clients "the same thing" (under another title) for fifty dollars per week—as against Ripley's fee of two hundred and fifty. He wound up with almost as many papers as his former boss and tutor formerly enjoyed.

Ripley's hefty list of papers—and income, of course—was considerably diminished.

"Imitation is the sincerest form of flattery"? My foot! It's the sincerest form of burglary.

★

HIS HONOR, THE MAYOR OF NEW YORK

James J. Walker ("Jimmy" to those who liked him and didn't) was the living spirit of the terrific 1920's . . . way back to when we saps believed a rising stock market was taking us nearer to heaven on earth; when everybody thought the lottery had more prizes than tickets. When flaming youth and lights of Broadway were the vogue—and the torch of the Statue of Liberty was a forgotten, burned-out electric bulb—Jimmy Walker led the parade. He was more than a product of that age. He was the expression of it. To pussyfoot around and say Jimmy was below the conscience of the American people is sheer, unadulterated bunk.

Mr. Madden was Number One Man of the New York top mob throughout Mayor Jimmy Walker's terms. He and Big Frenchy—Number Two Man in the Hudson-Dusters—not only were the landlords of twenty-two prosperous nightclubs, restaurants and speakeasies. The Mob also "owned" the politicians, who really mattered.

When Walker was an assemblyman in 1924, and then ran for the mayoralty, Madden asked me: "You for Jimmy?"

"Yes, very much. He was the principal speaker at the testimonial dinner for me at Billy LaHiff's Tavern the night before I started my first newspaper job on the *Graphic*. He said he felt sorry for me, saying: 'I just found out you will also be the dramatic critic! Oh, you poor man,' clowned Walker. 'Look at all these stars here tonight to honor a crrrritic! I can only predict, Walter, that if you give them good notices, you will keep all these friends, But if you are faithful to the playgoer who reads your reviews, you will lose all these false friendships!' "

It got a Large Laugh and Big Applause. Jimmy's prediction, of course, eventually came true.

Madden said, "Puddit in the paper that you like Jimmy and that people should vote for him."

I didn't need Madden's advice or suggestion. Jimmy Walker knew I was "for" him all the way. When I left Madden's offices (in the old Publicity Building at Forty-seventh Street where Broadway divorces Seventh Avenue) I mused, "Jeezuzz. Gangsters really run this town."

The Wall Street investigation five years later by FDR proved that Jimmy was not a statesman. He was a politician. But in place of a statesman's vision, he had instead, a politician's sympathy and understanding. He was not only elected mayor, he was expected to be the city's master of ceremonies.

In the 1920's the American people were hell-bent for prosperity and riches. And they wanted a politician who was hell-bent only for reelection . . . in short, a guy who would go along with the times—a man who would respect the national rush to get rich, who would accept greed, avarice and the lust for quick gain as a legitimate expression of the will of the people.

As a politician, Walker knew what the people wanted. And as a mayor, he gave it to them.

Once Walker entered a nightclub and was jostled by a small-town big shot who didn't recognize him. Walker bowed, then smiled, but the big shot would have none of it. "Do you know who you are talking to?" he asked Jimmy very belligerently.

"No," said Jimmy, "but take my chair and I'll go out and find out for you."

One of the best exchanges occurred when La Guardia opposed Mayor Walker's raise in salary from twenty-five to forty thousand dollars. La Guardia said forty thousand a year was too much. "Think how much it would cost," said the never-punctual Jimmy, "if I worked full time!"

Mr. Walker, a handsome hunk of he-man had been parted (for decades) from Mrs. Walker, a devout Catholic. It cost him the goodwill of the Church—and of Governor Al Smith, also a devout man. Jimmy fell in love with former show girl Betty Compton. Their courtship was Topic A in Manhattan and elsewhere.

Fiorello La Guardia, the Fusion candidate for mayor of New York, was running to dispossess "Mr. New York." La Guardia's team heard about Jimmy and Betty and breathlessly reported the scandilly to "The Little Flower." "Fahevvensakes!" exclaimed respectable La Guardia, "don't let that get into the papers—it'll get Walker another hundred thousand votes!"

Jimmy shrugged off the criticism by the Church, the Governor, and Catholics in high and low places. One night at the Stork Club, he told me: "I make my private life pretty public. I don't sneak in and out of restaurants, nightclubs, the Central Park Casino [his pet spot], the fights at Madison Square Garden, or the opening nights at the Broadway theaters. I take Betty with me everywhere—always where the lights are brightest. Right down front at ringside in Madison Square Garden or in Row A at the plays! The whole audience sees me and Betty. I have nothing to hide. I'm in love."

The newspapers published pix of their hand-holding almost daily. When editorialists and others condemned Walker for the romance—and the way he flaunted it—he went into the New York history books with this oft-quoted crack: "I'll match my private life with any man's!"

Nobody ever risked it.

When Walker ran for reelection the last time, he did so under great pressure from Tammany Hall, every New York Democrat's Svengali. He didn't want to run.

Tammany chiefs insisted that the party couldn't win unless he did. He finally was persuaded and told them he would run—providing he didn't have to make any speeches.

In the final week of that campaign they told Walker that unless he was willing to get out and do some campaigning, the ticket would flop. Angry as he was, Jimmy obliged his bosses and during the last week made several glib speeches daily.

The traditional last Democratic rally in the mayoralty election was always held at the Savoy Ballroom in Negro-populated Harlem. At that event Jimmy ("Mr. Unpunctual") arrived at the Savoy about an hour tardy—after making about a dozen speeches in the five boroughs of Greater New York.

By this time Our Hero was pretty squiffed but—with a little assistance from aides—he made the podium and delivered what I have always considered to be the shortest and sockiest political speech in the history of American politics.

"Ladies and Gentlemen . . . [the usual Walker pause] . . . and I mean Ladies and Gentlemen . . . [lusty hand clapping] . . . while I was driving up to this last big and most important rally of my campaign, a man on one side was telling me about all the things I did for the Negro while I was in the State Assembly. A fellow on the other side of me was telling me of all the things I did for the Negro while I was mayor of the City of New York.

"Well, I'll tell you the truth. In all my political life I never did anything for the Negro! . . . [big Walker pause—with consternation on all sides] . . . I never did anything for the Catholics either; I never did anything for the Jews or Italians or the Germans—because, Ladies and Gentlemen, I don't know the difference! Good night."

☆

When Gene Fowler wrote *Beau James* (about Jimmy), some of us thought he knew the above story and would make a highlight of it. However, Fowler later said he never heard it or he would have used it.

I do not think it ever got into print because the reporters covering Walker that long day had become exhausted. They quit to file their reports before Jimmy Savoy, showstopper.

Jimmy's faults and his virtues were too fully dramatized not to be very well known to the voters. They wanted what Jimmy had—a debonair, shoot-the-works guy to lead the grandest show in the history of the Big Burg. And Jimmy wanted to give them just that. The people thought Jimmy was exactly what they wanted—and that's proved by the fact that he was reelected by a larger majority in his second campaign.

So why all this hypocrisy? Jimmy was a Tammany mayor, and proud of it. He ran on the Tammany ticket and millions of people who voted for him knew it. You can't cast a vote with your eyes shut . . . neither can you blame a politician for giving you what you want. But it is pure fakery to say you didn't want it in the first place because it turned out you didn't like it after you got it.

From a book published many years ago by Putnam: "George Jessel and Winchell were comrades in greasepaint (when they appeared in a vaudeville act in 1910) but took separate routes to fame and fortune. They remained good friends until Jessel told a friend, 'I have a speech ready for Walter Winchell's funeral, and I hope it's this afternoon.'"

That's not as funny as what Jimmy Walker, still mayor of New York, said about my funeral.

He was waiting for his car in front of a supper spot. So was I.

A drunk came out of the place and hiccuped: "Well, well, well, Mr. Winchell! The man who will go into the books for the things he has printed!"

To which the mayor intoned, "You are wrong, sir. He will be remembered by some of us for the things he did not print!"

He meant several stories about his private life with Betty Compton. And the drunk continued, "How come someone hasn't shot you?"

A cop took him away.

56

"Jimmy," I chuckled, "would you come to my funeral?"
"What!" he ejaculated. "And get killed in the crush?"

★

BLESSED EVENT

From the book *The Fifty Year Decline and Fall of Hollywood* by Ezra Goodman, page 287: "One reporter asked Lucille Ball how Winchell got a big news story about her.

"She replied, 'I don't think it is difficult for Mr. Winchell to have access to anything. He told me I was pregnant before I knew it.'"

That brings us to my most unusual Blessed Event.

Lillian Hellman, playwright (*The Little Foxes, The Children's Hour* and other smash hits) and her ex-husband, playwright-humorist Arthur Kober were among the Broadway people I called on almost daily seeking anecdotes, quips, trivia, gossip, and news for the column. Miss Hellman was in her husband's Shubert Theater Building office over Sardi's. Kober was one of the press agents for the Shubert empire.

I came in like a mendicant begging for alms. "What do you know I don't know?" I greeted.

Lillian watched her husband jot down a few items and cooed: "I could tell you something—but I shouldn't."

I persuaded her.

"Peter Arno of *The New Yorker* and his wife, Lois Long [she authored the breeziest banter, signed "Lipstick," in that mag], are having a baby."

"Oh, brother!" I ejaculated. "That's swell! Thanks. Are you sure?"

Remorse set in. "Oh, you had better not print it," she hedged. "I really do not know."

"Then why did you say it?"

"I was talking to Lois last night," explained Lillian, "and she sighed, 'Wouldn't it be just my luck? I think I'm in a family way!'"

"Is that all you know about it?" I grimaced, as I crossed the item from my notes.

As I started colyuming, *The New Yorker* was on my desk. I skimmed through it, but paused to read "Lipstick" and her devastating reports on new shows in the swank night spots.

In her review of the new show at Barney Gallant's Greenwich Village bistro, she groaned that "a smart aleck named Winchell ruined the fun

57

for many women at Barney's on opening night. He went around squirting a bottle of seltzer at the people. He splashed a lot of it on my new dress."

William Randolph Hearst, Sr., had a slogan on his city room bulletin boards which shouted: "Get It First, But First, Get It Right!"

Seeing Miss Long's scolding, I sizzled. It happened all right. I saw it happen. But I was not the smart aleck who did it. The party pooper was practical joker Borrah Minevitch, a vaudeville headliner. It was he who soaked Lois' new frock with his Little Boy prank.

Newspaper competitors and others were talking about my Blessed Event items—and how they were "usually" accurate. And now *Time* magazine had been telling the *News* (the nation's Number One Circulation) to take lessons from Walter on baby reportage.

The column was almost done—and looking it over I noticed that it didn't have one Blessed Event.

The Machiavelli in me made me chuckle.

Lillian had said she "assumed" Lois was preggy because Lois told her she thought she "might" be.

Intelligent newsmen never take themselves too seriously. They know newspaper people always have one foot on a banana peel. I decided to print "a baby is expected over at the Peter Arnos' (Lois Long) of *The New Yorker.*"

"I'll run it, anyway," I shrugged, "and let Mrs. Arno yell her head off. I'll show the beautiful bitch how it feels when someone gets it wrong!"

The *Graphic* was on the stands about 11:00 A.M. Lois had gone to her physician two hours before. She told him she wanted an examination. "I think I'm pregnant."

He dismissed her with a pat on her shapely fanny. "Go home. No baby!" The relieved Lois hastened home.

About 11:15 A.M., her three phones clanged like fire-engine gongs. Every caller exclaimed, "Lois darleeeng! What wonderful news! Winchell says you and Peter will become Three!"

"But he is wrong, dammit!" Lois shrieked back. "I just came from the doctor. I am not having a baby!"

The phone calls came in bunches. One after the other.

She couldn't sleep that night. All that day Lois had kept worrying— what if the doctor is wrong and Winchell isn't? She was her medic's first visitor next morn.

"Oh, Doctor," almost wept Lois "Lipstick" Long, "I know I'm a fool worrying like this, but Walter Winchell's column yesterday reported I was having a baby. Please examine me again to make certain? I wouldn't make such a thing of this, Doctor, but that bastard's accuracy is deadly!"

She got on the table for the exam. It seemed endless. "That fellow's accuracy," was the doc's verdict, "embarrasses me!"

Nine months later, husband Peter phoned me the skewp: "It's a Girl for the Peter Arnos (Lois 'Lipstick' Long) of *The New Yorker.*"

This is the first time Lois will learn that the source was pal Lillian Hellman—despite the fact that Lillian and Lois' doctor were inaccurate at the time.

Lois landed in the papers again when her baby was vaccinated—the first time (I think) that a baby was not vaccinated on the arm. The source for this was the great wit, dramatic critic, and television-movie star, Robert C. Benchley, also of *The New Yorker.* One midnight at Tony's (a popular saloon in the West Fifties) Benchley invited me to his table for a drink. Between his howls of laughter, he related that "No daughter of mine," decided the mother, "is going to have her vaccination where it can be seen! Put it," she instructed the physician, "under one of her feet."

My favorite Blessed Event epic.

★

DROPOUT GETS TO COLLEGE!

Over forty years ago the late literary editor, critic, and genius Burton Rascoe thumbed his nose at his detractors and mine—and invited me to do pieces for *The Bookman,* one of the more popular publications for intellectuals.

Mr. Rascoe's contributors were topflight writers. The checks were always mini. No author, renowned or newcomer, expected more than "your usual rates." The Big Idea was to get your stuff into *The Bookman.* Status. Up-there-with-the-importants. Being in with the In-Crowd.

The piece of mine Rascoe published in 1927 brought immediate invites from *College Humor* (for which I did an article every issue); the old *Life* (when it was a humor mag); *Dance* magazine (because they thought I was a dancer when I was really a soft-shoer in small-time vaudeville theaters); *Collier's, Cosmopolitan,* and other magazines.

But the one ride I most enjoyed was getting into *Vanity Fair*—then one of the most popular publications. Its byliners included George Jean Nathan (at the time the nation's top drama critic), Dorothy Parker,

Robert Benchley, Ring Lardner, and many of the other Big-Timers. I sold it several articles.

Many weeks after *The Bookman* introduced me to its subscribers, I got a letter from a stranger. A student at Ohio State told me he desperately needed a good grade in his English class. He hoped I didn't mind that he had "borrowed" a piece I had done for *The Bookman* and submitted it under his own name.

The young man later sent me—a dropout from the sixth grade at P.S. 184!—this thrilling news: "Congratulations! You got an 'A' in English at Ohio State!"

Many years later I received the following letter.

> Dear Walter: My name is Lester Biederman. I'm a sports writer with the Pittsburgh Press and spending my vacation at my brother's in Los Angeles.
>
> You may not remember me but several years ago (1925–30) when I was a student at Ohio State University, I told you about a story I picked up of yours, for which I was credited with an "A" in English class. You often commented on it in your column—omitting my name—but happily after I graduated and therefore, no kickback from the faculty.
>
> Although I'm with a Scripps-Howard paper I still heartily enjoy your columns and am glad to say that I was one of the first discoverers of yours on the old *Graphic* when I was a college student. —Lester Biederman.

In 1966 I was pecking away at a portable in the press box at Dodger Stadium, Los Angeles. A man approached and smiled a Hello, There! "Does the name Biederman ring a bell?" he asked.

"Oh, my goodness!" I ejaculated. "You are not the boy from Ohio State?"

"That's me," said Les Biederman. "I want to thank you in person for the help you gave me to graduate."

"What are you doing here?" I asked.

"Covering the Dodgers for my paper, the Pittsburgh *Press.*"

Well, whaddaya know? Time Sur Do Fugit!

"Look," I told Biederman, "I came through for you. Now you can do the same for me. I pledged I would never reveal your name. I may do a book some day and I'd like very much to include you in it. Go right back to your Underwood or Remington or Royal or whatever you use and write me a note telling me you release me from my pledge. Okay?" Which he did.

An "A" in English at Ohio State!

Who, me??? Hahahahaha. Principal Kidd and my favorite teacher, Miss O'Donnell, must be in stitches.

The fellow who really won that "A" in English was not the kid who was "left back" four times in the same class at P.S. 184 for being the dunciest dope in that school on West 116th Street, Harlem. The winner of that "A" was Mr. Burton Rascoe, the first literary giant to give me space in his reputable mag, *The Bookman*.

I hope his daughter (who sent me a postcard from Europe early this year) has her attention summoned to this chapter. I want her to know that this winchellectual has never forgotten her wonderful father.

Years before I got my first reportorial job on the weekly *Vaudeville News*, O. O. McIntyre parlayed a gimmick into the most widely syndicated newspaper column.

McIntyre (we never met) conducted "New York Day by Day," which enjoyed syndication over five hundred papers according to the "Literati" page in *Variety*. It was not a gossip pillar the way you know them today. No Blessed Events, marriages, divorces, romances, etc. Mr. McIntyre, who had spent his boyhood in Ohio, was enchanted by New York City —the Broadway First Nights, the swank cafés and restaurants, and the high and low whose stories supplied "human interest."

McIntyre served his apprenticeship in Manhattan as a press agent. His first client was the Majestic Hotel, now an apartment edifice on Central Park West between Seventy-first and Seventy-second streets. He dwelt there rent-free and returned the compliment by mailing a column of New York paragraphs gratis to newspapers in which there was a mention for the Majestic Hotel, plus plugs for cafés and restaurants which picked up the tab. That, I suppose, was the birth of the colyuming Freeloaders. Many byliners inherited Odd's "racket."

McIntyre's daily stint dealt with celebrities in The Big Town and the activities of his glamorous intimates. Many of the latter included well-knowns in the allied arts. His best paragraph, we thought, was christened "Purely Personal Piffle," and is still imitated by brain-pickers coast to coast.

Columnist Franklin Pierce Adams (FPA), monitor of "The Conning Tower" in the New York *World* and other Manhattan gazettes, did not appreciate McIntyre's fascinating trivia. FPA twitted and kidded his stuff a good deal of the time. He especially ridiculed his reports about

New York's Chinatown—when McIntyre breathlessly reported "the slant-eyed characters slinking in and out of alleys" and ominous'd that "nobody knows how many white girls have been attacked, molested, slain and buried under Chinatown's tenements."

Readers in the hinterland devoured every word. McIntyre died wealthy, FPA died broke.

Now prospering, McIntyre frequently used anecdotes, quips, and wise-cracks from the *Vaudeville News* column. So did S. Jay Kaufman, Bide Dudley, Karl K. Kitchen, and other chroniclers of Broadway. All of them gave due credit. "Walter Winchell," prefaced one of Mr. McIntyre's paragraphs, "tells the one about the actor who . . ."

This was peachy. It was good promotion for me. I thanked him every time he mentioned my name—specially since I was not yet syndicated.

For many years, however, his column could not connect with a New York newspaper. Hearst's New York *American* finally took him on in 1928, ironically four years after my column appeared in the New York *Evening Graphic*. His friends later told me that it nettled him to wait "so long to be published in Manhattan—and only because a former vaudeville hoofer [thaz me] made it first."

That is not a fact. S. Jay Kaufman's column about New Yorkers, First Nighters, opera notables, social climbers, and other characters en-joyed a long run in several local gazettes. No syndication. (It was Kauf-man, by the way, who introduced the Guest Column. He persuaded the most popular and best-known writers, novelists, play-authors, stars of Hollywood and Broadway to fill his space every June or July so that he could cover the goings-on in Vienna, Berlin, Rome, London, Copen-hagen, etc.)

Then, with great regularity, the McIntyre column lifted several of my notes—with no mention of the source.

After I landed with King Features Syndicate, I asked him to stop doing it. "Some day," I memo'd McIntyre, "I hope to put some of my stuff in a book—or when I am stuck for material, I may have to repeat from my files. Your editors and readers will then accuse me of swiping your stuff. Please cut it out."

Odd Oscar McIntyre didn't stop pilfering. I goosed him with: "The Very Odd McIntyre" and "Odd McIntyresome" and similar nonlibelous shin-kicks. Eventually he quit using stuff from the column. But more anon.

☆

Debunking the Bunk: from the puff-piece biog of Ed Sullivan: "Bitterness between Ed and Walter Winchell began in the 1920's. . . . In 1928 the managing editor [of the *Graphic*] treated Winchell in almost sadistic fashion and Sullivan appealed to a vice-president of the paper. The editor found out and vented his fury at Sullivan, who was bitter when he was told that the informer had been Winchell himself."

Impossible. I had stopped talking to the louse editor years before. Gavreau treated me sadistically, because that's how I treated him first. He had removed me as drama critic to appease the Shubert showmen, who were threatening to stop their ads. (George Holland went into the show biz history tomes as another of the drama critics barred by the Shuberts from their theaters. When he was drama sentinel for a Boston newspaper, Jake Shubert banned him for his insolence toward incompetents. Mr. Holland got himself appointed a city fire official, which got him into every Boston theater at will.)

In the old show biz days a popular gag went: "Who called that piccolo player an S.O.B.?"

"You mean, who called that S.O.B. a piccolo player?"

The now very dead Gavreau had a hobby—playing the piccolo. The following ackchelly got into my column in his own paper:

"Two reporters were rapping an editor. One said, 'Who called that editor an S.O.B.?' 'You mean, who called that piccolo player an editor?' "

It ran three editions until Gavreau read it and almost choked with fury. This may give you an idea of how fierce our battles were.

And so, I could never have "informed" him about anything. The fact is I told O. J. Elder, the Big Man at Macfadden Publications (owners of the paper), about my nemesis, the editor. Mr. Elder stopped him from chopping punch lines out of the column, etc.

★

WORKING FOR HEARST

Bill Curley, top editor of Mr. Hearst's New York *Journal,* was the one who hired me at five times the wages I got on the New York *Graphic.* Hired me, that is, two and a half years before my contract with that rag was up. He gave me a thousand-dollar "gratuity" (he called it) just to sign the contract two and a half years before he could get me.

Curley never got me on the *Journal* because Mr. Kobler, then newly made *Mirror* publisher, persuaded The Chief—William Randolph

Hearst—to "let me borrow him for one year to get things humming around here and I promise to give him back to Bill Curley." The Chief agreed. And because I never got there, it opened the way for an "echo" of mine to land the job. He had practiced imitating the gossip-column format I "introduced to journalism"—an editor's quote. When Mr. Hearst signed me in June, the *Graphic* hired five men at a hundred dollars each to do the five jobs I'd been doing for a hundred dollars a week. Louis Sobol was assigned to cover the Broadway scene and review the plays. (Months later, Mr. Sobol was also lured from the *Graphic* to do a Broadway gossip pillar for the *Journal.*)

☆

Hearst's *Mirror* imitated the New York *Daily News* and wound up losing ten million dollars yearly for ten years.

The late Captain James Patterson, publisher-founder of the New York *Daily News,* enjoyed being a reporter between editions. He would leave his executive duties to turn up unexpectedly where news was being born and inform the reporter covering the story, "Here I am. What's to be done? Understand now, you're the boss and I am working for you. What angle do you want me to take?"

Ruth Snyder and her uh-huhney Judd Gray almost got away with murder, but for one of Patterson's underlings. The police suspected them of killing husband Snyder while he slept, but they had Gray's "alibi" to confound them. Lover Gray said he was nowhere near New York or Queens County at the time of the crime. He told lawmen that he was in Syracuse on a business deal. He invited detectives to take him there to document it.

Gray, it appears, had put a "Do Not Disturb" sign on his hotel room doorknob. Hotel maids reported that the sign had been there for at least two days and nights. Gray explained that away by saying he had wanted to catch up on lost sleep.

The sleuths searched his room and bath but found no clues. They were on the verge of giving up and returning with Gray to New York when *Daily News* reporter George Kivel handed them a small bit of paper that he had found floating in a spittoon. It was a Pullman car receipt for a lower berth from New York to Syracuse dated the evening of the murder.

It became Gray's one-way ticket to the Chair.

Colonel Frank Hause, one of the early editors at the *News*, didn't believe in keeping news a secret. He argued that people who told things in whispers and who added, "Don't repeat this, it's a big secret," kept misquoting the secret until it became libelous.

Colonel Hause reminded, "The safest place for a secret is page one."

Murray Kempton, writing for the New York *World Telegram Sun* in March 1966, said in part: "Capt. Patterson's single great defeat was his failure to develop a Broadway column [in his New York *Daily News*] to compete with the *Mirror's* Walter Winchell. He used up several lone troopers in this battle; when he finally conscripted John Chapman, his managing editor told Patterson that no one could keep up with Winchell, and that the only remedy was to give a $5 bonus to every reporter who turned in an item that could be used in Chapman's column.

" 'No,' Patterson answered, 'we'll ruin one man at a time.' "

When I moved over to the *Mirror,* Miss Cambridge began complaining that the work was too heavy for one girl.

Ruth's salary was still fifteen dollars, but I got her another fifteen from *Mirror* publisher, Albert Kobler, whom she hypnotized with her girl magic the first time they met. Mr. Kobler assigned her to "moonlight" as a reporter in the mornings.

Her first assignment was a "probable jumper," a young woman out on a ledge of a hotel—high up. Ruth hastened to the address, but arrived too tardy to see the poor woman Let Go.

She joined other newspaper people in the backyard to "get the story." What Ruth saw made her swoon. Back at the paper, she was still weeping—and in shock. "Oh," she sobbed, "it was awful, so awful."

A reporter took down what little she had learned and devoted a "side bar" to the reactions of our "Girl Reporter" on her very first assignment. It made excellent human-interest stuff. When the publisher heard about it, he sympathized, and told her she was now the paper's first book reviewer—same salary, fifteen bux. Thirty, with the fifteen I paid her. When I began to earn more loot on the air, she got a lot more.

Ruth Cambridge's luck stayed with her. I introduced her to Buddy Ebsen, whose act (with his sister Vilma) I boosted almost daily until they landed in their first Broadway show, the *Ziegfeld Follies.* Buddy Ebsen and Ruth Cambridge became a steady-date.

From the *Denver Post* and other gazettes of November 2, 1929:

"Gilbert Miller has suggested to Walter Winchell, critic and story-teller of the *New York Mirror,* that he remain away from the Miller plays and theaters for a while. Mr. Winchell already is exiled from several other New York playhouses. It is his sense of humor, always acute, that gets him in trouble with producers and managers, and Walter very likely soon will find himself a critic always dressed up with no plays to go."

But it wuzzon so. Mr. Miller, who called our attention to the spurious report, added that if it were true, it would indeed be the Millernium.

For reviewers only! These insults were made by Anthony Pasquin in his book *Children of Thespis* in 1792:

> When I first undertook to write this poem, it was through a thorough contempt for the opinion of those persons who have arrogated to themselves the high and mighty title of Reviewers, and this contempt originated from my having a perfect acquaintance with the vices and weaknesses of the men; being superior to their jurisdiction, I dare tread upon their assumed authority. I know them to be blockheads of the first magnitude, envious and stupid, cowardly and corruptible. When a man destitute of feeling is fit for no other purpose in society, he may make a tolerable executioner; so a literary dunce, when denied the advantages of genius, may make a respectable reviewer; the requisites are dullness and malignity— the ends, profit and dishonor. Their interference with the productions of men of wit is a circumstance of the highest presumption, and somewhat like the conduct of unprincipled old maids; for though they have not sufficient merit to win a husband for themselves, they possess an adequate portion of ability to sully the virtues of those who have.

So there, you old virtue-sulliers!

Miriam Hopkins, the legit star, opened in a new opus in Boston, where dowagers sniffed at her role — rich man's keptive. Miss Hopkins sighed, "It will be great to get back to Broadway, where the mistresses in the first night audience always outnumber the wives."

Walter Pritchard Eaton's wise words: "That we all may dismiss the oft-heard sneer of actors, writers and painters who say that the critics are those who tried to paint, write or act and failed. The critic reacts to the finished product. It isn't his job to teach the craft."

Aristotle settled this matter over 2,500 years ago when he observed, "A pilot, not a carpenter, is the best judge of a rudder; and a guest, not the cook, the best judge of a dinner."

When Broadway's favorite son, George M. Cohan (playwright, star producer, director, and writer of hundreds of song smashes), decided to holiday at a swank inn at Lake Placid, New York, he telegraphed for a reservation.

When Mr. Cohan arrived he was informed, "Sorry, this place is restricted. No Jews."

Cohan, as Irish as the shamrock, went to another hotel and wired the bigot, "You thought I was Jewish and I thought you were gentlemen."

★

"NO PARTNERS"

Shortly after I started working for Hearst's New York *Mirror,* I exposed a Mr. Big, a top mobster, behind a scheme that exploited just that kind of intolerance. The story dealt with a planned hotel at Long Beach, Long Island.

"For the people whom restricted hotels bar," was one of the come-ons in the prospectus. The promoters had paid $15,000 for the land (all beach sand) and then peddled "charter memberships for $100." Mark Hellinger (my best pal) of the *News;* Harry Hershfield, a popular cartoonist for the Hearst papers ("Ish Kabibble" was his best comic strip); Bugs Baer, Hearst's Number One humorist; and several other "names" in journalism and show biz were made "Honorary Members"—window dressing to lure suckers.

When one of the promoters came and asked me to be on the "committee," I told him I never joined anything—because of a bitter experience.

Hellinger and some others on the committee said: "What's happened to the Winchell we grew up with around Broadway? Your head's gotten too big for your hat! Why won't you do what we're doing to stop the barring of Catholics, Jews, and Negroes from membership in certain clubs and hotels?"

I gave in. "All right," I agreed, "providing they drop my name if I don't like the way they run things."

"That's okay with us," I was told. "If you hear that they are doing something you are against, just send a letter and tell them to declare you out and off the honorary membership rolls."

Sure enough, a few days after I agreed to the use of my name, a young reporter named Nathan Zalinsky paused at my open-door cubbyhole on the editorial room floor and said, "Walter, thanks for asking me to join your new club. But where will I get a hundred dollars to become a charter member?" That was my first clue that it was a promotion scheme. My name—and the names of other well-known people—were being used to peddle membership, perhaps stock, and so on.

A few nights later the mayor of New York City, James J. Walker, telephoned me at the paper. "What the hell is your name doing on that Long Beach joint's stationery?" he scolded. "It's being run by a Bronx mob!"

"Jeezuzz!" I exploded. "I didn't want to be on it! My pals talked me into it because they were on it! The names on that list include many of your best friends in politics, judges, lawyers, actors, and leading citizens!"

"I don't care who and what judges are on it!" the mayor boomed back. "You get *your* name off it fast!"

I sent a registered letter to the promoters requesting they remove my name at once. It was ignored. I mailed two more. No dice.

Then one 3:00 A.M. while I was alone in the *Mirror* office fighting a column, in walked three strangers—immaculate appearance, fancy duds, clean shaven, boots shined, and nails manicured. You'd never suspect they were gangsters unless you looked at them.

"What's with you?" one said sarcastically.

"Who are you?" I asked.

"Friends of friends of yours. They like the way we are doing this thing at Long Beach. Why don't you?"

I told them about Zalinsky showing me a letter from the outfit which said in part: "Walter Winchell of your paper recommended you for membership in our beach club. For only $100 you can be a charter member."

"I never recommended him or anyone to be members!" I shouted at the trio. "Take my name off your list. Your promotor promised you would do so if I changed my mind."

"Well," I was informed, "we are not going to take it off. We've invested a lot of dough in this thing, and you behave yourself."

"Okay," I said, "see you in the paper tomorrow!"

"You go ahead and do that," another said, "and we will sue you and the paper for all you've got!" They left.

Editor Charles A. Dana's reply to an interviewer who asked him the best way to edit a newspaper: "Print the news and raise hell!"

Before their arrival I had finished a column titled "If I Were King." I was so furious about being "taken in" by my pals and these bums that I tossed out the leading paragraph and inserted this:

"November 23, 1929—

If I were king I would throttle the swift-talker who got me to consent to serve on the Board of Governors for the planned Fleetwood Beach Club at Long Beach, N.Y., just because Eddie Cantor, George Jessel, Bugs Baer, Mark Hellinger, and others were so gullible. The enterprise, it appears, is being worked along the lines of another "racket" to which I am opposed, and I hope others won't invest in the damb thing because our names are being prostituted."

They started a suit for two hundred and fifty thousand dollars. My first libel suit.

No lawyer in town would take their case. *Variety* reported "no legalite wants to get mixed up in this argument. They fear reprisals by Winchell and his newspaper." *Variety* kept running the same item for four years.

My lawyers, one of the finest legal firms in New York, were O'Brien, Malevinsky and Driscoll. They numbered George M. Cohan, Jack Dempsey, play producers Klaw and Erlanger, and other big Broadway names among their clients.

Four years from the serving of the summons, a man in that firm was dropped. He had apparently heard about or read the item in *Variety*. Here was his chance to even things with his ex-employers. He was quoted as saying to intimates that he would be happy to take the case— without a retainer or any pay.

"I might get lucky," went the alleged quote, "and win! I would enjoy meeting my former partners in a courtroom and beating them."

I met him again in the courtroom.

"What," he asked, "does the word 'racket' mean?" (The word had not yet landed in common usage.)

I was half-asleep and irritable. I had worked all night and got no sleep, fearing a contempt charge if I overslept or didn't show up in court. "Oh, you know," I grumbled. "You know what racket means, don't you?"

"Do you mean by racket," he persisted, "make a noise? Make a racket?"

69

"No, I do not!"

"Did you mean it to mean a tennis racket?"

He swept the air as one would if he had a tennis racket in his paw.

"No, I do not."

"Well, will you please tell the judge, jury, and me just what you meant by the word racket?"

"I guess," I testified honestly, "that it comes from racketeer."

"Ohhhh!" he ohhhh'd lustily, "Racketeer, eh? What's a racketeer?"

My patience was at an end with this bloke who looked like a comedian when he wore a derby. It came down over his ears.

"A racketeer," I defined the underworld word, "is someone who is illicit, illegal, crooked—like you!"

That diddittt! He actually covered his eyes as though on the verge of tears. The ham then went into a long pause—as though I had hurt his feelings terribly—and then stated: "The plaintiffs rest."

The jury fell for his histrionics and found me guilty and awarded the plaintiffs fifteen thousand dollars—the actual sum they said that they had invested in the planned inn.

I lost the case, but I won my point. My "If I Were King" expozay had put them out of business four years before the trial. They never, so far as I know, ever tried to pull that racket again.

And the Irony Of It! About a decade later this same Scalise, the Bronx hood I exposed as being the man-behind-it-all, was "exposed" by "Scoop" Pegler. Pegler was awarded the Pulitzer Prize for exposing the very same gangster I exposed ten years before—and my reward had been losing the lawsuit!

Scalise screamed that the columnist "Peglerized me!" It made the wire services and papers coast to coast. The word was quoted for many years. Still is, now and then.

Justice isn't Blind. It is Deaf, Dumb, and Stupid—especially that ignorant jury, bless 'em. Cuz if it weren't for that sappy jury, I would never have enjoyed what no other reporter got: a clause in my contract holding me blameless for "damages and costs of any kind."

How did I get that clause? That's another saga.

My publisher on the *Mirror* then was A. J. Kobler, a genius at getting ads. Mr. Kobler came into my office the day I lost the case and sighed: "Too bad. Your first libel suit, too. This will get other people you go after to go after you and the paper. But, so what? Only fifteen thousand. That's seventy-five hundred for me and seventy-five hundred for you."

"You're kidding!"

"No," said The Boss. "You got us into this trouble, so you will pay half."

"You mean," I asked him, "that every reporter on the paper must pay half if they lose a lawsuit? Like Nathan Zalinsky?"

"Zalinsky," replied my boss, "makes a lot less than you. We will take it from you in small amounts every week!" He was serious. He was a blunt man. He was not making wiz me zee joke.

"Say it again, Mr. Kobler," I requested. "I can't believe my ears!"

"Seventy-five hundred for me," he said, "seventy-five hundred for you!"

I reached for my Cavanagh, put it on my conk, pulled down my old-fashioned rolltop desk and took big steps out—and over! My column did not appear. I didn't write any. Imagine doing that to one of your staff.

Mr. K. had wooed me away from Bill Curley at the *Journal* because it was unanimously agreed by all publishers, editors, and circulation managers in New York that my *Graphic* column was responsible for considerable circ. Herbert Swope, the executive editor of the New York *World,* had put it at "over two hundred thousand."

Sime Silverman, the founder of *Variety,* wrote: "At least 150,000." And the circulation manager for Hearst's New York *American* was quoted along Park Row (where the newspapers were then bunched): "All this crap about Winchell's circulation is guesswork. We know what it is! He's selling over two hundred and fifty thousand *Mirrors* a day!"

And here is Mr. Kobler, a better advertising man than a diplomat, practically chasing me out of the place. I just got lost. The hell with all of them.

Three days later Harry Bitner, Mr. Hearst's Mr. Big (about such things) phoned me from Pittsburgh, Pennsylvania. "What happened?" he asked.

I told him.

"You stop being a little boy," he said. "Go back to work. I will attend to it. I'm too busy now."

"No, sir, Mr. Bitner," I said. "I'll sit this dance out until the contract ends. Bye-Bye!" And I hung up on him.

I didn't go to the Stork Club to avoid running into other Hearst brass. The Stork was their pet place, too. Richard E. Berlin (Number One man for The Chief in San Simeon) went there often. So did W. R. Hearst, Jr., Number One son of the Hearst-chain founder.

One afternoon during my AWOL from the paper at about four o'clock, when I was "sure" none of them would be there, I had a sandwich and some java with the owner, Sherman Billingsley, a favorite with many Hearst execs. I was seated at Sherm's Table 50 (as you entered the Cub Room) when I was suddenly surrounded by two Hearst execs——Jack Lait, my editor ("Better Lait Than Never!" I once heckled him in print in his own paper), and my favorite syndicate boss, the late Joseph V. Connolly. Mr. Connolly (he died at fifty, too young to die) was a tall, handsome man, who had a way of making you feel that he meant every word he said. He chief'd International News Service and King Features Syndicate, Hearst branches. Joe got me out of many a jam with The Chief. He was for me; most of the other Hearst execs weren't. They got a thousand dollars a week. I got twelve hundred plus all that syndication loot.

You can't like people who get more pay than you get. I mean they can't.

Billingsley must have tipped them off that I was there. Lait sat on my right; Connolly on my left. I was surrounded by "the enemy."

"Hello, Sonny-Boy," greeted Connolly, "where you been?" Both men kept up a running patter of clowning and kidding. They were waiting for the phone to ring from San Simeon and The Chief.

Before coming to the Stork Club to make me their prisoner, they must have phoned Mr. Hearst, Sr., to call me "in about fifteen minutes"—the time it took them to cab to the Stork. About ten minutes after Jack and Joe sat down, the phone on the maître d's shelf rang.

"It's for you," said a waiter, handing me a phone.

"Hello! Hello!" said the voice, "Is Walter there?"

"Yes, here I am. Who you?"

"This is W. R. Hearst. I work for newspapers!"

"Oh, hello, Boss!" I greeted.

"What is all this trouble about, anyway?" he asked.

"I found out, Mr. Hearst, that I am a partner in the *Mirror's* liabilities, but not in its profits! Mr. Kobler told me I must pay half of a fifteen-thousand-dollar lawsuit we lost for exposing a gangster's racket!

"I couldn't do another column or a story for the city desk under those conditions, Mr. Hearst," I breathlessly continued. "I haven't got seventy-five hundred dollars! If we lose a million dollars, where am I going to get five hundred thousand? The words won't come out of my fingers. I guess I will sit out the contract, which has a year and a half to run. I won't get any wealthier, but if I don't write any more for the *Mirror,* I certainly won't get poorer."

"What do you want us to do?" he said.

"I'd like a letter from you or your lawyers saying that I am to be held blameless for damages of any kind. Why should I pay any lawsuit damages? Your lawyers and editors go over my stuff with a butcher's cleaver. They know the libel laws, I don't. It's their fault if they let me put things in the paper that shouldn't be in it."

He said to put Connolly on the phone.

I got that letter the same day.

That's why the contract with Hearst was unlike any given to their other headliners. I wrote my own contracts: Give me this, give me that, etc. Twelve hundred dollars per week for five columns plus 50 percent of the gross—not the net, which is the standard contract.

A friend of our longtime boss, W. R. Hearst, Sr., was miffed over an item I ran about him. He wired me: "I am complaining to Mr. Hearst about you. I will see to it that you are put back in the soup line where you belong."

We informed Mr. Hearst about the complaint, saying that we had double-checked the item and were convinced of its accuracy. But I knew the aggrieved man was a good friend of the Hearst family, and what did my boss want me to do about it?

He telegraphed back: "We newspapermen have a lot of troubles, don't we?"

★

PEOPLE WILL TALK . . .

Walter Winchell column, New York *Daily Mirror,* November 25, 1929: "Of course it will be vigorously denied, but the Col. Chas. A. Lindberghs (Anne Morrow) anticipate a Blessed Event!!! . . ."

Now how would I know that? The Lindberghs had requested "no publicity, please." The medic never told it to anyone. But people will talk.

One of the nurses confided it to another nurse in another city. The latter revealed it to a chap she liked. He told it to a girl he was trying to impress. She, a column fan, told it to me in an anonymous letter. I threw it into the nearest basket.

A few days later, a couple of friends were recommended to the same obstetrician. They learned of the approaching Blessed Event for the Lindberghs from one of the nurses. The husband (a newspaper columnist who said he didn't print "such things") told it to me.

73

"You'd better check it," I was cautioned.

"Why?" I said. "People usually deny it or give a scoop to one of their favorite newspaper friends. I heard it before, anyway. All that can happen—if it is wrong—is that I gooft again."

New York *Daily Mirror,* January 28, 1930: "The most famous baby in the world will be born in the Harkness Pavilion of the Presbyterian Hospital, where Anne Morrow Lindbergh will go through the most sacred and dangerous experience of woman.

"The definite news confirms the report printed in the columns of the *Daily Mirror* two months ago by Walter Winchell, the columnist, who set the world guessing with his oracular paragraph."

Baby Charles Augustus Lindbergh, Jr., arrived June 22, 1930.

One of the all-time greats in the craft, Ring Lardner, was another who found himself strapped because the banks were ordered to close after several crashed. Ironically, about a week after Mr. Lardner (one of the most underpaid of all writers) borrowed a few hundred, one of his sons (who, of course, didn't know) auth'd an article about columnists and guced me.

★

PORTRAIT OF A MAN TALKING TO CAPONE

In September 1930, Al Capone was living in a luxurious mansion on Biscayne Bay in Miami. The government was preparing its income tax case against him.

A mutual friend arranged an exclusive three-hour interview between Capone and me that filled a column in the New York *Mirror* on October 28th of the next year:

> Something told me at the time I wouldn't see Capone for a long spell . . . I mean the last time I met him in his Florida mansion. He seemed pretty glum after he got that call from Chicago. They told him that local politicians, aspiring for the heights, were re-opening the Colosimo thing again. He never dreamed that they would finally trap him via the income tax gag.
>
> A mutual friend asked me if I would like to meet Capone, and I said I would. I might have made a lot of coin from all those magazines that asked for an article on the visit titled, "The Capones

at Home." But I told Capone I wouldn't go commercial on the call—and I didn't, even though he said he didn't care if I did or not, that he never met a newspaperman yet who didn't cross him. Wonder if it is true what I heard about him?—that before retiring each night, he cried like a baby.

The size of Alphonse was what impressed me more than anything about him. I had always pictured him as a small and fat person. He was over six feet! . . . When I was entering his place, he saw me coming up the three steps leading to the parlor. He was playing cards with three huskies, their backs to the door. Capone faced it. "Oh, come in," he called as he saw me. In the same breath he must have said to the others "Scram!" . . . because they disappeared quicker than the bird cage that magicians use.

He was sweeping the table clean of cards and chips. I sat down on a settee near his side of the table. "Sit over here," he said.

"No, this is all right," I countered.

"No, sit over here, please," he persisted, but I didn't move. My orbs had caught sight of the largest automatic I ever saw. It was resting in one of the table nooks where they keep the chips, I guess. He didn't want me to be startled. He covered the gun with one of his immense paws, and hid it on the other side of the table.

"I don't understand that," I said for want of something to say. "Here you are playing a game of cards with your friends, but you keep a gun handy."

"I have no friends," he said as he handed me a glass of grand beer.

Every time you referred to "his gang," he corrected you with "my organization." "Why don't you guys ever put it in the paper about my breadlines and soup lines?" he asked me. Then he told with great pride how his Chicago philanthropies so congested traffic that the police urged him to stagger the hours.

He argued long and loud about being blamed for everything—most of which he never did . . . "All I ask is that they leave me alone," he said once. I didn't tell him so, but I thought of a lot of people who wished *he* would leave *them* alone.

His beautiful mansion was really another prison for him. He couldn't leave it without a heavy guard. When he moved, it was done secretly by plane or boat—both of which were anchored in the waters adjacent to his home there. He told me of a doctor down in Miami who crossed him for the Government—who told the officials he wasn't sick at all when all the while he thought he'd die from pneumonia . . . "Once," he was saying, "I was so sick I fell down a whole flight of stairs!" The doctor's fee, he thought, was too stiff, and he paid him only half. "So he told the Government," said Capone, "that I was never sick." He sighed heavily and with a prop smile, added: "That's the funniest thing. Anybody I have wined and dined right in my own house has crossed me." He handed me the third beer—Swelegant!

Before the call from Chicago came, Capone was in a gay mood . . . he likes to talk, it seems, and he was defending his reputation against A First Impression. After the phone call he came back into the parlor and seemed away off. "What's the matter?" I asked. "Nothing good?"

"Aw," he said, "that bunch in Chicago is trying to pin the Colosimo murder on me. That was years ago! All of us had a hearing! The hell with them!" He told me about the time they nailed him in Philly, where he did time. "I was buying tickets back to Chicago," Capone said, "and I told the ticket guy in the cage at the station to keep the change. It was a fifty-dollar bill. So that's what I got for being helpful. He must have recognized me. So he phoned the police, I guess, and kept my fifty dollars . . ." The detectives, it appears, traced him and his companions to a movie house where they had gone to kill time between trains, and bagged him when they came out. "What crazy cops they were," Capone barked. "They might have started a panic in that lobby with all those people! That's no time or place to get excited—and maybe a lot of people could get hurt!"

I was looking at him through one eye—his beer was too good. "Yeah," I said, "that's pretty dangerous—with all those people around."

One of the cops said, "Hello, Al," and Al returned the salutation. "Got a gun on you?" the officer queried.

"Sure," said Al, "go and get it." Capone explained to me that it was a good thing he didn't remove the gun himself, for that is what the cops wanted. "They'd have shot me down claiming self-defense, get it?"

They took him before a magistrate there. "Oh, boy," said Capone, "you should have heard the call down he gave me. He called me everything in the world. I was a bum, a rat, a this and that. He missed nothing. All the time I thought he was putting on a show —for the benefit of reporters and others in the courtroom. So I took it all. But he wouldn't stop. He told me he was sorry that he couldn't put me in the electric chair right then, himself! Finally, I promoted a lawyer and figured the bail would be low. But the judge, who once was my pal, was trying to crash the spotlight with me. He continued giving me a piece of his mind. When he said thirty-five thousand dollars bail, and I started to peel it off my bankroll, he changed his mind and said the bail would be higher. In the time I spent in that jail it cost me a hundred and ten thousand—all over the fifty-dollar tip!"

"What I can't figure out with a guy like you," I said, "is you are in a big business. The biggest business men cheat a little, but they rarely give the Government a chance to catch them clowning with their income returns. You should have used your nut and paid it!"

"Why?" he snapped. "I have no business."

"Then," I countered, "how are you going to explain all this— and your wealth?"

"Presents," he said. "My friends and cousins gave me it all."

I realized then that Capone wasn't so shrewd, and his beer gave me the courage to tell him so. A newspaper was brought in . . . "Hah!" I hah'd. "This is good. Look! It says people in New York saw you today on a train. And here's a report that you just passed through Albany!" It was amusing to read those statements sitting with him in Miami Beach.

Then he tossed the paper to a couch . . . The paper's front page carried another tale about him being wanted in Chicago for the Colosimo murder.

"That's another thing about you I can't figure," I said, "you're nuts over that boy of yours. Still, you leave newspapers around the house like that where he can see stories about you. That's not nice!"

"Don't mean a thing," Capone replied indifferently, "he knows that anything they put in the papers about me is a lie."

God bless Mr. Volstead—if it weren't for him, there would have been no marvelous Capone beer. I think I know the recipe . . . it must be flavored with lightning.

☆

Alan Hynd, a highly respected newspaperman and author, wrote a feature on Al Capone for *True* magazine in July 1945. Mr. Hynd's affidavit included the following:

Walter Winchell, the columnist, was one of the few men in the country who correctly diagnosed the real menace of the underworld, and he had the moxie to point out repeatedly, often at the risk of his life, just what was going on in Chicago, New York and other metropolises. Herbert Hoover had often scanned Winchell's column, before and after his election to the presidency, to keep abreast of the latest underworld activities, and Chief Elmer Irey of the Intelligence Unit had, in fact, first become thoroughly alarmed,

77

as a private citizen, through what he had read in W.W.'s daily chronicles.

☆

In October 1929, when some people had been jumping out of Wall Street windows following the stock market crash, Ed Sullivan and I were luckier. We both had had by-lines, in the New York *Graphic* and *Mirror* respectively.

And still respectfully.

Ed's later boss, Captain Joseph Medill Patterson, invited me to join the *Daily News* before Ed got the job. The first time was in 1930 when his M.E. (Colonel Frank Hause) ran the errand. The second time, the offer was made by Captain Patterson, in person, same year.

"When we found out over here," Patterson told me, "that you were responsible for considerable circulation over there [meaning the *Mirror*] we decided that if that was what readers wanted, we would give them so much of it perhaps they'd get sick of it!"

As I got up to leave, I thumb'd the pages of his Monday edition. When I got to the pages that featured three gossip columns, I clowned, "Where would you put me on this page?"

Captain Patterson closed the paper and hmmmm'd, "That should be the least of your worries."

I suppose that he planned dumping them all.

Every bid from Patterson to desert the *Mirror* (where I was fussing with the bosses and they with me) got me a hefty raise. One raise included a twenty-thousand-dollar bonus to sign for seven years. My wage was now higher than any other Hearst "star" and executive. Total: Over a hundred thousand per annum. (Oops! Arthur Brisbane got five thousand per week. Because he also solicited department store ads.)

Would the *News* have permitted me the latitude I enjoyed on the *Mirror?* Many newsmen didn't think so. They pointed out that none of the chatter columnists were allowed to fight legislators, government policy, etc. That was reserved for the editorial page, the Letters to the Editor department, and the political writers.

Leo C. Rosten's book *The Washington Correspondents* (Harcourt, Brace, and Company) states that the "so-called gossip column" is a phenomenon of recent years. He refers to the Washington chatter pillars. They sprang up, he adds, during the Hoover administration "as a necessary device by which the correspondents could speculate about news which the government presented in unreliable fashion."

Mr. Rosten quotes Paul Mallon as estimating that "no less than 125 columns of political gossip have been launched in four years."

The author blamed the entire catastrophe on us.

★

ED SULLIVISION

One rainy sundown in 1931 Ed was buying a paper at the newsstand on the Forty-seventh Street and Palace Theater corner. He turned to leave and saw me behind him. "Think of the devil," he said, "and there you are! I was going to call you. I have a problem. Tell me, how do you survive all the fights you've had with editors and publishers?"

"What's the matter? You have trouble?"

"We have a new managing editor. He was a sports editor in Philly. He takes my ringside seats to the fights and world series. He covers them himself. My column doesn't run. It's humiliating. I found out that when you lose your by-line you also lose your false friends. I don't know what to do."

"You have a contract?"

"Yes."

"Well, live up to it. Keep turning in the column. If you don't, he'll use that as a reason to say you broke it. Give me some time to think. I'll call you."

In 1929 I had landed on the air for CBS thanks to owner William S. Paley. He is to blame for me getting on radio.

My radio sponsor at the time was Gerardine, a hair tonic for women. The wage was a thousand dollars per week. George Washington Hill, the boss of American Tobacco, heard me one Sabbath evening and phoned his ad agency, Lord & Thomas: "I just heard a fellow who talks very fast over CBS about Hollywood and theater people. I want him for Lucky Strikes. Deliver him Tuesday night!"

The deal was a thrice-weekly (Tuesday, Thursday, and Saturday nights) one-hour NBC program. Chatter, anecdotes, and show biz gossip about the celebrities—between dance music with orchestras from all over the world. The salary was thirty-five hundred dollars.

My radio contract with Gerardine had nine weeks to go. Lucky Strikes paid the obscure firm thirty-five thousand dollars to release me immediately. But Gerardine had one provision: "Winchell must get us a replacement who can do what he does and bring guest stars, too."

I phoned my pal Mark Hellinger, who reported the Broadway Beat for the New York *Daily News.* "Get me off the hook, Mark. Take this job, so I can be free to get my first coast-to-coaster. It will pay you a thousand dollars a week!"

"Thanks," said Mr. Hellinger. "I wouldn't be known as a Winchell imitator for ten thousand a week."

I suggested Sidney Skolsky of the same newspaper. Sidney's audition disappointed the agency involved. "His show business stuff is fine," they said. "But he has a thin, squeaky voice." Too bad.

I phoned Sullivan. "Go over to CBS and tell them I suggested you to replace me on the Gerardine program. It pays one thousand per."

Months before, Louis Sobol had been lured from the *Graphic* to do a Broadway column for the New York *Journal.* With Ed's new exposure, his managing editor felt he now had his Broadway vacancy problem solved. He told Sullivan, "You are the new Broadway columnist and dramatic critic!"

When Sullivan got into radio newscasting, his format was a facsimile of my one- and two-liner flashes. It soon died from natural causes.

None of the above truth appears in a biography of Ed by a man CBS later assigned to press-agent the Sullivan show. Perhaps that Forty-seventh Street corner newsstand conversation and my recommendation to Gerardine (that he replace me on the air) eluded him.

When Ed inherited the colyum style I introduced in the *Graphic,* his opening paragraph on July 1, 1931 Elmer Gantry'd: "I charge the Broadway columnists with defaming the street. I have entered a field of writing that ranks so low that it is difficult to distinguish any one columnist from his road companions. I have entered a field which offers scant competition. Phonies will receive no comfort in this space. To get into this column will be a badge of merit and a citation. Divorces will not be propagated in this column. No kindly gossip via keyholes."

It was a neat way of attracting attention and starting a feud. Ten days later Ed started printing divorces, people having babies, romancing, busting up, and the keyhole stuff he "condemned." .

At Billy LaHiff's Tavern that same night, Ed joined the table where many show biz celebs and I were swapping quips. I couldn't resist heckling him about his sudden switch from altar boy to scandalmonger. He was carboning my whole act!

"Eddie," I cooed, "what happened? Did your editor tell you to get interesting or get out?"

"No," he sighed, "my wife did."

No dope, Sylvia Sullivan. The feud was on.

The *Graphic* finally went out of business following libel suits (none because of my stuff) costing seven million dollars. I had gone to Hearst three years earlier.

"The Old Maestro" Ben Bernie and I fooled most radio listeners for over 7 years, swapping brickbats over the air. That was when I was doing three one-hour broadcasts a week for *The Lucky Strike Hour* in 1931. Amazing the way many people thought it was a real feud.

The publicity for us both got Bernie back into the Headliner Dept. (vaudeville was dying or almost dead). It got me a big bundle headlining at the Palace (at last!) on a bill featuring "real stars" such as Harry Richman and Lillian Roth. Then with Bernie for two fortnight engagements at the Paramount Theaters on Broadway and Brooklyn. The show we did at the Paramount on Broadway attracted overflow throngs and nearly every stage, screen and radio personality in town. They came in to see us "in action" and to be introduced to the audience. Later came solo appearances for me (at $15,000 per week) in Detroit, Chicago and San Francisco—and then $150,000 for each of us co-starring in two of D. F. Zanuck's money-makers for 20th Century-Fox, *Wake Up and Live* and *Love and Hisses*. The first movie's leading lady was Alice Faye, the other leading lady (*Hisses*) was Simone Simon. Both Ben and I got wealthier.

Many other radio and teevee stars later employed the same exchange successfully: Bob Hope and Bing Crosby, Eddie Cantor and Rubinoff, Jessel and Eddie Cantor and many others. I often heard some of them snap the same quips Bernie and I used.

Almost all through the "insult-exchange" I would pause and say to the outfronters, "Just a minnnitttt! Would you all like to see what a real champion looks like. There he is on the 2nd Row aisle, *Jack Dempsey!*"

Or: "Oh, we have a darling out front. The First Lady of the Theater! *Miss Helen Hayes!*" . . . And so on. This became one of Ed Sullivision's teevee features. Introducing celebs in the audience.

★

OBSTETRICKERY

From the WW col'm of August 10, 1931: "The Gene Tunneys (Polly Lauder) are rehearsing lullabies in Maine."

Mr. Tunney, the Associated Press, and the United Press all carried vigorous denials on front pages.

From a note written by Mr. Tunney on Nov. 16, 1931: "Dear Walter: We expect the 'blessed event' on Thanksgiving Day. Sincerely. Gene Tunney."

A word that I created and has been swiped a lot was "phffft." Many people say "pift." It's ph-f-f-ft, just like it's spelled.

Frances Williams was the leading lady in a show. I think she was the one who sang Cole Porter's "Love For Sale." She was romancing with a guy whose name by rare coincidence was also Williams—Bob. They came into Texas Guinan's one night to catch the midnight show, which had already started, and Mark Hellinger, my pal (who died too young, at forty-four, from a heart condition), said: "It looks like Frances and Bob are having a spat." At that moment a waiter brought them a bottle of champagne. Frances was yelling (in her loudest tones) as the waiter opened the bottle which, with a sizzling pop, went phfft, as did their romance soon after.

One day I found a long list of memos Ruth Cambridge left in my Royal.

Trivial things: "Your mother phoned. She'd like her check two days earlier next week. Gone to Atlantic City . . . Your dentist phoned. He cannot wait for you to wake up so late. He has to make a speech tonight at 8 at some affair . . . Hey! Did you take my box of aspirins from outta my top drawer? . . . Big squawk from producer of show you rapped last night. Threatened to jerk his ad from theater page directory . . . Syndicate wants two columns at once early next week. They don't work on holidays. Just us slaves! . . . Killed first two items. El Punko again double-planted with imitators . . ." And so on.

I had trouble trying to fall asleep that night.

Six columns a week then, and I was on *The Lucky Strike Hour,* three one-hour programs weekly—Tuesdays, Thursdays, and Satdees, ten to eleven . . . I was also doubling at Columbia Sabbath nights for a hair tonic sponsor—a fifteen-minute newscast. I kept tossing and turning. Mainly because I hadn't done the col'm. I'd expected to get a few hours sleep—and then do it. Now it was 7 A.M.

The idea for a "different" gossip column came in my fitful semi-dozing. The notes Ruth left for me! I got up and hastened to the paper.

I copied Ruth's memos, opened the mail, used some of the press agents' stuff, titled it "A Columnist's Sec'y Jots Down a Few Notes" and signed it "R.C."

Next day in the *Mirror* elevator I was complimented by the big Hearst syndicate boss, Joe Connolly, chief of International News Service and the syndicate. "Liked the column this morning," said Joe. "Good idea. Do it once a week."

"Gee, Joe," I said, "thanks. I was worried you all woudn't go for it."

"Goodgahd!" Joe ejaculated. "He doesn't even know when he has a ticket seller!" The elevator reached his twelfth-floor offices and he got off.

I had no intention of ever doing one again. I'd been stuck for a col'm and did it to get one done. But I started doing the secretary column every Friday and began signing it "Your Girl Friday" in 1932. In 1934 I changed the title to "Memos of a Girl Friday."

The format served as a gimmick to make retractions. Ruth "retracted," not I: "Soandso called. Says not true!"

Brain-pickers pounced on it in papers coast to coast. Nobody ever sassed back, "What's so new about it? It's the old Dear Boss gimmick." Which, of course, it was.

Newspaper readers to this day say, "You'd better watch out. Your Girl Friday is often better'n you." They actually believed that every word of it was written by my secretary. When some article writers revealed that I auth'd them—with a few memos Ruth jotted down—it took the fun out of it for me.

Other columnists on papers with more circulation than mine brazenly lifted it. I got letters from the carboncats' readers—who had apparently just read me for the first time. They slapped me with, "Stop stealing that Girl Friday idea from my favorite writer, Ed Sullivan!"

Oh, dear.

As summer vacation time approached, Ruth asked, "May I have three weeks instead of two?" Okay, Have Fun.

She never returned. She eloped with Ebsen.

Anon: "A career is all right for a woman, but she can't run her fingers through its hair."

Their first image, a girl named Elizabeth ("Libby") was born April 7th. My birthday, too. I am godfather to Ruth's and Buddy's second daughter, Alix, another darling. Both girls landed in Las Vegas show-girl lines (like Mama was on Broadway) when they were teeners.

The Ebsens divorced many years later.

MURDER FOR A PAL

Owney Madden hated newspapermen, and for sound cause. Two reporters on the New York *Herald Tribune* were in the gent's room when Madden was liquidating a foe named Patsy Doyle in a saloon on West Forty-first Street—a stroll from the newspaper plant. As they started to come out, the shots sent them back to the pissoir.

Madden didn't see them.

Their "surprise" testimony sent Owney (also nicknamed The Duke, because he came from England) to Sing Sing. He got ten to twenty. And so he despised anyone on a newspaper.

Madden was never seen at Tex's place—before or after his confinement in prison. He rarely came to his Cotton Club.

I had never seen or met him until he picked up my barbershop tab in Spinrad's where mobsters and some nightlife columnists got prettified. This shop stayed open until midnight and after. One of the mob always picked up the tab for every person in the place. It was a form of grandstanding.

That day I borrowed a thousand dollars from the Morris Plan, a finance firm. Our firstborn was due any hour. I borrowed the money for the bills.

I was making a hundred dollars a week at the time. You paid back the loan with twenty dollars weekly for fifty weeks.

When I went to pay my barber tab, I had the Morris Plan coupon book in my hand. The lady cashier shook her head. I lip-read her "It's paid."

"Who?" I inquired.

"Mr. Madden," she signal'd—directing her orbs to the nearby mirror, where he was straightening his cravat.

"I beg your pardon," I said, "are you Mr. Madden?"

"Yes."

"Thanks," I said. "I've heard so much about you and wondered why we hadn't met."

He recognized the Morris Plan thing in my hand and took it from me, saying, "What's a wise guy like you doing with a sucker thing like this? You know you can get a G whenever you want it from George and the other guys." He started to tear it.

"Oh, please! Don't do that. You're embarrassing me."

"Then take this," he said, offering a thousand-dollar bill, "and pay it off. Miss Guinan told me how helpful you and Hellinger have been to her in the paper."

"Oh, look," I told him, "thanks very much, but I can't be under obligations to a man like you. I'm a newspaperman."

"You can't be under whaaaatttt?" he asked, puzzled.

"Under obligations. I couldn't do you any favors."

Glaring at me icily, he flung the book of coupons at me—and with great contempt in his tones, walking away, he nastied, "What the phuc could *you* do for *me*?"

The episode circulated throughout the plunderworld. "You shouldn't have done that to The Duke," I was told by other hoods. "You hurt his feelings."

It didn't hurt my reputation among the mobsters. They had been under the impression that newspaper people were always "on the take." Many were.

About two years later Madden "sent" one of his staff for me to come see him at his office in the Publicity Building, located at Forty-seventh and The Big Street, (where Broadway divorces Seventh Avenue.)

"A guy has written a book," he prefaced, "and he is running all that stuff about me that was in all the papers long ago. Don't you guys ever let up? I paid my debt to society. When do you people stop?"

The book was authored by a newsman on the *Herald Tribune*—the late Herbert Asbury. He lived in the same building I lived in—the Whitby Apartments on West Forty-fifth Street between Eighth and Ninth avenues. (So did Bing Crosby.) Madden gave me the impression that he planned on dealing with that reporter and Knopf, the book publisher.

"I hope," I offered, "you won't do anything about the book. You will help make it a big seller with the publicity."

Two days later the front pages reported that Knopf's publishing place had been "shot up."

I ran the following in the *Daily Mirror* column: "Mobsters named in the new book about the gangs in New York told me they wondered when newspapermen stopped digging up their records and making them public again. I am fearful for the safety of the author."

The same afternoon on my way to Broadway, the author, on his way home, stopped to say, "I read your piece this morning. You can say for me that no mobster worries me. I've been over the top in a war. Put that in the paper!"

"Okay," I replied, "will do."

We parted. A second later he returned to request, "Walter, don't put in where I live."

I ran that, too—his quote, not his address.

The *Herald Tribune* started a series about Madden's mob. The initial article reported that they had muscled in on several business firms in Brooklyn.

This enraged Madden. He sent for me again. "I thought," he thundered, "you were a friend of mine! Why do you let them say those things?"

"I work on the *Mirror,* not the *Trib,*" I reminded him. "I can't stop stories about anyone in any newspaper."

"But these bums got it all wrong!" he complained. "We didn't muscle in on any place in Brooklyn or anywhere. We invested two hundred and fifty thousand in a chain of laundries, and lost it fast!"

"Why don't you tell that to the editors of the *Trib*? I'll introduce you to them." To my surprise, he agreed.

I phoned Stanley Walker, the city editor, and requested he interview Madden. Mr. Walker said, "Bring him over."

The setting was a huge conference room. Walker and his top men sat around a long table—the way the Cabinet does when the President of the United States summons them. The *Trib* people included a dozen reporting greats.

After I brief'd them on why Madden was there, the aggrieved man said, "Ever since I turned Catlic, I lost money!"

"Ever since you what?" I asked.

"Catlic, Catlic, Catlic!"

I deciphered it to mean "Catholic"—turning "straight" for the first time in his life.

They all howled. His testimony was so convincing the *Trib* ran his story and stopped the series.

When we left the *Trib* building Madden said, "Let's walk back up Broadway."

"I have to return to my apartment for something," I told Owney, directing him toward Eighth Avenue on Forty-first Street. He went along reluctantly. I wondered why he was so glum.

As we approached the corner (to turn north on Eighth) he blew his top and hollered, "Gahdammit, I never go anywhere near here. That's where it happened!"

It was the saloon where he had committed murder.

Several years later Madden retreated to Hot Springs, Arkansas, where he lived with his wife, a lovely girl, daughter of a Post Office official.

Internal Revenue alleged Madden owed eighty thousand dollars in tax arrears. They dropped the case when he paid eight thousand. When I asked a tax man why Madden got off that cheap, while the rest of us paid the full tariff, I was told: "What do you want us to do—put him in the can and get nothing?"

Years later, the author of a book on the mobs reported that Madden "even took Winchell for $100,000."

That was not true. The sum was ten thousand dollars. And I wasn't "taken" for it.

The gangster who was once a multimillionaire was broke. He was gravely ill and he long-distanced that he'd appreciate a loan. He asked for five thousand. I sent ten. For over fifteen years I had feasted at his various nightclubs every night in the week, where they wouldn't give you a check if you had syndication. I figured that the ten thousand dollars Madden "borrowed" made us even.

The irony of it! Madden, who was offended when I rejected his offer of a thousand dollars when I was poor—and told me, "What the phuc can *you* do for *me*?—found out the definition of a friend: one who walks in when the rest of the world walks out.

I waited seven years (when you can write off a bad debt) but decided the Helwithit. I would have had to name him. I had already been paid back Big.

His orders to have Vincent Coll ("The Mad Dog of New York") assassinated, following Coll's kidnapping of partner Big French (who was ransomed for $35,000, paid by Madden), had given me the biggest newsbreak I ever had.

My column in the *Daily Mirror* on February 8, 1932, said: "Five planes brought dozens of machine-gats from Chicago Friday to combat

87

The Town's Capone. Local banditti have made one hotel a virtual arsenal and several hot-spots are ditto because Master Coll is giving them the headache."

The *Mirror* was on the streets at 8:40 P.M. Sunday, February 7. Coll was dead at 1:15 A.M. February 8.

When Vincent Coll, former stooge for Dutch Schultz, was done in by a machine gunner as he took a planted call in a phone booth, the only witness, a drug clerk, said the slayer "made the sign of the Cross" on Coll's frame with his rat-a-tat-gat. The avenger strolled away and was never apprehended. Nor has his name ever appeared in print or on the air in connection with the murder.

The police, however, knew it. They never tried to question him. Because gangster Coll was a cop-killer.

The killer had been released from the can only a few weeks before the snatch of "Big French." Madden and Frenchy befriended the ex-con when he got out of Sing Sing. Theirs was a warm friendship. To show his gratitude, the ex-con suggested he deal with Coll alone.

They were so thankful to the avenger they gave him one of their many Broadway nightclubs. It went out of business three weeks later.

★

THE VERY ODD McINTYRE

Most of the nation's radio listeners and newspaper readers apparently liked the way I "took them all on." The fan mail (long before we had ratings) told the story. Their written applause must have impressed the networks and sponsors.

Andrew Jergens, for instance, one of the most devout Republicans in the land. I was for FDR publicly in 1932, so he knew I was an FDR man when he signed me.

Jergens Lotion . . . "with *lotions* of Love!"—my favorite sponsor. I started with them on December 4, 1932, and went on for sixteen consecutive years. The record steady job on the air, until Jack Benny matched it—and Ed Sullivision outdistanced the field with his twenty-one straight seasons over CBS.

Then tragedy struck at our home.

Gloria was age nine. Her very last words to me were "baby-talked" at breakfast time two weeks before she was stricken. Gloria walked across the parlor on her heels with outstretched arms, as though to make me her prisoner. She giggled as she teased: "I'm gonna get my daddy and let him take me to breakfast!"

Then we knew something was wrong. She couldn't eat it. "I don't feel good, Daddy," she said.

The doctors and specialists said pneumonia. The crisis would come in eleven days. The doctor slept on a sofa alongside her oxygen tent. Gloria was gone exactly eleven days later—December 24, 1932. It couldn't happen today, they say, with all the miracle drugs.

I remember seeing the exact time Gloria left us. It was 7:50 A.M. Every time I wake up, it always seems to be 7:50 in the morning or night. Thirty-six years later, it still makes me think of her.

The doctor summoned a pneumonia specialist "to make sure." He turned Gloria over once on her stomach. "She's gone," he said. His bill was twenty-five hundred dollars.

The Winchells have "faked" Christmas ever since.

It was a Sunday. I did my radio program at 9:00 P.M. I did not report that "our" baby had died. I couldn't have said it. It would have made me choke.

A column or so after the funeral, this verse led off the col'm:

Gloria

> *Her "Garden of Verses" and all of her toys*
> *Had been placed in an orderly row.*
> *Her dollies and tea-things had all been arranged*
> *For a Christmas Eve "party," you know.*
>
> *"Right after your broadcast, please Daddy, come home,*
> *Or the tea will get chilly," she said.*
> *"My dolls will be hungry and weary for sleep*
> *And they have to go early to bed."*
>
> *Oh, Little Boy Blue, whose tin soldiers don't sleep,*
> *Holding vigil with never a noise;*
> *Please send me a few of your trustiest guards*
> *To watch over Gloria's toys.*

Following the wire services' flash, thousands of condolence cards, letters, and telegrams came from readers and listeners in the forty-eight states. From folks in faraway places, too, like Johannesburg, South Africa, where a family apparently read about Gloria in the papers. They sent me a ring made of ebony, the inlay of solid gold—a mourning ring (size of a wedding ring) I seldom removed, not even when I washed my hands.

One of the very first telegrams came from a confrère with whom I had feuded publicly. The wire read: "Walter and June Winchell, *N.Y. Mirror*: Your great loss has made us very sad. Ed and Sylvia [Sullivan]."

For some time the daily mail had contained anonymous insults handwritten in green ink on postcards. They were always signed: "From The Old Copyreader." I suspected that the sender was one of my former *Graphic* editors with whom I had feuded. I was not certain who sent them until a young man came to the New York *Mirror* and told me.

He was a new postman who delivered and collected mail from buildings along Park Avenue. One of those apartment buildings was 290 Park Avenue. He said that there was only one occupant in the "brand-new" place—the first to dwell there.

The reason he came to tell me, he said, was that he thought the sender "had gone too far"; that he had told his very old mother about the postcards every time he picked them up at 290 Park Avenue and read another few lines of my anonymous correspondent's mean streak. One day, said Mr. Postman, he put the "meanest" postcard in his pocket and took it home. "I would like to show Mr. Winchell this one," he told his mother, "but I don't know what to do."

He said his mother instructed him to mail it, then go see me that night and tell me it was to be delivered next morning—and the name and address of the source.

The card arrived on schedule. It shattered me. On that postcard was pasted a newspaper photo of our nine-year-old daughter, Gloria, who had died from pneumonia two nights before. Under the picture of Gloria was one word: RETRIBUTION?

It was signatured in green ink: "The Old Copyreader"—the same cowardly, anonymous poison-penman who had been needling me for many months.

"There is only one tenant so far at 290 Park Avenue," reported the postman. "His name is O. O. McIntyre. He always uses colored ink—usually green. I hope," he sighed, "you will not get me in trouble by revealing your source for this. I did it because I read about you and your wife losing your little girl, and it made me very angry with Mr. McIntyre."

I assured the postman I would never reveal his name or complain to the Post Office Department. And I didn't.

90

After Gloria died, I ran a daily blind item for a week. It read: "This is to let the anonymous postcard-sender (who signs his needling 'Old Coypreader') that I know his name. He is a syndicated columnist!"

The cards never came again. McIntyre, who made the Stork Club—my fort—one of his stops when he made the rounds, stopped coming there. His health failed shortly after, and he went to Heaven. I spoze.

The Very Odd McIntyre, who won the hearts of animal-lovers all over the nation with his tender and touching tales about his dog (and other pets), was honored by his Ohio hometown with a tablet reading "Birthplace of O. O. McIntyre."

When McIntyre passed on, various news personalities were rumored to succeed him.

"It just won't look right," sighed a McNaught Syndicate executive, "to let that space go without someone like McIntyre."

"Well," said the other, "who is there?"

King Features brass reminded us that when Arthur Brisbane died, his daily front-page column was never inherited by anyone. "There was only one Enrico Caruso," said Hearst exec J. V. Connolly, "and when he died the Metropolitan Opera House kept announcing new tenors—but never another Caruso." The *Reader's Digest,* I don't suppose, will consider this charming chapter for its "Memorable Characters I Will Never Forget."

★

MY SECOND GIRL FRIDAY

Rose Bigman started working for me when both of us were Young and Beautiful. She's still photogenic. I'm photopathetic.

One fourth of December Rose wistfully said, "I've been with you for over thirty-five years, did you know that?"

"How do you figure that?"

"Ruth Cambridge hired me the day you started for Jergens Lotion in 1932."

"I simply have to have an assistant," Miss Cambridge ultimatumed. "I know a girl named Rose Bigman, very efficient. She's fast at taking dictation and at the Remington."

I took on Rose Bigman at twenty dollars per.

But that was then. Un¢le $amuel began getting ninety-one cents of each dollar I earned on the radio for Lucky Strikes, Jergen's Lotion, Phillies Cigars, Gruen Watch, Kaiser-Frazer cars, Hazel Bishop Lipstick, and TWA.

The Jergens job lasted sixteen years. We made each other big taxpayers.

The Hearst Corporation (New York *Mirror* and years later, the New York *Journal-American*) also overpaid me. For a long spell my annual intake was over a million.

From the job at ABC-TV-Radio (simultaneous newscast) the per annum wages totaled $650,000. Paid 52 weeks—and broadcast 45. Seven weeks' holiday.

Nobody's Girl Friday, I am sure, has taken so much from a boss who can blow his top faster than I—before orange juice. "Fercrissakes! You let me run the leading item when two of the opposition rags had it the day before! I thawt you read all of them. I can't read every paper every day. I don't mind getting it second. I just don't like getting it *third*!" (Bang! Hanging up.) Why she didn't resign years ago is a puzzlement.

When she cries (Rosie cries like a girl!) my schizophrenia shows. "Oh, stop crying! You're a grown-up woman! Jeezuzz!"

After working for maniacal me all those years, she recently asked me for an autographed picture!

I inscribed it with affection. Next day I almost killed her for omitting a skewp I feared would "leak."

Character? You bet. Rose has never let fickle press agents of night spots and restaurants pick up her tab without first asking me if okay. She refused to return to the Stork Club for months when the owner refused to give her date a check. But they all know, especially at the theaters, that if she enjoys a show—she's on the Second Night lists—she will send a memo saying so. I quote her if I am out of town when it premièred.

And that, Mr. and Mrs. America, winds up another edition—with *lotions* of love to Rose Bigman. The only other wonderful "wife" in my life.

WINCHELL FOR CONGRESS?

That's What The Man Said.

The man was the national chairman of the Democratic party at the time, Ed Flynn, who was also the "owner" of the Bronx. He told Stork Club proprietor S. Billingsley, "Find out if Winchell would be interested in running for Congress."

"*Are* you?" queried Mr. Billingsley, whose intimate friend Flynn kept mobsters from muscling in on Mr. B.'s swank saloon. "Run for Congress—and take a cut?"

"Sherm," we told Mr. B., "you are making wiz me zee joke, no?"

"It's no gag," he said, "Flynn asked me to ask you. He's the most powerful politician in town, you know that."

"What!" we replied in astonishment plus laughter.

My wage from Jergens Lotion was then $7,500 weekly for newscasting a mere twelve and a half minutes once a week; the New York *Mirror* paid $1,200 per week for five columns weekly; King Features Syndicate gave me 50 percent of the gross; and there was sugary income from magazines (now and then) and personal appearances in New York, Brooklyn, Chicago, Detroit, and San Francisco theaters (weekly stands), some of which paid me as high as $15,000 a week—the Fox Theater, Detroit, frixample.

The most overrated and overpaid man in the news and show biz. As we have noted often, "Get it while you're hot. You stay cold a long, long time!"

"Guarantee it?"

"Flynn said you couldn't possibly lose. He has this town sewed up."

" You mean they don't count the votes for the other fellow? Please tell Mr. Flynn I said thanks for the compliment, but I do not prefer politics to the newspaper craft."

Politics, hmmm. I've known too many politicians who stay in office taking orders from Murder, Inc., what is left of the Capone mob, and other gangsters. (It was newspaper ace Asa Bordages of the defunct New York *World Telegram* who coined the name Murder, Inc. for the Lepke-Luciano Mobfia.)

Three-Finger Tommy Brown wouldn't allow anyone in Brooklyn or the other boroughs of Greater New York to "get" elected if the candidate didn't go along with his "organization"—the gangster's word for mob.

So, thanks again to the ghosts of Ed Flynn and Sherman Billingsley for the invite to run for Congress—and for dropping the subject after I did.

Can you imagine me running for Congress in the 1930's, long before it became "fashionable" for former song-and-dancemen to run and win —the way Senator George Murphy and Governor Ronald Reagan did?

The foes I later made in both houses—Senators Borah, Burton K. Wheeler, and Bilbo; Congressmen Rankin, Dies, Hoffman, Lambertson, and others—and the ones on the flopposition newspapers would have laughed me back to the small-time Circuits.

Jimmy Walker's song-plugging and Tin Pan Alley career didn't stop him from becoming mayor of New York, you say? I know, but he had Ed Flynn, Democratic Chief, and Owney Madden, Gang Chief, for his Big Backers!

★

FDR

A week or so after Franklin Delano Roosevelt took office as President in 1933 I was summoned to a Stork Club phone. The time was about 2:00 A.M.

The caller said he was Joe Kenenan of the Department of Justice. "Your presence in Washington is desired," he said, "very early this morning. Be here by nine—before the press conference at ten."

"How do I know you are a Government man?" I challenged.

"Call the FBI or SS in New York. Ask for me—and they will put you through."

I did that.

Mr. Kenenan continued, "I know you sleep all day and are full of zing for fifteen to eighteen hours. Take the Pennsy train that leaves for Washington—about three-twenty A.M. Gets you here in four hours. Come to the East Gate of the White House. The boss doesn't want the press to see you. You will be met at the East Gate."

"What've I done now?" I chuckled.

"See you about eight forty-five or nine, okay?"

"Okay."

I couldn't wait to make the trip. I napped three hours. I was going to meet my first President. Why, I wondered, while waiting for the departure, did he send for me? Perhaps to say thanks for the support I gave him over the air and in the papers.

With Lucky Strikes as my sponsor, I had borrowed the Battle Page feature from the New York *Daily News* which gave presidential (and

94

local) candidates half a page during the campaigns to argue things out. My one-hour radio show (thrice weekly) plus name brands from all over the globe devoted six minutes to FDR and Herbert Hoover in their race for the presidency. Three minutes each. It had never been done before on the air. This ran for many weeks before Election Day.

We are now at the White House. That morning, an agent escorted me to the office of Grace Tully, his prettiful Girl Friday. He had several, but Missy LeHand was chief sec. Marvin McIntyre and Steve Early were the Chief's press commanders.

The President greeted me warmly. "Good morning!" he boomed, smiling the famous smile I saw in the newsreels and papers.

"Good morning, Mr. President!"

He told me to sit in the chair alongside his desk. "How's your fan mail holding up?" he queried.

Fan mail? FDR was under the impression that fan mail was the barometer on how many listeners you had—and readers. On the papers, yes. But on the air, the mail doesn't tell you or the sponsors and networks how many people tune you in. The Crossley, Hooper, and Pulse ratings gave you the sweet or sour news.

I told FDR that.

"Really?" he said, as his eyes widened and his eyebrows lifted. "I know," he went on, "about the cooperation you've been giving Naval Intelligence and the FBI."

I had forgotten for a moment that he had been Secretary of the Navy for many years before he became Commander in Chief.

The President then said that whenever I heard anything I thought he alone should know (Hitler was on the way up at the time, and Mussolini was another threat) I should tell it to him in person—not via letter or any third person. "That's an order!" he kidded.

After another ten minutes or so he said the Secretary of State and other top execs in government were on his appointment list.

I got up. He shook hands with me and again said to report "only to me!"

When FDR's initial press conference was about to end, he was asked: "Where does your administration stand? To the left or right?"

The President replied: "Let us say this administration is a little left of center." Meaning, of course, that he was not on the side of the Axis or for any of the Hitler-Mussolini comreds and traitors in the United States.

The President recognized Russia in 1933, shortly after he took office.

"Russia," he reminded critics, is an ally." He knew that Russia would have to be an ally—since Hitler and Mussolini kept attacking "the Russian Communists." And so those of us on the papers (and on the air) who were FDRooters (and ferociously anti–Nazi-Fascist) used our syndicates and networks to help the President and our government fight the maniacs who were bombing little countries like Holland, Belgium, and Ethiopia.

☆

Months later I dug up a helluva thing that only FDR's ears could hear. I found out that one of his bitterest foes in the newspaper business had disturbed the peace and quiet of other Union League members in the famous New York Club—so veddy excloosiff.

The man, who had been drinking heavily, bellowed, "The time has come for somebody to assassinate that crippled sonofabitch in The White House!" The four oldsters lazying in their huge cushiony chairs were appalled. All were GOPeople. They walked out on him.

I phoned the Secret Service in New York City to tell them I was on my way to Washington and to please inform FDR's press chiefs that "it is urgent I see him."

After an exchange of trivia and a joke I knew was a knee slapper—FDR was an "easy" audience for a funny one—I told him about the man in the Union League Club. I gave him the name of the louse, since deceased, boss of a news syndicate.

FDR pursed his lips and said, "Well, well, thanks." As I left, he stared at the floor in deep thought.

Shortly after I gave FDR that info Mr. Louse and the National Press Club were divorced. I was told the late John O'Donnell, star Washington man for the New York *Daily News* (then wed to pundit Doris Fleeson, a lovely lady) made a motion for the man's expulsion.

Another National Clubber seconded—and bye-bye "Mr. Syndicate."

John O'Donnell and his paper were top boosters for FDR's election. They fell out before FDR's second term—a bitter feud.

Just when some of us thought that O'Donnell, his boss, Captain Joseph Medill Patterson (who served bravely in World War II) and the President might be reconciled, FDR humiliated O'Donnell at a press conf when he said, "John, I have something for you. You've earned it!" He held up one of Germany's Iron Crosses.

Oh, brother! It made front pages in the forty-eight states. The New

York *Daily News* and cousin Chicago *Tribune* (published by Colonel R. R. McCormick) then let the President have it every day on the editorial pages and elsewhere.

The *Trib* included me in its front-page editorial cartoons (in color, yet!) as one of FDR's "stooges"—out "to wreck the U.S."

Harry Hopkins, FDR's right arm, and playwright Robert E. Sherwood were included. The *Trib* purchased Hearst's Chicago *American* in recent years—and so my col'm is paid for by the Chi *Trib*. Funny woild.

Presidents, and men who aspire to the job, jass do not cooperate with Secret Service agents, local police, and other boy-dee-guards.

In Miami in 1933, FDR was President-elect. Minutes before Zangara shot at him—hitting and fatally wounding Mayor Cermak of Chicago —Mr. Roosevelt told all White House correspondents, "Get on the train so we can get out of here quickly. Nothing is going to happen!"

Washington newspaper people enjoyed spinning this one. A group of them accompanied FDR to a show. During intermission they thanked a Secret Service man for providing them with excellent seats.

"Don't mention it," was the federal man's retort. "Just notice the seating arrangement. No one can take a shot at the President without hitting one or two reporters first."

I never bothered to request a White House press pass when FDR was President. "*You* need a pass?" he kidded. One day I went to one of his press conferences.

Mr. Simmons, the reception desk man, put me up front right behind Merriman Smith, dean of White House correspondents (United Press) and the AP man. I decided to leave that choice position and strolled to the rear of the group. I didn't want them all to say, "Hmf, teacher's pet."

As we all slowly strolled into the Oval Room, Secret Servicers were stationed every few feet along the way. One agent, not seeing any press pass (which all reporters held high in the air) grabbed and pushed me into an office. Another agent rescued me.

During the press conference I was still shaking from the embarrassment. Steve Early, FDR's press chief, told me to "linger." When the President motioned for me to sit down I stood before him—pale and livid.

"What's the matter?" he asked. "You look white as a sheet."

"Oh, Mr. President," I almost wept, "don't they know who's on your team around here?"

"What do you mean?"

I told him what happened.

"Well, well," he chuckled, "that shows you how well they protect me."

"Not so very well, Mr. President," I said, displaying a loaded .38.

He threw up his hands in mock surrender.

That was also when I found out that a longtime legend was bunk. There are no secret peepholes in the President's office for his guardians to watch every visitor through.

When FDR ran for his second term published polls revealed that "66% of the press" was opposed to him. I suppose that explains why they romanced me at the White House.

My Sabbath evening newscasts then led the ratings—not just for news'casters, but right up there with the Top Ten shows. The program, according to Hooper, Crossley, etcetera, often was first, second, or third. Decimal points separated the leaders.

I never believed the damb'd arithmetic. I knew before they did when I won or lost listeners. If I said something people didn't agree with, the next rating showed me in a "dive," often by a tenth of a point. If I submitted a stock tip that enjoyed plus signs the following week, the ratings had me back leading the field again.

Tony DeMarco: "Meet the wife. My Ball and Charm."

Chip Roberts (one of FDR's favorite government appointments) and his beaut-of-a-wife, Evie (a witty wench), were leaving the Stork Club one night when they spotted me in a far corner of the Cub Room annex having breakfast about 1:00 A.M. They walked over to say hello and contribute a quip. Evie was summoned away by a gal-pal.

As she and her gorgeous figger strolled off, her adoring mate gave her the up-and-down and said, "Hot damn! That gal looks just as good goin' as she does comin'." Evie Roberts' oft-quoted sallies and snappy rejoinders to wisecrackers won her the title "The Dorothy Parker of Washington."

Drama critic Alexander Woollcott (whose word magic made *The New Yorker* mag easier to enjoy—and whose drama essays appeared in the New York *World* and then *The New York Times*) was at a party in Washington where he documented that he was a two-drink-drunk.

He was introduced to Evie.

"I understand," said the acid-tongued Alex (pressing his plump belly against her), "that you are the Dorothy Parker of Washington. Say something clever."

"You say something clever first!" Evie rebuttled.

"Veriwell. Button my fly."

"Why?" slashed Evie. "Have you something to conceal?"

LEONARD LYONS

The date for this one is March 1934.

I was invited by Captain W. D. Puleston of ONI (Office of Naval Intelligence) to visit him at his office in Washington. G-men J. Edgar Hoover and his chief aide, Clyde Tolson, brought me in.

"You were in the Navy when you were a youngster in 1918," he said warmly. "Have you ever considered re-enrolling?"

"No, sir."

"Well," said Captain Puleston, "think about it. If you decide to enroll, and you pass the required studies and courses, you will be commissioned a lieutenant."

On September 24, 1934, I was appointed lieutenant in the Reserve and assigned to ONI 'cause I had got the top rating (4.0) filling out the difficult Q. & A. they give applicants. (Leonard Lyons helped me considerably with the answers.)

I had named his column "The Lyons Den" when Leonard first started. One night he told me: "I must be a success. I've been doing this for a month and I'm being threatened with a lawsuit because I'm using the title 'Broadway Medley.' "

"That's corny, anyway," I said. We were at a table in a nightclub owned by Billy Rose. I was doodling on the tablecloth. While doodling

I wrote "The Lyons Den." "It takes a long time to get your name on the top," I said. "They usually put it somewhere in eight-point type, and here you have your name in the title."

In all the articles I have ever read about Lyons, this story never appears. I once asked him: "How come you never tell interviewers that?" He replied: "I do, but they just don't print it."

Which is a likely story.

Leonard told me a long time ago that he was a law clerk when he proposed marriage to his wife, Sylvia. It was she who designed his future and not he hers, according to *Pic*. "No," she said, "I don't want to be married to a law clerk. That's too dull. I want you to make like Walter Winchell and do a column and put things in the newspaper so we can get free tickets to all the shows and movies and go to fancy places like the Stork Club and never have to pay checks." They came from Rivington Street—but never left it.

When Jimmy Cannon started I took him by the hand and put him on my team. One day Leonard Lyons came along with his wife and said to Cannon: "I'm Leonard Lyons. I just started on the *Post*."

Cannon said: "Screw, bum. Come back when you have a reputation."

I said to Cannon: "You screw, bum. *You* come back when you have a reputation."

Then Jimmy wrote a book and autographed a copy: 'To my dearest friends, Sylvia and Leonard Lyons." Nowhere was there any mention of me getting him a job.

Lyons, who tells my "Mafia" that I am a swell fellow, pans the hell out of me to his chums and any listener in the United States and abroad —tells them stories that I told on myself, and distorts them. He doesn't say the source was Little Ol' Me.

One of the top news stories of the decade was the 1934 birth of the Dionne quintuplets in a small Canadian town.

The country doctor who saved their lives was Dr. Allan Dafoe. He was brought to New York City for high honors. He addressed medics from all over the world at the Academy of Medicine. Government sleuths and Manhattan detectives were assigned to protect him from crowds and autograph pests.

After several days and nights of being toasted by the elite and others, newsmen and photographers took the doctor to see the New York sights—winding up at the Paradise nightclub winkside.

The star attraction was Sally Rand, one of the pioneer strippers. Sally really revealed nothing. Her figure was draped in skintights from chest to ankles (the law in New York prohibited undraped femme cuticle) and she covered her casabas most of the time with the largest white-feathered fans you ever saw.

To tantalize the male patrons, her Form Divine was "hidden" by a curtain made of peekaboo material that reached from the stage to the ceiling. Plus dark blue lighting!

The newspaper people phoned me at the New York *Mirror* to rush over and join them. "It wouldn't be right," said Hy Goldberg of the New York *Post,* "for Canada's Number One Blessed Event man to be in town without meeting Broadway's Number One Blessed Event reporter!"

They introduced me to Dr. Dafoe and sat me alongside him. On came Sally and her silly fans. She did the familiar "strip" slow-walk (accompanied by pashy soft music) around the ringside.

As she passed Dafoe, I whispered, "Doc, she's really a nice girl."

Without turning his head, he mumbled, "Nice ass, too."

From page 163 of the "Tender Loving Care" article scribbled by my old foe's historian: "Sullivan wrote an open letter to Barbara Hutton in his column suggesting that she sponsor a Christmas party for some of the underprivileged children of New York. The heiress (then one of the richest girls in the world) sent a check for $5,000 and Winchell devoted his next two columns to characterizing Sullivan as 'a black-mailer.' This increased the bitterness."

In Ed's biog, the "author" neglected to print that open letter.

Wellll, let's get it right, son. At the time, Sullivan's stuff appeared in very few papers. Mine ran in over a hundred. Ed's letter in the New York *Daily News* of December 13, 1934, began:

> An Open Letter to Princess Mdivani. . . . The unreality of your existence must be boring, Princess. You have a husband who has little or no relation to everyday life. I read that he has bought himself a new string of polo ponies, and that after the polo season has ended, he will hunt tigers. I believe it was he who insisted that a band be flown across the English Channel to play tango music for one of your parties.

101

With people in distress all over the world, such reports create a sinister undertone. . . . I have heard grim and resolute men say some nasty things about your husband, Princess. . . . I would dislike to turn him loose along the waterfront of New York, or the south side of Chicago. They might do some dreadful things to him and make it impossible for him ever to play polo again. I have heard underworld chieftains speak about him and his apparently callous disregard for human suffering. . . .

So in asking you to distribute 1,000 Christmas baskets to the poor of New York, I . . . believe this is a . . . grand opportunity to wipe the slate clean. . . .

Come on, Princess, what do you say? Sincerely, Ed Sullivan.

The New Yorker's "Talk of the Town" department complained: "We think the time has come for someone to do something about the Broadway columnists [-ists!] who write open letters to people for money, etc."

No columnists wrote it—a colum*nist* wrote it. I wondered why that magazine didn't mention the open-letter writer's name. That mag's readers in the sticks probably jumped to conclusions (a good way to break your neck) and surmised, "They must mean WW."

Miss Hutton phoned me a few days later. She wondered what I thought she should do.

"Wouldn't you say," she said, "it is a form of blackmail?"

"You said that, lady, I didn't!" I told her.

For making Miss Hutton's statement public, Mr. Sullivan's Boswell quotes Ed as saying: "I will never forgive him [W.W.] for that."

Bugs Baer's quotation marksmanship reminder: "If you want to be a good newspaperman, you've got to be a harpoon—or a whale."

The Seabury Investigation documented that Jimmy Walker and some of his City Hall people had been trapped with their hands in the tambourine.

After being reduced to nothing by the investigation, this wonderful man was exiled for two years and then came back. When the Walkers returned via ship, reporters gathered about them as Jimmy devoured the Manhattan Island skyline and Miss Liberty in the harbor.

"Jimmy, how does it feel to be back?"

Always ready with a wisecrack or pepigram, the former Most Popular

Man In Town sighed and chuckled, "It is awful to find that New York City can function without me."

I checked the ship and announced on the air: "Mr. and Mrs. North America and all the ships at sea. This is Walter Winchell, who has this greeting for His Honor, Mayor James J. Walker, on board the S.S. *Mauretania*. He was always a friend to the many, who were only a pal to him."

Betty Compton told me: "You go to the Mayfair and tell Jimmy that if he doesn't call me by eight forty-five, I will shoot my brains out on the steps of City Hall."

Jimmy shrugged and walked away from me. I said: "Jimmy, please do it."

He replied: "Walter, butt out of this," with the fury of a lover.

His wife, to whom he had dedicated his only song, "Will You Love Me In December As You Do In May?" finally stepped aside so he and Betty could wed.

In the Stork Club Cub Room weeks later Jimmy chatted about his career, his golden hours, and the heartaches.

"I'd like permission," I said, "to print what you told me about being seen with Betty where the lights were brightest—how you both didn't try to hide the affair."

"Go ahead," he said, "but run this, too. At a Midwest steel company, a man who had never taken a day off or come to work late was rewarded for twenty-five years as a loyal, hard worker.

"His boss told him he could take a month's vacation anywhere in the world—all expenses paid by the firm. The Milquetoast fellow decided on Paris, France. He had never been abroad.

"The first night in Paris, he flirted with a beauty in the lobby, invited her to the bar for a sip, and before he knew it, she had him in her suite. She 'neglected' to shut the door. It stayed open several inches.

"The woman's 'husband' [pimp] walked in and pulled the old badger game bit. He demanded money to keep the story from the papers. Our Hero said he had no big money—only a few hundred dollars—and gave it to him.

"The con man's arguing was so noisy that disturbed tenants complained to the manager. A house detective came to shut them up. The story landed in the Paris papers, then over the cables. The poor sucker's name and photo were front-paged in his hometown. His boss cabled him to hurry back.

103

"In the plant, the boss denounced him for disgracing the company and himself.

" 'I didn't do anything out of the way,' was the reply. 'The door was open all the time!'

" 'You damb'd fool!' barked the boss. *'Doors were meant to be closed!'* "

★

THE LINDBERGH BABY KIDNAP

Charles A. Lindbergh's baby was kidnapped in 1932. Many people on and off the papers and networks were not convinced that Bruno Richard Hauptmann, later electrocuted for the crime, did it. Wherever I go, coast to coast, newspapermen, police, and readers still ask, "Do you really think he was guilty? How could one person do it alone?"

I reported the story from March 2, 1932, until February 1935, when a jury in Flemington, New Jersey, found Hauptmann guilty. Penalty—the Chair.

How did the kidnapper know the exact location of the nursery? Probably because one of the most popular slick paper magazines (months before the crime) published the layout of the Lindberghs' new Hopewell, New Jersey, home. The captions revealed the exact location of the Lindberghs' bedroom, the room occupied by the baby's nurse, the nursery, etcetera.

Moral: Whether you are celebrated or not, never permit any publication to print pictures of your house or apartment.

I want to tell you about a man whose amazing deductions—from studying the ransom notes—were confirmed.

His detective work is saluted in many books written about the Crime of the Century. The best book, in my opinion, is *Kidnap* by George Waller, who told me that he was a kid of eight when the story broke on the world's front pages.

You may find the book that Dr. Dudley D. Schoenfeld himself wrote about the crime in the public library. The title: *The Crime and the Criminal—a Psychiatric Study of the Lindbergh Case.* The publisher, Covici-Friede. "It was," says the flyleaf, "upon his concept of the crime and the criminal that the Police Department in New York City devised its plan of apprehension."

Several months before Hauptmann was arrested I learned about Dr.

Schoenfeld, who had confided to intimates: "My fear is that someone like a Winchell will reveal the role I played at the very start."

In my *Daily Mirror* column I ran this: "When the Lindbergh baby kidnap is solved, which it will be eventually, it will be revealed that the one person who did more than all the law enforcement agencies put together was Dr. Dudley D. Schoenfeld, the eminent psychiatrist of Mount Sinai and The New York Academy of Medicine."

When Schoenfeld read this it was, he said later, "with a sigh of relief." He was pleased, he added, "that it was done with dignity." ("Like a Winchell," eh?)

Following publication of my paragraph about Dr. Schoenfeld, he spent hours tracing the Winchell family doctor. He located the late Dr. Sidney Reiser at his West End Avenue apartment about 1:00 A.M.

"Doctor," said Schoenfeld, "I must meet Walter Winchell. He will never again have an inaccurate report about the kidnapping. He's had a few unfounded rumors. Please tell him to call me any hour day or night. Now, if you can find him . . ."

Dr. Reiser phoned me at the *Mirror* and relayed the message. I phoned Dr. Schoenfeld at his home.

"Please," he said, "come now."

I spent several hours with him. I came away with enough inside stuff on the case to last a long time.

How did Dr. Schoenfeld get permission to study the ransom notes? He knew people who knew the Lindbergh lawyer, and offered to help. He read the notes through plastic coverings, of course.

"The kidnapper—not kidnappers, this was a Lone Wolf job—was not Scandinavian," said Schoenfeld (to me—and to police) right from the beginning. "Dr. Condon, who handed the ransom to the man behind the St. Raymond's Cemetery gates told police 'he seemed Scandinavian.' "

"He is German," continued Schoenfeld.

"How do you know that?"

"His first ransom letters were addressed to 'Mr. Police Commissioner Mulrooney,' 'Mr. Colonel Henry Breckinridge' [Lindbergh's lawyer], 'Mr. Captain Lindbergh,' and 'Mr. Dr. Condon.'

"Scandinavians never say or write *Herr*—Germans use it! 'Mr. Colonel' and 'Mr. Doctor' correspond to the Germanic expressions '*Herr* Colonel' and '*Herr* Doctor.' "

The first note found on the sill had assured "the baby is in gute care." Schoenfeld said, "*Gute* is German for 'good.' Scandinavians don't say *gute*. This is not the work of any Detroit Purple Gang or Capone mob or gansters," he continued. "It is the work of a loner. He lives in the Bronx."

"The Bronx? How did you arrive at that?"

"Because when Dr. J. C. Condon, a Bronx teacher [in his seventies] invited himself into the headlines by writing on 'Open Letter to the Kidnapper' to contact him, the letter was only in the *Bronx Home News*. The Condon address was in the letter. The kidnapper responded to that appeal by Condon the next day.

"No Detroit or Chicago mobsters would see that paper. It circulates only in the Bronx!"

"Well, whaddaya know!" I astonished.

"But," I reminded Dr. Schoenfeld, "the second ransom note—following the one found on the nursery windowsill—was postmarked Brooklyn."

"Yes, Brooklyn," replied Schoenfeld. "You could take the subway in the Bronx and get off at Borough Hall in Brooklyn, mail the letter, and get back home on the subway. Very simple deduction."

Schoenfeld deducted that the baby was dead because "kidnappers do not tell you the victim is all right. They threaten, 'If you tell the police or don't do what I say, we will send you an ear!' "

Then there was my second-favorite figure in the entire kidnap: the man who followed the kidnapper's instructions about the ransom money.

Lindbergh had phoned President Herbert Hoover: "Mr. President, please don't let them mark the money. I want my baby back."

The President so ordered one and all. But President Hoover's order was ignored. A clever government official jotted down the serial numbers of the ransom. It included thirty-five thousand dollars in gold seal notes.

Bruno Richard Hauptmann was trapped passing one of the ransom gold notes.

That self-effacing man was rarely mentioned, if at all, in any newspaper, magazine, or newscast. If so, it eluded me. He was the late Elmer T. Irey of the Treasury Department.

I doubled-checked the above with his brother.

The fifty-thousand-dollar ransom money kept popping up only in New York City for several years. Bank tellers, shop cashiers, and others wearied of studying the government's long list of serial numbers.

The kidnapper was a frugal man. Police told me that he was so cheap, such a penny-nurser, that when he drove from his Bronx home every day down to a Yorkville (Eighty-sixth Street) stock brokerage firm, he never bought more than a few gallons of gas.

Hauptmann crossed the bridge at 138th Street (Harlem Ship Canal) which brings you from the Bronx to Manhattan. He could have purchased his gas at an Esso Station at 130th Street.

But no, he drove three blocks to another gas depot, made a U-turn to enter it on the uptown corner, and ordered five gallons—the fee for which was two cents cheaper than the place at 130th Street.

He presented a ten spot to Walter Lyle, filling station attendant at the Warner-Quinlan station at 127th Street and Lexington Avenue. Mr. Lyle made the change and said, "You don't see many of these around anymore since we went off the gold standard in '33."

"Oh," said the driver, smiling, "I haff only about a hundred left." And drove away.

Lyle jotted down the license plate on the gold note.

Good-bye, Charlie! That was the beginning of the end of Bruno Richard Hauptmann. Thanks to Elmer T. Irey and gas station man Walter Lyle.

When the gold ten spot was spotted by an alert bank teller, William R. Strong, in the Mount Morris branch of the Corn Exchange Bank Trust Company at 85 East 125th Street in Harlem, he checked it against the list of ransom bills. He found the serial number and immediately notified the Justice Department's Bureau of Investigation.

Hauptmann, to save two pennies, paid for that gas with his life.

I had the arrest of Hauptmann all to myself for fourteen hours and did not make it public—as G-man Chief J. Edgar Hoover certified. The following is an excerpt of a three-part series on Hoover by Don Whitehead for the Associated Press. The articles appeared on page one of *The New York Times* for three days.

Reported Mr. Whitehead: "Referring to leaks from the FBI, Mr. Hoover recalled that many people thought the FBI had leaked information from time to time to Walter Winchell . . . who is a friend of Hoover's."

Hoover recalled after the Lindbergh kidnapping case was broken and Bruno Hauptmann had been arrested, there was a meeting in New York City Police Headquarters in which we worked out the final details of how the case was broken.

"Someone brought me a note saying Winchell wanted to see me outside the conference room," Whitehead quotes Hoover as saying, "I had never seen him—but I was just Country-Boy enough to want to see what he looked like.

"I came out of the room and he came out of a crowd of about two hundred reporters. He asked me if I had received a letter he wrote me the day before, in which he gave me information on where the kidnap ransom money had been found and other details of the case. I suspected he was trying to . . . trick me into giving him a scoop on the story we were about to break. I told him I had seen no letter. I was pretty annoyed with him.

"I got back to the hotel that night and called my office. The letter was there and Winchell had all the facts in the case just as he said he did. Next day . . . I apologized for my suspicions. I asked him why he didn't print the facts he gave me in his letter, since he had them correctly.

"He said he hadn't wanted to do anything that might hurt the case or hamper the investigation—and that he had sent it to me to be helpful. Imagine, a newspaperman not making public every newsman's dream of a scoop—the arrest of the Lindbergh baby kidnapper—so that confederates, if any, would not be alerted to escape.

"That was the beginning of my friendship with him."

The only thing I wrote was the following on September 14, 1934:

"The federal men are convinced that they will break the most interesting crime on record—the Lindbergh snatch. A squad of handpicked aces still are working on it 24 hours a day. I hear they have collected some definite clues."

Westbrook Pegler's columnar comment at the time: "Imagine WW calling himself a newspaperman! He told his alleged beat to the FBI instead of to his city desk!"

When Hauptmann's Bronx home was raided by the Bureau of Investigation (later the FBI) and New York police, the lawmen found about $14,600—what was left of the $50,000 ransom money—in Hauptmann's home and garage, most if it tightly rolled into tiny holes made with a carpenter's drill in beams, closets, and elsewhere.

After the ransom money was found, detectives made another discovery. One alert sleuth found a minicloset with space for only a broom, mop, and pail. It was so tiny the detective couldn't turn around in it.

He threw his flashlight into it and found open letter-writer Dr. Condon's phone number scribbled on the wall. Most important, it was Dr.

Walter Winchell as a very young man, before 1908

Winchell at age 13, in costume for Gus Edwards' Song Revue *(1910)*

WWith James J. ("Jimmy") Walker, Mayor of New York City

Mr. and Mrs. Winchell, just arrived on the train to Hollywood, with Ben Bernie ("The Old Maestro") who was then making his screen debut in Shoot the Works *(1934). Bernie and WW's ersatz feud hoodwinked the public for years (King Features)*

Condon's old number—which he had changed ten days after the kidnapping to a private listing.

The Detroit *Evening Times* saluted me on September 21 with: "Last Friday Walter Winchell . . . predicted that a break was near in the Lindbergh kidnapping. Today, the news of the arrest of Bruno Hauptmann proves Winchell right again."

The kidnapper had figured out a way to convince the Lindberghs and police that he was The Right One. He said his "singnature" was in the two interlocking circles outlined in blue ink. The inner oval formed where they overlapped was colored solid red. They were punched with three rough-edged square holes, similar to the hole punched on tickets by train conductors.

So what? When arrested Hauptman was asked to write the word "signature." He spelled it "singnature."

After Hauptmann's apprehension, "I believe" said the clairvoyant Schoenfeld, "that Bruno Richard Hauptmann signed his 'name' like this: The blue ink on the circles stood for *B* for 'Bruno'; the red oval, for *R* like 'Richard' and the *H* for 'Hauptmann' was in the three punched holes—*H* for 'hole.' "

Pretty good, even if it was not offered as evidence.

After the kidnap, Violet Sharpe, one of the Lindbergh's kitchen staff, had been interrogated by top New Jersey detectives.

She had a spotless reputation. This was attested to by everyone.

"Don't give me any of that good girl stuff!" one of the detectives allegedly yelled at Miss Sharpe. "You know you're a whore!"

One day, hearing she was going to be questioned for the fourth time, she rushed to her room and swallowed cyanide chloride, killing herself almost instantly.

I never let the cruel man forget it. I told the story to my readers and radio listeners for weeks.

Reporters, photographers, and others on the New York *Daily News* and other papyri warned me, "Don't ever set foot in New Jersey again, if you are smart. The guy you've been attacking swore he'd knock out your teeth the first time he sees you."

When Hauptmann was arrested three years later and the trial was to start, the *Daily Mirror's* newest managing editor, Arthur Brisbane (Hearst's top-salaried staffer), sent for me.

"Runyon will cover the Q and A [questions and answers]. You will do the sidelights, side bars [human interest], and I will be there daily. The *Mirror* has only three passes to the Flemington Courthouse. Here's yours."

"Mr. Brisbane," I told him, "I've been warned by many newspapermen not to go to New Jersey because of my blasts at a detective who drove Violet Sharpe to suicide."

"Now you see here!" Brisbane icily replied. "I'm the general around here. You're a soldier. I command you to go there!"

We had adjoining suites at a hotel in Trenton—miles from Flemington. At 6:00 A.M. he rang my room and told me to see him at once. "Give me your pass," he said.

"How will I get in, Mr. Brisbane?"

"Oh, I'm not worrying about that," he general'd, "I know about you. You can get in anywhere! I have to have your pass for Bernard Gimbel —he is one of our biggest advertisers."

Oh, Brutha!

Brisbane limousine'd me to Flemington. It was a frigid day: snow everywhere, retarding the speed.

We got there a few minutes before the Curtain Went Up. Brisbane stranded me on the congested courthouse steps—walking in with Mr. Gimbel.

"You look lost, Walter," said a man I had never met. "Come with me, I'll get you a seat right down front alongside the defense table." He was one of my newspaper-radio fans, I assumed.

Dr. Schoenfeld, who did so much to help the lawmen from the day the ransom notes came, couldn't get in. No pass. At the first recess I saw Schoenfeld in the hotel dining room across the street. "I can't get in," he sighed.

"I'll get you in, Doc," I assured. "Watch and see."

After lunch I found the man who had got me in and told him my problem. He arranged a pass for Schoenfeld and a seat alongside mine.

"You're a very nice guy," I told the stranger who had opened all doors for me and Schoenfeld. "Let me know how I can return the compliment."

He turned out to be the brute I had attacked for driving innocent Violet Sharpe to suicide. He became my third-best tipster on the trial.

Item in the Miami Beach *Tribune,* Sunday, December 16, 1934:

"JAFSIE CONDON THREATENS TO HORSEWHIP WINCHELL. Dr. John F. Condon [JFC—Jafsie] threatened last night to horsewhip

110

Walter Winchell if and when he can find him. His gray head shaking wrathfully, the aged intermediary in the Lindbergh kidnapping case sat in a downtown Miami hotel room and vowed vengeance on the columnist for his attacks on Condon's unimportance as a witness in the case."

One day during the trial the Philadelphia *Ledger* carried the following story:

"Special to the *Evening Ledger*: Flemington, N.J., January 3rd: Bruno Richard Hauptmann, whose courtroom seat is directly in front of the *Ledger's* reporter, broke his courtroom silence this morning to ask the *Ledger* reporter a question.

" 'Listen,' he said, 'who is Walter Winchell? Is he in the court?'

"A reporter pointed him out and the defendant said: 'He shouldn't be allowed in the court. He is not the right man.' "

Hauptmann had to pass my seat to get to his own each morning. Two state troopers escorted him.

Looking at me one morning, he German-accent'd, "Vich vahn iss Valter Vinchell?"

"Right here," I said.

"You tell *lies, lies!*" he exploded, as they pulled him away.

He was a carpenter, he testified. His last job, he also disclosed when arrested, was at the Majestic Apartments, Seventy-second Street and Central Park West, Manhattan.

The kidnap took place March 1, 1932.

The ransom was paid April 2, a month later. Hauptmann said he worked that day at the Majestic. The Majestic timekeeper said Hauptmann had not turned up on April 2.

He never returned to the Majestic after April 2—nor to any other job.

Mrs. Hauptmann, who bore him a son, testified that "about that time" her husband gave her an extra five dollars weekly.

Editors are recommended to the article "How We Trapped the Lindbergh Kidnapper," by Elmer L. Irey, former Chief of Intelligence Unit, United States Treasury Department. Mr. Irey debunked all the Letters-to-the-Editor writers who "couldn't believe one man did it alone." "Hauptmann," Irey testified, "was the guiltiest man I ever knew. . . . He had kept records," wrote Irey, "of his savings and expenses. We proved that he spent or owned $49,950.44 more than he ever earned since coming to America. . . . We came within $49.56 of the $50,000 ransom by one method and within $14 by another. . . . Haupt-

111

mann insisted he had gotten the money from Isador Fisch, his deceased business associate. We were able to prove Hauptmann had been spending the money two years before he even met Fisch!"

What about Isador Fisch, the man Hauptmann said had left him a valise "to care for" while Fisch returned to Germany to visit kin? This was thoroughly debunked in the Flemington courthouse. A sister of Fisch testified that her brother died on March 29, 1934, in Germany; that when he returned from the United States to live with her, he owned five hundred dollars in American cash and fifteen hundred marks in traveler's checks.

The ladder found under the baby's nursery was the work, said experts, of an amateur. The ladder contained a piece of "new" wood nailed to the side of a lower rung—apparently to give it more support —when the kidnapper, rehearsing his crime, discovered one rung to be very weak.

That piece of wood (our top newsbreak on the case) came from Hauptmann's attic floor. Wood experts from all over the nation so testified in court.

In my column in the *Mirror* on December 10, 1934, I said:

> Flash! Exclusive! Jersey's 'ace' evidence against Bruno Hauptmann for the murder rap will be this astounding fact hitherto unpublished: In the Bronx home tenanted by the Hauptmanns— state troopers just discovered that one of the wardrobe closets has a removable ceiling, which leads to a trap door and then to the attic . . . In this attic officials found that a strip of flooring board had been carefully sawed away . . . A patch of wood used to strengthen one part of the crime-ladder fits exactly into the place in the attic floor. The wood in the ladder patch is identical to the attic floor wood, as are the nails and markings!

"Oh, my God!" exploded the prosecutor (Attorney General David Wilentz). "Why did you make that public? It was to be my closing line in the summation!"

A newsman couldn't do that today. It would result in a new trial.

The reason I made it public? Because I had already lost the scoop on Hauptmann's arrest.

How did I get the scoop? I got it from a man I later put high on my Drop-Dead List—the late Governor Harold Hoffman of New Jersey.

What madman would invade the home of a national hero? Bruno Richard Hauptmann, an alien from Kamenz, Germany, according to his police record there, also used a ladder to burgle the upper-story dwelling of a neighboring town's most important person, the Bürgermeister.

Following Hauptmann's conviction, Schoenfeld came to my apartment (in the same Majestic Apartments where Hauptmann had said he "vass in sharge of the Tower Floors." We lived there at the time of the crime on floor twenty-nine.) "We helped convict him," said Schoenfeld, "now we must keep him from going to the electric chair."

"Ofercrissakes, doctor! Why?"

"So that men of science may study him like a bug under glass."

"How can I do that?" I asked, giving him a "look."

"You can contact the governor of New Jersey and tell him what I suggest."

"But the governor," I reminded, "said from the very beginning that he would never intervene—that 'Jersey Justice Would Prevail Again!' "

"I know all that," said Schoenfeld, "but if anyone can get his ear, you can. He gave you that big scoop about the extra piece of wood in the ladder coming from Hauptmann's attic floor, didn't he?"

I reluctantly phoned Governor Hoffman's aide at the Hotel New Yorker, where Hoffman was making a speech.

The governor called me half an hour later.

I told him I had something about the trial that only he must hear. He fell for the bait and came to my apartment.

I introduced him to Schoenfeld, who told him what he told me—about saving Hauptmann for science.

Hoffman was impressed. He wanted to save Hauptmann, according to newspaper articles, because he had given him two reprieves—and when criticized for not keeping his pledge to let "Jersey Justice Prevail," he sought an Out.

As he waited for the elevator to reach my twenty-ninth floor, Governor Hoffman paused to ask me, "How can I depend on you not printing what I may do?"

"Oh, Governor," I groaned, "don't you remember? It's our idea! I only hope you don't let it leak to anyone on your staff. That's how newspaper people get stuff: usually from somebody who promised to keep it a secret!"

Imagine my astonishment and disgust a few hours later when the final edition of the New York *Daily News* hit the stands.

The "War Declared" type of headlines screamed: "GOV. TO SPARE

HAUPTMANN!" "KIDNAPPER TO BE STUDIED BY SCIEN-
TISTS!"

That ended another warm friendship. I never spoke to the publicity-
mad governor again.

★

LUCKY LUCIANO, GANG CHIEF

Charles "Lucky" Luciano was chief of the Italian mob in Greater New
York. He got the nickname Lucky after foes took him for a ride and
left him for dead one dawning. While making deliveries, a milkman
found Lucky, bullets from head to ankles, dumped in an alley of a Long
Island house. He summoned police.

An ambulance medic found Luciano's pulse weak, but beating. He
survived. Thus, "Lucky."

The first time I met Lucky was in Spinrad's barbershop, practically
in the subway entrance at 47th Street and Broadway, where we Night
People could get a shave or trim until midnight. One of his hoods told
me Lucky wanted to talk to me in a far corner of the shop.

The night before, I had been slugged by two Nazis over my opinions
of convicted Lindbergh baby–kidnapper-killer, Bruno Richard Hauptmann. Mr. Luciano, who looked like one of *The Untouchables,* asked,
"Who hitchew?"

"Two Nazi guys," I told him. "They let me have it from front and
back—and then ran. Chipped a front tooth."

"What makes you think Nazis did it?"

"I had a column this morning saying Hauptmann should burn. They
must be Nazis. They had German accents."

(This was confirmed a few days later by the late Johnny Broderick,
then New York's most feared detective.)

"You know," continued Luciano, "none of my boys did it, don't-
chew?"

"Oh, I know that," I told him. "Why would any of the boys do it?
I never did anything to them."

"Well, just so long as you know," said Luciano. "If you find out who
hitchew," was Lucky's ta-ta, "be sure and lemme know. Okay?"

"Yes, thanks," I said.

A few nights later at the Hollywood Restaurant (Forty-eighth and

Broadway, later the site of the Latin Quarter), Luciano and his top aides caught the midnight girl show. They remained for the 2:00 A.M. stanza. They were champagne buyers, the top tippers. All the babes in the chorus sat with them between shows and long after the last show, too.

Except one Doll. She had gotten the job a week before. A lovely thing named Mary Lou Dix, a grad of Carnegie Tech. High-class gal. She simply said to the girls who invited her to join them with the Mobfia: "Okay, I'll be there after I make a call home." But she never showed.

One midnight the management brought her to my table in the rear. She told me she was worried. "Those fellows might be angry with me because I keep turning down their invitations to join them."

"Don't worry about it or them," I told Mary Lou. "Just tell the boss to tell them I'm dating you. I hope it helps."

And it did.

A Luciano staffer named Pretty Boy Amberg (because he was so ugly) decided to be the judge and jury about Miss Dix. "What's with that ritzy-bitzy Dix dame?" he complained to the brother of the joynt's owner. "We always invite her to sit with us and she never does!"

Frank Moss, the owners' brother (and manager of the place), tried to calm Pretty Boy.

He whispered, "She's got a feller. He waits for her every night."

"I don't care if she's got a feller," argued Pretty Boy Amberg. "The hell with him!"

Mr. Moss told the gangster, "He's Walter Winchell, the newspaperman."

"Big deal!" hmf'd Amberg. "I'll knock his teet' down his troat!"

This was too much for manager Moss. He feared he'd get a shellacking. Moss sent word to Lucky he had to speak with him—urgent.

Lucky went to Moss's office and was told of Amberg's threats.

Luciano returned to his table and audibly reprimanded Amberg.

"Just forget it!" Lucky ordered. "And *never* hit a newspaperman. It's hard luck!"

Pretty Boy was credited by mobsters with inventing the latest fashion in One-Way Rides. After murdering a person in a car in a deserted area, he'd pour kerosene or gasoline all over and inside the car—then ignite it with a book of matches. That's the very way Pretty Boy went to hell.

☆

115

Novelette at "21": People who belonged to the inner circle at the renowned Manhattan restaurant gave the creeps to intimates with this alleged lowdown on what killed owner Jack Kriendler.

The storytellers rarely note that Mr. K. had suffered numerous heart attacks. They prefer this legend: Two weeks before he succumbed, Kriendler had a scene with a man in his place. The man had no police record but was influential in both the upper and underworlds.

Kriendler signal'd a captain to seat this man and his lady on the third floor in the far rear so he wouldn't be seen. The man was incensed. He sent for Mr. K. and told him off. "Why did you do this to me?" he thundered, "I will kill you, do you hear? I will kill you!"

Kriendler, pals insist, tossed every night in bed for two weeks worrying about the threat—killing himself.

The late Polly Adler was New York City's Number One Madam. Her clients included the top gangsters (Dutch Schultz, Legs Diamond, *et al.*); politicians, newspapermen, and celebrities of the stage and screen.

Polly was a respectable girl when she worked in the sweatshops at a sewing machine on the Lower East Side. But this bored her and she decided to "hustle" and make some better money than sweatshop girls get to support her very poor immigrant family. So she became Queen of Hookaville in midtown and prospered. Her Call-Gels were the most attractive and the most expensive in town.

Now and then her elegantly appointed apartment (she had a private elevator) was raided by police. But Polly and her cast of Prostipretties were invariably dismissed by one of her magistrate clients for "lack of evidence."

In her sunset years Miss Adler improved her neglected schooling by enrolling in an English class at the University of Southern California.

She wrote a book christened *A House Is Not A Home,* a best seller. It became a film. She died in her sixties from The Big C.

My favorite paragraph about her: When she escorted clients to the exit she always said (in a slight accent), "Denk you. It's all-vays a business doing pleasure mit you!"

Later in the decade a New York maid, employed by a couple in the Fifties, came to work with an unsightly rash on her face. Alarmed, the couple admitted that they'd be more comfortable if she went to a doctor. In order not to embarrass the girl, the husband suggested in an offhand way that the three of them go to have a blood test. Yesterday the report came back from the Board of Health. The maid passed, but her employers flunked!

★

WHY DUTCH SCHULTZ WAS SLAIN

When *New York Times* star reporter Meyer Berger was introduced to gang potentate Dutch Schultz, the mobster refused to shake Berger's hand. Squinting at the scribe, Shultz pouted. "Aintchu the guy who wrote that I was a pushover for blondes?"

"Someone," gulped Meyer, "told me that."

"That isn't the pernt," admonished Dutch sternly. "I don't think that 'pushover for blondes' is any kind of langwidge for a high-class newspaper like the *Times!*"

The Dutchman (as Arthur Flegenheimer was nicknamed by colleagues) was too tough for Murder, Inc. He quarreled with them all.

Mad Dog Coll, one of his aides, got so miffed with Dutch for refusing to let him become part-owner of the brewery he governed that he defected. Their feud resulted in the exchange of shots near Central Park in the vicinity of 102nd Street, where nurses and mothers wheeled their babies at noontime.

Coll's poor marksmanship killed a baby in its carriage. The headline hunters then gave him the label that stuck to him: "Mad Dog."

Shultz was not killed because he turned down Coll. The other mobs (Italo, Irish and Jewish) learned that he planned on killing Thomas E. Dewey, who was then investigating organized crime. Lepke, Gurrah, Shapiro, Bugsy Siegel, Albert Anastasia, and other members of Murder, Inc., kept cautioning Schultz to forget-the-whole-thing.

He told them to go to hell.

That's where they dispatched him. Dutch was dealt with by members of the Mob as he quaffed beer with other hoodlums in a Jersey saloon.

Some of his lieutenants were also hit in other spots in Manhattan at almost the same moment. One of them who survived still has a damaged wing.

Police who saw Schultz as he lay dying in the hospital told us that they had never seen such a frightened person in their lives. As we have often noted, gangsters, like dictators, always look good until the last ten minutes.

117

The Dutchman's assassin served twenty-three years in gaol. He was released a few years ago.

I see him occasionally in restaurants.

He is now one of New York's better-behaved citizens and is prospering in "Catholic" enterprises—to borrow Owney Madden's synonym for legitimate business.

★

FIRST-NIGHTER

Then there was drama critic Percy Hammond, another must-read word magician in the Long Ago, who never gave the back of his neck to this newcomer on the papers. His counsel, his help with anecdotes about the theater greats, and his warm words in his corner of the New York *Herald Tribune* cushioned the climb to the Broadway Heavens.

Mr. Hammond, who had a Santa Claus shape (and a face as benign), was one of the most feared play- and actor-appraisers in town—in Chicago too, from whence he came reluctantly because, as he confided, "I expected these New Yorkers, the wisecrackers at the openings and on the *Trib*, to label me a hick and laugh me back to Chicago." Imagine this very talented man with words being fearful of what his confrères and other show-oafs at the premières thought of him and his essays!

One of my pet quips about him: He walked out on a new opus after Act II. As he labored up the steep (for his tonnage) aisle, Percy put on his millinery. To which a First Night-Fraud seated next to me mumbled to his lady: "Get that Hammond guy. Putting his hat on. What awful manners!"

I ran a paragraph about it next morning, adding: "Mr. Hammond was apparently showing his contempt for the audience as well as the play."

One First Night, just after he started on the *Tribune* assassinating actors, actresses, playwrights, and producers, I returned from a stroll to the corner after the first act. On that bitter cold evening the audience at the Maxine Elliott Theater on Thirty-ninth Street had gone back to their pews. Only Hammond and I remained on the pavement.

I was finishing a cigarette.

"Mr. Winchell," he prefaced, "have you a match?"

"Yes," I answered nervously, lighting his pacifier.

He must have noticed my hand tremble as I tried to steady the match.

"May I tell you something, son?"

"Please do, Mr. Hammond."

"I think you are trying too hard. Trying to make each paragraph in the column a punch line."

"I guess," I replied, "that comes from my vaudeville training. In the three-and-four-a-day theaters, Mr. Hammond, you have about ten or twelve minutes in which to get over with the audience. So you try to make everything you say punchy. You know—make good."

"You make your point," said Hammond. "But remember this. No matter how good you think your stuff is, there will always be people who will say it is only pretty good. And when you think your stuff is pretty good, there always will be those who will call it lousy."

I thanked him as we both went back to our aisle seats. He was the first of the critics to give me more than a casual nod, and it was the beginning of a Long, Long Romance.

We did the late spots together often, winding up at around 4:30 A.M. in Reuben's, then open around the clock. Then, one sorrowful day in 1936, I read his obituary.

He passed suddenly. His Letting-Go like that saddened many of us in New York—but none mourned more than I.

Every drama sentinel eulogized him. His son put the write-ups in a thin book. Mine was the next to last.

I assume his son had me next to closing because of my punch line—to wit: "For me he was The North Star of Broadway."

But I was not the author of those beautiful words. Percy himself was. I borrowed them from one of his pieces. One day when he had no play to cover he devoted his entire space on the drama page that morning to writing about me. The last line of his patty-cake was, "For me, Winchell is The North Star of Broadway."

Quite a writer was Mr. Percy Hammond. Chinese Proverb: One more good man on earth is better than having an extra angel in heaven.

One big story I didn't remember owning exclusively was the merger of the Duke of Windsor and Wally Simpson.

The collaborators of a planned television series invited me to be the narrator. At their offices on the Twentieth Century-Fox lot, one of them said, "We can't pick up a book written in the past thirty years that doesn't mention you in some way. Your scoop of the marriage plans of the heir to the British throne and an American girl, for example. We came across that one yesterday."

"Oh, I didn't have that one," I said.

"It's in two books about the Windsors!" they informed.

"Oh, really?"

The titles of those tomes elude me now. The collaborator who told that to me has since shelved Hollywood to be a Professor Wotzizname in movie writing, etcetera, at UCLA.

Reviewers and others who may want to check with him, please look him up. I'm too bizzy. I'm not interested in what happened yesterday anyway. I never was. "What's going to happen tomorrow?" is my theme song.

★

"YOU BOTCHA ME . . ."

Oh, I have had some dillies that blew up in my red face many times. Name me a newspaperman that hasn't.

Some actor, actress, producer, director, some government, city, or state executive, or some pest invariably comes up and says, between hiccups, "You don't like me, do you?"

That's enough of a warning to put on my best false-face, smile courteously, and say, "Sorry, but I didn't hear your name. Did I ever offend you?"

"Oh," said one silly woman, "that's the trouble! You never mention me!"

"Haha," I usually say to people like that, "the big idea is to keep your name out of the papers!"

I don't always get off that easy. A few times a woofled belligerent guest spoiled the fun by complaining about some long-ago comment I made in print or on the air—and challenged me to a duel.

One night at Lindy's restaurant on Broadway, a maniacal drunk flung insults at me as I was leaving. He challenged me to a fight.

He sat with three powerful-looking men as he kept yelling at me.

Leonard Lyons, a confrère, was with me. I recognized a detective nearby and mumbled: "I think I'm in trouble—keep your eyes on his friends."

That detective's duty was to stop a fight from starting: "keeping the

120

Peace, etc." I had never met this sleuth. I had been told he was a copper, that he was a swell fellow—that he appreciated the many benefit shows I emceed (and staged) for widows and children of policemen and firemen killed in the line of duty. But he just sat there waiting for me to get decked, looking like a fight fan waiting for the kayo.

All this happened in a few tick-tocks. My critic was now standing on his table spewing profanity plus "Look at all these Jews in this place!"

This character was Jewish himself, the son of a respected and wealthy New York businessman. His father supported him all his life. It was four against one! I didn't know what they would do next.

Now he stood on the table—making a perfect target. I picked up a bottle of ketchup from a nearby table, took careful aim, and opened his skull.

As I stood there after flinging the ketchup bottle, his tearful wife moaned, "Oh, Mr. Winchell! He's been angry with you for a long time."

"Who is he? What's his name? What did I write about him that made him hate me so?"

"You never wrote about him," she explained, "but three times we were refused admittance to the Stork Club. My husband wrote you several letters about it and when he gets intoxicated he brings it up and says 'That Winchell never showed me the courtesy of a reply!' "

"Oh, lady," I told her, "I never see that sort of mail. My Girl Friday usually answers stuff like that without even telling me. Perhaps she was very busy. So that's the reason for his wild hollering? What's the reason for his Hitler-like opinions about the Jews?"

"He is a very sick man, Mr. Winchell, can't you see that?"

She divorced him, I later read in the papers, because during an estrangement he would climb the building like a fly to her first-floor apartment, smash in the window, and beat her up. The newspaper accounts included: "She charged that when intoxicated he often tried to kill her" and said that he was "a maniacal drunk."

He needed eleven stitches at a nearby hospital.

At that time I did not know it is a felony in New York State to do what I have seen gangsters do in brawls—pick up a chair or bottle and open an antagonist's head. A thrown bottle, chair, or anything that causes injury is the same as a concealed weapon.

Yes, concealed, because the "target" didn't know it was coming. Knowledgeable law enforcement people said I might have gotten ten years in prison on a felony rap—for defending myself.

Detectives from the main office of the New York City Police Department visited him in the hospital and asked: "Who hit you? Don't be afraid to say. There is nobody so important in this town that he can get away with this kind of assault. Who did it?"

The terrible-tempered mental cripple said: "I dunno. I don't even remember where it happened."

So I was not arrested. I got away with it, mainly because several people in the restaurant (friends and strangers) told me they'd be my witnesses. "We saw him provoke you," they offered.

What's more, the basstidd had done the same thing at one of the Longchamps chain of fooderies some time before. He was with a group in the upstairs section of the place and started a wild scene. When the captain of waiters told him to pipe down or leave, he took a swing at him.

They flung him down a long flight of stairs. That incident cost him several teeth, and other injuries. He "loved" to be beaten. When that detective's superiors learned that he hadn't stopped the bloody encounter but remained in his chair, he was demoted to patrolman. For all I know, he is still pounding a lonely beat somewhere on Staten Island.

Moss Hart and Oscar Levant also went to it at Lindy's once. They threw newspapers at each other.

Restaurateur Lindy sighed, "In the good old gangster days when Dutch Schultz and Legs Diamond dined here we never had such things!"

So please don't invite me to parties. I have a terrible temper—I believe it is called homicidal. "You Botcha Me, I Botcha You!" Simple as that.

Nobody is going to take a sneak-punch at me any more and get away with it.

In my over four decades on the papers, I got two sneak-raps in the mouth.

Once from paid Nazi sluggers during the Lindbergh-Hauptmann trial and once in Hollywood when Al Jolson (a pal for many decades) threw one when I wasn't looking. He'd been told my first movie for D. F. Zanuck dealt with him and his wife, Ruby Keeler. My movie made a Hero of the Star and a Heroine of the Chorus Girl!

He apologized in print the same night. But I didn't hear his apology for five years. When Jolson learned I was suffering torture from a pain that wouldn't go away, he gave a mutual friend some salve, saying: "Don't tell him I sent this or he won't try it. But I know the agony he is having—it's a toothache in the rectum. Just tell him to rub it on before going to bed and he'll sleep like a doped baby."

It was the first eight-hour sleep I had had in months. I went looking for Al that night and found him with Ruby at the premiere of a new show at the Trocadero in Hollywood.

The large crowd hushed as they saw me approach his table. I threw my arms around him and kissed him, saying, "Thanks, thanks, thanks. What *is* that stuff? Please send more."

He sent me enough to last a lifetime.

I didn't need it weeks later.

☆

From Frederick James Smith's thesis on me in *Liberty* mag, circa June 1937:

> The office walls are covered with pictures, a large number being of Mrs. Winchell and the children. Then there are autographed photographs, interesting framed letters and wires.
>
> One of the important wires is from William Randolph Hearst, the newspaper publisher. Winchell had published a column called If I Had a Newspaper, in which he told what he would do if he were a publisher. Mr. Hearst's wire in part, reads:
>
> "When I get so I can produce something fine every day as you do, I will apply for the promised position on your paper."

☆

Excerpt from a letter we wrote to Abel Green, editor of *Variety,* on March 2, 1938:

> Truman Talley offered me a job as news commentator along with Lowell Thomas and the others for Fox Movietone. He said: "I know you don't care about that, but I don't know what amount to offer you," but we tentatively agreed on a minimum of $500 a week for me to just give my voice and have his staff prepare the material once a week. I was on the verge of doing it when my tax accountant told me that out of the $25,000 I would be allowed to keep about $6,400, so the hell with it.
>
> It's a far cry, isn't it, Abel, from the days of hustling around trying to sell ads for *Vaudeville News* to get enough money to pay Billy LaHiff the rent, to turning down $25,000 because I would only get $6,400 out of it. This is a concrete example of what the heavy taxation is doing to stifle ambition and stopping people from wanting to work harder.

☆

On June 19, 1938, I broadcast the exclusive flash that Max Schmeling would fly to New York from his upstate training camp and that famed aviator Dick Merrill would handle the stick.

Next day's New York *World-Telegram* headlined: "SCHMELING NOT TO FLY. PHONY STORY ON BROADCAST EXPOSED BY SCHMELING AT HIS CAMP."

Harold Conrad in the Brooklyn *Eagle*: "Someone must have been pulling Winchell's leg. Max happened to be listening to the broadcast and that was the first he knew about it." A sportscaster got into the act with: "Strictly a spurious story faked by a desperate for news radio flasher. Max personally told me 'It isn't true! Why do they make up such lies?' "

From all NYC newspapers June 21, 1938: "Schmeling Flies To New York With Merrill!"

Oh, dear.

★

NEW YORK NOVELETTE

She was a beautiful young thing and very happy, too. Her beaus were abundant and she had many parties and dances to attend. But every nighttime she yearned for "the real one" to enter her life.

Then one nighttime, he did. It was at an ice-skating rink. He was a tall, handsome, well-to-do lad, intelligent and the other nice things a girl likes in a guy. He fell for her, too, and they began to live.

Not long after they set the day for the wedding. But three days before the tie was to be knotted his doctor told him the marriage couldn't be allowed by law—he had "flunked" his premarital health test "and the treatment would take years." He went home and shot himself dead. The next day the doctor received a letter from a laboratory apologizing for mixing up the blood samples and saying the patient was okay!

★

BROWNSHIRTS AND BRICKBATS

Byliner star Leland Stowe was with the New York *Herald Tribune* for ten years.

Back in 1933 Mr. Stowe visited Germany. When he returned to the United States he wrote a book titled *Nazi Germany Wants War*. Some of his editors considered it very funny.

It must have been a satisfaction to Stowe to know he was six years ahead of his betters. But when World War II began and he asked to be assigned to it, he was told he was too old to cover wars.

☆

Occasionally, government chiefs suggested I do pro-Russian pieces for the papers. One of my contributions was titled: "Things I Never Knew About Russia." A similar column was headed "Things I Never Knew Till Now About Stalin."

That was all the isolationists in the United States (the Peglers, the Reverend Winrods, the Coughlinites, the German-American Bundists, and the America First committee) needed. "He must be a Commy!" was their hysterical yelp.

The same week I ran a column debunking Stalin and his gang. This outraged the United States Commies. Some of them were editors. They ran expozays about me regularly. One New York paper devoted six weeks to attacking me.

One of President F. D. Roosevelt's inner-circlers, Leon Henderson, was sent to Buenos Aires to cement "good will" relations with Argentina's dictator, Juan Perón, playing footsy with Hitler and Mussolini. Mrs. Evita Perón, a former call girl, was really that nation's Fuehreress, according to many newsmen and women.

Mr. Henderson invited me to join his table at the Stork Club the evening he returned from Washington and Buenos Aires. "I thought," he said, among other things, "that this would amuse you. Evita Perón, alongside me at the dinner in my honor, suddenly pouted, 'Why does your Walter Winchell hate me so?'"

The Far Righters were no little confused. "Where the hell," some of them editorialed, "does he stand anyway?"

The "America Firsters" and their misled followers (General Leonard Wood, Captain Charles A. Lindbergh, and other celebrated Americans) started romancing me. But not for long. I let them have it, too.

One of the greatest newspapers, I reported, had the largest Communist cell in the world outside of Russia. One of our top weeklies, I added, had the Number One Red cell among mags, plus a senior editor that I helped expose. "He is Joe Stalin's Number One courier in the United States!" I reported to Mr. and Mrs. United States. That weekly retaliated almost every issue for years, reporting my corrections and never mentioning my Firsts.

I was unloved (and unliked, too) by both sides, the Lefts and the Rights—the kind of a fight I enjoy. In nobody's hip pocket.

From the Letters to the Editor column of a Los Angeles newspaper: "I guess he is one of those unnecessary evils. But the biggest shock came when I went to get my children from the classroom and there on the walls were several Winchell Americanism editorials. Do some school teachers really think the man is to be taken seriously?—Indignant Subscriber."

The New York *Herald Tribune* in 1938 quoted a staffer who belittled our efforts to alert the public. Said the heckler, "1938 will go down in history as the year that W. Winchell discovered America."

That newspaper also predicted a landslide for W. Willkie. But that wasn't so much of a gaffe.

In 1940, when Wendell Willkie ran for FDR's job, the President told me that Mr. Willkie was the only competitor he ever considered "a big threat."

"He's grass-roots stuff," FDR declared. "The people like him very much. His sincerity comes through with terrific impact. The people believe every word he says. We are going to have a heck of a fight on our hands with him."

From an interview with Ben Grauer, the announcer for *The Jergens Journal*: "A book titled *The News and How To Understand It* on page 140 observes that American editors warned our nation about Hitler's real plans to conquer the world 'too long after Winchell had warned a larger public about Hitler's threat to the American way of life.' "

Statement by Assistant Secretary of State A. A. Berle, Jr.: "Some day when historians go through the State Department files they will come across a paper which certifies that when Walter Winchell was recruited by his country to wake the sleeping public to the dangers ahead he did it—singlehandedly—starting in 1938."

Oscar Levant: "I'm a controversial figure. My friends either like me or hate me."

Following is a part of a letter we wrote to our radio sponsor in 1938:

> I do not want you to become unduly alarmed when I become controversial. Controversy, as you know, brings circulation. In radio it brings more listeners. There will always be people who don't agree with us, no matter what we discuss. Today it appears to be European politics and domestic politics. Not long ago, during the Hauptmann case we had people opposed to us because we were frank about the trial. It seems I have always been in the middle of some controversy. I thrive on it. It seems only yesterday that my critics condemned me because I mentioned that people were getting divorced or having babies. Now it is usually someone who thinks I have insulted Franco, Hitler, Mussolini, Roosevelt, Landon, or someone else.

> The best advice I ever got from an old editor is this: "Keep raising hell." One day I did, was worried about the reverberations, and I asked my editor what he wanted to do about it. He said: "Nothing." He once told me how he had fired a very nice columnist who worked for him, "because after two years I realized that no one was reading him, or that those who did did not care, because in those two years the paper didn't receive one letter of compliment for him—or criticism."

When George Putnam, Oregon's fightingest editor, retired, his quotable ta-ta was: "A newspaper without enemies has no friends."

Fritz Kuhn was Hitler's man in New York City in the latter 1930's when Hitler was on the march. In 1939 Mr. Kuhn was the fuehrer of the German-American Bund. I mentioned many of Kuhn's undercover activities almost daily in the paper, and on the air Sabbath nights. He rated me his Number One foe.

The German-language *Free American,* a weekly, called me "Kuhn's worst enemy."

The wire services quoted Fritz as threatening to "blacken Walter Winchell's eyes because of all the lies he has written about Germany and the Nazi Party."

After his conviction for the theft of over five thousand dollars from the Bund cash register, he was sentenced to two and a half to five years and wound up at Sing Sing Prison.

Fritz was finally deported to his hometown of Munich, Germany.

Two U.S. military policemen who escorted him there came to see me when they returned to New York.

"We have a message for you," said one, smiling, "from an old friend of yours, Fritz Kuhn. We promised we would relay it.

"Fritz said, 'Tell Herr Vinchell, I vill liff to piss on his grafe!' "

But the poor man died on December 14, 1951. A pity.

The inside story on why Britain's Prime Minister Neville Chamberlain appeased Hitler in 1938 (leading to the Munich Pact) was exclusively disclosed by this reporter in the New York *Mirror* on January 2, 1939.

My source was U.S. Ambassador Joseph P. Kennedy, who had just returned from London for a holiday in Florida. He wanted the facts made public.

Colonel Charles A. Lindbergh was widely blamed for Chamberlain's "surrender" and Ambassador Kennedy said the charge was unfair; that Lindbergh had informed him that Nazi Germany had 9,700 fighting planes as against Britain's 1,500, only 500 of which were dependable. In sum, Germany outmatched Britain in the air by six and a half times.

Lindbergh reported his findings to Chamberlain at Ambassador Kennedy's request. Lindbergh revealed that the Nazi leaders had permitted him to fly over fortifications and other restricted areas in Germany— the only visitor given this privilege.

From a Berlin newspaper when Hitler became Europe's top villain: "Since all of Vienna's beautiful parks are closed to Jews, hundreds of Jewish mothers may be found day after day taking their babies to cemeteries for sunshine and fresh air."

The dead being better company than the intolerant.

When Eugene Meyer published the Washington *Post,* the opposition blatt was the Washington *Times-Herald.* Mr. Hearst, for reasons many of us in the craft never learned, sold it "for a song" to Cissy Patterson, sister of the founder of the Number One giant newspaper in the land, the New York *Daily News,* and kin to Colonel R. R. McCormick, the landlord of the mighty Chicago *Tribune.*

Cissy was a powerful enemy to make, and I made her a ferocious foe with just one remark. But I am ahead of my tale about Cissy and her newspaper.

When she visited New York, which was often, she snubbed many of her socially registered friends' parties to join me "chasing the burglars" in my car, which had the police-signals contraption that all prowl cars have. She loved the excitement, plus the breathless anticipation waiting for Signal 1030—"Crime in progress! Use caution. They are armed!"

When the signals were dull ("1020—female down at Ninth and Fifty-fourth Street"; "Twenty-fourth Precinct. Car B-for-Boy. A noisy party fourth floor, address next to El Morocco"; and so on), I had to ad-lib a running commentary to keep my guests from being bored. "Now that house over there, number eight-fourteen. That was where a murder happened and was never solved. A playboy named Serge Rubinstein was done in—with the Chinese torture bit. Every time he moved, he choked—until he was dead. His killer was never caught. Big mystery."

And so whenever Cissy came to town she "romanced" me (she was lots senior than I) to take her riding in the car along the crime beat and tell her anecdotes and tales of the Beautiful People and the not-so-beautiful gangsters and the others who populate Broadway. She liked me so much that when I brought my daughter (then about twelve) to Washington, Cissy insisted that we not return to Manhattan in a "silly little old regular chair car," but in her private Pullman.

"Oh, Cissy," I begged, "don't squander money that way. All I need is a room to take a nap in. You'll never stay rich throwing it away like that."

Anon: "Some people think they are worth a lot of money because they have it."

One day FBI chief J. Edgar Hoover told me that I was "very rude" because every time Evelyn Walsh McLean, another rich-bich, had invited me to one of her elegant soirées, "you always manage to have some excuse not to show up. Mrs. McLean likes you a lot and asked me to find out why you are probably the only person invited who never comes."

"Thanks, John, but I don't enjoy parties. Besides, I could get a column done in the time wasted with a bunch of people I do not know. I'm a one-drink-drunk. Two make me dozy. Sorry, but the hell with it."

Art Weem's advice: "It's all right to drink like a fish if you drink what fish drink."

129

"Mrs. McLean," Hoover continued, "is giving the biggest affair of the Washington year next week—for your Washington publisher, Cissy Patterson. Cissy has told me that she rides all night a lot in your car and would love seeing you again."

And so I reluctantly went to the gahdamb'd affair and what always happens (when I rarely go to a party) happened again. I got into an argument—this time with My Boss.

I was seated at the Number One table with Cissy, Mrs. McLean, Senator Alben Barkley (later Truman's veep) and some other Big Shots. And don't dot the *o*.

My boss, who had had a few, suddenly said, "Why the hell don't you quit looking under the bed for Nazis?"

"You mean," I kidded, "and finding them?"

"I mean," she said in raised tones, "your column, which is read by only servants down here, is becoming a bore the way you keep after Nazis!"

"Mrs. Patterson," I caustically cracked, "why don't you get another boy?"

She got up and left the table. Barkley and the others asked me what had happened. I shrugged and said: "She gave me a piece of her mind and I gave her a hunk of mine—so she got into a swivet."

Mrs. McLean left the table, was gone a few minutes and returned to report: "Walter, Cissy is in the kitchen crying over whatever you said. Now be a good fellow and go in there and apologize."

Apologize? That'll be the day. My files include a favorite line: "Only A Fool Apologizes But A Bigger Fool Accepts One."

Anyway, the night was wrecked for me. I got up to dance with a lady who invited me to show her how to do a rumba. It was an ordeal.

The poor thing had three left feet. But is was better than staying at Table Number One, where I felt I was surrounded by pro-Nazis plus FDR–New Deal-Haters, excluding, of course, the man who later became vice president.

I never returned to the table. I made a sotto voce exit and have ducked parties in Washington and most other places since.

☆

Following the bout, Mrs. Patterson began chopping my column to splinters. She instructed her editors to kill the punch line of all paragraphs.

You can lose more readers that way.

But she wouldn't fire me. She kept me on the paper, butchered my stuff, loaded the Letters to the Editor columns with letters she wrote herself, saying the column was lousy, etc.

That was tame. You should've read the editorials she wrote about me.

One of her kin had one of them in a tome about her dear Aunt Cissy. The head over the idiotorial was: "WINCHELL THE COCKROACH!"

Hell hath no fury like a pro-Nazi with a pro-FDR columnist on her staff. She used her power to intimidate men high in the Navy Department to "strip Winchell of his uniform—he's a disgrace to the Navy!" Crapaganda like that.

The bigots in Congress and elsewhere put her opinions about me in the *Congressional Record.* That was what the hate-racketeers needed. They could reprint them under the title "From the *Congressional Record"* and be immune from lawsuits.

One night I received a phone call from Eugene Meyer, the publisher of the Washington *Post,* the rival paper that Cissy's rag couldn't match for circulation or Class. "I want to talk with you," said Mr. Meyer, "where can I see you without people recognizing us."

"In the barbershop upstairs in the Stork Club," I told him. "I'll be there in half an hour. It's Mr. Billingsley's private barbershop."

He was punctual. "I see," he said, "you and Cissy are miffed with each other. Can you keep your mouth shut for once and not say you are going to be in the Washington *Post,* as soon as you can get your syndicate to get you out of her paper?"

Cissy learned of his offer. That determined her to keep King Features to its contract with her. "I want to make Winchell miserable," she said.

She couldn't stop me on the air—which is where I returned the compliment. She started a lawsuit but dropped it. I served notice I would sue her and her paper for criminal libel, etcetera. Not because of what she said about me—but to get out of her paper so I could go over to the Washington *Post.*

P. F. Healy, on the staff of Cissy's Washington *Times-Herald* many years ago, wrote a puff book about his adventures working for her— all pro-Cissy. And when he got around to me, "Mr. Ethical" distorted what actually happened.

One of his inaccuracies is "Hailed into court for a pre-trial examination in the [Cissy's] libel suit, Winchell did an about-face and said meekly under oath that the editorial he had singled out was 'indeed a patriotic piece.' "

This is news to me, Daddy. Nobody could ever get me to be meek

131

about anything, you silly man. Very likely the lawyers for the Hearst Corporation gave Cissy that statement to get her to drop the suit.

In return for the indemnification holding me blameless for damages and costs of any kind my Hearst contract stipulated that "Winchell agrees to co-operate to the hilt with Hearst lawyers."

The editorial in Cissy's rag (long dead, as is Cissy) had been printed two years before in the *Congressional Record,* as Mr. Healy notes. "On his radio program," adds Cissy's puff writer-historian, "Winchell noted that the *Times-Herald* editorial was inserted in the *Record* with praise by the late Senator Ernest Lundeen of Minnesota, who was shown in court to have worked with the convicted Nazi agent George Sylvester Viereck. 'It fascinates me,' Winchell commented, 'to see how the pieces of the jigsaw puzzle fit together.' Winchell added his customary complaint that the paper which printed the editorial 'buys and suppresses and handcuffs my column.' " Biographer Healy neglected to mention that I first exposed Nazi agent Viereck when he operated undercover for Hitler in the United States, and that I also belted the bejaberz out of Senator Lundeen on the air (and along the syndicate) for giving aid and comfort to the Nazis here and abroad.

Senator Lundeen's widow was also aggrieved. "Why does Winchell keep kicking my husband's grave?" she lamented. I quoted her and added: "Why didn't her pro-Nazi husband stop kicking the graves of our war dead???"

Careless Mr. Healy's final reference to me in his dreary tome was "Winchell never did succeed in following Drew Pearson to the Washington *Post* and, indeed, never got another daily newspaper in Washington. In this sense, he was a Patterson-feud casualty."

Izzatzo? I got on the Washington *Post!*

About two weeks after my column began running in the *Post,* the son-in-law of Eugene Meyer (Philip Graham, another who died too young) invited me to Washington to have lunch with him and some of his friends including Clare Boothe Luce in the Post's private dining room.

The Women still brings playwright Clare Boothe (later Mrs. Henry Luce) sugary royalties she doesn't need. Her 1939 *Margin For Error,* which was not appreciated by some reviewers (but which I embraced often), was the first to caricature Adolph Hitler & Company.

Clare was elected to Congress from New York, giving the House of Representatives some Class. One evening while I was in Washington she phoned to alert me.

"You are going to be attacked on the floor tomorrow by some of the

132

people [Representative Rankin and other pro-Nazis] you've attacked on the air and in the papers. If they get too rough, I will get up and answer them for you."

But Clare just sat there on her shapely derrière, apparently enjoying their barrages, and I never had to scratch her back for scratching mine.

She was eventually punished for not keeping her promise. The rich thang got demoted to Rome, Italy, as U.S. ambassador.

It was (I read in the papers) privileged pot-shotting—but I always wince when anyone disgraces me with a defense. George Jean Nathan, dean of the drama critics, once told me why he "never answers attacks." "When you're in the brick-throwing business, you must expect to get hit by a brick now and then."

I was waiting to meet Graham in the office of Mr. Wiggins, the *Post*'s top editor. Mr. Graham came in, shook hands warmly, and then escorted me to the feasting place. Between his offices and the dining room, he paused and called my attention to a huge blackboard on which was chalked: "SUNDAY CIRCULATION UP 4000. DAILY CIRC UP OVER 10,000."

"You helped do that," complimented Mr. Graham.

That was, as noted above, two weeks after the *Post* started using the col'm. So I was off to a good start. Doesn't Mr. Healy check the clips in the reference room? Or does he find it simpler to kiss a boss's dead behind? (Every man to his own taste.)

"March 10, 1939: My Dear Mr. Winchell: I listened in last Sunday night to your radio broadcast and I want to congratulate you for the great work that you are doing in presenting affirmatively the case of Democracy, and at the same time fighting the vicious influences of Communism, Nazism, Fascism and bigoted movements in this country. Sincerely yours,

John J. McCormack, Congress of the United States."
To bad there weren't more of him.

There was a pained expression on Happy Chandler's face when he paused at John Edgar Hoover's table in Harvey's (Washington) one supper time. Happy, twice the popular governor of Kentucky, was the newest senator in the Capitol. Happy was very Unhappy that evening.

Mr. Hoover said, "Where's your contagious smile? You seem low."

He was invited to pull up a chair. He explained why he was so blue.

"I didn't know," Chandler began, "that my colleagues were so petty. One vote defeated my first bill today! And he was one of my close friends. It was a tie vote, and he killed it! I couldn't wait to see him in the cloakroom and ask him why he voted against my very first bill. You know what he said? He said, 'You did not vote for mine last week—so ah didden voht fo' yo-urs!'

"That's little boy stuff. Imagine being so mean to kill a bill that would help the poor of Kentucky!"

You hear things like that a lot. Not only in Washington—but almost everywhere.

☆

Never-deny-the-other-feller's-skewp-it-may-be-trooo!

From Elmer Sunfield's "Hollywood Newsreel" column in *Hollywood Magazine,* a Fawcett branch, in the February, 1939, issue: "Walter Winchell columned recently that Wayne Morris, Warner film star, would wed Bubbles Schinasi, society deb Dec. 1st or thereabouts. Which must be in error since Wayne's first romantic move upon his return to Hollywood was to escort Jane Wyman to a swanky affair."

From the already yellowing newspapers of January 9, 1939: "Wayne Morris and Bubbles Schinasi Wed."

★

WAITING FOR LEPKE

Louis "Lepke" Buchalter, who hid from the police and G-men for over two years (his hiding place for a long spell was in a furnished room next door to Police HQ in Brooklyn), had no desire to surrender. "Let them find me first!" he shouted at his cabinet.

But all of his gang agreed to persuade him to take a rap for a short term because the pressure by the lawmen on all of them (their families and business associates) kept the mob from thriving. "We can't even make a two-dollar bet at the tracks without being cased by cops!"

"Look," one of the Murder, Inc. commanders argued, "we are losing our shirt in Baltimore [where the Raleigh Clothing Company was one of their legitimate enterprises] because every time a buyer comes to our floor, he's stopped and questioned by the FBI guys."

The G-men would present their credentials and challenge: "What's your name? Where do you live? What are you doing here?"

The flustered customer might respond: "My name is Schmule. I'm a buyer from Pottsville. I come here twice a year to look at the spring and fall line."

"Do you realize," he was told, "that you are dealing with killers? This bunch is using this company as a cover. The real owners are chiefs of Murder, Inc. in Brooklyn!"

This was enough to scare buyers and other legits away from the Raleigh Clothing Company. The same pressure was employed by G-men on all Murder, Inc.'s other "companies." Besides, the FBI agents summoned them (via phone) down to the U.S. Courthouse daily for over a month, where they were deposited in a huge room about a city street long and wide. They went slightly daffy waiting to find out why they were there.

But that was The Big Idea. Keep them sitting, sitting, sitting, and sitting from 9:00 A.M. until 5:00 P.M. (with an hour for lunch), getting on each other's nerves. At 5:00 P.M. a marshal would come to the door and politely announce: "Gentlemen, you are dismissed for today. Please be here at nine A.M. tomorrow as usual."

The FBI, they also complained to Lepke, was making their children and wives miserable, asking schoolmates: "Do you know little Shirley's father is a gangster?" To neighbors: "Do you know that Mr. Buchalter is a member of Murder, Incorporated?" And so on.

Lepke was unmoved. He couldn't care less. But the Mobfia decided "something had to be done" about the Lep. "You are wrecking everything we all own," he was informed.

On Saturday night, August 5, 1939, I was approached on Broadway near Lindy's by a man "on the fringe of gangdom." Not a gangster, sort of a gang buff. "I have something important to tell you," he said. "Lepke wants to come in. But he's trying to find someone he can trust. Someone who won't turn him over to Governor Dewey." Dewey wanted him to fry in the chair. "He's heard so many different stories about what will happen to him. Talk around town is that Lepke would be shot while supposedly escaping. He can't trust anybody, he says. If he could find someone he can trust, he'll give himself up to that person."

"Would he trust me?" I inquired.

"I'll find out and let you know," said the fellow.

He did so the next midnight, when he called to suggest that I broadcast FBI Director Hoover's assurance to protect Lepke's rights.

"Sure," I assured. "I'll tell John Edgar Hoover about it. I'm sure he'll see to it that Lepke receives his constitutional rights. Nobody will cross him."

135

"If you can get that promise, OK, put it on the air tomorrow night." And then he disconnected.

The next night I started the newscast slowly—instead of the machine-gun tempo I usually employed: "Attention, Public Enemy Number One, Louis "Lepke" Buchalter! I am authorized by John Edgar Hoover of the Federal Bureau of Investigation to guarantee you safe delivery to the FBI if you surrender to me or to any agent for the FBI. I will re-peat: Lepke! I am authorized by John Edgar Hoover . . ." Etc.

I said it again just before sign-off.

Mr. Hoover and his Number One aide, Clyde Tolson, sat alongside as I appealed to Buchalter, whose WANTED! picture was prominently displayed in police stations, post offices and other federal buildings in every state. In those days I had to repeat the broadcast at midnight to get the 9:00 P.M. listeners on the West Coast. Hoover and Tolson were in the studio for that one, too, in case a phone call came in.

That night, about an hour later, I got a phone call at the Stork Club. "Walter?" said the voice. "That was fine. See you!" The caller hung up.

For almost three weeks—nearly nightly—a different voice phoned to arrange "a meet" to negotiate Lep's coming in.

The next caller—another voice—asked: "You got your car with the four lamps?"

"Four lamps?"

"Yeah, the four lamps!"

"I don't know what you mean."

"You got a pair of fog lights under the big lights, right?"

"Oh, yes. But that car is in Scarsdale, my wife is using it. I can borrow a friend's car—Mr. Billingsley's Caddy, a convertible. It has a license plate with an X on it— just an X."

"No, no good!" said the voice. "Get the car with the four lamps!"

"It's now almost one-thirty in the morning," I told him. "It takes at least forty minutes to get to my home. Why is it so necessary to get that car?"

"That's the one we know!" he exclamation-pointed.

"Then what do I do?"

"If you leave now," I was told, "you oughta be there by two-fifteen, right? Then another forty minutes back down to New York, okay?"

"All right. Then what?"

"Did you ever go to Philly or Atlantic City through the Holland Tunnel?"

"Yes."

"All right. So when you come outta the tunnel, you make a left. And at the second light turn right. We'll pick you up somewhere after you make that right turn. Understand?"

Sherman Billingsley drove me in his car to Scarsdale along the West Side Highway until we got to Ardsley for the off-ramp that leads to Greenburgh, where our home, Twelve Acres, was located. (It became twenty-three acres after we purchased adjacent property.)

Mrs. Winchell, who was still up reading a book, called out: "Honey?"

"Yes, Sherman is with me."

"What is wrong? Why are you home so early?" I usually got home at dawn after covering the Night People.

I told her I had to have the car for a big story. I told her it had to do with the surrender of a famous fugitive, "Oh," she oh'd, "why do you get yourself involved with such people?"

"I don't get myself involved with them—they get involved with me!"

I went to wash my hands and get my topcoat.

Months later, my wife told me that while I was washing up she hurriedly searched the kitchen and found a tiny box of thumbtacks. She emptied the box near the front wheels of our car. Of course they fell into the gravel on the ground.

"Why did you do that?" I asked her.

"I was so worried," she said sheepishly. "I hoped you'd have a blow-out before you reached the gate"—1,000 feet from the door—"and it would keep you from going." Another of June's demonstrations of her great love for her undeserving husband.

Darling, I don't care what happens to me, just so long as nothing happens to us.

Sherman followed my car back to midtown Manhattan. I proceeded down to the Holland Tunnel. It was now about 3:30 A.M.

At the second light from the Jersey side of the tunnel, I found myself in a deserted swampland. Not a streetlight or house light in sight. It was eerie. The night was very foggy, like an Alf Hitchcock melodrama.

I had turned on the fog lamps and was prepared to meet the stranger who insisted I use the car "with the four lamps." I kept driving slowly, wondering why nobody was there to meet me.

After driving about fifteen minutes I got the jitters. Was this a trap by the Nazis to get me alone and even matters for my daily and Sunday night assaults on Hitler? It could very well be. I had made public (on the air and in the papers) that the G-men had authorized me to guarantee Lepke safe delivery if he surrendered.

I locked all doors, turned, and sped back to New York.

The next night, about 2:00 A.M., I got another phone call in the lobby booth at the Stork Club. Another voice. They never used the same person twice.

"What happened?" I said. "I was there. I turned at the second light and drove around the area for a long time."

"We saw you," was the indifferent reply.

"You saw me? Why didn't you *stop* me?"

The weeds and other shrubbery in that spot are thick and tall. Their car, apparently with lights doused, was purposely hidden from view—to make sure, I suppose, that I wasn't tailed by lawmen.

The charge, if caught there, could be "harboring a criminal."

"So what now?" I asked the caller.

"You got the same car with the four lamps?"

"Yes, it's parked across the street."

"Okay, can you leave soon?"

"I can leave right now. To where?"

I was told to cross the George Washington Bridge, keep driving ahead for about half a mile, and park the car opposite a bar and grill with blue neons. Go into the place and order a drink at the bar. Someone would take it from there.

Halfway through my Scotch and soda, a man took a bar stool alongside. He chatted quietly about sports for a minute or three, and then softly instructed me to join him in his car a few feet from the joint. It was Saturday night—almost 3:00 A.M. Sunday.

"Ask your friend the G-man," said the impeccably groomed stranger, "what the possible sentence will be if the Lep comes in."

"What else?"

"That's all, just ask him that. Then put what he says on the air tomorrow."

Back in New York I phoned Mr. Hoover's suite at the Waldorf Astoria and told him I had a message for him from the mob.

He told the hotel security people to permit me to come to his rooms. One escorted me up. I echo'd the one question from the mobster.

"I'm not a lawyer," Mr. Hoover began, "I'm just a policeman with a badge. But there are two serious charges against him. Narcotics and

138

being a fugitive from justice. He probably will get between twelve and fifteen years."

That was good arithmetic. Federal Judge Knox later sentenced Lepke to fourteen years. But I didn't broadcast or publish what Hoover said. I waited until I got another call to tell it to Lepke's men in person. I feared that making it public with Lepke listening might kill the whole thing.

The call came after the midnight repeat broadcast at the studio. "What did the man say?" said the voice.

"I was instructed by Mr. Hoover," I fibbed, "to tell it to one of you in person."

He asked where I could be reached in about an hour. I told him to try the same phone booth at the Stork Club, or at Lindy's, or Reuben's —all-night restaurants at the time.

A call came exactly an hour later at the Stork. "Can you leave right away?"

"Yes. To where?"

"Just start driving north along Fifth Avenue. Enter Central Park at Sixtieth Street and keep on going. Okay?"

Halfway through the park (to the exit at Seventy-second Street and Fifth Avenue), I stopped for a red light. A car with two men stopped near me. One of them smiled and said: "Keep driving along Seventy-second Street and stop at the curb at Madison."

I did.

The man who had greeted me with a smile got into my car.

I reported what Mr. Hoover had told me about the probable sentence.

The man told me to wait until he conferred with his friend. The friend then got into my car. He was the first person I recognized—one of the top men in Murder, Inc.

"Where can you be reached on a pay-station phone in an hour?"

We went to the nearest phone booth, where the stranger marked down the number and instructed: "This is about Lepke. This time it's important. Please be here in an hour."

He hastened away, hailed a passing cab, and taxied north.

I never told that to Mr. Hoover. I told him I had never seen any of the persons who negotiated.

After I'd been running errands for the mobsters for several weeks (with only one query a night to ask Hoover), John Edgar finally blew his top before hundreds of Stork Clubbers and thundered: "I am fed

139

up with you and your friends! They can make a fool out of you, but you are not going to make a fool out of me and my men!"

"They are not my friends, John."

"They are your friends! They are your friends! And don't call me John! I'm beginning to think you're the champ bullshitter in town!" And so shouting, plus a finger in my face, he yelled: "You tell your friends that if Lepke isn't in within forty-eight hours, I will order my agents to shoot him on sight!"

The humiliation in front of all those people had me on the verge of tears. "Gee," I said, shaking with embarrassment, "you guys sure fall out of like with a fellow fast. You know I've been a good friend of the FBI for years. Calm down, please."

But Mr. Hoover was livid with rage. "TELL YOUR FRIENDS," he boomed in capital letters, "I will order him shot if he doesn't come in within forty-eight hours!"

Hoover's blast included this barrage: "Why are you doing this to us, anyway? Your radio ratings slipped or something? Did you do it to get your rating back up?"

I replied: "You are treating me like some criminal. I'm the one who raced to your defense every time some critic knocked you on the editorial pages. How can you forget this way?"

Oh, man. The newspapers and broadcasters would have all this via a tipster. The Number One law enforcement officer in the nation had denounced me publicly. The publouseity would surely destroy me. My newspaper and broadcasting career would end.

I walked away as the Stork Club elite and other rich-raff witnessed my disgrace.

Clyde Tolson, Mr. Hoover's aide, followed me to the door, grabbed my arm, and said: "Do what he told you! Don't be a fool."

"No," I told Tolson, "I'm through being the goat-between! He said if the Lep wasn't in within forty-eight hours he'd order him shot. You people haven't been able to find him for two years. How you gonna find him in forty-eight hours?"

I broke from Tolson's grasp, got my hat, and walked along East Fifty-third Street, knowing I had lost one of my best friends and that he really believed I had concocted the whole story.

Strangely, not a newspaper or broadcast mentioned the Stork Club episode.

Being a devout coward, as the nightclub comics say, I thought of suicide, but that would have confirmed Hoover's argument.

Promptly an hour later, right on the button, that pay-station phone tinkled. I didn't give the voice a chance to talk. "I just spoke to Hoover," I said breathlessly. "He's fed up. If Lepke doesn't surrender by four P.M. tomorrow, Hoover says no consideration of any kind will ever be given him. For every day he stays away it may mean an extra two years added to his sentence."

The voice interrupted: "You simply have to wait until he can arrange things."

The following midnight a phone caller said: "They want to have another talk."

"Oh, no," I responded, "I'm through. Last night Mr. Hoover called me everything under the sun in front of hundreds of people. He accused me of faking the whole thing. He said if Lepke didn't come in within forty-eight hours, he'd have his agents shoot him on sight!"

The caller giggled a phony giggle and calmly said: "Take it easy, take it easy. You may get lucky. Where can you be reached tomorrow night at six?"

I "knew" from the way he said "you may get lucky" that this was going to be *It*—that Lepke would come in.

Two nights later, while having an early supper in the Stork's Cub Room, I was phoned by one of the mob. "How soon can you get away?"

"I'm finished eating. I can leave now."

He told me to drive up to Proctor's Theater in Yonkers. Before I reached Proctor's, a car loaded with strangers—faces I didn't recall ever seeing before—slowly drew alongside. I heard a voice say, "That's him."

One of the men got out, holding his handkerchief to his face as though he intended to sneeze. He got into my car, sat alongside, and kept the kerchief to his face. "Go to the drugstore on the corner of Nineteenth Street and Eighth Avenue," he instructed. "There are some phone booths there. Get in one and look busy. About nine P.M. somebody will come up to you and tell you where to notify the G-men to meet you."

Oh, brother!

This was It, indeed—the actual delivery of the nation's Most Wanted Public Enemy! My reputation as a newsman with Hoover would be restored. I got so nervous I shook from head to toe.

I parked in front of the drugstore. I don't know why I did it, but I took the car keys with me. (Habit, of course.)

In the drugstore were three phone booths—all occupied! Jeezzzuzzzz! One booth contained a teen-age girl laughing and laughing and laughing. The second booth had a woman gabbing her head off. The third was filled by a noisy drunk. Time was being squandered by three strangers I hoped would choke or drop dead.

I tried not to appear tense. The youngster behind the fountain asked did I want anything. "Yes," I said in my softest tone, so he wouldn't recognize my radio voice, "a small Coke."

As the kid prepared it, he stared at me with a "you look familiar to me" look. I kept turning to see if the phone-booth occupants had stopped yacking. As he put the Coke before me the soda jurq inquired: "Mister, ain't you a movie actor or somebody?"

Finally one of the phone booths emptied. I didn't get a chance to appear busy in it. As I turned to look through the open door, a face met mine. The stranger jerked his head as though to telegraph "Come here." I joined him outside and walked to my car slowly.

"Go back in there and tell Hoover to be at Twenty-eighth Street on Fifth Avenue between ten-ten and ten-twenty," he instructed.

How did the mobster know he was there? What if Hoover wasn't at the hotel? Hoover and Tolson usually weekended in New York, but were in Washington during the week. I called the hotel.

"I want to speak to Mr. Hoover!" I almost shrieked. "It is urgent!" Hoover got on. "Yes?" he said coldly.

"John, this is the champ bullshitter. My *friends* have instructed me to tell you to be at Twenty-eighth Street and Fifth Avenue between ten-ten and ten-twenty tonight. That's about half an hour. They told me to tell you to be alone."

"I'll be there," he said, and hung up.

I came out of the drugstore shaking. The thrill of it! The man wanted by the State of New York for over one hundred murders committed by his gang, and by the FBI for lesser charges, was surrendering to me! Ka-riiist, what a story! But more important: Hoover and Tolson would know I hadn't faked it. My reputation would not be demolished.

When I returned to the car the man was there. My hand trembled. I aimed the ignition key at the lock and couldn't find the damned thing. My companion chuckled. "Whatzzamatta, you nervous?" he twitted. "Gimme the key." We changed seats.

He drove south along Eighth Avenue down to the Battery and then north—snaking in and out of side streets. He was stalling for time so that the "meet" with Lepke would be punctual.

142

I kept trying to remember scenes along the way in case I had to testify in court. And hoping the surrender wouldn't flop. The date was August 24, 1939: one week before World War II started in Europe.

Now we were going east along Twenty-third Street near Broadway and the Flatiron Building, once New York's tallest skyscraper. Now we were at Twenty-third and Madison Square Park. The driver made a left turn and pulled up at the southeast corner of Twenty-fourth—four blocks from Twenty-eighth and Fifth where Hoover was waiting.

At the time, there were no shops in the building between Twenty-third and Twenty-fourth opposite Madison Square Park (opposite the original Madison Square Garden where architect Stanford White was shot dead by Harry Kendall Thaw, zillionaire husband of show girl Evelyn Nesbit). No store where lights would be on so a passing cop could see if a burglar had broken in. I didn't realize until I got to my typewriter that the lamp post on the corner where we stopped was dark, too! Quite a coincidence. The mob even arranged that.

My driver, slipping out of the car, leaned back in and handed me a religious emblem—a mezuzah that Orthodox Jews employ to keep trouble away—and said: "Give this to the Lep. Tell him it's from Jake." First time any of them had given me his name.

I looked over his shoulder. Across the way in the park I saw two heavyset men in white shirts chatting on a bench. There wasn't another person in sight.

The time was 10:15. It was very humid. My clothes were dripping. The butterflies started to romp inside of me.

I reached down to turn on my shortwave radio for police signals— a silly thing to do, but I was so excited and nervous I didn't know what I was doing.

All of this, remember, took place in fractions of seconds.

While I leaned down to turn on the police box, a voice softly said: "Thank you, Volter."

IT WAS LEPKE! He must have come up out of the gutter, like the Devil appears suddenly in movies. I had never seen him in my life.

"Get in the back, get in the back," I told him, "in the back!"

His felt hat was pulled down over his ears like a comedian's. He wore the longest sideburns I ever saw. And he wore an overcoat—not a topcoat, an overcoat—in August, on one of the most humid nights of a long heat wave!

I released the brake to keep our rendezvous with Mr. G. Man.

143

"We'll be with Mr. Hoover in a minute or two," I told Mr. Murder, Inc. "He's waiting at Twenty-eighth Street and Fifth."

"Yes, I know." Lepke sighed. "I just passed him."

The next few moments seemed like years to me. What if some stool pigeon on the fringe of the mob knew that I was to meet Lepke? Stoolies trade information with police in return for a break in case they get into trouble. How awful if I lost my "prisoner" to a cop or patrol cruiser team, with Mr. Hoover waiting only a few streets away!

As I made a left at Twenty-seventh Street and Madison, a 13th Precinct car appeared. "Oh, nutz!" I groaned to myself, "I'm going to lose him!"

But the police cruiser kept going west.

The lights turned "Go." I proceeded to Fifth Avenue on Twenty-seventh doing about four miles an hour—fearing some cop might accuse me of speeding and recognize my guest.

Another red light. And oh, dammit, another police car going south slowly along Fifth Avenue!

All of a sudden I saw two prowl cars in a few seconds—and I hadn't seen one or a foot cop until the final few seconds.

The police car kept going south. The light was still red. I could see Hoover's license plate a block away. My very dry mouth got drier.

Suddenly an atomic blast almost blew my bones through my skin.

"What the hell was *that*?" I said.

"I threw away my eyeglasses," said Lepke.

That's how shaky I was. He had flung his dime store-disguise spectacles to the gutter. But to me it sounded like an explosion.

As the glasses hit the ground, two well-dressed men strolling by were also startled. Both looked up as though something had been thrown from a window. They would have been $50,000 wealthier if they had known that Public Enemy Number One—for whom the FBI and the State of New York had each offered $25,000 reward dead or alive—was right there within touching distance.

The light turned green. I stepped on the accelerator and made like a rocket to the Twenty-eighth Street corner behind Hoover's car. I left the motor running, doors open, and ran to open Lepke's door.

Holding him by his right wrist like a parent holding a child, I escorted him to the FBI limousine. Hoover was unarmed and without handcuffs, disguised in dark sunglasses to keep him from being recognized by passersby.

I opened the car door and looked at Hoover like the cat that had swallowed a canary. I cooed: "Lepke, this is Mr. Hoover. Mr. Hoover, *this* is Lepke." I didn't mean it to sound like dialogue from a Noel Coward drawing room comedy, but days later it broke me up when I was telling it all over town.

"How do you do?" said Mr. Hoover affably.

"Glad to meet you," replied Lepke.

"Get in the car!" ordered Hoover. Lepke complied.

I took the jump seat.

"Where are your high and mighty friends now?" caustically asked John Edgar. "You did the smart thing by coming in," he comforted.

Lepke was a little excited. He seemed anxious to talk to anybody new—after being in the shadows for over two years with so many hunted men.

"I am beginning to vonder if I did," sighed the captive. "I vould like to see my wife and kids, please?"

(Hoover had arranged for Lepke's family to visit him shortly after he was booked, fingerprinted, and Kodaked. He had $1,700 on him. He gave $1,100 to the boy and $600 to the jailer—for "expenses.")

"To the Federal Building [United States Courthouse] at Foley Square," commanded Hoover. His colored pilot turned swiftly south.

At Thirteenth Street and Fifth Avenue, where we stopped for the light, Hoover devastated me all over again with a lusty command: "Get out of the car!"

"Oh, John," I oh-johnned.

"Get-out-of-the-*car*!" he repeated. "What do you want to do—make an entrance with me and this man, so the reporters covering the courthouse will know who he is?—you'll lose your story, you fool!"

"Oh! Thanks, John. I never thought of that."

I got out and raced back to Fourteenth Street looking for a phone booth. Very few shops or places were open in that deserted district.

I found a bar, rushed in—and into a phone booth. I dialed the *Mirror* city desk. The assistant managing editor, Hinson Stiles, answered the phone. Recognizing his voice, I yelled: "Hinson, this is Winchell! I know we only have time for a box bulletin. Lepke, Public Enemy Number One, just surrendered to the FBI!"

"How do you know that?" was his astonished query.

"How do I know? I just turned him over!"

"Oh," was the rejoinder, "you and your gah-damb'd scoops. A world war is starting!" And he hung up.

A newspaperman's dream-of-a-skewp only made the final edition's

145

replate. The New York *Daily News,* our chief competition, and the Associated Press beat us to our own beat. Is that one for the book, pal? I ask you.

I returned to the *Mirror* city room to jot down the story. The phone rang. It was Hoover's chief assistant director, Clyde Tolson.

"How do you want us to handle your part in the story?" he asked.

"Tell what happened, Clyde. I don't care how you do it."

The lead in the next edition of *The New York Times* reported the surrender plus: "Walter Winchell gave the FBI considerable assistance" —about two lines of linotype. Oh, dear. That's also the way it was written in an authorized book about the FBI.

Weeks later, a well-known crime reporter authored the alleged "inside" on the surrender in a hokey article for a magazine. He reported that "rumors had it that the whole thing was pre-arranged by the G-men so that their friend and stooge [thaz me] could look good." The author snidely added that "although Hoover and Winchell deny that they split the $50,000 reward, the skeptics wonder."

It is wonderful being a newspaperman. You meet so many envious crap artists. A check with the State of New York, the District Attorney, or Congress (which had authorized the FBI's reward) would have shown the heel's reporting to be inaccurate.

In 1949 Simon and Schuster brought out a book titled *A Treasury of Great Reporting.* In his preface to the book, Herbert Swope said it was a collection of "one hundred and seventy-five of the greatest examples of literature under pressure." My story about Lepke's surrender was included.

The day after Lepke was convicted and confined in the federal detention pen, his mouthpiece came to the *Mirror* office.

"Lepke," he said, "would like to see you. It is very important that he have a moment's talk with you. You must get permission to see him from the sentencing judge—Judge Knox."

Next morning I went to Judge Knox's office. I brought my wife along to make me look respectable.

"Your Honor," I said, "Buchalter's lawyer told me that Lepke would like to ask me one question. I understand I must get your permission to visit him. I do not know, sir," I added, "if you know about the small part I played in his surrender."

His Honor nodded that he did know. He gave permission. I sent Mrs. Winchell home and went to see the former president of Murder, Inc.

The scene was not set in his cell. It was in a smaller cell where Lepke

146

sat between his wife, Betty, and his lawyer. A dilapidated kitchen was between us.

"I vant to ask you one thing," Lepke said calmly. "Did you ever tell my friends that if I came in I would get only ten years—and if I had a good behavior record, I'd get out in five or six?"

I realized for the first time that he had been double-crossed by his own "friends." Suspecting that the cell was bugged, I replied in a raised voice: "Lepke, my name is Walter Winchell of the New York *Mirror*. I never told that to anybody. I said between twelve and fifteen!"

Lepke leaped from his chair and almost broke the table with one mighty blow. "That's what I thought! I knew it, I knew it!" he yelled like a mad animal.

The lawyer motioned me to leave. I heard Lepke's profanity all the way down the corridor.

After a restless time of it trying to get enough sleep that afternoon, I phoned a mobster I knew. "It is very important that Abe see me tonight," I said. "I will be in the Stork Club barbershop on the first floor around seven P.M. Later I will be at the *Mirror*—but he'd better make the barbershop. They'd recognize him at the *Mirror*."

Abe appeared promptly at seven. I told the lone barber to leave the shop.

Alone with Abe (one of Lepke's most trusted aides), I reported what happened in the cell. "I thought you should know, Abe. Lepke will surely even matters."

Abe, six feet four, a handsome fashion plate, looked at me with iceberg eyes as he puffed on a long cigar. Walking out, he sarcasmed: "He's tired. Very tired."

Abe didn't even say thanks or ta-ta.

Abe who? The second man in the car that stopped when I did at Seventy-second Street and Madison Avenue. The man to whom I gave Hoover's reply about the probable sentence. Abe was so respectable to his neighbors in a swank sector of New Jersey that he married a beautiful girl described in the society pages as a "Junior Leaguer." She was his second wife. They raised lovely children.

To look at him, you would never know that Abe was a gang chief. But his business acumen was superior to that of the others in the mob. It was Abe who told Lepke that Hoover had said not more than ten, "and if you behave yourself, you'll be out in six."

From the moment that Lepke blew up in his cell, I felt that Abe was not long for this world.

Abe was in excellent condition. His health was inscribed all over his powerful frame and in his face. One day he was found dangling with a noose around his throat in the cellar of his fashionable New Jersey residence. "Suicide" was the coroner's verdict.

Married to a Junior Leaguer, pretty children. Why would he want to kill himself?

"Why should he hang himself?" became "Topic Abe" all over Broadway. "He wasn't ill. It wasn't cancer or anything terrible. Why did he do it?"

He didn't do it. He was done in by Lepke's loyalists, if you asked me and even if you didn't.

Abe who? Abe "Longie" Zwillman—the only person in the mob (and I only saw him once during the negotiations) that I knew. I had known him for a long time.

It probably was Longie who suggested to the mob (and Lepke) that I be used to find out from Mr. Hoover if a deal could be made. It was Longie who directed every move and query made to me by his agents in those breathless weeks. And so John Edgar Hoover was right when he thundered in the Stork Club: "They are your friends!" But I did not know Longie was behind it all when Hoover lost his cool.

WAR

The reason there can never be permanent peace: "There are more dogs than bones."

Hitler's hateful hordes had conquered most of Europe when a show girl at the Versailles nightclub on East Fiftieth Street, in New York, told me she feared for the lives of her father and three little brothers in Poland. "Is there anything," she wept, "you can do?"

"Where are they in Poland?"

She didn't know. "They haven't written for months."

"I know Joseph P. Kennedy, our ambassador to Britain. I'll ask him to help."

A few weeks later the father of Senator Ted, the late Senator Bobby and the late President JFK suggested the youngsters (ages ten, thirteen and fifteen) be shipped to the Azores. "Send $300 for transportation," Joe cabled.

I did so, and then requested a friend (an official of United States

Lines) to bring them to the United States. The line never sent a bill. Ambassador Kennedy arranged their visas and pocket money.

I feel sure it will please the State Department and Mr. and Mrs. America to learn what later happened to those three youngsters. When each became seventeen years old, he enlisted in the U.S. armed forces to show his gratitude. They served in the front lines.

☆

From our Sunday night newscast of November 5, 1939:

> Ladies and Gentlemen: Tonight as I have been speaking to you —even at this very moment—the voice of your New York correspondent is being recorded by engineers in Pittsburgh, Pennsylvania, where today the world's most ultra-ultra radio transmitter was dedicated by that grandfather station of them all, Westinghouse KDKA.
>
> This recording, ladies and gentlemen, along with some fifteen others, will be hermetically sealed in a crystal crypt near the base of KDKA's seven hundred and eighteen-foot antenna tower. These records, I am told, will be made by big shots of science, education, religion, and government, predicting what this world of ours will be like in twenty years.
>
> Your reporter has no objection to his voice being used as a record of what's going on in the world of the present. But he does refuse to become a fortune-teller. As to the future, I can only hope that in 1959 when that glass case is opened at KDKA this world will have come to its senses, and that the only appeasements with which we Americans are ever confronted are peace, patriotism, and prosperity.

★

WHITTAKER CHAMBERS, RED SPY

Whittaker Chambers was one of the editors of the *Daily Worker,* Moscow's voice in the United States, in the late 1920's and an editor of *New Masses,* a Far-Left publication, in the early 1930's.

One of America's brainiest intellectuals, Chambers joined the Communist Party in 1925 and became part of the underground in 1931. FDR "recognized" the USSR in 1933. In 1937 Chambers allegedly "began to break away from communism." In April 1938 Chambers deserted the party and went into hiding with his wife and two children.

At the time of his break, Chambers was contact man between Soviet espionage in Washington and his superior, Colonel Boris Bykov, known as Peter, in New York City.

Chambers landed on *Time* magazine in April 1939. He was so clever that publisher Henry Luce elevated him to senior editor. Mr. Luce, we assume, had no idea Mr. Chambers was a Communist, but surely his editors knew that Chambers had worked for Lefty periodicals.

Now here was Mr. Chambers, one of *Time*'s top editors, molding American public opinion in the nation's leading newsmag. Under "Press" this reporter was downgraded almost weekly: " 'Keyhole Peeker' Winchell last week was sued again" and shin-kicks like that. When other detractors let me have it, *Time*'s press page mentioned it. Never a note of a big beat, or even a little one. When I won a lawsuit (almost all of them), *Time* neglected to make a note of it.

These blackballs, of course, became fodder for attackers on the Left and Right. They quoted: "Even *Time* magazine denounced him for his inaccuracies and opinionated, biased and reprehensible reports."

Then came my turn at bat. My critics and poison-penners on *Time* and elsewhere were agonized when I reported on the air and in the column: "Whittaker Chambers, *Time*'s senior editor, is Josef Stalin's Number One courier in the United States!"

"Winchell," Chambers later wrote, "was the only one who wasn't fooled."

After Chambers turned American again and "exposed" Alger Hiss (who had a high post in government) before the House Committee on Un-American Activities in 1948, Chambers wrote a book, *Witness*, about the Communists who had infiltrated the State Department and other government branches.

Ralph de Toledano, an anti-Red syndicated pundit, and co-author, Victor Lasky, ditto, in their book *Seeds of Treason* (published in 1950 by Funk and Wagnalls and revised in 1962 by Regnery) devoted considerable wordage to Chambers—and to Alger Hiss' conviction for perjury in denying that he, Hiss, had passed on secret information to Moscow.

This is how I got the beat about Chambers being Stalin's top U.S. spy. Early in May 1939 Chambers made hesitant contact with Isaac Don Levine, editor of *Plain Talk*, a magazine aimed at liberals. Chambers sought counsel on how to alert the State Department that the U.S. Government was infiltrated with respectable-appearing Americans working for the Kremlin.

Mr. Levine told Chambers: "Without names, dates, and places, no one will believe your story."

Russian General Walter G. Krivitsky was collaborating with Mr. Levine on a series of articles in *Plain Talk* that revealed Soviet espionage in Europe and the United States. Chambers agreed to meet with Krivitsky.

Not long after, General Krivitsky was found mysteriously shot dead in a Washington, D.C., hotel room. Chambers knew he could not tell his story to anyone in our State Department. Mr. Levine persuaded him to tell it to the President, and offered to arrange an audience with FDR.

White Housers were sympathetic, but felt that this was not something that could be taken up "directly" with Mr. Roosevelt. They suggested Levine see A. A. Berle, then Assistant Secretary of State—also in charge of State Department security.

Levine and Berle were friends, so this was easily arranged. Chambers and Levine were invited to dinner at the Berles' home in Washington on September 2, 1939.

But Hitler invaded Poland on September 1. Jittery Washington waited for France and Britain to declare war on Germany. This was no time for busy Mr. Berle to take on another burden. Nevertheless, Mr. Berle informed FDR of Chambers' revelations about oh-so-many trusted people in top security posts in various government branches. According to Mr. Berle (in de Toledano's *Seeds of Treason* and Chambers' *Witness*) the President told Berle to "go jump in the lake." That was a laundered quote. FDR's language was profane. Berle's closest friends said that that exchange between FDR and Berle was not made public until nine years later, in 1948.

When Don Levine got no action from the White House or Mr. Berle, Levine spoke to Loy Henderson, chief of the Russian section of the State Department and a staunch anti-Red. He had been on the staff at the U.S. Embassy in Moscow. Mr. Henderson did not act because he would have been signing his political death warrant.

Levine went to his friend Senator Warren Austin, later chief U.S. representative at the United Nations. Senator Austin did not feel it was up to him to "carry the explosive information" to the American people.

In March of that year, Levine gave sufficient evidence to Congressman Martin Dies (Texas), chairman of the House Committee on Un-American Activities, to start a full-scale probe.

151

"But," reported Levine, "though the scatter-brained Texan issued a public statement that he would soon hear testimony from the head of the OGPU [Russia's Gestapo] in America, he seemed more interested in pursuing hapless liberals and belaboring fellow-travelers than in busting open the spy ring."

Page 89 of *Seeds of Treason* has this footnote: "Robert Stripling, then a Dies Committee investigator, was also present [when Levine told the story to Congressman Martin Dies] but the name of Chambers never registered with him either." Stripling was Westbrook Pegler's "hero" (so were Dies and other anti-FDR lawmakers); all of them belted the hell out of me for attacking Mr. Stripling and his chief and other no-nothings.

Levine's next stop was at the office of William C. Bullitt, former ambassador to Russia and one-time Soviet partisan. Mr. Bullitt went to FDR with the startling lowdown.

Bullitt told intimates that FDR laughed and said, "Don't worry." State Department executives to whom Mr. Bullitt repeated the warning reacted with shrugs.

Now the time is March 1941—Pearl Harbor months away.

Don Levine flew to Miami and came to see me at the Roney Plaza Hotel's cabanas and laid before me a lot of the Chambers disclosures. They included the intelligence that there were at least six Soviet agents operating freely in our government. (I was a lieutenant commander in U.S. Naval Intelligence at the time, but Levine did not know it.)

The same page of *Seeds of Treason* reports: "Winchell, who for some time had been using his powerful and widely syndicated column as a stick to belabor anti-American forces, both Communist and Fascist, held a reserve commission in Naval Intelligence and was a frequent guest at the White House. Aghast, he too agreed to take the matter straight to the President."

I flew to Washington in time for a presidential press conference. Marvin McIntyre, FDR's press chief, told me to "linger as usual" and the President would give me a few moments.

The President, years before, had told me that whenever I had anything he should know, I should not relay it through a third person but report directly to him.

After about two hundred newspaper and radio-teevee reporters raced to their phones and cameras, I started to tell FDR about Chambers and Levine—and how they could not get Mr. Berle and others in government to do anything about the spies.

The President didn't let me finish the first sentence. Leaning closer and pointing a finger in my face, he angrily said, "I don't want to hear another thing about it! It isn't true!"

My middle almost turned over from the shock.

He had never talked that way to me before. Christ! The President of our country doesn't know or believe how deeply Russian agents had bored from within! "Thank you, Mr. President," I said, making a hurried exit.

I couldn't wait for my next Sunday night broadcast. That's when I broke the exclusive story about Whittaker Chambers being Joe Stalin's Number One courier in the United States.

Page 739 of Chambers' epic says, in part:

> I concluded that there were powerful forces within the government to whom such information as I had given Berle was extremely unwelcome. I believed that they had no intention of acting on it, and that, if I made myself troublesome, any action would be taken against me.
>
> From time to time [continued Chambers] rumors and reports had reached me of what I could only regard as a fitful struggle going on—out of sight—among those who sought to bring the facts behind the [Alger] Hiss case to light—and those who strove to keep them hidden. Sometimes, the struggle reached a peak, as when shocked by what Isaac Don Levine had told him of my story—Walter Winchell again took it to President Roosevelt. Again nothing happened.

Every Red cell on the biggest newspapers in New York and around the nation—and the Commy cells on important news and public opinion-molding magazines—opened a tremendous barrage calling me everything a worried enemy calls you.

Now I had lost the confidence, I feared, of the President. I didn't go to the White House for several months. Until I was summoned.

FDR told a joke or two. I told him a few. Then he inquired, "What's going on up in New York that I should know?"

"Something I am not happy to tell you—it's about you."

"Really?" he replied, pursing his lips and raising his eyebrows.

"I found out the source for the slander your political and other foes are spreading—that you have paresis."

I jotted down the name of a famed Democrat, once close to FDR, who "went off the reservation" (FDR's phrase) when the Democratic

153

party chiefs refused to consider him for the Veep spot in 1936, for FDR's second term.

He thanked me warmly. I was out of the White House Doghouse.

The irony of it! The vengeful Democrat who started the unfounded gossip died a few years later—from paresis.

★

UNMAILED LETTER

My Navy duties included being a spy for our country—and writing speeches for top naval people in New York City attached to public relations. The P.R. work was part of my "volunteer active duty" six months before Pearl Harbor.

Washington newsmen Evans and Novak, in their book, *LBJ: The Exercise of Power,* reported the following bunk:

> Just before World War II, high naval officers, angered by the fact that syndicated columnist Walter Winchell seemed to be exploiting his lieutenant commander's commission in the U.S. Naval Reserve, encouraged Carl Vinson (chairman of the House Naval Affairs Committee) to launch a congressional investigation.
>
> No friend of Winchell, and usually attentive to the naval brass on such a question, Vinson was willing. But Roosevelt wanted no congressional man-handling of one of the few columnists supporting his interventionist policies toward the European war.
>
> "Daddy" Roosevelt used Johnson [LBJ] to quash the investigation, requiring Johnson to differ with "Daddy" Vinson. There was no investigation.

I wrote this letter which wound up in the files instead of the mails:

> Dear Evans and Novak: Regarding the reference to me on page eleven of your book, one phone call to me would have rewarded you with the facts. The incident you referred to followed my Sunday evening radio attacks on several solons. They included Bilbo, Borah, Rankin, Lundeen, Clare Hoffman and other isolationist legislators . . .
>
> Congressman Martin Dies and I fell out of like with each other when he posed for a news photo with German-American Bund chiefs. I attacked Dies almost every broadcast. Months before that feud began, Mr. Dies visited me in my cabana at the Roney Plaza

154

in Miami Beach and said: "I want to shake hands with a real American."

Later that same month Mr. Dies phoned from Washington. "I'm just a country boy," he said, "and I am always fearful that some city slicker is putting one over on me. I have an invitation to address a group called The American Fellowship Forum. Is that bunch okay?"

"Congressman," I replied, "that outfit is a front for Hitler's Nazis in New York. Please ignore them."

Imagine my astonishment when Dies posed for news photographers standing between Bund leader Fritz Kuhn and Hitler chief named Kunze, Kuhn's Svengali. I told my readers and listeners about Mr. Dies' stupidity.

Dies and some other lawmakers fought back ferociously in the House and Senate. None knew I was a reserve officer in U.S. Naval Intelligence (since 1934) until they read, in the newspapers, the wire I sent to the Navy Department on Pearl Harbor Day requesting active duty. It was this group who charged me with exploiting my uniform; they demanded I be cashiered out of it. No naval officer or navy brass accused me of anything. Rep. Carl Vinson was a good friend of mine. So you were wrong when you wrote, "Vinson, no friend of Winchell."

Frank Knox was then Secretary of the Navy. He was on leave from his job as a Hearst publisher. Mr. Knox summoned me to his office.

Before I kept the 10:00 A.M. tryst at Mr. Knox's office, I went to see FDR at 9. The President was busy signing letters. He motioned for me to sit down alongside his desk. When he was done signaturing his mail, he asked why I came. I placed my letter of resignation on his desk.

"What's that?" he asked.

"My resignation from the Naval Reserve, sir."

He swept it off the desk to the floor without looking at it. Then I told FDR about Knox sending for me.

He got Congressman Lyndon B. Johnson on the phone and said, "Lyndon, a good friend of ours, Walter Winchell, is to appear before Frank Knox at ten this morning. Please get Warren [Senator Magnuson] and sit in on this and see that he gets a fair shake."

The reason there was no probe was not that Johnson and Magnuson (both on naval affairs committees) were present, but because of this exchange:

"I still do not know, Mr. Secretary, why I am here. Are there charges against me?"

155

"Oh, nothing like that, Walter. Just thought we should have a talk." A talk, he said. The office was populated with over a dozen top naval people.

Knox suggested I lay off controversial things because he had received many complaints from Congressmen.

Knox, ill at ease, continued, "You are quite a controversial fellow, you will agree, and I know of your devotion to the President."

"Are you suggesting I resign?" I interrupted.

"Welllll . . ." hemmed Mr. Knox.

I didn't wait for him to haw. "I submitted my resignation less than an hour ago . . ."

Knox almost jumped from his chair and excitedly said, "You did? To whom?"

"To the Commander in Chief."

The silence that fell over that spacious room was deafening. Then I blew my cool and told them all what I thought of them for cowering before congressional people on Hitler's team. Mr. Johnson and Mr. Magnuson, seated in the rear, shook their heads. I lip-read LBJ's: "Shut up, you are talking too much."

I never mailed the above to Evans and Novak. I simply wrote them that their comment about me was completely untrue.

They sent me an apology, but putting it all in this book may stop other careless people from using their bunk. And in January 1957 I was appointed Commander, U.S. Naval Reserve.

★

BISHOP SHEEN'S FAVORITE COLUMN

A mutual friend was telling Bishop Fulton J. Sheen a quip. The storyteller prefaced it with, "I'm Jewish, you know."

To which the popular padre replied, "I am always happy to hear a person say that. Because my Lord was, you know."

Fulton J. Sheen was Monsignor Sheen in December of 1940 when the following pillar appeared in the New York *Daily Mirror*.

The padre distributed many thousands of reprints to Catholic institutions, convents, and parochial schools. The title: "Broadway Alien":

She believes everything she reads in the movie mags. She once went to a nightclub on New Year's Eve and didn't enjoy it. The only time she stays up all night is when she has a toothache. Marriage, in her opinion, is something sacred, not just a breathing spell between gigolos. She thinks "Lucious" Beebe is the name of a perfume. If she wasn't true to the guy she cared about most, she'd never be able to sleep. It would worry her too much.

When she sees a girl snubbing others or being insulting, she doesn't consider it being sophisticated, but downright rude. She doesn't do charity work just to get her picture in the paper. She's never been to a horse show or dog show at Madison Square Garden—and when she sees scenes from them in the newsreels, they make her yawn. She is familiar with all the latest styles, but cannot afford to wear them.

You never see her sitting in the corner of some Broadway joynt drinking and smoking and trying to appear interested in the conversation of a man who looks as though he might be her father. If you see her at 5:30 in the morning, she isn't on her way to some after-hours spot in Harlem. She's en route to the 6:00 A.M. Mass. Tommy Manville never asked her to be his Girl Friday or any day of the week. She thinks a sweater is something you wear at home—to high school or at a football game. Not at the Stork Club.

When a fellow asks her if she'd like a silver-fox stole, she replies: "What for?" When she goes to the theater, it is to see and hear—not to be Seen and Heard. The only Daddy she knows is the one who married her mother.

She remembers everything she did on New Year's Eve since she was ten years young—and there's nothing she did that she's trying to forget. She thinks a powder room in a restaurant is a place to powder your nose, not to stab a gal-pal in the back. Macoco never took her to El Morocco or on a trip to Acapulco. She heard the risgay lyrics of Dwight Fiske and Belle Barth and blushed. Her name has never been bandied about in a Broadway Column or in some comic's routine at The Copa. *Life* and *Look* photoggers have never tried to get pix of her with her dress up to her hips. They know what a waste of time that'd be. The only time she ever got her picture in the paper was when she helped Coney Island reach the "Million on the Beach" mark. She thinks "Tony's" is a shoe-shine place. She detests double-talkers, double-crossers, double-entendres, and double-Scotches. To her "going on the wagon" means a hayride with a boyfriend and the gang.

You won't find her father rated in Dun and Bradstreet. In fact, he may not even be listed in the phone directory. Her finger nails never grow to claw-length because they'd get mixed up in the typewriter key-

157

board. When you talk about "heels," she thinks you mean part of your shoes. The fur coat she wears was purchased by herself on the installment plan. It's almost paid for, too. She doesn't go slumming on Second Avenue. She lives there. An "Escort Service" would fail if it was up to girls like her.

She wore the colors of The Flag as an ornament on her dress or coat long before it was fashionable to do so. She thinks phony eyelashes look exactly like phony eyelashes. She never bothers people in the public eye for an autograph. When Joan Crawford gets a bum notice, it makes her ache. Nobody from the fashion pages ever writes up what she wore at the Opening Night because she goes to the theater after she's read the reviews. And, anyway, they'd never see her because she sits in the balcony and stays there during intermission. She smells sweet, not because of any cologne, but because she washes her neck, too. When she says she loves you it comes from the heart—not from a Cuba Libre.

You seldom hear her pulling any of Dorothy Parker's best quips, but if she does she prefaces them with credit to Miss Parker. Nobody ever goes to the bother of telling her shady gags because they'd lay an egg. Her vocabulary of cusswords is limited. When she gets real angry she says "Holy Smoke!" She reads the best books and understands them, not just an occasional detective story. At the movies she considers it perfectly normal and proper for the boyfriend to hold her hand—not her knee. If you told her you were a press agent she'd respond: "What's that?" If a fellow ever pinched her any place but the cheek, she'd never say "Fresh!"—she'd haul off and bang him one. She's definitely not in the Social Register. She couldn't be—she's the kind of gal who always says "Thanks" to waiters and busboys.

She's a strange little creature, this kernel of alien corn. She doesn't like being called a dame or a broad. She buys Ernest Hemingway's books to read them, not to have Mr. Hemingway autograph them. On her way to the "Little-Girls-Room" she never pauses to shout "Daaahhhleeeeeng" to Brenda Frazier or Tallulah. For the very simple reason that they do not know her. She thinks *The Great Dictator* and *Fantasia* are swell, and that the critics are whacky. Two highballs are enough for her and she won't let you pay nightclub prices for a doll or toy. I don't know how she lasts in this town. She stops eating bread, butter, and potatoes when she's getting chunky. No avoirpoison for her. She always goes home with the fellow who brought her and she's never called anyone "Stinky."

Saroyan, Stein, and Dali are not up her alley. She adores Toscanini or Kostelanetz recordings and detests "Gloomy Sunday." Her grandfather wasn't with Clive in India and none of her kin came over on the *Mayflower*, but they all made darn fine buck privates when they were needed. Jane Kean would find her dull material for mimicry or satire, but she would have made a swelegant heroine for Harold Bell Wright. She eats onions with hamburgers. She doesn't know Peter Arno or Lois Long and vice versa. She's her own Emily Post and insists you use your knife on that impossible hunk of lettuce. When she goes into a phone booth, it is to call her mother to report she'll be later than she thawt—not to phone some other guy to meet her after she drops the date she's with. She applauds when the American Flag is flashed on the screen. She closes her eyes when she dances with you—and stays on key when she hums in your ear. You can bet your life she isn't flirting with the sax tootler over your shoulder. She's the gal your mother was and your sister is.

★

BLACKMAIL

That's the title of a book published in 1944.

Henry Hoke, a businessman esteemed as a leader in his field (according to the publishers, Reader's Book Service, Inc.), witnessed Fascists and Bundists brazenly march, demonstrate, and slander "decadent Americans" and our form of government, à la Hitler, Mussolini, and Tojo. He decided to become "involved" and fight back. His book, *Blackmail,* enjoyed eight printings: a best seller.

The publisher's statement reads: "It is now issued after months of careful checking to guarantee that every statement is documented and verified. . . . The Nazis are relying on their active sympathizers within our border. . . . They continue to plant propaganda on a vast scale, conceived like a time-bomb to explode at the right time and in the most effective place. . . ."

From page seven of *Blackmail*:

> I began to pay more attention to . . . Walter Winchell's broadcasts. He was the first of the "Paul Reveres" to warn against the men involved in the plot against America. . . .
>
> By March of 1940 [author Hoke had devoted five years to his

159

personal investigations] the pattern seemed clear. We learned from a person working on the top floor of the Ford Building . . . in New York that Ford Company employees were compiling a list of appeasers, anti-Semites, pro-Nazis, and Fascists from fan mail addressed to Colonel Charles A. Lindbergh, former Senator Rush Holt, and Representative Hamilton Fish.

The lists, when compiled, were delivered to Bessie Feagin, circulation manager of Scribner's *Commentator* magazine. That explained how some of the dummy names used in writing to radio orators eventually got on the list of the America First Committee and Scribner's *Commentator*.

Your reporter interrupts to remind yesteryear's oldsters and today's youngsters that because of founder Ford's violent anticommunism (and anti-Semitism) and affectionate profascism, we rebutted with "FORD: F-or-D—Fascism or Democracy?"

The rabble-rouser radio commentator hired by Henry Ford, Sr. was on the air Sunday nights opposite my Jergen's newscast. The Jergen's Lotions-of-Love ratings drowned him.

Another excerpt from Mr. Hoke's *Blackmail* book:

The battle of words continues in print, in the mails [Mainly letters enjoying various pro-Nazi, anti-Red congressmen's franking privilege—free!], on the floor of Congress. Senator Burton K. Wheeler demands a Senatorial committee to investigate certain books exposing Reds in the U.S.

Wheeler is appointed chairman of the investigating group. Congressman John Rankin rants against Negroes and Jews. Clare Hoffman [Congressman from Michigan] rails against Walter Winchell . . . Congressman Martin Dies charges that the book *Under Cover* is a "plot" to smear him and Congress.

Dies subpoenas Winchell's broadcast scripts . . . demands and gets time to deny that his Committee has been inactive against the Fascists. Congressman Fish attacks those who try to expose the dangers of native and foreign fascism. Dies charges that an organized "smear bund is directing a dangerous movement to destroy representative Government" and then retires from the fight!

All of which happened while your kin were bleeding and dying fighting the Axis—Hitler's Germany, Mussolini's Italy, and Hirohito's Japan.

Congressman Martin Dies, after frightening my network chiefs into giving him "equal time" to "expose Walter Winchell," kept making

160

many front pages with what he promised Americans he would say and do to me.

It didn't worry me. I knew that Mr. Dies was running scared; that he had nothing on me, politically or otherwise. And I was confirmed. Instead of exposing me, Mr. Dies squandered fifteen valuable minutes of prime radio time denying what I had said about him being a dupe of Fritz Kuhn's German-American Bund and other U.S. Nazi-saluters.

Dies demanded that I go on ahead of him in my regular 9:00 P.M. Sabbath eve time—so that he could pop off about me and I would not be able to rebut him the same night.

And what happened? The stupid soandso delivered a meek alibi, waved the flag, and turned his free fifteen minutes into a political speech. (He was up for reelection in Texas.) His tepid "blast" at me resulted in the first defeat of his long career. Dies defeated himself with that broadcast.

I merely assisted.

Some of my favorite pamphleteers were Gerald L. K. Smith, who called himself the Reverend Gerald Smith, and an echo named Joseph Kamp. Their various "expozays" about FDR and anyone on the President's team invariably included Walter. Smith had a large mailing list at the time.

Some of the wild things they wrote about me belonged in a criminal libel case. They quoted the pro-Nazis and Far Right people in both the Senate and the House of Reprehensibles. That gave them the same immunity solons enjoyed.

I hoped I would encounter the Reverend and Kamp some day so I could return the compliment in person. Then the "Winchell luck" came along again: devastating lowdown about Smith's sources—which I made public.

His subscribers became fewer. His income considerably less.

Since the early 1940's, Gerald Smith has been filing financial reports under the Federal Corrupt Practices Act of 1925.

Here is a sample of the libel some of them went to in their attempts to get something "on" me.

The pro-Commy and pro-Nazi and anti-FDR stupids danced with joy when I was "exposed" as a sex maniac (some skewp!) "who brought a very young and pretty girl from New York to a Washington hotel." They demanded I be arrested under the Mann Act (white slavery).

The girl *was* very young and very pretty—my twelve-year-old daughter.

161

When we tangled with U.S. Senator Burton K. Wheeler of Montana, one of FDR's severest critics (six months before Pearl Harbor), the solon's supporters flogged us. The following flak appeared on the front page of the *Pink Reporter* at Three Forks, Montana, on June 21, 1941:

> World's Public Rat Number One Walter Winchell, a lowly cur who commercializes rotten news, insults mothers, smears honesty, deals in filth, associates with the worst criminals, grins at adultery, lives by his wits, produces nothing but scandal and trouble for others, screeches for bloody war, a human gila monster, a cowardly jackel, a war-mongering, labor-baitor who condemns strikes which he says are shameful so long as a million soldier boys get 21 bucks a month, but who fails to tell you that he, the unhung rat, reported a net income of 261 thousand 892 bucks and 45 cents for the year 1940.
>
> Gaze at the mug above, folks, and observe the features of the dirtiest louse alive today; a preposterous liar. May the worst that may befall a person overtake this damnable creature!

From the editorial page of the Miami *Herald* two years later:

> We particularly liked something Winchell said a long time ago in defending U.S. Senator Burton K. Wheeler of Montana from his egg-throwers: "This is what we are fighting against—those who stop us from freedom of speech. And although Senator Wheeler doesn't agree with anything I say, I will fight for his right to be wrong!" Wheeler sent Winchell a telegram thanking him for his American spirit of fair play, etc. And then saw that he was prevented from broadcasting over stations in Montana friendly to the Senator.

A few months before Pearl Harbor, some Americans were worried about me. Sample: The America First Committee of Colorado distributed bulletins signed "Harry C. Schnibbe, Public Relations Director, suggesting that a letter campaign bombard our radio sponsor:

"The way we must fight the foul-mouthed assaults by our Commercial Patriot No. 1—Walter Winchell—is through his sponsor. Write that you have purchased your last bottle of his product until the unfair warmongering tactics of Winchell cease."

My radio chief ignored them all. He sponsored me for sixteen years.

My radio contract was renewed annually by the Jergens Lotion spon-

sor for sixteen consecutive annums. The column inherited dozens of
new branches from border to border and coast to coast, plus over a
dozen papers in foreign countries.

Many still publish it: the Athens (Greece) *News,* the Manila (Philippines) *Evening News,* two papers in Germany, a tabloid in Mexico
City, a paper in Brazil and, before Castro arrived, my piffle ran daily in
three Havana blatts—two in Spanish, the other in American. The syndicate people told me they did not recall any paragrapher ever appearing in three newspapers in the same city simultaneously.

In the early 1940's, besides King Features Syndicate, we were also
syndicated by Western Newspaper Union. The latter supplied features
mainly to farm-belt weeklies. On November 22, 1941, the service
editor for WNU wrote me: "Don't know whether you know it or not,
but you're probably the first columnist whose writings were purchased
for publication in a prison newspaper, the *San Quentin News.*"

★

THE DURATION

George Norris' merciless fact: "We have wars because the human race
has learned how to improve everything—except people."

On December 7, 1941, while living at the Roney Plaza, Miami
Beach, I telegraphed the Navy Department: "REQUEST ACTIVE
DUTY IMMEDIATELY. WALTER WINCHELL, LT. USNR."

I was commissioned a lieutenant commander on December 18, 1940.

This meant (I was told) that I could command a battle cruiser.
(Me?) I can't even keep from getting seasick in a Central Park rowboat.

My duties included being a spy for our country and writing speeches
for top naval people in New York City—attached to public relations.
The P.R. work had been part of my "volunteer active duty" six months
before Pearl Harbor.

The Navy Department's first order was: "Stay on the air and in the
papers. We will tell you when to go on active duty. Navy Relief needs
money. Tell the people—your listeners and readers."

I did so on the coast-to-coast network and via my syndicated papers
in every state. The big money avalanched in from "Mr. and Mrs. United
States and All the Ships At-Sea!"

Navy Relief got nearly $250,000 from a one-night show at the old Madison Square Garden on Eighth Avenue near Fiftieth Street.

Irving Berlin wrote a special song for the Navy: "I Threw A Kiss Into The Ocean." He gave all royalties—all—to Navy Relief. It still receives checks.

The Navy was immensely pleased. So was Commander in Chief Franklin Delano Roosevelt, a Navy man.

I told my superior officers in Washington and the President (after a press conference one matinee): "I am going to do the same big show in San Francisco in a few weeks."

"You're going great, Lieutenant," said Admiral Leland P. Lovett. So did other Big Brass in Washington. They also told me to ask boat owners—of any kind of skiff ranging from a motorboat to a yacht—to loan them to the navy for inshore patrol for the duration. The patriotic owners would receive one dollar payment.

After one broadcast requesting those boats I got a phone call from the Navy: "For goodnessakes, don't say it again on your next broadcast. We got over two thousand boats from your first newscast. We have too many!"

Okay, no more boats or yachts.

My next assignment: "Talk up enlistments for Naval Aviation—V-seven Cadets."

Same response. After three such appeals, I was ordered: "No more! No more! We can't handle the ones we have, thanks. You have performed another public service."

Then, to my amazement, one afternoon following an FDR press confab, the President said: "Cut out the Navy Relief stuff."

"Good Heavens, Mr. President, why?"

"Getting too many complaints from other worthy causes. The Red Cross is not happy about it. They feel Navy Relief is getting all the money. Nine million dollars is enough, anyway."

That was the first I had learned how much money came in.

"Oh, gee," I oh-geed, "please let me do one more show for the Navy in San Francisco. I already have it set, Mr. President."

"All right," he said happily. "Then cut it out."

One day after Pearl Harbor, Ben Bernie phoned from a theater in Pittsburgh about our long-playing "feud." "No more, no more," he said. "I'm afraid of being stoned by patriotic people. One little old lady stood up in the front row and bawled me out for taking a poke at you. She said, 'Don't you know there's a war going on, Mr. Bernie? Mr. Winchell is a loyal American!' "

So the "feud" was over, our juicy racket at an end.

One day in FDR's office he asked, "What's new?"

I told him that a story making the rounds in Manhattan was about the "real reason" he and Captain Patterson, patriotic publisher of the New York *Daily News,* had Phffft.

"The story," I reported to the President, "is that Captain Joe flew to Washington a few days after Japan's 'infamy' and asked to see the Prez.

"He was kept waiting for over one and a half hours and when he finally got in he was not invited to sit down.

"You glared 'Yes, Joe?'

"Patterson saluted and said, 'Reporting for duty, sir.'

"You supposedly said, 'I assign you to go back to your paper and read all those rotten editorials you printed about me in the past six months.'

"Captain Patterson saluted and walked out, hurt, Very hurt."

"Well," sighed the President, "that isn't what happened. Quite an exaggeration. It is true that he waited a long time, but we didn't expect him—and there were many government people on the list to talk to about the war.

"The day after Pearl Harbor," continued FDR, "I told Steve [Early] to do something about all the small-town publishers and other people I never met before, who get in with the press and stay on to shake hands or request an autograph or photo. 'Keep them all out! Think of something to do about them all—they give me a headache or bore me stiff.' "

Steve Early, a trigger-thinker, dreamed up a beaut. "Let's remove all the chairs but yours," he giggled.

FDR laughed and laughed and complimented Steve for his "brilliant" idea. "Soooo," sighed the Prez, winding up his version of the estrangement, "Captain Joe went off the reservation.

"What about your boss, Mr. Hearst?" he said. "He went off the reservation, too. Because I didn't stop the Securities and Exchange Commission from investigating the Hearst newspapers and magazines. The SEC had complaints and alleged evidence that Hearst stock was being watered. Something like that.

"Then Roy Howard's papers [Scripps-Howard chain] went off the reservation because of a stupid thing they did around here. The Internal Revenue went after the rich who set up corporations in the Bahamas and other Caribbean places—to avoid higher taxes. Nobody told me that the number three name on the list of tax dodgers was a pal of Roy Howard!"

FDR said that if he had known the name was on it, he certainly would have ordered them to forget making the list public; that he could not afford to lose any more newspaper people who had helped elect him.

In 1942 I put on a show for Navy Relief at the Opera House in San Francisco. Every name in Hollywood appeared—besides the many headliners who paid their own way to San Francisco from New York, Chicago, etc. We wound up with another triffic bundle of loot.

It was very dark backstage as I squeezed my way through the crowd of entertainers waiting to go on. I was in uniform: a two-and-a-half striper. As I inch'd my way through the throng backstage, a voice whispered: "Walter?"

"Yes, who you?"

"Irene Martin."

It was so pitch-black back there I could not see her face. I just knew I had found her again—the dear friend who had saved my job at Yonkers in 1910. We embraced. "Why are you here?" I asked.

"I'm with Joan Blondell, a longtime friend." Now I could see That Face. Her smile, still beautiful, beautiful . . .

I learned that Joan Blondell employed Irene; Girl Friday sortathing —a good job. She was more like a gal-pal. They probably met in Hollywood when Irene was the wealthy Mrs. Pat Somerset.

"What can I do for you, Irene? Get you a job in the studios or on the air? I know so many people, but I rarely ask them for favors. You always have to pay back double. I'm also drama critic for the New York *Daily Mirror*, so I hate asking producers, actors or directors to do anything for me. They might be afraid to turn me down. But I have some real friends in show business. Mr. Zanuck is one. He'd give you a job for me. He's done it for several guys and gals who found the going rough."

"Thanks," she said, "but I'm okay. Joan pays me well. I live at her house. Everything is fine, Walter, really."

"Look," I persisted, "you helped me out when I needed help. You'll make my day, Irene, if you just say what I can do for you."

Several months before, I had played the role of the reporter in *The Front Page* on *Lux Radio Theater,* one of the standouts at the time—and for a very long time, too. Cecil B. De Mille produced it, a weekly program high in all the ratings—or, as *Daily Variety's* ace critic "Helm" Hellman said: "It was tops in the Rate-Race."

The network version of *The Front Page,* a prosperous long-run stage play by Hecht and MacArthur (and also a movie), was so popular that Mr. De Mille reprised his show. This time he cast me as the managing editor. But I was more comfortable playing the reporter.

And so I told Irene that I knew Mr. De Mille. "How about me asking him to put you in one of his shows?"

She lit up. "I love that show," she said. "I'd like very much appearing on it."

I lost no time phoning De Mille. At his office I made the long story short—about Irene Martin saving my job when I was a kid. He got The Point immediately. "Send her over," he said warmly, and he made Irene a permanent member of his troupe.

Thank you, Agnes De Mille, for having such a dandy Daddy.

The Affairs of Dame Rumor by David J. Jacobson, published by Rinehart and Company, later revealed that Nazi propaganda chiefs used a shortwave radio in Berlin to "debunk" Americans. The news programs included one that "came from the American midwest" and was patterned after those of Walter Winchell.

"The Stars and Stripes Forever" prefaced the broadcast, which started with "Good evening, Mr. and Mrs. America and the ships at sea." That was almost like our own salute on our newscasts.

The rest of the spurious news flashes dealt with American troopships being sunk by German U-boats, etc.

Mr. Jergens, my sponsor, never instructed me to change my tune. One dinnertime in the Stork Club his guests (top Jergens execs) groaned a little. Said a Mr. Nelson, now gone to his heavenly harp, "Walter, you keep criticizing people we like very much, friends of ours. Senator Taft ('Mr. Republican') is our firm's lawyer. Did you know that?"

"No," I said. "I just disagree with many of Mr. Taft's policies."

"Look," continued Nelson, "you've helped Roosevelt get elected three times. Why not let us Republicans try to elect a Republican?"

Mr. Jergens interrupted by putting a hand on my arm and saying: "You pay no attention to any of this. Just keep peddling your papers, and we will peddle the product." Quite a man. Quite an American.

One of the most unhappy moments for me came some time after that Stork Club scene. Hitler's submarines landed eight saboteurs on the Florida and Long Island coastlines. It was my painful duty to report that a woman in Ohio was the saboteur's contact. She was an employee in Mr. Jergens' Cincinnati home!

It was a Sunday evening—an hour before broadcast time. I telephoned my sponsor and said: "Mr. Jergens, the FBI quietly arrested a woman working in your home. She is charged with being a Nazi contact. The FBI will announce the arrest momentarily. If I don't make that news public tonight, you and I will be denounced by the American people."

"Go right ahead," said Mr. Jergens calmly. "By all means do so."

Mr. Pegler and his colleagues on the papers and airwaves did not mention that *The Jergens Journal* reporter made that exclusive news public. Nor did any of the Commy editors on our top magazines.

Another missive that slept in our files since the World War II years is this one from a New York *Herald Tribune* editor:

"While shooting some train action shots along the Boston and Albany at Brighton I was apprehended as a German spy. The tracks are just across the river from the Watertown Arsenal and a citizen phoned the police who arrived six deep from all sides in squad cars and very menacing, too.

"When I identified myself by my police card the officer in charge of the detail snorted: 'He can't be no Nazi; he's a friend of Walter Winchell; always in his column.'

"Thanks, pal."

★

ST. CLAIR McKELWAY AND HAROLD ROSS

"Paint me as I am," Van Gogh once told another great artist, warts and all!" Then there was Alexander Woollcott's order to his bioger, Samuel Hopkins Adams: "Print what you like! Don't prettify me!" I've said the same thing to an army of biographers, and most of them sure didn't.

168

A new magazine published in Southern California assigned a faggity newcomer to do an article about me. It was crowded with many of the true and false things others had written for decades—an amateurish rewrite job. But it was what the new mag wanted—to get itself on the map. It was publishing similar raps about movietown stars and producers.

Months later another article-writer phoned me. He said: "I had a talk with the publisher of that magazine. I suggested he assign me to do one on you. I know your history better. I was told to work it up. That he'd like to see it first."

" 'We are always interested,' said the publisher, 'in a piece about WW if it is unfavorable.' "

What a shmuck that publisher was to admit that. The word is "malice." If the writer he spoke to was subpoena'd as a witness in a libel action and so testified on the stand (and I won the case), the punitive damages probably would be considerable.

St. Clair McKelway, a former headliner for *The New Yorker,* did a "profile" on me in the early 1940's. It ran six weeks—one of the longest articles ever published about a target in that mag. McKelway told nothing that I had not read about myself before.

His main theme was a long list of "wrongos" (boners) to show my columns were "not always accurate." He got the "wrongos" from my published "corrections."

One of his researchers sent postcards to many of the persons mentioned in the column. Ethel Merman, the popular musical comedy star, was one who received a card.

One after-theatertime in the Stork Club, Miss Merman showed it to me. It said: "Mr. Winchell in his column of (——) reported that an admirer presented you with a yacht. Is it true, false, or partly true?"

"Put down the truth," I said. "You did get a yacht, didn't you? Your sweedee told me he gave you a yacht."

"Oh, it's only a boat," she technical'd. "A yacht is a big boat."

"Well, then put down 'partly true' or 'partly inaccurate'.

One day at the White House, Marvin McIntyre had whispered, "After the press leaves, linger as usual." When more than two hundred reporters had rushed to their phones and typewriters, and FDR's inner circle (about six "Brains Dept." men) departed, the President motioned for me to sit down.

"Boy, have I an item for you!" he said for openers.

169

When I told that to Ernest Cuneo, then my lawyer (who told it to one and all in Washington), it became the leading paragraph in a series of articles in *The New Yorker*.

The profiler belittled it, as though to say, "Can you imagine a President saying a thing like that to a gossip columnist?" But that's what the Man said, and *The New Yorker's* editor went to hell, where I told him to go. The author and I now share a laugh about it.

McKelway's *New Yorker* boss was the late Harold Ross. It was Ross who ordered the series written. Ross liked me, believe it or don't. He liked me so much he dropped my name to cops several times when 17th Precinct (midtown East Side) police cars were often summoned to subdue his maniacal drunken episodes in the wee hours.

In front of Reuben's late-spot restaurant, editor Ross made such a nuisance of himself kicking in shop windows and screaming like a psycho that he was about to be arrested when he name-dropped: "I'm on Winchell's staff!"

The police in that precinct believed it and drove him to his nearby cave. They told me about it an hour later when I got to Reuben's.

About a year before the series ran, Ross phoned me and said: "I've always told you that if you laid off me and checked things you are told about me, I'd give you a good story some day. I have one for you now. My wife is divorcing me. But you must promise that you will not put it on the air. Just in the *Mirror*."

"Oh, then the hell with it," I said. "Forget it."

"No, no," he countered. "I want you to print it, but my folks in Aspen, Colorado, listen to you every Sunday night and dammit, I don't want them to be shocked. Promise you won't put it on the air."

"Okay, I promise."

He told me the story on a Saturday evening. My broadcast was the next night at 9.

I used his abrogation item in the New York *Mirror* Monday. The bulldog edition was on the midtown streets at 8:40 P.M. Sunday.

He was a cutie, Ross was. He knew what he was doing. He knew the Monday papers would be crowded with local pre-election news, and so would the Tuesday—Election Day—papers. Editors would not, he figured, bother following up gossip in columns.

I ran his item. Not one paper picked it up. He phoned his kin in Colorado Sunday night after I went off the air and informed them of his marriage splituation.

This whole incident was the basis for McKelway's final chapter in the series about me. I always suspected Ross wrote that one himself.

McKelway's finale was titled "Legacy of an Ex-Hoofer." It told about an advertising executive who had made up his mind to resign from the department store for which he worked and form his own agency. He feared it would leak to "someone like Winchell" and wreck his future.

"Oh, stop worrying about it," he was told. "Just call up or go see Winchell. Tell him your problem and he'll lay off."

To the man's amazement, said McKelway's report, he did tell me of his concern and that was the end of his needless ordeal. Thus, "The Winchell Jitters" were erased.

Not a bad notice for me, at all. It was *The New Yorker's* way of giving me pattycake after five articles of goosing.

The *New Yorker* series also started the untrumor that Sherman Billingsley ("Mr. Stork Club") had banished editor Ross and the mag staff. Thereafter, in the magazine's weekly index to restaurants and night spots the Stork Club was either omitted or given a rap.

The meanest news that could have been recorded about Mr. Ross was ignored by me.

His habit of not paying the waiter on his excursions there almost got him barred from the Stork Club.

Owner Sherman Billingsley told me that Ross was the "god-dambdest" check dodger in the history of the place. Ross, drunk, would pick up his tab and table-hop—but never so drunk he didn't forget to bring along his bill. After another few rounds he staggered out—leaving his check on some other fellow's table. Clever?

My favorite gag about him is this one. I ran it during his series about me and many times since.

"A man dashed into the Stork Club," went the quip, "and breathlessly said: 'I must see Harold Ross at once!'"

"He's in the Cub Room," the excited one was informed.

"But I don't know what he looks like!" said the fellow, "How will I know him?"

"He'll be the one," was the retort, "with his back to the check!"

McKelway's series was put into a minibook and went down in the literati history tomes as a big Zero. The public didn't want to read about boners. They wanted to read about my sinfulness along Broadway and about the many ladies of the stage and chorus I raved about in print.

His series was meant to blow me down, but it blew down the author

171

of the articles. He enjoyed a brief time in the spotlight "taking on Winchell." It won me many papers I hadn't appeared in before.

Letter from a newspaperman in the oh-so-very-long-ago:

> Dear Walter: This will give you a laugh. I ran into St. Clair McKelway on the street the other day. He started talking about the *Post* and said he understood they had lifted quite a bit of material from his (*New Yorker*) series.
>
> He remarked that if they thought they could hurt you with such a series they were crazy, and he told me this story. About a year after his series ran in *The New Yorker,* the whole staff was at a meeting when editor Ross declared: "We are all a lot of fools. I have learned that in the year since we did our series on Winchell, his income has increased by a hundred thousand dollars a year!"

About a decade later I received a very long, very warm telegram from Hollywood. It was signed St. Clair McKelway. It said (in part) that it had taken him ten years or so to realize "what you have been trying to do for our country" and so on.

I read it with my best eyebrows raised high. Now a decade later—after I survived his bombardments—a wire says he realizes "what you have been trying to do for our country."

My satisfaction was short-lived. That midnight I picked up *The New York Times* and read on the movie pages that St. Clare McKelway of *The New Yorker* was in Hollywood and his new movie was to premiere on Broadway shortly.

So that's why Mr. Fearful wired me that love letter! No matter. If his movie was good I would so report. But I didn't have to mention the movie, after it opened and closed fast.

THE NINETEEN CANNONS

The first time I went to sea since World War I was as a press officer on the shakedown cruise of the largest American warship at the time, the U.S.S. *North Carolina.*

Roy Alexander of *Time* magazine and dozens of other news gatherers were on that maiden trip, six hundred miles east of Cape Cod—the first time that nineteen guns were fired simultaneously.

172

Winchell, Bernie, and a trio of Los Angeles chorines cavort on the grounds of the Ambassador Hotel (King Features)

In Miami Beach, 1938: Joseph P. Kennedy, then Ambassador to the Court of St. James's, talks to Damon Runyon (center) and WW about conditions in Europe. The shirtless gent at lower right is N.Y. criminal lawyer Samuel Liebowitz (King Features)

J. Edgar Hoover and WW at the Roney Plaza, "when we were much younger"

First reproductions of the ransom notes from the Lindbergh Baby kidnapping. From these letters alone, Dr. Dudley D. Schoenfeld was able to tell Winchell of the then-unknown kidnapper's German background and general whereabouts — and that the Lindbergh child was already dead.

At a 1940 luncheon at the Capitol, WW clowns with J. Edgar Hoover and Vice President John Nance Garner. The occasion: the Arlington American Legion Post No. 139 awarded Winchell a gold medal in honor of his patriotic writings and broadcasts (King Features)

In 1940, WW saunters with his son, Walter Jr., on the Roney Plaza's Cabana Row boardwalk (King Features)

Wearing his Lieutenant Commander's uniform for the first time in public, WW talks with some sailors aboard the U.S.S. West Point *arriving in New York with a load of Americans evacuated from Europe, 1941 (King Features)*

Being interviewed by Jimmy Kilgallen (King Features)

WW saluting the flag as he goes ashore at Recife, Brazil, from the flagship of the South Atlantic Command, 1943. "The reason my sleeves were rolled up, against regulations, was the extreme heat and humidity. But I had gotten permission from Admiral Jonas H. Ingram to do so."

WW on extreme right, arms folded, in the flagship's war room. Others in photo are high commanders of the American, British, and Brazilian navies, planning strategy to combat Nazi submarines in the area

December, 1943: Lieutenant Commander WW on right, prior to takeoff from Recife on a Navy PBY plane on a "killer group" looking for enemy submarines

A year after Runyon's death, the Damon Runyon Memorial Fund presented its first check of $250,000 to the American Cancer Society. Robert E. Strawbridge, Jr., watches as WW presents the check to Brigadier General John Reed Kilpatrick, Chairman of the New York City Cancer Committee, at the Stork Club (King Features)

At the ABC microphone

Benedicto Macri was sought for more than a year following the slaying of a union organizer. In 1950, Winchell broadcast a plea that Macri surrender to him so that the $25,000 reward posted for Macri's capture could go to the Damon Runyon Memorial Cancer Fund. Here Macri and WW are shown a few minutes after they met, one hundred feet from the West 20th Street Police Station

WW stands by as Macri is booked (King Features)

On the air — but most likely this was a posed shot, since his watch read slightly before 9:00 P.M. (King Features)

At Dwight D. Eisenhower's inauguration, 1952. Mamie and Ike are at lower right foreground (Bill Mark)

The new ship sailed under "darkened war conditions"—all lights doused. Nazi submarines were in the area. Mr. Alexander said: "We want you to see the skipper and ask one question: What does he think will happen when all nineteen guns go off?" I went to the Admiral's quarters and relayed *Time*'s query.

"How in hell do I know?" boomed the Loneliest Man on any battle-wagon. "We might break in two! No navy in history ever shot nineteen cannons off at the same time!"

When the nineteen guns lit up the ebony night, the great new battle-ship hardly budged. You felt only a very slight "oops!" to the right.

One of the cameramen for the New York *Mirror* gave me a camera. He told me to hold my right index finger on a color-camera button. "Don't press it," he counseled. "The blast will push down your finger and we might get a helluva picture."

"My" photograph of the historic moment made the *Mirror*'s front page in black and white—and in color a week later on the cover of the paper's magazine section.

★

TOUR OF DUTY

Following tours of duty at various naval bases in the New York area, after a White House press conference I asked the Commander in Chief to "please send me to sea." He notified "BUPERS" (Bureau of Personnel) to do so. Before, in December 1940, I'd been promoted at Opa Locka, Florida, to three-striper: Lt. Comdr.! This meant, I was told, that I could command a battle cruiser. I was ordered to report to the Commandant, South Atlantic Command, Recife, Brazil.

"What," boomed the late Admiral Jonas H. Ingram (former All-American) "were you ever trained at?"

"Public relations and ONI, sir."

"Ever shoot a gun?"

"No, sir."

"I thought not. How'd you like to go on a killer group?"

"I would like that," I said, trying to disguise my apprehension.

Jay Allen's Chicago publisher insured him for fifty thousand dollars during the early months of Spain's Civil War. But so far as I know, none of the news wire services insured their men during World War II. Webb Miller, then of United Press, said glory should be enough.

173

"Report for PBY duty tomorrow," he ordered.

PBY duty? That's the slowest-moving plane in the Navy. Hitler's subs were out there. It would be ironical, I said to myself, for a Nazi sub to surface, the skipper of which would megaphone, "Just sent Herr Vinchell. Ve vant he should meet our Fuehrer!"

I told that to the crew. They said it was the best laugh they had had in many months.

In 1944 Curt Riess edited a book, *They Were There,* for G.P. Putnam's Sons. In this book about World War II Riess included articles by many American war correspondents: Edgar Ansel Mowrer, H. V. Kaltenborn, John Gunther, Ernest Hemingway, William Shirer, Quentin Reynolds, Dorothy Thompson, Howard K. Smith, Brooks Atkinson, and WW. Thaz me.

Riess said: "Walter Winchell was born in New York City in 1897. Although never officially a war correspondent, he gave some lively accounts of his missions for the Navy which rank with some of the best reporting done by regular correspondents." Riess then reprinted my "Tour of Duty" column from the January 25, 1943, New York *Mirror*:

> January, 1943—Aboard a Navy patrol plane over the South Atlantic: Some men are more fortunate than others. Some men are richer than many. Some men stay in love longer than most— and most men never experience the wallop that goes with being at the bow gun of a Navy patrol plane (a PBY) a few feet over the submarine-infested South Atlantic.
>
> How even a veteran bombardier can keep his eyes open or focused on a target out there in the open bow—with the fierce wind blinding and bayoneting him—is something I do not savvy. The powerful gun kicks the way Joe Louis punches and shakes you violently the way Lew Fields shook Joe Weber. At any rate, there you are out there under the huge propellers—several feet ahead of the pilot—alone—except for the hurricane-tempo'd wind and perhaps a Nazi sub hiding below.
>
> I was reminded of the time Senator Holman of Oregon and Senator Chandler of Kentucky flew to the Aleutians through heavy fog and storm most of the way. And picked up a soldier at some Alaskan base, who immediately took his battle station and trained his guns on the skies.
>
> "Son," said Senator Holman, "watcha fussin' with that there weapon fer that-a-way?"
>
> "I'm being ready," replied the gunner, "in case we meet some Jap planes."

The white-as-a-sheet Holman turned to the whiter-than-that Chandler and intoned, "Ain't it silly what some of us Senators will do to get into trouble—when we don't have it?"

My good break came from missing connections with the plane that was to take me to the next port on the tour. Had I made that plane I would have missed one of the biggest thrills of them all. That thrill was not my first flight in a PBY—a huge and comfortable Catalina (one of which helped sink the *Bismarck*); or firing the bow gun—or circling low over oil specks that stained the beautiful aquamarine below. The big wallop came several hours later when we reached the base.

I am not permitted to divulge the excitement I witnessed at this place. . . . The four paragraphs about it were blue-penciled even before I had the chance to correct the spelling. It was my first experience with an official gremlin. For the first time in many years of newspapering, I realized how tame the toughest editors are.

All I was trying to jot down was that some fellows were luckier than other fellows . . . that some pilots had reasons for being happier than others. And that the United States now has fewer enemies than it had. And so I cannot reveal at this time what all that excitement was about . . . I cannot even elaborate that the excitement was enjoyed by a lot of very happy men, and that the reason they were so exicted and happy was that certain other men, with dialects, were unhappy or dead.

The PBY on which I hitchhiked was manned by the most youthful fellows I encountered down there. Most were only twenty-one. Some were twenty-three or twenty-five, and some were a little more seasoned . . . but all featured beards that must have been months in blooming. All the other fliers I met at various places were clean-shaven. "Why the whizgers?" I asked.

"They haven't been as lucky as other chaps," explained an officer, "and so they agreed not to shave until they got a sub."

I kept wishing that on this routine flight I would not prove a jinx to them—and that they could all get a shave.

The Atlantic seemed as tame as any Florida lake. I was instructed to occupy one of the copilot's pews—handed a helmet containing earphones, and some dark specs. I just sat there wishing hard that they'd all get lucky. Now and then the captain brought the plane down to a few feet over the water, to circle over oil specks. They are really huge gobs of scum from tankers and ships, they said. Sometimes it might be from an ill-fated merchantman . . . but not always.

At the Admiral's morning conference I was shown a dispatch that told of a merchant ship sunk the night before, and that a

175

PBY patrolling the area had radio'd seeing two lifeboats with survivors . . . but when he returned to the scene later he saw only one. We were instructed to keep our eyes open for those survivors, that saving them would be even better than sinking an enemy sub. . . . But there was no trace of them. I never learned whether they had been rescued or not. I kept thinking of them throughout the flight—knowing that brave men somewhere were suffering, not only from the suffocating humidity and heat, but from the blinding sun. Even with dark specs, my eyes ached from the glare.

About a hundred miles from our destination the earphones crackled. The plane was ordered in. Enemy subs were reported—and a squadron of PBYs were on the way for the attack. Ours was too far from the scene to join the killer group and still have enough fuel to get back. The disappointment on the faces of the crew was painful to see. . . . I was their jinx, after all. They were "out of the money" again. Other fellows had all the luck.

As the PBY came down gracefully, the crew was greeted with more sour news. They were to get their chow while their ship was being readied to relieve one of the killer group. But by the time they were ready to climb like homesick angels—a flash radio'd that the "show' 'was over. PBY COMBAT DUTY SQUADRON VP-83, RECIFE, NATAL.

On the flight one of the crew asked if I would like to handle the 50-calibre bow gun (machine gun). I outranked them all. How could I shudder and say "Nh-nh?"

I crawled on my belly to the frightening weapon, out in the open about ten feet over the water. I was a sitting pigeon for an enemy sub's marksmen.

I followed instruction. I put on the huge "ears." I was told to tightly grip the lead handles on the gun and press the gadgets that fired it.

When the damb miniature cannon rat-a-tat-tatted at a "million miler per hour," it shook me from skull to toes. I felt that the crew were in stitches. The wonder of it is that the body-shaking weapon didn't shoot one of our own ships.

But the adventure was recorded in my naval record. Admiral Ingram's report to the Navy Department included, "Lieutenant Commander Winchell manned the cannon of a PBY."

Just before I returned to the United States, the crew of that PBY presented me with a gold identification bracelet. The inscription on it reads: "Lt. Com. Walter Winchell. PBY Combat Duty, Squadron VP-83, South Atlantic Command. Recife, Natal."

Some hours later a radio flash ordered the PBY I had been on to join other planes about eighty miles off Natal. Our planes had spotted an enemy sub. "My" PBY got there in time to help sink it—the first enemy submarine sunk off the Brazilian coast.

Admiral Ingram, who had flown there following the first report that an enemy sub had been traced, was delirious with joy. A huge man, he kept jumping up and down, yelling: "Just bring me a hat—one little Nazi hat! Just one!" (to prove that it was a Nazi submarine). Miniature pictures of the sub sinking (still wet from the darkroom) were hastily tacked on a bulletin board in Commander Phillips' offices.

Our Navy also captured two of the sub's crew, who had been deserted by their skipper when the sub submerged to escape the approaching PBYs—and their sailor hats!

Ingram kept shouting congratulations to Commander Phillips. "Everybody up a grade!" hollered the joyous Ingram. Addressing Phillips, Admiral Ingram gratefully cooed: "Just name it! Just name it! What can I give you—name it, Phillips!"

"Thank you," replied the happy commander; "but I want nothing. You know that, sir".

"Just name it," Ingram persisted. "I want to show you how happy and proud we all are!"

Phillips sighed deeply and finally said, "All right, sir. Please don't take Winchell with you. He brought us such wonderful luck!"

Admiral Ingram was rewarded with a thirty-day leave—a holiday back home with his kin at Coronado, California. When he returned to Natal, he sent for me. "Your tour of duty is about up, right?"

"Yes, sir."

"Why not stick around here a few days or so? You may enjoy a delightful surprise."

A naval observer, walking by the open tent, spotted me. "Well, aren't you the lucky one, though!" he exclaimed. "One of the ferry command just set down to pick up some gear. It is bound for Miami. Get aboard!"

Ingram looked at me and shook his head. "You'll be sorry when you read about it," he said cryptically.

I got my laundry and toothbrush and followed the observer to the "prop" plane aiming home. As we hastened to it, a civilian jumped back into an open shack.

I learned weeks later that the "civilian" was a Secret Service man who was casing every spot (with other Feds) where some assassin might lurk.

Because the plane paused at various South American airfields where they close "the store" at sundown and go home, I was waiting to be checked by quarantine medics at Miami (a twenty-two-hour hop from Natal) when I was greeted by reporters from the Miami *Herald.*

"Mr. Knight [John Knight, publisher]" said the reporter, "wants to see you at once."

"I have to report to the Commandant of the Seventh Naval District first," I reminded him.

He waited until I reported to Admiral Kauffman at HQ on Flagler Street. At the *Herald,* Mr. Knight with his other chiefs excitedly said: "Did you see him? What happened?"

"See who?" I asked Knight.

"Oh, my goodness!" he exclaimed. "He doesn't know!"

"I don't understand," I said.

My publisher in Miami then told me.

Ingram had kept telling me to stay a while for a "surprise." The big surprise that Admiral Ingram wanted me to enjoy was the arrival at Natal, a few hours after I left, of FDR; Harry Hopkins; FDR's son, General Elliott Roosevelt; the President's physician, Admiral Ernest King; and a few others! They were on their way to Casablanca for the historic conference with Churchill and Stalin! As Admiral Ingram's temporary Intelligence aide, I would have accompanied him when he greeted the presidential party. Hopkins, who liked me (he told Robert E. Sherwood, who put it in one of his books), or perhaps FDR might have invited me to go along.

Dammit! What rotten luck! History almost touched me.

Mr. Knight, I prefer to believe, still thinks I was being a good Intelligence agent for our country—that I kept my mouth shut when our President was making a secret plane trip.

During the war, no newspaper (or any publication) may report or reveal the movements of naval vessels or officers. But I didn't know. Mr. Knight knew! And he was twenty-two hours by air from Natal.

In 1947 the "civilian" who had jumped back into a shack as I hastened to the Miami-bound plane wrote a book, *Reilly of the White House,* with William J. Slocum for Simon and Schuster. In it, the Secret Service bodyguard for FDR mentioned the scene:

"At Natal I inspected the Pan American Airways base where the President was to disembark from his plane. I started to walk out on the pier, when I saw a man at its end looking over a Clipper lashed to the pier. It was Walter Winchell, then on Navy duty. I quickly ducked into a near-by warehouse, out the opposite side, into my car, and got out of there pronto. Winchell was a great friend of FDR's, a frequent presidential visitor, and I knew my maneuvers were unnecessary. Just reflex action, I guess."

Michael F. Reilly also sent me this: "The reason I didn't stop to say hello in Natal was that I didn't want to burden you with an additional secret [FDR's trip to Casablanca] if that was a secret to you. Knowing your admiration for him, I knew then as I do now that you would be the last to use the story if you thought it would jeapordize him in any way. In a sense, you too were his bodyguard."

Mark Twain always thanked people who wrote words to or about him with this brief reply: "Thanks for your kind letter. Some people can live three months on a compliment—and so can [signature] Mark Twain."

I used Twain's words to thank that Secret Service man.

★

ALEXANDER WOOLLCOTT

Back in the Prohibition era, Cornelius "Sonny" Whitney of the Social Register—one of the world's richest walking banks—had made a wager of twenty-five thousand dollars with another wealthy New Yorker that he could make the rounds of the Broadway places for a fortnight and not be recognized.

Whitney's disguise, I was tipped, was very dark Hollywood-movie-star specs, plus a red wig. I printed it twenty-four hours before he would have won the bet. A dirty trick (as the saying doesn't go), but triffic Winchelliana.

Steve Hanaghan, then press agent for Coca-Cola, Sun Valley, the Union Pacific, and the new city of Miami Beach, Florida (in the early 1930's), came to see me about the item. He was very mizzable about it. He said that Sonny Whitney was one of his new clients. Would I promise that I would never again mention Sonny's name in the paper—without first "checking" with him?

I reported that, too. "Steve Hanaghan," ran the item, "who is supposed to be a press agent is really a suppress-agent!"

The above happened over forty years ago. I never met Sonny Whitney until one night recently at El Morocco, midtown's popular swank sip-and-sup spot for show-offs.

"I don't hold it against you, but you ruined my bet. I've always wanted to ask you," he said, "how you knew."

"I never reveal a souse," I kidded.

"Was it Neysa?" he cross-examined.

"No, it was not."

"Okay," he said affably, returning to the dance floor.

Of course I did not "recall" the source. Actually it was Alexander Woollcott—one of his Best False-Friends.

Drama critic Woollcott was once buttonholed by an actor he had panned the night before. "Despite your opinion of my acting," protested the aggrieved one, "I had the audience glued in their seats."

To which the critic said, "How clever of you to think of it."

Mr. Woollcott's reviews were more entertaining than the plays he assassinated.

When I asked why he wasted so much space on plays he detested, he once told me, "Just because a show is dull is no reason my opinions should be."

Playgoers and other drama-page readers read Woollcott before they read his competitors, albeit *Variety*'s annual box score on critics invariably had him last.

When he finally was persuaded to read his true-murder-mystery sagas on the radio, he told the network chiefs, "I'll do it if you get Winchell to introduce me at my first broadcast."

I did so, happy to be his straight man.

His weekly program caught on with listeners coast to coast who had read his tales about famous slayers (Lizzie Borden was his pet) in his articles and books. Alex had found a new career. Very happy man.

None of us at the First Nights suspected that he was so ill he would soon die. In 1943 he collapsed at the microphones—the way I suspect he wanted to make his Big Exit—Going to Press.

Woollcott's will requested that his ashes be interred on the campus of his alma mater, Hamilton College, in Clinton, New York. Classmates, alumni, faculty members, chums were present at the interment. It was a miserable day. Torrential rains flooded the grounds. The ankles of mourners were deep in mud. Their clothing was drenched. That was nothing compared to somebody's Big Goof. As they lowered the urn containing Alex's ashes, they discovered the string was too short. The urn was dropped into the rain-filled hole, where it made such a plopp that it splashed muddy aqua in the faces of the mourners. To which a wag Woollcott'd a crack Alex would have loved:

"A critic to the end!"

★

OKLAHOMA!

As I said at the Lambs Club salute to Richard Rodgers in 1968, he and I go back a long time to when Rodgers and Hart's score for the *Garrick Gaieties* lit up the skies—from the Garrick Theater to all the other Enchanted Evenings along the Grandest Canyon by Dick and Larry, Dick and Oscar, and Dick and Dick.

The time: When we covered the First Nights as dramatic critic on the New York *Evening Graphic* in the early 1920's.

Our notice was a rave. But so were all our other quotes about their clix—up through Dick's *No Strings.* "The Sweetest Sounds I Ever Heard Are Still Inside My Head"—and Heart.

"The Height of something or other," I once colyum'd, "would be for Walter Winchell to get sore because somebody wrote something about him!" But when I wearied of reading a bit of bunk pinned on me about the wonderful hit musical *Oklahoma!,* I wrote the editor of *Harper's* requesting that the record be set straight. The request was ignored.

It all began when Helene Hanff, a woman attached to the Theater Guild press office, wrote the misinformation for *Harper's,* which introduced Miss Hanff's article with: "A reformed theatrical press agent recalls a chapter in her past which taught her—among other things—that even a Broadway columnist can miss a hit."

Miss Hanff reported that when the great production, originally christened *Away We Go,* was trying out in New Haven, "Winchell's Girl Friday came to see it and wired her boss, 'No Legs, No Jokes, No Chance!' " Miss Hanff also reported that I had shown that telegram to one of the show's top backers, who "was at the moment to be pulling his $30,000 out of the show."

Reader's Digest reprinted the article. The Dije editors also shrugged off my protest. One of the *Oklahoma!* stars (Celeste Holm) did a piece for *Look* magazine in 1968 and echo'd the same erratum.

The facts: My Girl Friday has never seen a show outside of New York. She has never been in New Haven. She never sent me such a telegram. It was the late Mike Todd who didn't give the new musical a chance. In the New Haven lobby at intermission, Todd was heard to say: "No jokes, no tits, no chance."

181

Miss Hanff apparently didn't look up the *Oklahoma!* files and research my rave review. One paragraph began: "One of the most startling things about *Oklahoma!* is that the tardy arriver is the sufferer—for the first seven minutes of the show offer two of its best melodies. Imagine that . . . two hits almost before you've made a memo of the first. These delightful songs are called 'Oh, What A Beautiful Morning' (which is sure to sweep the land) and 'The Surrey With the Fringe on Top.' "

Six months later—after *Oklahoma!* had been a daily sellout from the First Night (and for many years)—composer Richard Rodgers invited me to share his table for two in Sardi's. He was dining solo.

"Remember the paragraph I ran after all the *Oklahoma!* notices embraced it? When I revealed how you listened to the New Haven lobby crowd to hear what was being said and you heard Mike Todd tell a group of Broadway people: 'No Jokes, No Tits, No Chance!' "

Richard smiled and said yes.

"And now," we quipped, "NO TICKETS!"

I ran that exchange with Richard in next day's column.

Of course I laundered it: "No Jokes, No Legs, No Chance."

Imagine my astonishment years later when Helene Hanff put that wrong guess in my mouth instead of Mike Todd's big one.

Talk about getting a good gag scrood up. Wow! And so her inaccurate lulu is in the show biz history tomes. (Dammit.)

☆

Playwright Noel Coward, a longtime favorite with Americans, alienated many of them in 1944 with snide comments about soldiers from Brooklyn in his book *Middle East Diary*. The slurs were challenged by this reporter.

Many organizations complained to officials in Washington, D.C., demanding that Mr. Coward be listed persona non grata. There was no official action taken, but Great Britain's Home Office contacted friends of mine to find out "if Winchell would accept a written apology for all Americans" from Coward.

The written regrets were played big in *Stars and Stripes,* the official U.S. Army newspaper.

Mr. Coward's apology, in part: "Dear Walter: I am deeply sorry that any offense was construed from my book particularly by the good people of Brooklyn. I hope that my sincere and lifelong friendship for America, so often expressed, will be taken into consideration. Whether a mere author ever visits your country again is unimportant; it is important that our enemies fail in their unceasing efforts to cause misunderstanding between us. I am sorry my careless words—for that is all they were—provided some opportunity for misunderstanding. Won't you please convey my regret?—Noel."

I quoted him on my coast-to-coast newscast and in my syndicated column. To which I added: "Dear Noel: All people of goodwill understand goodwill in others. Some mighty unkind things, too, have been said about England in America as well as about America in England.

"But what are a few paragraphs by us writers when our armed forces are writing such mighty chapters together?—Walter."

★

MURDER, INC. PROBE PHONY?

A newspaper editor friend of mine on the late New York *Journal* was "permanently" assigned to cover District Attorney Thomas E. Dewey until Dewey left office in 1942 for Albany and the governship. So what my editor friend told me may be rated authentic.

When William O'Dwyer's office launched its Murder, Inc. probe, Mr. Dewey's staffers immediately labeled the inquiry a phony and correctly judged it an attempt by the mobsters to try to offset the tremendous job that Dewey was doing with his able assistants, Murray Gurfein, Sol Gelb, Frank Hogan, Jake Rosenbloom, *et al.*

If newspaper people look back, they will agree the judgment of Dewey and his aides was correct and will find that O'Dwyer's men did not get a single big-name gangman in their entire inquiry—except for Lepke, chief of Murder, Inc. The mob ordered Abe Reles and other gangsters to give the remarkable Burton Turkus, the prosecutor of Murder, Inc., enough information so that Mr. Turkus could prove Lepke guilty of murder. And they got him only because the Lep surrendered to the FBI through this errand boy for the lawmen and the mob. All the other criminals trapped in the Murder, Inc. net were punks of no stature—merely evil men.

Mr. Reles was the principal canary. He kept "singing" because he had official permission to do so by Albert "Mr. A." Anastasia. But Reles sang lustily—too lustily. His vocalizing made top gang people realize that they had created a Frankenstein monster. It suddenly dawned on them that once Reles ran out of songs for Mr. Turkus, he could and would be taken over by Dewey's people and made to sing on more important gang leaders—far more important than Lepke, who was rotting in a cell and who eventually went to The Chair.

And so Reles had to be done in. But who did it?

He was being protected in a Coney Island hotel by several detectives. They said Reles fell from his room window. The legend persists, however, that Abe was flung from it.

Mr. Dewey and his staff had a low opinion of O'Dwyer. They cited an incident at the height of the Murder, Inc. investigation when O'Dwyer was as much of a hero as Dewey.

This was some time before mobster Bugsy Siegel was carbine'd to death in Beverly Hills. O'Dwyer summoned the press to his office for a conference. He announced that the Kingpin of the Rackets in New York was Bugsy and that he, O'Dwyer, personally was going to California to arrange for Siegel's extradition to Brooklyn, where he could be tried for murder.

The day O'Dwyer left for Los Angeles, the source for the above (a *Journal* editor) luncheoned with three of Dewey's staff. They predicted O'Dwyer would return empty-handed—that "he had no intention" of bringing back Bugsy because the Murder, Inc. landlords "wouldn't allow Siegel to be touched." And they were exactly right. O'Dwyer returned to New York alone.

About ten days later he told the press that he had been wrong in his earlier opinion of Siegel—that Siegel had nothing to do with New York rackets and had no part in the continuing inquiry of Murder, Inc.

And the continuing Murder, Inc. inquiry continued to bring in exactly nothing—as was intended from its inception.

After the final curtain had dropped on a new play, I was strolling along Broadway. I paused at a newsstand to look at the front pages of the *News* and *Mirror*. Both devoted the entire front page to Lepke's covered corpse being wheeled into a mortuary wagon at Sing Sing— after he had fried in the electric chair.

I shuddered and turned away. If he hadn't surrendered, maybe . . .

Why did he burn in the chair, you may wonder, if the FBI had authorized me to announce publicly that he was guaranteed safe delivery to the G-men if he surrendered? That's another creepy saga. It follows.

The New York *Herald Tribune* was the Voice of the Republican party. The *Trib* thumped Thomas E. Dewey—its choice for President in 1944. It was District Attorney Dewey who became governor of New

York following prosecution of Lepke. It made him governor. Why not President?

When Dewey competed for the White House against Roosevelt, the President told me, "He's the dirtiest pool shooter I ever saw."

He despised Mr. Dewey. And Mr. Dewey vice versa'd.

As the 1944 national election was coming up the *Tribune*'s leading editorial one morning lead off with this barrage: "What is this unusual camaraderie that appears to exist between Murder, Incorporated, the White House, the FBI, and Walter Winchell?"

President Roosevelt, who had read New York City's only GOP newspaper, sent for Steve Early, his press chief. "What is this?" he demanded.

"Politics, Mr. President," said Steve. "Dirty politics."

"I know that," said FDR irritably. "But why do they drag me into it?"

"Dewey wants to be President," testified Steve. "He became governor following conviction of Lepke and other gangsters in Murder, Inc. The mobsters asked Winchell to find out if John Edgar would be interested in Lepke's surrender. Winchell told John. John told Walter to proceed, but no deals of any kind."

Of course Lepke and the mob had wanted their leader to come in to the Feds. Dewey's lawmen were also breathing down the necks of the whole gang—and a stretch in a federal clink would be a lot cozier than Dewey's electric chair at Ossining.

"Lepke," continued Steve Early, "was given fourteen years by Judge Knox at Leavenworth. But the *Tribune* and Dewey hope to smear the Democratic party and this administration by implying that we all grabbed Lepke to hurt Dewey's chance of election."

The President's fury atomic'd. Waving his right arm in a sweeping gesture he bellowed: "Tell the Attorney General to turn him over! Turn the sonofabitch over!"

Louis "Lepke" Buchalter, president of Murder, Inc. (former Public Enemy Number One), died in the electric chair on March 5, 1944. Not for over 110 murders by his killers—but for the slaying of a Brooklyn merchant.

How did they trace the murder to Lepke? An alert detective, inspecting the unlucky's man's body, exclaimed: "Welllll, look who was here. The Signature!"—the New York Police Department's affectionate nickname for a hoodlum who was never satisfied that the victim was very dead. He always stood over the body and emptied his gat to make sure.

The bullets always were in a straight line: one-two-three-four-five-six, between the groin and throat. Thus: "The Signature." When he was arrested, he copped a plea. For revealing that it was Lepke who got him to kill the man, he was rewarded with a short sentence.

I presume they have since met again in hell.

☆

FDR surrendered to the delegates at Chicago in 1944 when they booed every mention of Henry Wallace's name. He told them—in a note read to the conventioneers—"As you know, I have run and won with Wallace before . . ."

The booing was thunderous and endless. Bob Hannigan, reading FDR's message to them, could not continue for nearly an hour. Every time he started to read the rest of the message and got to Wallace's name, the booing got louder and longer. Deafening.

Hannegan, who was Harry S Truman's pal and booster for the veep slot, wanted to report to the throng that FDR said, "In the event you do not want Mr. Wallace to run with me, I have five other names for you to consider."

The first name was Mr. Justice Douglas of the High Court.

Mr. Hannegan (when the mob of delegates wearied of booing and shouting No, No, No!) yelled: "How about Senator Harry Truman?"

The roof of the Convention Hall almost blew off from the blast of cheers—as delegates have a habit of doing when they have a gat at their back.

Then there was the time FDR gleefully told me about Commissioner Elrod, a Chicago Democrat chief.

"You know Elrod?" asked the President of the United States.

"Met him once between trains in Chicago on the way to Hollywood. Pleasant person, I thought. I was introduced to him by one of Al Capone's top men."

"Pleasant?" edited FDR. "He's a magician! Elrod's ward controls three thousand, nine hundred and ninety-eight votes. But he's generous to the Republicans. He always gives them two!"

Our President enjoyed bragging that elections out there were gimmicked! I couldn't believe my ears. Politics. Hmmmm.

I eventually met all of FDR's family except his wife. Met Mrs. R. years later. Introduced to daughter Anna. Knew the four sons, Jimmy, Elliott, Frank, and John, who were Stork Club habitués. John, you may recall, voted Republican.

In the bitter fight on foreign policy in 1939 no one remained more

186

objective than FDR. He had paled with anger only once: when Senator Burton Wheeler charged that he planned to plow under every third American boy.

Recovering his composure, FDR had remarked: "A strange policy for a man who has four sons of his own."

Now, one day after a press conference, I told Mr. Roosevelt that his sons' war records were being attacked daily by several solons in both houses; that I knew about Jimmy having lost three-fourths of his stomach following several major operations from wounds; that Elliott and his crew had had to come down in the Newfoundland wasteland while on a mission to rescue another plane in trouble—and how they had all suffered many days and nights until both planes and crews were found; that Frank had jumped over the side of a destroyer in mid-Atlantic in a vain attempt to save a Negro sailor blown overboard in a storm; and that John, their baby, had also served.

The President pointed his index digit at me and said, "Forget it."

"But Mr. President," I persisted, "I think their war records should be made public—to shut up their stupid and uninformed critics!"

"I said," FDR admonished, "forget it."

I slumped in my chair alongside his desk. Disappointed, defeated. As I got up and requested "permission to go ashore, sir," FDR motioned for me to sit down. He opened a desk drawer, picked out a letter, and read part of it.

"Dear Pop," it began, "I only hope one of us gets killed. Maybe then 'they' will stop picking on the rest of the family."

I had seen and heard FDR laugh at jokes and stories, but I had never seen a President weep. His eyes filled. He tried to swallow a lump that stuck in his throat. He put the letter back in the drawer.

I turned my face away, so he would not be embarrassed about his tears. I always suspected that the letter he read had come from Elliott.

The next day was Saturday. My weekly newscast was the next night. Saturday evening I picked up a helluva beat. But I couldn't use it without also reporting what FDR had told me to "forget."

So I telegraphed his wife at Hyde Park: "WILL YOU PLEASE GET YOUR HUSBAND TO RELEASE ME FROM A PLEDGE NOT TO MAKE PUBLIC WHAT HE KNOWS I KNOW ABOUT YOUR SONS' BRAVERY IN ACTION. THANKS. WINCHELL."

She responded immediately: "IF HE TOLD YOU NOT TO DO IT DON'T DO IT. ELEANOR ROOSEVELT."

I had never violated a confidence before. Now I did that very thing to our President. Because of that darling-of-a-scoop I got Saturday night. It ended the newscast like so:

> I have some exclusive news for the few members of the Senate and Congress who keep picking on the excellent war records of the four Roosevelt boys. I also have unhappy news for Congressman Lambertson, the most persistent attacker of FDR and his sons, all of whom performed heroic war duty without publicity.
>
> Congressman Lambertson of Kansas! Your son was arrested last night for dodging the draft as a conscientious objector! Good night!

Following the newscast I did the Washington rounds with newspaper people—winding up at the Hotel Shoreham about 3:00 A.M. I read the papers, did a column, and got to sleep around 6:30.

I told the hotel phone operator that I had been fighting a typewriter all night and was pooped. My only protection from people who always want something is the phone operator. "Please," I said, "no calls of any kind, not even if there's a fire in the next room! That goes for the President of the United States!"

The girl laughed.

"I understand," she chuckled. "Not even if the President calls."

I guess I dropped off a few moments later. At 8:45 A.M. the phone bells sounded like gongs. "Sorry," said the chief operator of the hotel, "the White House is calling," and she connected the caller—Grace Tully, FDR's confidential Girl Friday.

"Goooood morrrrnnnninnnngggg," greeted Grace. "That was quite a performance you put on last night at nine."

"Did you hear it?"

"Everybody heard it."

"Every-Bodddeeeee?"

"Mr. Everybody heard it!" she giggled.

"Oh, brother! I guess I'm in the doghouse."

"I don't know, but you're wanted at the White House in a hurry—so you can come and go without your colleagues seeing you. They come in about nine-thirty or earlier sometimes. Hurry, please." She hung up.

I hastened into my threads. After a speedy face and hand wash, I paused at a drugstore for orange juice and black java—and got to Miss Tully's office (outside the President's) in minutes.

Oh, boy! (Whew!) He's going to give me hell or demote me back to apprentice seaman.

The usual greeting of "Good morning" (as you walked quickly to his desk) didn't welcome me. He was busy signing papers.

Grace ushered me to the chair I always sat in alongside of him. I sat there rigid, like a schoolboy hailed before the principal for misconduct or something.

"Why doesn't he look up and say hello?" I worried. On his desk right in front of me—to his left—were the Washington *Post* and *Times-Herald*. Grace or someone on his press staff had circled the front-page stories in green crayon.

The headlines were almost identical: "SOLON'S SON ARRESTED AS DRAFT DODGER!"

FDR pushed aside the letters he had signed, removed his eyeglasses and, with his long cigarette holder pointed to the headlines, smiled and softly said, "Thanks."

What a relief! I went limp in the chair.

"How did you know?" he asked. "How did you find that out?"

"I got it," I kidded, "from somebody who promised to keep it a secret."

From the front page of the Tampa *Daily Times*, December 18, 1944: "WINCHELL TALK NABS KILLER HERE. POLICE HOLD MAN WANTED IN VERMONT." The same day Tampa Chief of Police J. L. Eddings confirmed the arrest with this letter: "As a result of your broadcast the night before and the description of Harold Frotten, 26, wanted for murder of Robert Stratton at Bennington, Vermont, Frotten was apprehended in Tampa early this morning. He admitted his identity and the murder."

F. E. Jones: "Impatient soldiers overseas waiting for Returnity."

Wire from Dorothy Parker, January 6th, 1945:

"Dear Walter: This is a real SOS. There is a show called *A Salute to the Wounded* at Madison Square Garden Tuesday night January ninth at 8:30. It is sponsored by the Shipbuilders Union and it truly is of importance as laborers' earnest patriot efforts to do something—in this case to raise $50,000—to buy comforts for the wounded. Well, it would be cruel if the Garden is not filled and in confidence it looks a little rocky, mainly because through inexperience the shipbuilders did not place the project in good hands. Oh, if you would just mention it on the air tomorrow night you would do such a service for the servicemen, for labor and for all other decent people."

The afternoon of January 9 I received the following telegram from her:

"BECAUSE OF YOU THE GARDEN IS SOLD OUT FOR TO-NIGHT. HUNDREDS OF OUR WOUNDED WILL BE MADE HAPPY AND LABOR AND SERVICEMEN WILL BE FRIENDS FOR ALWAYS. GOD BLESS YOU, WALTER."

★

CURTAIN SPEECHES

The passing of Booth Tarkington, a popular author, was a radio scoop for me, thanks to Herbert R. Hill of the Indianapolis *News*, an "opposition" newspaper. Mr. Hill sent the following memo to my Girl Friday:

"Although Mr. Winchell's column appears in an opposition paper here, and although the *News'* radio station is not ABC, I acted on impulse in calling the ABC news room. W.W. got the flash on the air only a few moments after Mr. Tarkington died. It was a clean beat for you, as few here or anywhere (except myself) knew of the author's incurable illness."

Memo from ABC's newsroom manager:

"Walter might be interested to know that the Tarkington beat was a thirty-minute scoop over press associations, and naturally other radio guys."

Jimmy Walker died November 18, 1946. The following was my column in the *Mirror* a few days later:

> Jimmy Walker is dead . . . The papers are filled with accounts of what a great guy he was in spite of his faults. Because he was a friend of mine—and because I like to think I hate hypocrisy as much as he did—I want to offer a correction. He was not a great guy in spite of his faults; he was a great guy because of them.
>
> As a politician, Jimmy had three faults. One, he was too brave. Two, he was sincere enough to live up to his vices publicly. And the most important and final fault of all, he ran into hard luck. It's part of our tradition to make an unlucky politician our scapegoat.

190

But it is too much for the stomach of this reporter to see people try to turn it into evidence of their own virtue.

It might have proven too much for even Jimmy's sense of humor to watch the syrupy better-than-thou's pay glowing tribute to their own pseudo-virtue by assuming a forgiving and understanding attitude—for a man who had the courage to lead the colorful life they all secretly envied.

As a matter of fact, Jimmy could see so much of every side of a question that he was in frequent demand as an arbitrator. He wasn't anything but simply American. He wasn't pro- or anti-Franco, anti- or pro-Turks, Swedes, Russians, or Hindus. He took things as he found them.

He liked everybody and nearly everybody liked him . . . his most bitter critic, Fiorello H. La Guardia, recommended him years after as the impartial arbitration chairman for the garment industry.

The two men were warm friends until the end. They used to sit around and talk about old campaigns like two opposing generals explaining their battle plans to each other. Some men live to confound their enemies—but Walker loved to confirm them as friends.

One reason is that during the trying years, he maintained his sense of humor as well as his dignity. At his investigation, James Finnegan, Brooklyn Independent, accidentally struck Walker on the shoulder with a heavy chair. "Excuse me, Mr. Mayor," said Finnegan.

"That's OK, Jim," said Walker. "I was expecting your shoe—in a different place!"

While a great deal has been said of his affection for Betty Compton, little has been written of his undying devotion to her . . . Nelson for Lady Hamilton, Abelard for Heloise, Gabriel for Evangeline were not more constant. He loved her above mere possessiveness. He shared her memory with the man she later married. They became firm friends, occupied the same apartment and took care of the children she adopted. Both of them were broad enough to accept each other as friends because of their singular love for this remarkable and beautiful woman.

Few men in history are as widely liked as they are widely known —and he was once. His faults were the warm ones: There was nothing cold or calculating in his whole makeup. Love of his fellow man was his chief characteristic.

With this infallible credential there must be someplace, somewhere for someone who could even wear a halo jauntily.

So long, Jimmy. For once, you're too early.

☆

191

Damon Runyon had been a chain smoker for many decades. I had noticed his growing hoarseness. He was persuaded to have his throat checked, and in 1944 he did. Throat cancer.

They removed his larynx and from that time on Damon, unable to speak, communicated by scribbling memos on a pad of paper. His illness did not keep him from covering major stories. One of his very best was the passing of President F. D. Roosevelt in 1945. Editors and others called that one brilliant.

He had given up drinking several years before. Now he no longer smoked. His terrible illness was compounded by further heartbreak. His second wife, whom he adored, requested a divorce, which he did not contest. As a parting gift, he went to a bank vault and removed seventy thousand dollars in cash, which he gave her "for old time's sake."

Now, sensing his loneliness, I invited him to ride in my car outfitted with a police-call radio after we both got bored in Lindy's, the Stork Club, and the other spots.

We were practically inseparable the final two years of his life. These two years—waiting for "The Big C" to kill him—were mostly spent in my "police" car, from midnight to dawn.

"Little boy stuff—cops and robbers," he heckled on his pad. Reluctantly, he went along. Runyon found so much "copy" riding in my car "chasing the burglars" that his newspaper chief, William Randolph Hearst, Sr., telegraphed from San Simeon, "Your stuff lately is just great. Do it every day!"

One night two doctors came to the Stork Club and asked the owner to tell me to go to Florida as soon as possible. My taking Damon riding nightly in the damp air was not good for him. They wanted him back at Memorial Hospital instead of in his midtown room—where a nurse reported that his agony was so terrible he tried to jump out of the window.

Damon Runyon's syndicated column included this essay less than four months before his agony ended.

Winchell is like this:

"You shouldn't let me eat anything," he said at 2:30 o'clock the other morning when the pot roast and red cabbage and potato pancakes came along. "You know how I love red cabbage and how I will suffer from it later. Pot roast will lay on my stomach like a thousand o'brick at this hour," he continues. "How many calories in a potato pancake? Look how I have to unbutton my waistband . . . No, I don't want any dessert except a little lemon ice which is non-fattening with some vanilla ice cream mixed in it and one or two small cookies—."

This patter falls on deaf ears. I discovered long ago that it is designed to keep a dining companion so absorbed in the dialogue as to forget the food and Winchell nabs all the choicest viands . . . until I got wise and learned to continue advancing steadily on the chow even under the heaviest barrage of his remarks . . .

We had one argument when he made a tremendously fast and very short turn in the car . . . I said less than an inch stood between us and headlines shouting: "Runyon and Winchell Killed." . . . "What do you mean 'Runyon and Winchell'?" he finally asked . . . "Why not 'Winchell and Runyon'? Why should you bill yourself over me? It would be 'Winchell and Runyon Killed,' " he said. . . . "Maybe 'Winchell' in very large type and 'Runyon' in smaller type."

"What about seniority?" I said. "I have been around longer than you have. Besides, I know more newspaper editors and they would give me a break!"

"No," he said. "I would positively be on top. In fact, the headlines would read 'WINCHELL KILLED' . . . and underneath, a subhead saying 'Unidentified Man With Him.' "

"If you can persuade Mr. Winchell to leave town," one medic said, "perhaps we can prolong Runyon's life a little while longer."

Shortly before he died on December 10, 1946, Damon, who had never mentioned his illness, wrote this memo to me: "Give other men monuments of stone and steel. Just give me one man to remember me once a year."

Many stage stars and showmen have Broadway theaters named for them. George M. Cohan, "Mr. Broadway" in his heyday, has a statue bearing his name—if not his likeness—at Forty-sixth Street and The Big Apple.

Mr. Runyon has the most wonderful monument of them all. Five nights after December 10 I did my usual Sunday evening radio newscast —my first chance to make a coast-to-coast appeal for funds to do something to help cancer-fighters in their research. "Let's fight back!" I ad-libbed. "Please send me a nickel, a penny, a dime, or a dollar to fight cancer. No expenses will be deducted."

Mr. and Mrs. United States—and all the ships at sea—responded at once.

The Damon Runyon Memorial Fund for Cancer Research is at 33 West 56th Street, New York City, in one of the few mansions left in Manhattan: the one-time residence of Barbara Hutton's wealthy family. The Runyon Cancer Fund has received donations totaling almost $32 million. Most of it has been allocated to cancer-warriors in the fifty United States, the District of Columbia, and twenty-six foreign countries, except Russia and satellites.

That is the living memorial to a brilliant reporter, a brave man who asked simply to be remembered once a year.

★

"MY HUSBAND IS GOING TO DIE!"

Please don't read the O. Henry switch (at the very end of my addendum) until you get to it.

Larry Thompson, one of the star essayists for the Miami *Herald,* later wrote:

> The local outlet for Winchell's national network was WQAM, then owned by the *Herald.* We had a small studio in the news room. When Winchell spent his winters in Miami, he broadcast from there. We usually had a few tourists there to watch, joining printers, pressmen and *Herald* staff members, as his audience . . . Tim Sullivan was assistant city editor and was in charge of the city desk this particular night.
>
> One moment before broadcast time Sunday evening, December 31, 1946, the ABC network's Paul Scheffels put the following emergency item under my specs: "Rudy Kovarick, 36, from Dearborn, Mich.—visitor—arrived Miami last night, has blood hemorrhage—trying locate type AB-Rh-positive blood. None in blood bank. Miami *Herald* on presses—Dr. Meadow, Biscayne Hosp. source (signed) Tim Sullivan, city desk."

I used the flash twice, emphasizing that only donors in Florida should respond. As Larry Thompson put it, "Only a few blocks from the hospital, Nathan Dash heard the broadcast on his car radio. Within minutes he was at the hospital and within minutes a direct transfusion of the rare-type blood was being received by the dying tourist from Michigan.

"But Mr. and Mrs. America (particularly Mr. and Mrs. Miami) did not know this. Cars from all parts of the county headed for the hospital. Phones in the *Herald* city room, at the hospital, at the county blood bank began to ring."

This is what happened according to the TWX machines in Miami and

194

the WJZ newsroom, Radio City, New York, as I ended the newscast at 9:15.

"9:16 P.M. att'n WW: fones going wild here. Must had 75 calls already. Still ringing like mad in all ABC offices and out of town . . . You get blood?—Madigan."

"Source Tim Sullivan (Miami *Herald*) who urged flash on air. Can't get hosp on fone, clogged there too. *Herald* on fone now—wait min pls . . . Notify Dr. Ander, Post Grad hosp (NYC) has type blood. Notify INS and *Mirror*. Fones going wild here . . . Tell Rose turn over to city desk, *Mirror*—WW."

"Hesitate send out story til sure have donor—Madigan."

"Good story showing how newspapers and radio work together to perform a public service when someone needs help. Nearly whole nation responds to total stranger 1000's miles away. Shows people are basically good—all want to do human thing. Two on way hosp now—WW."

"WW says pls thank evbody . . . Okay, we been doing that . . . How many calls? . . . Lost track. Must be in hundreds all network—Madigan."

"Attn Paul and WW: What afraid of we get in hell of spot if we tell people in NY, Chi, LA, SF, Wash, Philly, Hwood, Detroit, etc. we have donors and not the type? Better check hosps again—Madigan."

"Attn Madigan: Cant get thru Dr. Meadow. Holding line 45 mins already. Herald called. Over 300 people at hosp. Cars congesting streets. Great chance to get their names and their blood for blood banks. Dont turn away any donors. WW says be sure thank airlines, donors, hosps in NY, etc. everybody. Also Capt Eddie Rickenbacker who ordered all Eastern Airliners to wait two hours everywhere in case someone had type blood."

"We have in all cases. Get donor yet?—Madigan."

"Standby Meadow on fone now. Newsroom! No kidding this on level. TWX machine on fire. Smell burning insulation. Goodnig. . . ."

"Tell Walter gotta get announcement on air before midnight. Every station in country (also opposition) report phone boards clogged. Ask Walter will he stay on air with followup story at 11? G'by—Madigan."

Eleven P.M. Eastern Standard Time, Miami: Attention, Mr. and Mrs. United States! Just as I went on the air tonight at nine I received word that a dying man needed type AB-Rh-positive blood; that the type had been exhausted and would not be available until nine tomorrow morning. The wife of the dying man phoned the Miami *Herald* and asked reporters: "Isn't there anything you newspapermen can do to help save my husband? My husband is going to die! Please?"

Tim Sullivan of the *Herald,* a trigger-thinker, rushed the flash to me. I used it twice. I have never witnessed such a remarkable demonstration of brotherhood. Brotherly love ... Or just plain down-to-earth willingness to help a man fallen by the wayside. Here is a stranger named Rudy Kovarick, thirty-six, of Dearborn, Michigan, suddenly stricken in Miami.

The local newspapers and radio aroused almost an entire nation ... Nobody stopped to ask, "Is he black, brown, white, or yellow? Is he a Jew, Protestant, Catholic, or atheist?" . . . Nobody said anything, just: "I have that type blood and I want to help."

I just learned that some man chartered a plane from Augusta, Georgia. In Georgia! . . . Imagine! Where they'd have you believe some folks hate people. But you see—they don't at all. They are, as sailors say, good peoples. People everywhere are basically good. It makes you feel good all over.

Thanks, too, to all the phone operators at the *Herald,* radio stations coast to coast, everywhere. Just a minute, please. They tell me Dr. Meadow phoned and has what he needs. So thanks to all, also airlines in NY, Miami, etc. Thanks also to Dr. Meadow from the man's wife for contacting my newspaper, the Miami *Herald*—Miami police wonderful help, too. Oh, yes, this is great! . . . They just told me that two Georgians (with type of blood) persuaded two others en route to Miami to give them their seats so they could help save a life. Hooray for the Georgians and the two strangers who gave up their seats. What a week for somebody to do a good deed —Christmas week! Talk about your Good Samaritans . . . People are beautiful . . . beautiful!

Now you-all looka here! You all wanted to give your blood tonight. How about giving it tomorrow or next week or whenever? So that never again will a human being have to wait until the next day when his life can be saved tonight! Oh, I almost forgot! . . . Most of the willing donors in Miami (as you might have suspected) are war veterans!

Flash! Miami! The stricken man received the transfusion just a few minutes ago. He is showing signs of recovery . . . I haven't yet found out the name of the donor. But I hear he is here visiting from New York City. So Mr. and Mrs. America thank you all very much and goodnight.

196

Hours later, we learned the donor's name. He is Nathan Dash. Lives at 1527 Northwest 59th Street, Miami. Thank you, Mr. Dash, from every American from border to border and coast to coast.

Now have some irony. Dr. Edward Meadow, owner of the Biscayne Hospital, Miami, died suddenly in October 1948. He was thirty-nine. The nurse, Mrs. Marie Reneger, was stabbed to death with a Japanese Marine dagger (a souvenir) by her husband (an ex-marine), a veteran of Guadalcanal, who went berserk. Nurse Reneger also was thirty-nine. Her husband was an escaped patient from a Hollywood (Florida) mental hospital. The Reneger story is in the Miami *Herald* files.

But this O. Henry twist-ending isn't in anybody's files.

Mrs. Nathan Dash gave birth to a boy on August 23, 1947—almost a year after her husband's blood saved Mr. Kovarick's life.

Three days after the birth, the baby died from erythroblastosis—which occurs when the mother has Rh-negative blood type and the father Rh-positive.

Medics tried to save the baby by transfusions—generously donated by a man named Jerry Riggs of Netcong, New Jersey, a stranger.

"Oh, Walter," wrote Nathan Dash in February 1948, "what irony. My blood saved a man's life—and yet, because of it, my son died."

★

WHO KILLED BUGSY SIEGEL?

Gang chieftain Ben "Bugsy" Siegel, who crashed "society" when he romanced American-born Countess Dorothy di Frasso, was slain in his Beverly Hills home while viewing television with a pal named Smiley. The killer was never caught.

The newspapers and other news media offered various "clues." None of them were confirmed. The big buzz was that Siegel was shot dead by gunsles hired by owners of a Chicago racing wire service that Bugs had reportedly tried to muscle in on.

Another wild legend: He was killed by the brother of his favorite sweetheart, Virginia Hill. Miss Hill's kid brother—an ex-Marine—was a carbine marksman. But Siegel and the young man were very friendly.

The gang chief made things comfortable for him: put him in good paying jobs, etc. There was no reason for newspaper people and others to suggest that he "did it."

Another "story" was that Siegel was done in by in-laws after Bugsy allegedly personally squandered a million dollars of their backing for a Vegas hotel. All bunk.

The following lowdown, relayed by one of my former editors, is probably the truth. He told me his sources were Thomas E. Dewey (when he was still district attorney) and Frank Hogan (when he was Mr. Dewey's chief aide).

Bugsy came to Los Angeles with $4 million given him by colleagues in "the New York Syndicate," a fancy name for gang. Siegel's confrères included the late Lucky Luciano, Lepke, and other mobsters with wealth. They instructed Siegel to arrange a syndicate setup on the West Coast, which up to that time (the late 1930's) had been left unorganized by the Eastern Establishment.

Bugsy, a handsome man, immediately became the playboy he longed to be. He housed his sweedee, Virginia Hill, in a classy home in Beverly Hills and crashed the Hollywood elite. He "romanced" the late Billy Wilkerson, publisher of *The Hollywood Reporter,* a daily movie-trade paper. Mr. Wilkerson touted Siegel that Las Vegas was going to become a boom burg.

Siegel, silly boy, used the New York mob's money to build the first elegant hotel in Vegas, the Flamingo. It was an immediate flop—mainly because Bugs knew less about running such a place than anyone. (One-armed Wingy Grober, former gaming house "stickman" [the fellow with the long hooked stick to stop the cube-tosser between bets], had the right idea—to keep up a running patter of gambling logic. Sample: "The less you bet, the more you lose when you win!")

A former gang partner interceded for Siegel with the mob. Bugs won an extension of time to return the $4 mill. But he couldn't raise that kind of money—and orders went out to the Brooklyn troops to "hit him."

Murder, Inc. tycoons assigned marksmen Happy Maione and Dasher Abbandando to execute Bugs. Bang-Bang-Bang! And Mr. Siegel went straight to the cemetery.

At the New York trial of Happy and Dasher, the State's witness was Sholem Bernstein. He testified that he had stolen a car in Los Angeles and used it to drive Happy and Dasher to Bugsy's home and back to the hideaway. Bernstein said he then disposed of the car. Maione, Abbandando, and Bernstein returned to Brooklyn.

All of this happened in three days. The slayers of Bugsy (Maione and "Abbadabba" Abbandando) along with "Pittsburgh Phil" Strauss were among the several Murder, Inc. chiefs who were tried, convicted, and fried in Sing Sing—for murders in New York City, not for Siegel's assassination. That was a California case.

Memo from my source—an editor on the New York *Journal-American:* "That's the Bugsy story in brief. I was saving it for a book I'll never do. If you want it, I will give you the details of the Dewey-Hogan feelings (backed by evidence) of the actual worth of Murder, Inc."

In essence, we learned the real story of what a Mafiasco the mob really was: a Big Phony. We are hoarding it like a miser for another nonbook. If, that is, we are ever invited to jot one down again.

★

LUCKY LUCIANO, JR.

This is another story never before made public.

Lucky Luciano was one of the smartest gangsters of them all—so smart he wound up getting thirty to fifty years in prison following conviction for almost everything.

But Luciano kept getting luckier. After World War II Governor Dewey commuted Luciano's sentence on the condition that he be deported to Italy, never to return.

U.S. Naval Intelligence, the Secret Service, and other government sleuths never confirmed the reason for Lucky's release. The newspapers, however, believed the never-denied "rumors" that Lucky had won his release because he performed a service for the United States.

The legend goes (and I believe it) that Lucky provided information to the U.S. Navy for the invasion of Sicily; that he convinced his "cousins" in the Mafia, Cosa Nostra, and the mobs to sabotage Mussolini's and Hitler's ships and ammo depots in Italy and do other helpful jobs—all of which helped shorten World War II and enabled the United States and our Allies to win it.

All of the above has been published in part. But not this: There was a Lucky Luciano, "Jr.," whom the mob chief "adopted" when the "son" was a grown man.

"Junior" was born in the United States . . . a personable fellow and well-mannered gentleman. His parents were Italians—from the old country. This man introduced himself to Lucky in a Broadway barbershop.

He told him his parents had been born in the same town where Luciano's parents once dwelled. He named streets, avenues, and places in that burg, names of neighbors, shops, stores, buildings, and so on.

Lucky reminisced with him about Italy, Sicily, Naples: Roma, the Via Veneto, etc. The barrier that Mr. Luciano always put up with intimates and strangers came down. A warm friendship followed.

The man became one of Lucky's "aides." He sat in on some confabs with Murder, Inc. and allied gangs. This respectable and charming man became one of the mob. A gangster!

Lucky was so devoted to him he adopted him. The Mobfia called him Lucky, Jr. This "ingrate" was the man who helped New York State send Luciano to prison.

He was not a stool pigeon or an FBI agent. He was a federal man, still living, whose real name would be a joy to Lucky's avengers.

He was an expert on narcotic smugglers, users, and sellers. He was also a very talented actor.

In 1947 the Chicago *Herald-American* requested a message from me to the over three thousand newsboys of Chiacgo. It was published in a small magazine, *Carrier's Voice:*

> I earn a living not because of what I write on a typewriter, but because millions of people read the newspapers you distribute. So, as far as I am concerned, you are engaged in the most important business in the world. For my money, the boy who puts the newspaper on the front porch is just as important as the man who puts milk on the back porch or the ice in the icebox.
>
> I was a carrier myself. I think anybody working around newspapers is in the best business in the world. Our job is to get the most perishable commodity in the world—fresh news—to market instantly. And that takes the best efforts of everybody, from the chief editor to the carriers. A deadline to a reporter is what the gong is to a prizefighter. You come out fighting and on your toes. But the pay-off is not on how quickly the reporter gets the story to the city desk, but how effectively you carriers get the story to the streets.
>
> We're the only profession in the world that puts a fresh idea on a man's front porch every day for a few cents. And the ideas of our free press are good enough that most dictators threaten to shoot anybody reading an American newspaper.
>
> This is not a word of encouragement to you, at all. It's a note of

appreciation to you as my fellow newspapermen and my fellow American citizens, doing one of the most necessary jobs in the nation today.

If the Statue of Liberty could have children, the first thing she'd want them to be would be newspaper carriers.

★

QUOTE UNQUOTE

"Winchell is America's No. 1 Warmonger."—Russian Ambassador Andrei Vishinsky.

From the editorial pages of all Hearst newspapers October 7, 1947: "WINCHELL ANSWERS VISHINSKY'S CHARGES."

"Following is the text of Walter Winchell's reply to Soviet Deputy Foreign Minister Vishinsky's charges of warmongering, as given by Mr. Winchell in his radio broadcast of Sept. 28:"

Attention, Mr. and Mrs. United States—

The Deputy Foreign Minister of Russia, Mr. Vishinsky, has charged that our country—the United States—is seeking war. And that I among others am a warmonger . . .

Mr. Vishinsky flatly stated that the Marshall Plan was an American attack on the nation of Europe. Now, let's look at some facts.

Mr. Vishinsky, you charge that American corporations made large profits during the last war. From whom?

It certainly couldn't have been from other countries—or lend-lease wouldn't have been necessary. Your country and a lot of others got much of the goods that these corporations manufactured. But none has paid back a cent. The American government paid for the goods and then gave the goods away to your country along with a lot of others. Therefore the American people will have to pay the bill for the whole war—over two hundred and fifty billions of dollars.

In the last two years those same corporations which you charge made such huge profits paid into the United States Treasury over thirty billions.

Part of these corporate taxes went to pay off the deficit of lend-lease. In short, these same corporations are making up in taxes the losses caused the American government because your country hasn't paid its bills.

201

You were glad to get the products of these corporations less than three years ago. Josef Stalin himself said that without American help Russia could not have survived. Well, these same corporations provided eighty-five percent of that help. We are not claiming a life-saving medal from Russia, but we don't deserve to be blackjacked from behind our backs either.

At the present rate that they are paying taxes, these same American corporations will put twice as much into the public treasury as they now have in profits. Since Americans will pay the whole cost of the war, how can you say—with a straight face—that Americans want war for profit? For what? So that we can owe ourselves more money? . . .

That is why you Communists are worried, Mr. Vishinsky. Your system can't compete with ours. The Marshall Plan shows you that our free enterprise economy can give away to other nations more than your communistic system can give to its own people. You are afraid to let the world and the Russian people know that, even with our high prices, an American worker gets over ten times as much as a Russian worker.

Official Soviet wage charts show that for doing exactly the same work, for every two pounds of bread a Russian worker can buy, an American worker can buy twenty-four.

For every pound of butter a worker gets in Russia, an American worker gets fourteen. For every pound of sugar a Russian worker gets, an American worker gets twenty-seven. For every pound of chicken a Russian worker gets, an American worker gets fifteen.

The same thing is true of clothing. For every dress a Russian housewife gets, an American housewife can afford to get fifteen. For every suit of clothes a Russian workingman can buy, an American workingman can buy seven.

That is why you are fighting the Marshall Plan, Mr. Vishinsky. Because it proves that a free industrial economy can feed its own people—and the world—better than any political monoply of machine guns . . .

A free press, by merely printing the truth, shows up communism as the greatest failure of all time.

You also remarked that the demobilization of our Army, Navy, and Air Force means nothing because we could organize that again. But you didn't even demobilize yours. Right now the Russian Air Force consists of twelve thousand first-line planes and eighteen hundred first-line reserves. The United States Air Force consists of sixteen hundred first-line planes and only eighteen hundred first-line reserves.

Russia has three hundred full-strength divisions in battle position from Berlin to the Bering sea. The United States has not more than eight full-strength divisions abroad and less than seven combat divisions at home. In the field—right now—you outnumber us twenty to one . . .

Yet every day, you tell three hundred million people that we are preparing to attack you. Even your schoolchildren are taught that we and our children intend to destroy your country. You are not only preparing your armed forces, you are preparing the minds of your people for war.

Who is the warmonger? Josef Stalin for maintaining such a force, or Walter Winchell, who merely reports the danger to his countrymen? Now, very notably, Mr. Vishinsky, you offered no plan to prevent the war which you say you hate and fear. Well, here are some concrete suggestions.

Since when is a loaf of bread for a starving man or a bottle of milk for a sick baby an act of war? Americans don't think so.

Suppose, Mr. Vishinsky, we let the people of Europe decide. You get every Russian soldier out of occupied Europe and we will get every American soldier home. And then let the people of Europe vote in open free elections whether Secretary Marshall is causing war by sending food and clothing, and whether they want American help.

Again, Mr. Vishinsky, you accuse America of threatening the world with the atomic bomb. But in open assembly we agreed to turn the A-bomb over to the United Nations, provided there was international policing and inspection of it. But Russia vetoed it.

Why no inspection, Mr. Vishinsky? Who's afraid of police but criminals?

We are ready for honest international inspection any time you are. But we will not trade our military secrets for your empty promises.

Now let's look at the personal side.

Your statement that I, and some other Americans, should be enchained is impractical. Chaining people, as a principle, doesn't work. Adolph Hitler tried that, and look where it got him and the world . . . Why don't you consider not more chains on Americans but fewer chains on Russians? Before you give us a piece of your mind, why don't you give the Russian people a chance to speak theirs?

You also said that Winchell would write more cleverly if he went to Russia. Well, all right. Open up Russia to an expedition of myself, the major news services, and the four major networks, and let us go anywhere in Russia that your reporters—right now—can go in America.

If you can prove that I am a liar you won't have to do anything else. My competitors will do the rest . . .

I do not flatter myself that you intended to attack me personally . . . because there is nothing in the world that you and Mr. Stalin fear more than a man with a free typewriter or microphone. . . . It is you, Mr. Vishinsky, who are in chains right now. I can speak my mind and you cannot.

Along with one hundred and forty million other Americans, I am free to criticize our government. But if you, the third-ranking man in the Communist dictatorship, criticized yours, you would be shot, and you know it.

Your chief worry is not keeping Americans from knowing what is going on inside Russia. You are afraid to let the Russian people know what is going on in the outside world. You and your atheist government know that one independent and honest American reporter inside Russia with a microphone is more dangerous to the Communist party than any atomic bomb. And, for once, Mr. Vishinsky, you are right.

In my column of October 15, 1947, I quoted an editorial from the Dover (New Hampshire) *Democrat:* "His memorable reply to Vishinsky is the essence of American freedom—the right of a poor newspaperman to tell a political boss where to head in. The right of an ordinary citizen to speak his mind, to combat graft and corruption in high places, to criticize inefficiency in public office, to supervise the expenditure of public funds, to tell the mayor how to run his town, to tell Mr. Vishinsky where he can go."

☆

In 1948 Commissar Eisler (in a speech at the Manhattan Center on West 34th Street, Manhattan) told his cheering audience: "That rat Walter Winchell, on the radio last night, called me a Communist!" (Lusty booing and hissing greeted his attack.) "I will sue rat Winchell and his dirty-rat paper, the New York *Mirror,* for millions!"

Mr. Eisler, who had been out on bail (following conviction on several charges by the United States) then eluded federal agents assigned to keep him under surveillance and fled the country. He stowed away on the Polish S.S. *Batory.* Back in the old country he was rewarded by the Kremlin. They promoted him to a high post in Red East Germany.

★

DON WAHN

From the *Daily Mirror,* March 5, 1948:

The Manhattan night was dreary, wet and cold . . . Over on Broadway at Fiftieth Street the Hollywood arc lamps touched the leaden sky—heralding the Big Town's major event. Famous people from both coasts came to witness Mark Hellinger's last thrilling movie, *The Naked City* . . . tragedy in the Big Burg. Ted Husing was at the lobby mike introducing Sonja Henie, Dorothy Hart, Bugs Baer, and the others. The happy spectators congested the four corners of 50th and our Main Street. A columnist tacitly saluted the scene from his midtown windows.

He opened the big envelope of mail on his desk. On top, as usual, was the final proof of his column as it would appear in another few hours . . . Plus the next-to-last proof of "Kills" and "Can Hold" paragraphs. "We are overboard," his Girl Friday had said on the phone earlier. "You have two poems tonight; if we can omit the Don Wahn verse, it'll just fit."

That verse (Philip Stack had been contributing over the name Don Wahn for twenty-five years) was actually his good-bye! . . . We never suspected that when it came in. He was such a very shy person . . . The two young ladies in our office knew him well through the many years. He never asked for anything for the many times he helped embellish the colum . . . Did we want melancholy verse? Or something to fit the occasion of a holiday? He could jot one down just like that . . . In the last years, that is. When his "torch" offerings first came in (about 1924) they were heavy with heartache. We signed them "Don Wahn," "Kid Kazanova," or "The Melancholy Don," after he objected to his name being signed . . . He never said why. We assumed he didn't want to be teased by his associates over at the Brooklyn Edison Company, where he then clerk'd.

Don Wahn's offerings (which originated here) popped up in other places . . . In an Army magazine signed by someone by some-one else, usually by a GI hoping his girl friend might see it. But many times a chorus girl or plain Jane Doakes would open her purse and reveal several of them clipped or torn from the colum . . . "Does this please your ego?" one of them once said. "I buy the

205

paper only for them. You don't run them often enough. He has such understanding. Who is it?"

"That's a military secret," we always said.

When Don Wahn's stuff failed to come in once, we tried to locate him and couldn't. We put some in the paper (copying his melancholy style as best we could) and signed them "Don Wahn" to see if he'd respond. "Hey!" he complained. "I've been very happy recently and just couldn't get in the mood. Now my wife sees some I didn't write and I can't make her believe it!"

"Then fergoodnessakes, Phil," he was told, "please don't strand me like that again. We reject all the other sad ballads because the torch-sonnet style is synonymous with your by-line!"

He promised never to disappoint his legion of readers again.

Philip Stack's name must be familiar to you. He wrote all those delightful bits of sassy and gay verse which appeared for so long in *Esquire* under the Varga portraits of lovely girls . . . The birthday greetings or the "Wish You Were Here" and other novelty cards you received (or sent) were usually from his pen. He turned them out like a machine for the Gibson people of Dayton, Ohio.

At ten minutes past midnight Phil jumped from the Gibson firm's offices at 20 East 35th Street and made sure he didn't hurt anybody else. He must have braced himself on the ledge and thrown himself hard into space—so he would land in the gutter. A cabdriver racing north said he saw the body plummeting down.

We were sitting alone in a pub . . . Enjoying the happy dancing couples and lovers at their tables-for-two. Less than a mile away was Philip Stack writing his very last words in a lonely skyscraper. A waiter brought a note: "The Associated Press wants you to call," it said. "Ask for Mr. Gleason." Now what would the AP want at this time of night? . . . Nothing in the column of import to any news service. "Mr. Gleason, this is Winchell returning your call."

"Er," said Mr. Gleason, "do you know a Philip Stack?"

"Yes, I do. Is he all right? Anything wrong?"

"He just jumped twelve stories on Thirty-fifth Street. He is dead. Could you tell us anything about him? He left a short note."

"I didn't really know him. He never came to the *Mirror* when I was there. Never wanted to be a bother, just sent in his stuff."

And then we gave the AP man what little else we knew about him . . . That he was a contributor who never sent his stuff to any other colum but ours. When, twenty-five years ago, we sent word asking him how we could return the compliment, he never took advantage of it. Once in a while he'd submit some obscure youngster's new book or recording, or mention a radio newcomer and wonder if we could find room for a plug for them.

His last note (which the police at the 35th Street station house showed us in the middle of last night) was in the handwriting we were so familiar with for a quarter of a century. "I am incurably ill," it said. "I leave everything to my wife. Goodbye, Phil Stack."

Now he is gone. The last Don Wahn he submitted was set in type for the very night he jumped, darn it . . . but not printed. Not that Phil could have thought we didn't think it good enough. When we delayed using his offerings he'd send a note saying: "Tell Walter to send back those two stinkers and I'll pep 'em up" . . . Here is his last contribution. He called it "Summary" . . . The familiar last two-line punch reveals, we think, that he meant it as his Good-bye!

SUMMARY

You who are prone to dream . . . remember this . . .
That lighted inns loom starkly in the day,
That mystery can fade from out a kiss . . .
That love can wear the trappings of decay.
We who have watched the roses in the dusk,
We who have sighed at muted violins
Have learned that age can wear the scent of musk
And that we pay for all our secret sins;
Songs that were ours have faded down the years,
Taverns and maids are ghosts within our hearts,
There is a time for laughter and for tears,
Now we must play the dull and listless parts . . .
This is a world of never-ending strife,
Dreams are a one-way passage out of life!

—Don Wahn

ONE MAN'S OPINION

Here is the editorial from our Sunday night, March 14, 1948, broadcast:

Good Evening, Mr. and Mrs. United States! Our Constitution recognizes only one authority higher than itself. That authority is you, the American people. The United States Constitution guarantees a free press, not to protect newspaper people, but to protect your right to know what is going on.

Secretary Marshall states that the crisis is very grave. The President states that his confidence in peace is lessened. The top staff officers of all U.S. armed forces are in heavily guarded conference at Key West.

I think you are entitled to know where you are at and how you got there. And I want to offer you my suggestions, as an American citizen, of where we go from here.

The United States has had a secret history for the past five years. I propose to tell it to you. This is not a case of "now it can be told." It is a case of "now it must be told." Obviously, you have not been taken into your government's confidence. During time of war, a government cannot tell all it knows. A government has the right to conceal from its people information that might be of use to its enemies. But no democratic government has the right to withhold information from its people to conceal its own tragic mistakes.

At first, the secret history of the United States was written out of wartime necessity. Then later it was written out of consideration and hope for peace. But now it is being written out of pure stupidity, blundering, and the government's fear of confessing its mistakes. The truth is that every one of the American policy mistakes was honorable. They were to our credit. The tragedy is that in an effort to cover them up, our government is losing both its dignity and integrity.

This is the truth. During the war we did not receive the co-operation of the Kremlin. On the contrary, they distrusted us completely. They even refused to accept delivery of lend-lease on Russian soil. They did not trust us on their land. They refused to permit inspection of their front. And they even kept our ambassador under guard. But there was a war on. And we were allies. Russia was certainly bearing the brunt. And after Munich we felt she had good reason to be suspicious.

So we went out of our way to prove that we were friends. As the tide against Hitler turned, Stalin made territorial demands. Once again we tried to understand. A man who has seen millions of his people slaughtered and hundreds of cities and towns burned can be excused for being fearful.

But this is where we made our first big mistake. Stalin demanded territory from people who had suffered just as much from Hitler. We made some bad commitments because we thought we could fully compensate the weaker peoples and thus establish world peace.

I was fully familiar with the arrangements. I had misgivings but, like every other American, I will support without question any American government in time of war. When victory was in sight I went to the San Francisco Security conference. I went to see what kind of a payoff the Four Freedoms and the little peoples were going to get. When I found, in the first few days, that Mr. Stalin was not giving back but asking more from these helpless nations, I reported that I was in strange waters known only to their experts. And even Mr. Stassen assured me I was wrong.

Here we made a second mistake. But it is a fine and honorable one. I am proud my country made it. We could not believe that, with millions dead and tens of millions still fighting, any government would dream of instituting a policy of force against little countries. We felt that if we could trust the Kremlin's honor, we could certainly trust its common sense to cooperate in preventing another war.

We were wrong. Mr. Stettinius and Mr. Byrnes, in an honest effort to effect world peace, made terrific concessions to placate the Soviet Government. The war ended. But not Marshal Stalin's demands. They increased. Mr. Byrnes embarked on an endless policy of explanation and yielding.

This was our next great and tragic mistake. We thought we were respecting the legitimate claims of the war-stricken Russian people. But we were not! Mr. Byrnes was appeasing a Communist dictator. I called those treaties "Byrnes' Blunders" at the time. And I still do. The Byrnes-Stettinius diplomacy marks the lowest ebb of American foreign policy.

By this time, in war and in peace, Stalin found us what in our language is called a soft touch. He devoured everything Byrnes yielded and growled for more. And at this very same time there started what Secretary Marshall has called (privately) the greatest diplomatic and military catastrophe in our history. We demobilized! Russian agents appeared everywhere near our forces. "The job is done" and "Bring the boys home" were Kremlin-inspired slogans. And we bit. We did more. We swallowed the Communist propaganda whole and dissolved our armed forces.

This, too, is a fine and honorable mistake. The world knows that we took off our arms. And this is not the act of a nation which wants or intends to rob its neighbors. From then on Stalin changed from demand to threat. We still tried. We urged Stalin to consider the United Nations. We offered to turn the atom bomb over to it. He demanded secret conferences instead and got them. And he refused atomic inspection. In the meantime he grabbed nearly a dozen countries and a hundred million people.

And this time we made a mistake which was more than tragedy. It was dishonorable. We bypassed the United Nations. And we ratified treaties which we knew were dishonorable. Before a mistake can be corrected, it must be admitted. We made the mistake of disarming and they rejected our plans for peace. We made an even worse mistake when we ratified their plunder.

Secretary Harriman has said Russia is at war with us though we are not at war with Russia. We still want peace. But if we have no force, we will have no choice. I repeat because it is so terribly important—if we have no force, we will have no choice!

That is the secret history. But this is Stalin's present plan. In the War Room of every General Staff is the North Pole air map of the world. All eyes are riveted on this map. But in the back of each General's or Admiral's head are photographs of Hiroshima and Nagasaki.

This air map explains many things. Stalin's operation in Italy is both defensive and offensive. Russian war planes operating out of Italy can cut the Mediterranean in two. This means Stalin can block us from counterattacking oil bases in the Caspian area.

Italy is Stalin's left flank. If he gets it (and everything indicates that he will) Stalin then automatically isolates Greece and Turkey. If he doesn't get it in April, he'll try again. The day Stalin takes Rome he has Athens, Ankara, and the Dardanelles in the back. Then he is in position to drive on to Paris. If Paris goes, Russia then has Switzerland, Belgium, and Holland. Because Russia already has General Von Paulus' Nazis (all war prisoners) ready on German territory to seize Berlin!

All this is bad—but it is only Stalin's European Plan! The arrows on Stalin's air map do not stop at Finland. They point south at Stockholm, Oslo, and Copenhagen. Sweden, Denmark, and Norway are under steadily increasing pressure. And they are looking anxiously to Washington. But the biggest arrow on Stalin's war map points to Norway's Narvik and the Lofoten Islands. They have big airports. They are what Stalin needs—an air base and submarine base—in the Atlantic.

Our military men know very well what the blackjacking of Finland means to us. It means that Stalin's offensive has started. That he is driving on Iceland, and control of the Atlantic sea-lanes. That will take time. Perhaps enough time to build an air force, if we start now.

Great Britain and France have already reached agreement to merge their air forces in the event of a showdown. The British will supply most of the planes for the French pilots, because the French General Staff is reluctant to depend on airplanes manufactured by Communist-controlled unions: a great fifth column victory for Mr. Vishinsky.

We too have a Red fifth column operating here—far greater and more effective than any Hitler ever had in the United States. Even as I talked against Vishinsky, Russian leaders ordered their fullest force out to protest against me. But the tons of mail from you

Americans outnumbered them one hundred to one in a week. From this (for my country's sake) I hope their masters in Moscow have learned a lesson. Never fight anybody who can fight back.

Addressing Citadel College yesterday Mr. Byrnes asked: "What are you going to do about it?" The first thing which should be done is that the government reverse its policy, admit its mistakes (including those of Mr. Byrnes), and take the American people into its confidence.

On October 24, 1945, Mr. Byrnes, you proclaimed the United Nations charter in effect. It had been ratified by twenty-nine nations then and many more since. Among those signatories was the United States of America.

Article Six, Section Two of the United States Constitution provides that all treaties made under the authority of the United States shall be the supreme law of the land. This means that the United Nations charter isn't State Department policy anymore, Mr. Byrnes. It means that it is United States law. Why don't you, its author, call upon your party to honor the moral commitment of the American people to the other nations of the world? By Supreme Court decisions the Truman administration (under Article Six, Section Two) has no more right to debate the United Nations secretly than it has a right to debate whether it will enforce the narcotic laws.

We need our own conscience and the conscience of the world. And that's why we need the United Nations. But we also need an air force. And we need it right now. We have the men to pilot the ships. Our immediate danger is from the ostriches who are piloting the Congress.

The Senator Tafts, the Marcantonios, the Clare Hoffmans, the Rankins, the Tobeys, the Langers, and the other petty politicians must learn that boundaries of the United States are more important than their respective election districts.

Mr. and Mrs. United States, tell them now that they must vote yes on every defense measure that comes up, without wasting any time on ridiculous debate—or you will vote no in November. Tell these exasperating men that you are worried about them tonight because their records on national defense proved how terribly wrong they were in 1941.

Good night.

The Cincinnati (Ohio) *Enquirer*'s editorial page challenged our "competence in matters of foreign policy" with this shove: "The radio shoutings of Walter Winchell have had us at the very verge of war with Russia almost every Sunday night for the last two years—and if war should come it would be quite possible that his constant poisoning at the well of public opinion would have had at least some small part in the precipitation of the conflict."

To which we colyum'd:

Among other esteemed journals that publish this literature is the Cincinnati *Enquirer,* one of the many newspapers which lulled readers to sleep when the nation was in peril.

We argue the editors and publishers did so because they just didn't know what was going on. And when we tried to alert them to the danger, they dismissed the warnings as so much poppycock—instead of getting on a telephone and trying to check with us.

"What," they might have inquired, "do you base your ravings on about the threat of war?" Instead, they poo-poo'd our reports as far back as 1945. We would have told them: "Such men as Defense Secretary Forrestal, and Assistant Secretary of State A. A. Berle, Jr., and FDR, provided us with the material in an effort to awaken the people" . . . In short, right from the Government.

Stu Symington, one of the Government chiefs, brought us to Mr. Forrestal's Georgetown home one night in March 1948. Before dinner the Defense Secretary said: "We are at peace. None of us in Government can say things that must be said. You have a wide audience. Would you consider performing a service for our country? Tell the people how serious things are with Russia. We are worried over the many newspapers and people who shrug things off. I will provide you with the facts and documentation. But you must not say at this time that you got it from us. Too many editors and readers are saying: 'Yes, we may have a war with Russia, but have the Russians the know-how?'

"Mr. Forrestal then outlined a broadcast for us. Address it to Stalin, he said. Tell him the American people will back up our President and fight if necessary. His agents apparently are telling him otherwise, the way Hitler was misled by his intelligenec men.

"Know-how? Oh, my God, Walter!" exclaimed the late Forrestal. "You are in a position none of us are. You can talk freely. Remind the people that the Russians have plenty of know-how. Remind them how two Red pilots flew from Russia over ten years ago, nonstop, bound for California. That hop took about sixty-two hours. Today with jets they can fly over the Pole in half the time and their first American city would be Minneapolis!"

And so the next broadcast from Washington I broadcast what Mr. Forrestal gave me. "Mr. and Mrs. United States," I prefaced,

"I am speaking from Washington, two hundred and fifty miles nearer the news." And I went into twelve and a half minutes of slowly paced talk based on information given by the one man who knew the peril.

The Cincy paper was one of the first to attack it. "We do not regard Winchell," it said in effect, "as an expert on international matters."

The Minneapolis editor called it Winchellitis and assured subscribers it was all "the hysteria of a New Yorker, a nonexpert who couldn't possibly know," etc.

And *Time* magazine reprinted this hokum, which could only mislead more Americans, lulling them to slumber, doping them into telling their congressmen not to fight for defense as it would mean higher taxes. That's why we charge these newpaper people with imperiling the nation. Who, me???? Quote from *Quick* (a minimagazine) September 26, 1949:

"Internationally, his influence and power reached the point where Russia's Andrei Gromyko called him a 'menace second only to the atomic bomb.' "

★

DID JAMES FORRESTAL JUMP? OR WAS HE FLUNG?

The death of FDR's Secretary of the Navy, James Forrestal, was listed "jumped or fell"—the usual line newspapers use to keep the deceased's family from suing for libel. The fact is that his body was found on the grounds below his sickroom at Bethesada Naval Hospital, Washington, D. C. The police and Defense Department sleuths called it suicide.

But his remains did not land directly under the open window of his hospital suite. And that's where the plot, if any, thickens.

Mr. Forrestal was a small, gentle man, married and the father of two handsome sons. I met him when he was a member of Dillon, Read stock market brokers. Forrestal was one of the several Republicans that FDR appointed to high posts. Roosevelt made him Secretary of the Navy in 1944.

When Vice President Harry S (no period, Mr. Printer) Truman became President on April 12, 1945, the day FDR succumbed at Warm Springs, Georgia, from a brain hemorrhage, the new President assured Forrestal that his job was secure. In 1947, when the departments of War and of the Navy were incorporated into the Department of Defense, Forrestal became Secretary of Defense.

At reelection time Truman's closest political counselors and other kingmakers did not believe HST could win. A close friend, Louis Johnson, a wealthy businessman, kept Truman's spirit high. "You are going to win!" he told Mr. Truman.

"But," sighed the apprehensive hell-raiser President, "the campaign money isn't coming in, Louis. We are way behind."

Louis Johnson wrote out a check for $1 million.

A few days later pal Johnson promoted another million from rich chums. This, of course, cemented their friendship forever.

At Mr. Forrestal's suggestion, Secretary Stuart Symington had invited me to Forrestal's Georgetown house many weeks before Election Day. Forrestal excused himself to the other guests—who included Symington, a Mr. Ludington of the airlines family, and General Toohey Spaatz— and with martinis in hand, we went into the parlor.

He lost no time getting to the point. "I would appreciate it," he said, "if you would tell me what happened between you and the President."

I paled from the shock of the query and he noticed my discomfort. "I thought," I said, "I was invited to have dinner with you. This is embarrassing, Mr. Secretary."

He was my Chief. I was a Lieutenant Commander in Naval Intelligence.

"Something happened to take you off the team. Your support of FDR helped him win the presidency four times. This President needs people like you. Your syndication, your radio audiences. You haven't supported him in recent months. You never come to a White House press conference anymore. What caused the rift between you and the President?"

I swallowed my drink and said: "It is a personal matter. Nothing political."

"Palestine?" persisted Forrestal.

This shook me up. "Oh, I don't operate that way, Mr. Secretary," I told him. "It has nothing to do with Palestine being deserted by the British . . ."

"Some of us down here," he said, "were trying to find out why you are no longer on the team, and wondered . . ." He didn't finish the sentence. "Very well," he said, filling my glass with another martini. "Will you see the President with me in the morning?"

I said yes. Reluctantly.

"I will pick you up at your hotel at eight forty-five. The President expects you at nine." He then said dinner was long overdue and we should join his guests.

At the table, I told them a story I had told Symington during the long ride to Forrestal's house. A twelve-line paragraph for the next day's paper had been killed by my lawyer, Ernest Cuneo, who had happened into my New York *Mirror* office, and read a proof of the column.

The theme was: If war was imminent, Mrs. Roosevelt would be performing a public service if she flew abroad to tell Marshal Stalin and his men (via our embassy phone at Oslo) that Hitler's intelligence department had made a big mistake when they informed the Fuehrer that the United States wouldn't fight—and so on.

My deleted paragraph concluded: "Even if Mrs. Roosevelt fails in her mission, the nation would applaud and cheer her attempt to prevent the 'imminent' war many believe is a matter of only days, if not hours away . . . Even if Mrs. Roosevelt fails to get Stalin or any Communist leader on the phone," I last-lined, "her attempt would make every American love her. She might wind up becoming the first woman President!"

"Oh, my gahd! Ernie aghast'd to Rose Bigman. "I don't want him to use this ridiculous paragraph. It'll make him a national joke!"

Miss Bigman told him that she never changed a word of my column without my knowing it; that she had tried all day to locate me in Washington to check something that troubled her and hadn't been able to find me.

"I tell you," demanded the barrister, "kill that paragraph! His critics will kid him about it on every editorial page!"

"It will make the column twelve lines short," she said.

"I'll write a dozen lines to replace it," yelled Ernie as he scribbled them.

That Cuneo chap was good at writing punchy and pithy political patter. He wrote nearly all of my "Mr. and Mrs. United States!" Thirty-second radiotorials for over twenty-five years. His Washington stuff embellished many of my broadcasts and columns. Front pages coast to coast confirmed the exclusives he gave me. His sources included the top giants in the Capitol. One of his best feeders was Thomas "Tommy the Cork" Corcoran, FDR's closest ally for the four terms.

Before leaving with Mr. Symington to motor to Forrestal's home, I had phoned Miss Bigman to check if all was okay. "Oh," she groaned, "I've had a difficult time with Ernie. He insisted that I omit the thing you had about Mrs. Roosevelt going to see Stalin!"

"Fercrissakes!" I boomed. "The hell with what Ernie says. Put it back in the second edition!"

But the editor said replating a page for just one short paragraph would be costly, and for me to Forget It.

"What worries me," I added, "is that someone in the composing room or city room or a proofreader, noticing that the paragraph had been deleted would, if he was a Pinko, tell other fellow travelers: 'Winchell had a helluva suggestion for Mrs. Roosevelt to fly to Oslo or some city close to Russia and contact the Kremlin and tell Stalin's chiefs that if Russian Intelligence had assured them the United States wouldn't fight if attacked, they were wrong—that she could guarantee that the Congress would vote for war.' "

Henry Wallace, the Vice President during FDR's penultimate term, had been dumped. The Reds and Far Lefts in the United States were giving him their support. I feared that one of the *Mirror* lefties (oh, we had a few) would relay that deleted paragraph to Wallace and his followers and arrange for him to fly to Oslo and make the same pitch.

☆

This got a lusty laugh from the guests. But Mr. Forrestal did not laugh or chuckle.

Next morning in the car to the White House he said: "I am going to ask you to tell the President that story."

After the "Good morning, Mr. President" was said, Mr. Harry S mentioned that I hadn't been down to a press conference since he took office; that I was always welcome and not to be such a stranger.

"Tell the President that story you told us at dinner last night. We found it most interesting, Mr. President."

The President listened attentively for about five minutes. When I finished relating it, I added, "Mr. President, would you consider flying to our embassy nearest Russia and telling Stalin . . . ?"

"I have been to Europe twice," he softly responded. "Let the Russians come here and see me. They have a river over there I never even heard of."

I couldn't believe this was the President. "The Volga?" I offered.

"Oh, some river," he shrugged. Then, raising his tones, he documented what many of us had read about his profanity. "No, I will not go over there. I never kiss anybody's ass!"

Mr. Forrestal, seated alongside me, paled. His attempt to reconcile the President with some of us who had "left the team" had failed.

216

I got up and, without the usual "Thank you, Mr. President," grabbed my hat and made my exit: probably the first and only person who gave a President the back-of-the-neck and walked out on him—another defeat for Forrestal, who had hoped to convince the Chief that despite his GOP affiliation, he was trying his best to help win back at least one newsman for the Democrats.

Opposite the President's Oval Room office, Clark Clifford, Truman's top aide, was at his desk. He must have noticed the forlorn look in my eyes. "How did it go?" he asked.

"Pretty bad," I replied. "Pretty bad."

"I'm so sorry," he said.

I didn't wait for Forrestal.

The story of my rendezvous with the President and our exchange never leaked. Nor did I ever hear that anyone but Truman, Forrestal, and Clifford knew what took place that unhappy—for me—morning.

Truman was elected, and one of the first souvenirs of the campaign that he saved (and made facsimiles of for many intimates) was the Chicago *Tribune's* first-edition front page election night. The eight-column banner headline: "DEWEY DEFEATS TRUMAN."

The first man Truman sent for the next morning was big contributor Louis Johnson. The President embraced Johnson hard and long. "I don't know how to thank you," he reportedly said. "I now want you to tell me what I can do for you to show my gratitude."

"Oh, Mr. President," responded Louis Johnson, "I'm just as happy as you are that my confidence in you was confirmed. I want nothing, sir."

"No, no," continued the happy President. "How about Secretary of the Navy? The Army? Secretary of Air?"

Johnson grimly replied, "Those jobs no longer are anything but office boys for . . ." He did not finish the sentence—and the grateful President "got" what Johnson was trying to tell him: that with the new post of Secretary of Defense, all other Secretaries in the Armed Forces became men who took orders from the Pentagon Chief instead of giving them.

Mr. Truman smiled knowingly. Holding Louis by the arms affectionately, he said, "Just give me time, Louie. Just give me time!"

I subsequently learned that Forrestal, the Republican, had donated $1,500 to Mr. Truman's campaign fund. But he was doomed and he must have known it. This, of course, contributed to his heavy melancholia. Months before he died he was the most unhappy man in the Capitol.

Another cause for his breakdown in spirit (and, they said, "his mind") was a Washington female gossip columnist. (She took a famed newspaper publisher for her second husband) whose leading paragraph became Topic A in the Capitol. The item ran: "The most intriguing gossip along the Washington cocktail circuit is that the attractive wife of a top government executive is the most popular person with the young Naval officers." Whether or not the gossipist meant to imply that the "popular person" was the wife of the Secretary of Defense, and that she was keeping trysts with her admirers, the item made juicy table talk and party patter. Persistent rumors had it that the Forrestals were estranged.

Not long after, the President replaced Forrestal with Louis Johnson, his $2 million campaign fund lifesaver. Jim Forrestal's breakdown came a few days later.

Pundits and other Capitol correspondents had been hinting in print that Forrestal was losing his mind, that he was incessantly looking under the bed for hidden "Reds" and believed the Communists were on the verge of "taking over."

After his death, his reward for his great service to our country was having one of the largest aircraft carriers named for him. Several books were written about his life by close friends and others. Nearly all of the authors blamed his tragic end on Washington political columnists. I was included.

In 1967, many, many years after he died, men once on Forrestal's staff told me that he did not jump from his hospital window. "He couldn't possibly have jumped or fallen," they said. "His body was not found directly under the window. It was about six to eight feet from it!"

"What are you trying to tell me?" I asked.

"That he was flung by two or more persons!"

I led off with part of the above in my Washington *Examiner* column. That newspaper published by O. Roy Chalk featured the paragraph with a banner across the top of the page.

If any reporter, wire service, or paper took it from there, it eluded me. Nobody at the White House pressroom or the news people who cover the Pentagon contacted me about it.

In the last week of January 1968, correspondent Jeremy Campbell of the London *Standard* long-distanced from Washington that his editors had assigned him to interview me about this book. "Are you," he prefaced, "planning to reveal the names of those who killed Mr. Forrestal?"

"I don't know their names," I told Mr. Campbell. "I don't know that he was thrown out of any window. I know only that the sources for that astonishing legend were men I know to be reliable."

218

Mr. Campbell kept coming back to it.

"If I told you," I said, "why my source is sure he did not jump or fall, you'd have a story I am saving for my book." I also told Campbell that I couldn't imagine how anyone could have gotten into Mr. Forrestal's hospital suite without nurses and other hospital staffers knowing it.

"You think they were strangers?" reporter Campbell inquired.

"I will use the reply to your question in the book." And this is it.

The persons allegedly responsible for Forrestal's death were Americans wanting to keep him, went the story, from recovering and jotting down his memoirs—revelations that would expose people in the highest government places.

★

HOLLYWOOD

Hollywood is where everyone dreams of becoming a success between the times they knock those who are.

A Girltown producer decided to do a boy-and-girl story of great simplicity and charm. He remembered *One More Spring* and put in a long-distance call to word magician Robert Nathan, who replied, "You know how I feel about Hollywood. Besides I do not need the money. I have just sold a sonnet to a magazine!"

British star Ivor Novello was mizzable in Hollywood mainly because Louella Parsons, the leading cinema columnist of her day, kept spelling his name wrong. One morning she spelled it "Ivan Novello," another day "Ivor Norvello," and then "Eva Novel."

Mr. N. became so exasperated with Miss P. that he wrote the following complaint to her editor:

"Dear Sir: I do wish you would do something about the way my name is spelled in your newspaper from day to day. My name is Ivor Novello, not Ivan or Eva. For the life of me I cannot understand how people can get names wrong as does your Lulu Pearson!"

Hedda Hopper, whose millinery often made "news" (I nicknamed her Hattie Hopper) was a former actress in the legit, who made it big in Hollywood, first as an actress—then as a Louella Parson's top competitor. Miss Hopper's pillar of gossip and guessip appeared in the Los Angeles *Times* and was syndicated by the New York *Daily News*-Chicago *Tribune* Syndicate.

When I was newscasting for Jergen's Lotion the sponsor booked

219

Hedda and several columnists in Chicago and New York to sub for me during my seven-week vacation. But my contract had a clause giving me the sole right to select substitutes. I had recommended Dorothy Kilgallen and Florence Pritchett, a lovely youngster who married a rich U.S. Ambassador. Florence (who died from The Big C too young) later clicked large on a popular teevee show named *Leave It To The Girls* and other vidiot programs.

So Miss Hopper didn't get the job. She threatened to sue Jergens and the network. They paid her in full for the seven weeks. End of suit. Years later in Hollywood she "forgave" me. Hedda patty-caked me for fighting Reds, Nazis, gangsters, and cancer via the Runyon Fund. At the GOP convention that nominated Eisenhower, we clowned it up for the newsfotogs. She wore my hat, I wore hers. But she never mentioned the incident (in print or to me) that kept her from getting her first crack at coast-to-coasting for Jergens.

A much-quoted show biz anecdote starring Hedda always gets a howl from actors. A former newspaperman who became a top Hollywood and teevee star had not yet met Hedda. He despised her for the stuff she wrote about him and his friends. At a cocktail party in Beverly Hills, Hedda was pointed out to him. She was surrounded by gushy movie people.

Our Hero gulped three martinis, elbowed his way through the group around Hedda, and planted the hardest kick-in-the-behind a female ever got.

The story never made the gazettes. Even her top feudest, Louella Parsons (who had invented the Hollywood gossip column for Hearst forty years before), refused to hint at it. When I tangled with columnists (never got into a fight I didn't start) mutual friends said, "Why take those guys on? You're pretty vulnerable yourself, you know."

"Oh," I said, "columnists wouldn't print what they know about other columnists. We know too much about each other!!!" Hedda later prospered with her own newsy-bitchy program.

Hedda wrote a book, *Nothing But The Truth*. In it, she carelessly reported that a popular married film star was a homosexual; that his "other wife" was a movie star homo. She mentioned their names. One of them sued.

The book publisher settled out of court. The actor was appeased with seven hundred thousand dollars—the tallest libel settlement at the time. That was the beginning of the end of Hedda's life. The humiliation had shock-killed her. Not long after, Hedda (seventy-three) died in bed.

★

LET HE WHO IS WITHOUT SIN, ETC.

Sir Laurence Olivier's flirtatious compliment when asked what he thought of Deborah Kerr's actressing: "Miss Kerr is a good actress. She is also unreasonably chaste."

During the filming of *Casablanca* the cast had fun with a parrot which had no lines to say. It was employed as atmosphere in a sequence. Ingrid Bergman and the other actors kept asking, "Polly wanna cracker?" Polly merely gave them all a blank stare.

One day Polly winked at Humphrey Bogart as though it wished to have a talk. Bogart obliged. "Polly wanna cracker?" cooed Bogey.

"Polly," was the retort, "want Bergman!"

In 1950 Ingrid Bergman, one of filmdom's finest and loveliest stars, was on the world's front pages following disclosure of her sudden romance with Italian director Roberto Rossellini. A married woman! And with a married man! Miss Bergman was so much in love with him she snapped her fingers at her "executioners" and other Glass-House-Dwellers.

The insults and abuse flung at her (not her lover) in many quarters— newspapers, columns, editorial pages, movie mags, periodicals, and some "Look-Who's-Talkin'!" radioafs—sent me to the typewriter to jot down my next broadcast editorial. I reprinted it in newspapers in all the states and in eleven foreign papers along the syndicate:

Mr. and Mrs. United States!

The only thing more brutal than a firing squad pointing its rifles at a man is the world pointing its finger at a woman.

Thousands of American girls this year experienced the same ordeal that Ingrid Bergman faces in Rome—with this exception: They, like Ingrid, were pelted with the traditional stone, but not with cutting headlines.

Every major newspaper knows that this social problem occurs so frequently that it isn't even news. Ingrid Bergman comes from Hollywood instead of Main Street, but that doesn't change her from an unfortunate girl into a wicked woman. If she weren't talented she wouldn't be famous. But if she hadn't been famous, the world wouldn't have stopped to sneer.

Miss Bergman is a very fine actress—some appraisers have called her acting great—but even public figures have a right to private tragedy. The very moral code she is supposed to have offended is her greatest defense.

There are few who can cast the first stone.

There are even fewer who can afford to fling mud.

All of us should be able to forgive sinners. Because none of us are saints.

Several weeks later (February 14, 1950) in the New York *Mirror* (and papers printing my reportage) I submitted this affidavit:

Following my broadcast about Ingrid Bergman, I heard from more listeners in the 48 states than all the radio ratings reveal. The very next morning at the office of the *Daily Mirror,* the mail was very heavy. Ten to one subscribing to my sentiments. But to be fair, let's start with a few who didn't.

Mr. and Mrs. United States write their New York correspondent:

Miami: "In speaking of the Bergman escapade last evening you quoted scripture very nicely. I have an idea there are many virtuous wives and mothers in this world who could qualify. Also the Holy Scripture says: 'Thou Shalt Not Commit Adultery.' This woman has a young daughter, also a lawful husband. If she has not committed adultery, I would like to know what is considered adultery? Yours sincerely . . ."

We didn't say she didn't commit adultery. We didn't quote any Scripture.

New York: "You defended Ingrid Bergman [which we didn't—W.W.] for her unfortunate conduct. She is not an ordinary woman: she is an actress who influences other people, and she should lead an exemplary life . . . She committed a sin against the Ten Commandments—the immovable mountain on which the world is built. Rita Hayworth is another bad example. Very truly . . ."

White Plains, New York: "To say Miss Bergman can be compared to the girl on Main Street is certainly ridiculous. When one reaches the fame of Miss Bergman, she becomes an outstanding figure in the eyes of the public.

You are quick enough, sir, to protect this wonderful country of ours from spies and atomic bombs. For Heaven's sake be as conscientious about our morals . . ."

Everybody has a skeleton in the closet. A celebrity's has no door.

Winston-Salem, North Carolina: "Dear Walter: I think you had too much to say about Ingrid Bergman last Sunday night. I am surprised at you for defending someone who has committed adultery. I have a 15-year-old daughter and I want her to have good morals.

Hence, I would not want her to support Bergman's pictures. I have been a listener for over 15 years. Sincerely . . ."

"It has been my experience that folks who have no vices have very few virtues"—Abraham Lincoln.

Kansas City, Missouri: "Mr. Winchell: Just why in the hell are you standing up for Ingrid Bergman? A fine example she is setting for the thousands of teenage girls and young women all over the country. Most of these girls have pictured her as one of the more saintly types of persons. For someone in the public eye she has really fouled up. These people that are in the public eye should be the ones that are more discreet in their private lives. I had planned on sending a check for $10 for the Cancer Fund, also my short snorter, but your statement tonight prevents me from doing so . . ."

Nothing personal, but Seneca said: "Other men's sins are before our eyes, our own behind our back."

Hollywood, California: "This letter is to doff my newest chapeau to Walter Winchell for his sympathetic handling of the Ingrid Bergman baby scandal. Very sincerely . . ."

Houston, Texas: "I have never bothered you with a card in all the years I have listened to you—but brother, you hit the nail on the head tonight about how few could justly 'cast the first stone.' " Yours . . ."

Paradise, Lancaster County, Pennsylvania: "I've been asking myself 'Can I sit in judgment on Ingrid Bergman, coming into court with clean hands?' It's an old twist of Jesus' query about casting the first stone. If he didn't consider Himself a qualified judge, where do the rest of us get off?

"Anyway, it's a pleasure to be able to agree with you occasionally and in this a lot more people will agree than will tell you so. Thanks again . . ."

Hampton, Virginia: "I was one of the millions of people who looked down my nose at her, until I heard your broadcast. Now I realize that self-righteousness is in itself a sin. Thank you very much for waking me up! Sincerely . . ."

Kalamazoo, Michigan: "Thank you so much for coming to the defense of Ingrid Bergman. No one has a right to judge her, because no one knows what he or she would do under the same circumstances. Sincerely . . ."

Santa Barbara, California: "Here is my short-snorter for the Runyon Fund. I hope you get that million. Glad to hear what you had to say about Ingrid Bergman. At least she had the honesty and courage to meet the consequences of her emotions. Cordially . . ."

Ingrid Bergman's fate [I went on] satisfies the moral code of the most severe moralist—that the way of the transgressor is hard. By her own actions, she is now internationally disgraced. To most people her shame is punishment enough. But now that she has fallen, that same moral law forbids that she be kicked and stoned while she is down. The great Man who taught us to hate the sin also told us to forgive the sinner. This means that when a woman falls she is not pelted with stones—but should be helped to her feet. Righteous people sometimes condemn the fallen, but good people always forgive them, because real virtue is always strong enough to be kind ... I repeat for the listeners who assumed I am indifferent to sin, I am not indifferent to it. I realize that a microphone is a great moral responsibility. I simply hoped for sympathy, understanding, and compassion for sinners—a basic tenet of every religion.

I don't recall sending any of the above to Miss Bergman, but someone must have. I received the following note from Rome, dated February 26, 1950: "Dear Mr. Winchell—Thank you! I want you to know how grateful I am. Sincerely, Ingrid Bergman."

Tallulah Bankhead was asked by an interviewer: "Do you ever smoke cigars in public? Or anything like that to attract attention?"

"No," said the star, "I don't have to smoke cigars to attract attention. I just stay at home and people wonder what I'm up to."

From our Sunday night broadcast, February 26, 1950:

I know that Maryland has long expected him to run—but George P. Mahoney will announce his candidacy for governor in a few days.

From the Baltimore *Sun,* February 27, 1950:

"George P. Mahoney, generally suspected of being a candidate for governor, last night claimed ignorance of a radio report . . . from Walter Winchell . . . that he would announce for governor 'within a few days.'

"Mr. Mahoney was asked if the Winchell report were true. His comment: 'Walter Winchell! Is he on now?'

" 'Winchell's speculating,' he said, 'like everybody else's been doing.'

" 'I met Winchell in Miami,' said the reluctant candidate. 'He said, "Hear you're going to run for governor. When you going to announce it?"

" 'And I said, "It will be shortly." ' '

"Then would Mr. Mahoney really announce this week, as reported by Winchell? 'Winchell,' said Mr. Mahoney, 'is just shooting at the moon.' "

Wire from Baltimore, Maryland, March 4, 1950: "Your prediction that I would announce my candidacy for Governor of Maryland will be verified when it appears in the Baltimore and Washington papers on Sunday, March the fifth. Thanks a million. George P. Mahoney."

★

MACRI

Lepke, chief of Murder, Inc., Public Enemy Number One, was not the only criminal who gave himself up to me. There were several—though none so notorious as Lepke.

Benedicto Macri and an alleged killer named Johnny Guisto (who disappeared and was never found dead or alive) were charged with the murder of a union organizer named William Lurye.

Lurye, police stated, had visited Macri's small dress factory in Manhattan's garment center and demanded that he run a union shop. Lurye was later found stabbed to death in a phone booth on a Saturday night, May 7, 1949. The police charged Macri and Guisto with the crime.

Macri's brother, Vincenzo, was one of the Murder, Inc. executives. Vince was always with gang chief Albert Anastasia, later slain in a barbershop in midtown's Park Sheraton Hotel. The inn was also where Broadway's wealthiest gambler, Arnold Rothstein, was found shot in the testicles during a high-stakes poker game. The shots were fired from under the table after a noisy quarrel about A.R.'s welching on a hefty bet made at a racetrack by one of the players, a gambler named George McManus. He was charged with the slaying. It was a sensational front-pager for days, but Mr. McManus, who had powerful connections with politicians, was acquitted. Not the hot squat at Sing Sing for him.

Minutes before I went before the mikes for my Sunday eve, June 19, newscast, police officials phoned me. "You can help us get Lurye's killers," I was told. "Tell them we know who we want for this murder. Their names are Benedicto Macri and Johnny Guisto. Guisto has a big X scar on his cheek. They might be listening to you from their hideout or in a car."

"Okay," I said, excited over the Exclusive. But the lawyers for the program's insurance firm, who scrutinized each word of my reports, deleted their names. "Libelous!" they argued.

"Oh, my Assss!" I argued. "I got their names from the Police Department! They asked me to do it because they want Macri and Giusto to know they're wanted."

"I don't care what the police told you," was the lawyer's rejoinder. "Maybe the police are mistaken. Then what?"

They tried to delete the entire story, but I compromised by agreeing to use only the men's initials—like so:

ATTENTION, B.M. AND J.G.! . . . B.M. AND J.G.! You are wanted by the New York Police Department as suspects for the murder of union organizer Lurye in a phone booth last night!

I am addressing this to you, B.M. I understand that you once read a book. That you went to school! That you have a lovely wife and darling children.

B.M., if you are in a car right now with the radio tuned into this broadcast, you are very likely looking back over your shoulder every minute to see if anyone is tailing you. If you are in an apartment or a house in another state, you are making it your own prison—and you know it.

Why don't you come in? Come in to see me, B.M. Take your chance with the law, which is fair. You might win!

A year later, on June 18, 1950, Macri surrendered to me against the wishes of his brother, Vince, and the family barrister, who feared that by giving up to a newspaperman instead of to Homicide Chief Monaghan Benny would ruin any chance of a deal. It was brother Vince who asked me to select the surrender location.

I told him I'd meet them at the corner of Eighth Avenue and 20th Street—a hundred feet from the 10th Precinct where Lieutenant Arthur Schultheiss was Mr. Big in the Detective Squad. I knew I could trust Arthur not to tip off the opposition papers.

I phoned my editor at the last moment to rush down a cameraman so the paper could have a helluva exclusive picture.

I parked my car on the corner. The long wait gave me the willies. Maybe they had changed their minds? Dammit-the-hell.

Macri and his brother were in the car in front of mine all the time, making their farewells.

226

Brother Vince stepped out first and came to my car.

"We are ready," he said, weeping. People in Murder, Inc. weep? Brotherly love.

Vince escorted me to his car, and out stepped the fugitive. He was smiling, impeccably attired. Clean-cut guy. Young, handsome. "Thanks, Mr. Winchell," he said. "I did hear you that night, in a car en route to a town in Pennsylvania—my hideout."

"I'm sorry," I said, "to meet you under these circumstances."

"You don't remember me," said Benedicto, "but we met during the war in Washington when you visited the Secretary of State."

"Oh, really?" I replied. "You were visiting his office?"

"No," Macri chuckled, "I was an assistant to Secretary of State Stettinius!" Later I learned that the accused slayer had become a multimillionaire through his connection with the State Department. He made $5 million, he told me, selling surplus ships at the war's end, still remaining in the rackets. Now he was broke, having squandered it at the tracks and elsewhere. He'd been reduced to landlording a small dress factory to support his family. And now—in another mintue or two—he would be under arrest for murder.

We started walking slowly to the station house. The *Mirror* hocus-focusers and their flashbulbs illuminated the street. The picture consumed all of page one. I escorted the former State Department staffer (as he claimed to be) to the bar before the police lieutenant's desk. "My name," I announced, "is Walter Winchell. I'm a reporter for the *Daily Mirror*. This man is Benedicto Macri. Wanted"—I started choking on the terrible words—"for murder."

"They are waiting for you upstairs," replied the lieutenant, giving Macri an icy glare.

In the squad room I turned him over to Schultheiss and I hastened back to the *Mirror* to make the last edition.

On June 20, 1950, the *Daily News* (the opposition) ran a short editorial with this headline: "NICE JOB, WALTER." The editorial said: "This is about the most uncustomary editorial we could possibly print today; but we want to congratulate Walter Winchell on having induced the alleged murderer of William Lurye to give himself up Sunday night. Fine work."

On the same day the New York *Post* editorial'd: "AN ORCHID FOR WALTER." The *Post* went on: "To coin a phrase, an orchid to Walter Winchell for his role in negotiating the surrender of one of the

227

men sought in the killing of William Lurye. As citizens and as newspapermen, we take off our hats to a columnist who has never been comfortable in an armchair."

On June 21, the editorial page of my paper, The *Daily Mirror* said:

How Does WW Do It? . . . Since Walter Winchell delivered the *Mirror* a fine scoop and the authorities a fugitive indicted for the Lurye murder, we've been asked by many people how he accomplished the feat.

The best possible answer is Winchell's column today, which we urge you to read as a true-life thriller and a masterpiece of suspense.

We're proud of W.W. We're grateful to the other newspapers which have congratulated the guy we know to be one of the greatest reporters of all time.

Our own memo to him on the exciting night of the scoop was:

"Dear Walter: Congratulations! Thanks! You're not an ace; you're the ace!"

On June 26 Bob Considine delivered the punch line in his column in the New York *Journal-American:*

I don't remember another case wherein rival New York papers ever broke down as readily and gave deserved salutes to a reporter as in the case of Winchell's recent feat. The *Times* and *Herald Tribune* gave the feat front-page play; the *News* and *Post* congratulated Walter editorially. But perhaps the finest tribute came from the *Daily Worker*. It refrained from calling the whole thing a Fascist plot.

Months later Macri went on trial. He was acquitted!! Newspapers disclosed that one or two jurors had allegedly been bribed by Murder, Inc. —either with money or threats on their lives.

But you can't try a man twice for the same crime.

My plea to Macri that night over the air was prophetic: "Why not take your chance with the law? You might win!"

I met him on Broadway weeks after his acquittal. I told him I hoped he knew how lucky he was; that his brother had wept not for him but for their mother, who had been promised by all her sons (who became gangsters) that Benny would be the Good Son. "Don't make waves," I counseled Macri. "Don't start anything that will make trouble for you and your family."

He promised.

Not long after, brother Vincenzo Macri was shot dead by foes. Benny's car was found with bloodstains on the back seat on the banks of the Passaic River in New Jersey—or so the underworld and Crepevine and the police were "tipped."

Was it Benny's blood? His car? Probably. He has not been seen since.

Seven years later, his very pretty wife approached as I left my hotel. "I am Benny Macri's widow," she said.

"Wellll, helllloh!" I greeted. "You live here?"

She said she worked there, but didn't say at what job. I didn't ask.

"Please do not tell anyone?"

"You can depend on it, Mrs. Macri."

"I do not call myself Macri anymore," she said. "I spell it another way—for the children's sake, you know. Do you believe Benny is dead?" she asked.

"All I hear is the scuttlebutt," I replied. "I really do not know."

About a year later she wrote me that the family "felt" that Macri was in a cement overcoat at the bottom of the Passaic River or in a grave buried under lime or some acid that leaves no trace of a body.

"I have a chance to be married again," she revealed. "They say I can do so because of some law about a husband being gone so long."

I said: "The Enoch Arden law. You have to get a court's permission, of course."

When I was writing and appearing in *The Walter Winchell File* for Desilu TV studios she asked me not to include the story about Benny. "The children watch your series. Promise, Walter?"

"I promise I will not include it in the series." And I didn't. Nor did I tell it to Desi Arnaz and his scripters.

Mrs. M. sent me a letter of thanks "from us all!"

Still later I reported the words of another fugitive from justice as I led him to the FBI offices in San Francisco. "You made a big boner about Benny Macri being in the Passaic River," he scolded.

"I didn't say he was!" I reminded. "I wrote that's what the underworld and cops believed."

"Not the Passaic River," he whispered. "He's in Gravesend Bay."

Then a priest wrote me to ask for verification of that quote.

I told the priest it was strictly hearsay—no judge would allow it in evidence, etc. "But," I told the padre, "Macri must be dead."

Widow Macri was given the go-light by her church to wed.

My wedding gift.

I also received some letters denouncing me for having written sympatico newspaper pieces about Macri's brother and his wife and children. "What about our family?" one letter screamed. "What about writing something nice about the Lurye family? Instead of writing nice articles about the Macri family? One of those Macris got away with murder!"

So true. So very, very true.

★

WORDS, WORDS, WORDS

Columbia Pictures planned a movie with the name "Burke" in the title. The Will Hays Office censors rushed a memo to the producers informing that the name "Burke" could not be used because in England "Burke" meant something naughty.

To which the reply was: "What about Burke's Peerage?"

Mickey Cohen, the underworld celebrity, cautioned me on many occasions not to use profanity or salty language in front of him because, he said, he didn't smoke, drink, tell dirty jokes or listen to them.

I quoted him on the subject in the column, adding, "Mickey Cohen is the first underworld toe dancer I ever met."

In Beverly Hills, where Mickey dwelled before starting a long term in prison, I related the conversation to former Police Chief Clinton H. Anderson of that elegant community.

Chief Anderson responded, "Did Mickey actually tell you he never uses profanity?"

"Yes," I told Anderson, "and Mickey emphasized that I mustn't use it in front of him because he just doesn't like it. His exact words included, 'I never use profanity.' "

To which the police chief punch-lined: "I once had to lock him up because he invaded my office and called me a no-good, dirty son of a bitch!"

On April 7, 1951, the leading editorial in *Collier's* magazine "Keep It Simple, Boys") discussed a feature of our column—heckling users of big woids.

Collier's noted in part:

> Mr. Winchell has been conducting a campaign for the last year or so against the overblown vocabulary. On this particular day he

was chiding the *New York Times'* drama critic for referring to a "satire on egalitarianism." "He means equality," the columnist helpfully explained. A few days later, Mr. W. teed off on the same paper's top movie reviewer for this sentence: "To pretend that the aural facilities are even remotely matched by the visual content of this picture would be senseless, however." Again Walter was on hand as interpreter: "He means that wot you hear is better than wot you see, see?"

On Sunday, April 15, 1951, the leading editorial in the Minneapolis *Sunday Tribune* said in its opening paragraph: "In the Tribune last Sunday, there was an outstanding job of reporting by Walter Winchell—an interview with Frank Costello, the gambling big shot."

A few days later a memo from my Girl Friday said: "Seymour Berkson, head man of International News Service, phoned to say your paper in Minneapolis nominated your Frank Costello interview for a Pulitzer Prize."

Not long after, my column was dropped by the *Star-Trib* and its sister paper in Des Moines, both owned by one of my former fans, the publisher of *Look* magazine. His former wife, Fleur Cowles, once devoted considerable space to me in his (and her) magazine, *Flair*. The long sugary article alleged that nobody "in the world has so many readers and listeners," etc.

Praps that's why *Flair* folded after a few issues.

From the *Congressional Record* of May 9, 1951, quoting pages eighty-one to eighty-three of the book *The Communist Trail in America:*

> In his Sunday night broadcast, Walter Winchell told of the secret Communist gatherings at which strike strategy was laid out. Because he had excellent sources of information, he was able to quote nearly verbatim just what was transpiring at these secret sessions . . . even the way in which they boasted of their success in particular plants then gripped by strikes.
>
> To erase Walter Winchell and his diatribes, a special conference was called in an obscure Chicago meeting room on April 8, 1941.
>
> Extra precautions were taken to insure that absolutely no one except the trusted hierarchy was admitted to that room. . . . The meeting, called at the insistence of Robert Minor, national secretary of the Communist Party, was presided over by Pat Toohey, then state organizer for Illinois.
>
> This was the plan: Hundreds of thousands, perhaps millions of letters were to deluge the radio network and Winchell's sponsor, all

231

protesting his attacks upon "an innocent political party." Organizations, thousands of them, some real but most of them fictitious, were to join to fight Walter Winchell's "persecution."

"Above all," Toohey warned, "the name of the Communist Party must be kept out. The protests should seem spontaneous and real."

The scheme, elaborately drawn up, was doomed to failure because Winchell exposed it before it got under way. His information about the Communists was accurate to the last detail . . . powerful ammunition.

★

FIRST LADY OF HOLLYWOOD

Marion Davies (née Douras) was sixteen when she met William Randolph Hearst. When their courtship began, he was the proprietor of twenty-three newspapers in the United States. Their idyll lasted for almost fifty years.

Their romance ignited when Mr. Hearst was a chief backer of several F. Ziegfeld, Jr., girl shows. She was one of the most beautiful babes in the *Ziegfeld Follies*. Her father was a New York City municipal court magistrate. All of them are gone. Mrs. W. R. Hearst, Sr., her class and dignity intact, survived them all.

Hearst, once wealthier than J. Paul Getty, Howard Hughes, H. L. Hunt, J. P. Kennedy, and other walking mints, squandered his fortune on imported Italian marble for San Simeon and art from the masters. On arrival in this country, most of it was buried in warehouses on both coasts.

His newspaper chain was suddenly decimated. Fourteen Hearst papers had to be sold or abandoned.

Many women whose men suffered great misfortune, failing health, and wealth deserted them. Not lovely, compassionate Marion.

Miss Davies, the mistress of Hearst's San Simeon and other estates, enjoyed Instant Stardom, usually in films produced by Cosmopolitan Studios, which her benefactor had built for her. Playing her finest role as a heroine, she documented her great love for the man who made her famous and rich when she handed him a certified check for $5 million plus every gem he had given her over the decades.

"Daddy," she told him, "you gave me all this. I don't want you to lose your last paper."

That fortune—and a little help from banker friends—saved his Boston branch. He retrieved many of the other papers with Marion's check. His sons and other heirs today are living like millionaires mainly because Marion Davies was loyal to her man—and his family.

In 1951, when Hearst expired after a long illness, Marion was asleep. She had comforted him in his final hours—the way she had from the time she was sixteen until she was sixty. When she wakened she was informed by servants that "Daddy" had died.

Hearst brass had The Chief hurriedly removed to a mortuary.

After she ran out of tears she plaintively said to a maid: "They didn't even let me kiss him good-bye."

★

BOY MEETS GIRL

One of the top stories in 1952 was the Denmark sex surgery performed on a former American soldier named George Jorgensen.

The New York *Daily News* scooped the world on that one. It was offered to the New York *Daily Mirror,* the paper my col'm appeared in, the editors of which rejected it.

George became Christine Jorgensen. The newspapers and their columnists, cartoonists, and editorial writers had a lot of fun kidding La Jorgensen. I called her Shim, He-She, She-He, and similar sassafrass.

The columns were packed daily with quips about Christine. She shrugged all of it off. Brave girl.

"The Bravest & Finest" benefit at Madison Square Garden was almost sold out. The event was to promote money for the widows and families of New York City policemen and firemen killed in the line of duty. I learned that the hundred-dollar, fifty-dollar, and twenty-five-dollar seats were sold almost within forty-eight hours after I announced in the *Mirror* and on the air that I would stage the show.

"But," said the box office people, "we can't sell the one- and two-dollar seats in the top gallery. Everybody wants to be downstairs and see the celebs out front!"

Miss Jorgensen's private phone number was furnished by the New York *News,* an opposition paper, after I explained why I had to contact her. She answered the phone.

"I'm Walter Winchell . . ."

"Oh, you!" she sarcasm'd. "What do you want?"

"I want you!"

"Drop dead!"

"Ladies first!"

It broke her up. "So what?" she asked.

"I'm putting on a helluva big show at the Garden Monday night . . ."

"I know, I read about it."

"All of the expensive seats are sold. We can't move any of the cheaper chairs in the gallery. If I could go on the air tomorrow night and say that Miss Jorgensen will be there Monday, I'm sure police and firemen's widows and children will—"

"I'll be there!" she interrupted.

"You're a doll!" I said. "It will be a neat way of taking your place in the community. You'll have to do that sooner or later, so why not do it for such a worthy cause?"

"The comedians will make fun of me, of course," she sighed.

"If they do I will just kill them!" I assured.

The Garden sold out completely Monday morning following my newscast. Backstage I cornered Milton Berle, Jackie Gleason, and all the other comics and told them of my pledge to Christine—that nobody would try to get a laugh poking fun at her or putting a hand-on-the-hip or mincing around like a whoopsy.

They crossed their hearts with their fingers that they wouldn't ridicule her.

"It would be a cheap thing to do," I reminded One and All, "like making fun of a cripple or the blind." All kept their word.

Now Christine (ex-George) waited in the wings to "take her place in the community" as a female. She was nervous, of course.

"And now, ladies and gentlemen," I said, wearing my best poker face, "Miss Christine Jorgensen!"—the cue for the orchestra to go into "A Pretty Girl Is Like A Melody."

Our heroine came onstage in tempo to the slow, dreamy beat the way a show girl would stroll, with arms gracefully stretched east and west.

I was sure the crowd would howl. But there wasn't a titter. Christine was welcomed affectionately with one of the heftiest hands of the thrilling evening.

That's all she did, just walk onstage to where I stood to greet her. Then I told the audience how we hadn't sold all the tickets—and that when I asked if I could broadcast the news that she'd be there to help us sell out, she graciously declared, "I'll be there!"

That won her another ovation.

Now backstage again, Christine had to go to the ladies' room. The Garden's uniformed guards refused to permit it.

Some of the actors, including Berle, escorted her to the gents. Other men kept watch at the door so that no males could enter.

In the washroom (after Christine had washed her hands) the following exchange took place between Miss Jorgensen and Mr. Berle, who had had a nose job months before. "Look," he said, as Christine rouged her lips, "I'll make a deal with you. I'll show you my old nose if you'll show me your old cock!"

Months later, in Los Angeles, Christine held a press conference at her hotel suite. She phoned to request that I be there. "They all make me so nervous," she said. "Please help me handle them."

The reporters and editors from the papers and networks were sympatico. No one made any wisecracks: just the usual Q & A.

One newsman, however, spoiled her day. His queries (no pun intended) got a bit rough. But she took his sallies like a lady.

"May I interview you for a moment or two?" she asked her heckler.

"Go ahead."

"You married?"

"Yes."

"Children?"

"Yes, a boy!"

"Well," she said—plus a frigid stare—"don't be too sure!"

One of the lustiest laughs by a crowd I ever heard.

Christine often announced her "engagement" to some heterosexual, but as this was written, she is still a spinster.

It's one of the risks a girl takes in acting like a lady. A standard human interest fable is the one that many newspapers echo every yuletide— based on mail addressed to Santa. Not all are penned by tots. One read: "Dear Santa: Please bring me a good-looking, ambitious man about 25 years old, six feet tall and very loveable: [Signed]: One of your best-behaved, good, hard-working girls."

HST–KKK

The rift between this reporter and the occupant of the White House worsened.

I disclosed Harry S Truman's long-ago membership in the Missouri Ku Klux Klan. I displayed his signature on his application for KKK membership on my television cameras.

Complete silence from the White House. No denial or confirmation.

I kept putting the application and the President's signature on the air for several Sunday nights. Then I received the following letter dated December 11, 1952, from Kansas City, Missouri. It should serve as a lesson to journalism students never to deny the other fellow's scoop (it might be true)!

> Dear Sir: About October 19, 1952, on your Sunday broadcast, you corrected Drew Pearson when he stated you were incorrect when you stated that Truman was once a member of the Ku Klux Klan. Thereafter . . . Republican Headquarters here received several calls—one from a deputy from Grandview and another from Lee's Summit, both indicating there were witnesses who would testify that Truman was a Kluxer.
>
> I motored out to Lee's Summit and there interviewed an old friend, who at the last minute refused to sign this affidavit; his family, two fine daughters and his son-in-law, remonstrated, being afraid of reprisals. However, all the facts recited in this document are authentic and my friend has a far better reputation in this community for truth and veracity than has Harry S Truman.
>
> The following story that made the rounds (which I do not wish to authenticate) was told me by a neighbor of Truman. When Harry was initiated in the Klan, he gave his check for $10 initiation fee and the said check bounced.
>
> Sincerely, John S. Cannon, Attorney and Counsellor at Law.

The unsigned affidavit alleged that Mr. Truman in 1922 had shown the writer his KKK card and revealed that he had kneeled and taken the oath being administered by John R. Jones at Klan HQ in the Baltimore Hotel.

A spokesman for Truman finally announced: "Yes, it is true. It happened when he was a very, very young man, when aspirants for political office joined everything—the Elks, the Moose, the Lions, the Rotary Clubs, and so on. He resigned long before he won his initial appointment as a county judge."

☆

Following Mr. Truman's historic letter to a Washington music critic threatening to beat him up if "the sunuvabitch" ever again wrote anything derogatory about Margaret's singing, Margaret was booked as

On live television (Bill Mark)

*WW and his Sunday night
ABC show staff (Bill Mark)*

WWith Ethel Merman, one of St. Clair McKelway's sources of "information" about WW for a six-part profile in The New Yorker *(Bill Mark)*

Chatting with an unidentified reader of his column (Bill Mark)

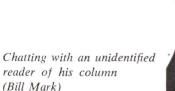

WW, Sylvia Sullivan, and Ed on the dance floor at El Morocco (Bill Mark)

WW showing off a copy of the Washington Examiner, *which had just picked up his column. From left to right: Miami Beach columnist Paul Brunn, Mrs. Ed Sullivan, an unknown woman, Ed Sullivan, and WW. This friendly scene ended a feud with Sullivan that had raged for years since WW's first days on the* Mirror *(Bill Mark)*

A good dancer, WW always enjoyed himself...(Bill Mark)

...But even as here, at El Morocco, he was constantly on the nearest telephone, checking and confirming (Bill Mark)

soloist with the Detroit Symphony. That program (on a Sabbath evening) went over the same network on which I did my newscasts.

I turned on my desk radio set to listen to Margaret. She came over like a pro. Not one sour note, as the critic and others had written about her tweet-tweeting. I jotted down the following brief item for my broadcast.

"Detroit: Margaret Truman, the President's daughter, made her debut with the Detroit Symphony a few minutes ago. She was very good!"

After my newscast, a staffer said: "The White House listens to you."

"How do you know that?"

"Just got a call from the producer of the Margaret Truman debut. He said Bess Truman, her mother, had phoned her: 'Walter Winchell just said he heard you and that you came over fine!'"

Some time later Robert Christenberry, then manager of Broadway's Hotel Astor (he became Postmaster of New York City and later a director of the Damon Runyon Cancer Fund), told me that Truman's pal General Vaughan had visited him. Mr. Christenberry related part of their chat.

"I said to Harry [Vaughan] I guess your boss doesn't think much of my friend Winchell."

"Matter of fact," Vaughan replied, "he mentioned Dubbleyu Dubbleyu only yesterday."

"In what way?"

"Something came up about Walter," explained General Vaughan, "and the President chuckled, 'You know I can't get mad at that New York sunuvabitch—he's always been so nice to my baby!'"

Sherman Billingsley, proprietor of the Stork Club, probably gave away more gifts than any other restaurateur. They invariably were cravats, fireman-red suspenders, perfume, gems, and other doodads of value. Billingsley's P.S. on the ties name-dropped "WW wears these ties, too."

Mr. B. sent me the following typewritten bread-and-butter letter he received from President Harry S Truman when he was presented with some Stork Club ties:

"Dear Mr. Billingsley: Thank you ever so much for your Christmas greetings as well as for your kindness in sending me the ties. You were most thoughtful. Best wishes to you for the New Year. Very sincerely yours, Harry S Truman."

The President's P.S. (in ink) needled, "Now inform me who W.W. is."

★

THE IKE I LIKED

"NEW YORK, June 19, 1947 (INS) The New York Daily Mirror today in a copyrighted story by Walter Winchell said today that Gen. Dwight D. Eisenhower has rendered his resignation to President Truman and will become President of Columbia University next Fall."

New York *Post,* same day: "Referring to reports that Gen. Eisenhower had resigned as Chief of Staff and would become President of Columbia University, Frederick Coykendall, chairman of the University's Board of Trustees, said today: 'No President of Columbia has been selected.' "

The New York Times, June 20, 1947: "Eisenhower gets call to Columbia."

☆

Rah, Rah, Rah!
From the *Harvard Alumni Bulletin,* May 14, 1949:

> Walter Winchell broke the news first. Some six weeks ago, he "flashed" a bulletin to his Sunday night audience: "He doesn't know it yet, but Archibald MacLeish, former Librarian of Congress, will be the next Boylston Professor of Rhetoric and Oratory at Harvard College."
>
> Since the election of a Harvard professor to permanent tenure is a matter of lengthy procedure, departmental recommendation, deliberation by an ad hoc committee, . . . and formal action by two quite separate governing boards, no one could be found in Cambridge who felt himself authorized either to confirm or deny Mr. Winchell's assertion. A week or two later, however, the Boston *Herald* repeated the story in a terse news item; the *Globe* followed suit. Later still the Boston *Traveler* published a commendatory editorial.

☆

From page nine of Dwight David Eisenhower's *Mandate For Change, 1953–1956: The White House Years* (Doubleday):

> One incident threw my personal staff into an uproar. Not long after I arrived at the university, Walter Winchell asked . . . each of

238

his radio listeners to send a card or letter urging me to seek the presidential nomination. The mail quickly reached such proportions —approximately twenty thousand letters, cards, and wires in the first week—that there was no convenient place to store it at Columbia. . . . Sure that the flow would stop as soon as the conventions had met and finished their work . . . I suggested that perhaps even my commodious office could be used for storage. . . .

When I arrived at the office the following morning, the staff had a measure of revenge; there was barely room for me to sit at my desk. . . .

I promptly announced a new plan: I was going off on a vacation until they could report that the place was cleared out. But for days my assistants had trouble even counting the inflowing letters and cards. In the end the Columbia University Bureau of Applied Social Research took over the task of analyzing this flash flood of correspondence.

☆

Things with the Washington *Post* were honky-dooly for several years. Then one matinee, while visiting the staff, one of them confided, "I think you have trouble coming up. They plan dropping you."

He suggested I go see the new editor in charge (Mr. Wiggins, always a friend, had been promoted to a softer job), and so I went into the office of Mr. Big, whose name was Friendly (Hmmmmm). I said, "I understand that our honeymoon is about to be over. What am I doing wrong? What is it you don't like that I'm doing? To be repudiated by an important newspaper such as the *Post* will probably cost me other reputable newspapers."

Looking out the window (because, I guess, he couldn't look me in the eye), Mr. Friendly replied, "Oh, Walter, we've changed. WHY HAVEN'T YOU?"

" 'Changed'?" I inquired, puzzled. "How do you mean 'Changed'? Do you mean politically? My attacks on Reds? What?"

Mr. Friendly stared at me blankly.

The *Post* didn't object when I was pro-FDR, pro-Democrat. Now I was an Eisenhower rooter. I am not a man who is for any party—I am for the candidate I like, Republican or Democrat: like many newspapers that call themselves "independent."

And so the Washington *Post* dropped me.

But why did Al Friendly dump me that way? Changed? In what way didn't I change, as he said à la double-talk? You Live and Learn. Months later it came out.

My rebuttal to the attacks by New York *Post* editor (at the time) James Wechsler was the chief reason Mr. Notso Friendly gave my column the Heave-Ho. During the "war" with Wechsler I disclosed that in his youth he had been the national secretary of the Young Communist League. Al Friendly, Sr., was unhappy about me finding an ex-Commy chief editing a New York newspaper.

I wear my scars and medals proudly.

When Ike was inaugurated I was the reporter chosen to be "pool" man for the hundreds of press people. I was then with ABC-TV and it was . . . my initial experience at ad-libbing on camera with a mike. All other news people were assigned to the roof of a two-story building about a hundred and fifty feet away.

As Ike and Mamie arrived—accompanied by several Secret Service agents—I got as close as possible (mike in hand) to describe the event.

The heftiest agent pushed me down. I jumped up and breathlessly told the national teevee audience, "Now you see how well the Secret Service protects our President."

Later I asked that agent why he'd spread-eagle'd me. "Nobody told me any newspapermen would be anywhere near."

The photograph of Ike arriving to take the oath, with me in the background—snapped by Bill Mark—is my favorite of all the pictures on my office walls.

Much later, after kibitzing one of the President's press conferenecs (always a fruitful orchard for anecdotes, quips, and items that White House correspondents cannot use in their grim war reports), I went to the cafeteria in a government building across the street.

Merriman Smith, the dean of White House reporters (the man who ended Presidential press confs with, "Thank you, Mr. President!") hastened in to breathlessly report, "Where the hell you been? Mrs. Eisenhower is waiting for you!"

Mrs. Eisenhower? I had never really met her, except for the time just after Ike was inaugurated and I was pool man for the press bunch, the only newsman within touching distance of the President and his wife. As their car slowly moved on, I shouted into my ABC-TV camera microphone, "Happy eight years, Mamie!"

She turned, smiled, and called out, "Oh, not that! Not that!"

Merriman escorted me back to the White House. One of the Secret Servicers brought me to where Mrs. Eisenhower was seated on a marble bench in one of the huge rooms. The East Room? . . . not sure.

"They never tell me when someone I haven't met is down here,"

240

Mamie said. "Hello!" The bodyguard kept looking at his watch, impatiently. She suddenly inquired, "Do you know why my husband likes you?"

"Because," I replied, "of that postcard poll I ran on the air for several weeks? When I asked radio listeners to jot down the name of a man they'd like to see President and he ran away with nearly all the postcard 'votes'?"

"No," Mrs. Eisenhower said, "this is why." She told of the time, months following the inaugural, when they flew to a friend's estate in the Southland and then motored from the airport to the retreat for some peace and quiet. The President had turned on the car radio at 9:00 P.M., as I did the "Mr. and Mrs. United States!" editorial.

"This is for the people of the South," I began, "where the folks invented hospitality! The President and Mamie are due to land at an airport any moment. They are on the way to a friend's home for a few days' holiday, some golf and fun. Wouldn't it be a novelty and hospitable of all of you in the area—especially the reporters and cameramen—if you all publicly demonstrated Southern hospitality and just let them relax? No interviews or autographers and crowds and so on?

"Thank you, Mr. and Mrs. Southerner!"

Ike and Mamie enjoyed a ten-day vacation there. Not one newsman or autograph pest bothered them.

When they were motoring back to the airfield to return to Washington, the President (Mamie told me) said how wonderful it was to be free for ten days and nights without the press pressure. "You know," Ike told his wife, "they really listen to that fellow!"

"That's why," Mrs. Eisenhower added, "he likes you."

The Secret Service man interrupted the First Lady with, "You are forty-five minutes late."

Mamie shrugged, "So I'm late forty-five minutes already."

I took the federal man's hint and got up to go.

"I want to show you around this place," Mamie said. And she did. For another half hour.

★

WESLEY WELLS

Shortly after my many weekly radio appeals to Governor Goodwin ("Good") Knight of California to commute Wesley Wells, a Negro, from death in the San Quentin gas chamber to the sentence of a life term—I was knotting my tie in the Twentieth Century-Fox barbershop alongside a man who was doing the same. Addressing me in the large wall mirror he said: "You're Mr. Winchell, aren't you?"

"Yes."

"I hope you feel better," he said, "now that you saved that nigger at San Quentin."

"Negro," I edited.

"He killed my brother, you sonofabitch!" And walked out sobbing.

Some time later, while in the San Francisco *Examiner*'s city room, I met a Pulitzer Prize-winning reporter named Ed Montgomery, who drove me upstate to Vacaville, also a facility for mental cases. I wanted to see the man I had helped save from the gas chamber. Wells had been assigned to waiting on table and doing other soft jobs.

To my great disappointment, Wells was far away at another California clink, transferred a few days earlier.

I met high officials of the Vacaville place. One of them sent for Wells's records. I was asked to read them.

I read a few pages—and was embarrassed. Wells, it appears, gave them plenty of trouble from the day he arrived: starting fistfights with other prisoners, sassing the cons, insolent to keepers and other prison executives, making homosexual passes, they alleged, and making himself disagreeable to One and All.

They told me that he was frenetic, frenzied, and more ferocious than ever after I went to bat for him on the air and in the papers.

The prison people, however, confirmed that the man he killed in prison had tried to kill him, after a long feud. That's why he was not given the gas chamber—"self-defense."

Wells's violence (hurling a spittoon at keeper Brown with perfect marksmanship) before the board meeting that heard his complaint about the keeper decided them on execution. California law at the time was: If you are doing life, and you attack a guard, you get the extreme penalty —death. But he was not doing life when he knocked prison guard Brown senseless with the cuspidor.

They gave him life for blowing his top and almost knocking off Brown's, and then ordered him gas-chamber'd.

That's when experts on constitutional law asked me to help them remind Wells's jailers that what they planned was not constitutional.

A year or so later I met one of the people who got me to do it. "Last time I was in California," I said, "I was told that Wells heard my appeals for him over his radio in the death row cell. He never wrote to say he heard me—or to say thanks—when he was spared."

"Oh," reported the man, "he wrote you several letters thanking you. The wardens apparently did not mail them."

I would enjoy knowing that Cassius Clay, H. Rap Brown, Stinkley Curmichael, and other "nonviolent" Negro spokesmen see this chapter. But I don't expect them to consider me a soul brother, just another "whitey" and "honkie."

None of the black power animals seem to remember "whiteys" like Mrs. Liuzzo, the Detroit housewife who was shot dead while driving—some negroes to a Civil Rights meeting or those two young Northern "whiteys" murder by klansmen when they demonstrated for "the cause" in the Deep South.

★

CLYDE HOLFORD

Another condemned man saved from the electric chair was Clyde Holford.

Jim Tully, the novelist, got me interested in Holford's plight. "It would take me at least six months to write it in a book," wrote Tully, "but you have a coast-to-coast microphone and a syndicated column and could help this fellow overnight—getting his story before the public." And so I did.

Holford landed behind bars when he was eighteen. He was shot full of holes before he was captured and got fifteen years for armed robbery. To ease his painful wounds he learned about narcotics while in prison. Along with two other convicts, Holford got into a fight over some dope and a prisoner was slain.

The others pleaded guilty. No one, up to that time, had ever received any severe sentence for a killing in prison. But Governor Marland of Oklahoma decided that Holford should burn. Holford was tried and sentenced to the Oklahoma State Pen's hot squat.

Mr. Tully persuaded many other citizens to intercede for the condemned man. All of us were called "sob sisters" by His Excellency. Following several coast-to-coast broadcasts by this reporter, Holford's death sentence was commuted to life.

I thanked all concerned, including the Oklahoma Court of Appeals and Governor Marland and then addressed these remarks to Holford: "If prisoner Holford is listening to me now at McAlester Prison, this is to urge him to never do anything that might humiliate—or make sorry—the strangers who helped save him from the electric chair."

Several years later Clyde Holford was released.

I told the late Wilbur Clark about him. Mr. Clark gave him a job as an electrician at his Desert Inn, Las Vegas, later owned by Howard Hughes.

Holford proved that an ex-convict can be rehabilitated. He has been there since the early 1950's—happily married, never in trouble with lawmen since, one of the most popular persons with the people he works for and with.

When I make my annual three-day visit to Vegas for the Runyon Cancer Fund Golf Tournament of Champions, the first man to greet me on the putting green is Clyde Holford.

He never says more than two words: "Thanks again."

Then there was my favorite bank burglar, Willie Sutton, still paying his Debt to Society.

A reporter once asked Mr. Sutton why he burgled only banks. Sutton logic'd, "That's where the money is!"

The following two-and-a-half-line broadcast tip to my paper in San Francisco (December 28, 1952) brought vigorous denials from many editors in California:

"San Francisco Call Bulletin: West Coast Commies are now running a school at a camp near Crestline, California. Under strict security regulations. Why is that?"

The San Bernadino *Sun*'s front page on March 26, 1953, headlined the AP's confirmation: "HOUSE UN-AMERICAN ACTIVITIES COMMITTEE REVEALS SCHOOL HELD AT CRESTLINE FOR TOP-RANKING COMMUNISTS."

The *Daily Sun* on March 30, 1953, headlined: "Winchell Has Last Laugh On Crestline."

The story concluded: "Winchell apparently used his private 'pipeline' to break the story of the camp's activities, which was news to many of the county's residents in the mountain area."

★

JOSEPHONY BAKER

Josephine Baker was one of the chorus girls in Harlem's Big-Timey Cotton Club in the long ago. Lovely Lena Horne was in the same line. Cab Calloway starred in the same show. Both show biz Greats.

Miss Baker soon became a headliner and the proprietor of a gay spot in the Broadway area. Her rivals alleged the place barred blacks.

She was happier abroad, where she became one of the rich-raff and the pet of royalty and celebrity parasites. She was acclaimed in Paris and in other European theaters and cafés. She married several white men. One was last-named Bouillon, which is OO-lah-lah for soup. The new generation (in the 1950's in this country) never really knew Josephine Baker—her beauty, class, and talent. She had stayed away too long.

Salaries in show biz changed overnight when Danny Kaye became the first headliner in a Miami Beach night spot (Copa City) to rate $22,500 per week. Copa City's only competition (down the street) was the Beachcomber. The brother of the Beachcomber landlord stopped me one day near the Roney Plaza hotel, my former home in Florida in the winter.

"I just came from Havana," he prefaced, "where I saw a girl who is just great. Her name is Josephine Baker. I can get her for seven thousand a week plus a contract to be her personal representative in the United States."

"I know Josephine," I replied. "I knew her when she was a kid in the Cotton Club chorus. Why don't you sign her?"

"That's why I came to see you," he sighed. "She was about to sign the deal when she put down the pen and said, 'Is Mr. Walter Winchell still vacationing in Miami Beach?' "

" 'I think so,' I said. 'He usually stays until mid-April.' "

" 'Well,' said Baker, 'you go back and ask him how does he feel about me giving up my American citizenship?' So how do you feel about it?"

"Oh, ferCRISSAKES," I capital-lettered. "How is her act?"

"Is that all there is to it?" he asked.

"Of course. Tell her I'll help all I can."

He told me the wild salaries demanded by popular top entertainers.

Damon Runyon on inflation: "What can money be worth when night-clubs pay some comedians $10,000?" Sophie Tucker, who heard about Danny Kaye's $22,500, said she wanted the same wage. The Copa City bosses met those demands, but the Beachcomber brothers couldn't match them. Getting Baker at $7,000 was like finding an orphaned gold mine. A bargain! He flew back to Cuba and signed her. She opened at his place shortly after.

With two hours to go until curtain time, she informed the management that she wouldn't appear "unless some of my people are out front." They frantically phoned me about her ultimatum.

I told them not to be concerned; that I would phone Champion Sugar Ray Robinson (holidaying there) to hasten over with his family and some ebony friends. They were seated down front—another "first" in Miami Beach. Negroes were rarely, if ever, welcomed in the city where a busy shopping street is named Lincoln Road.

Police and detectives surrounded the nightclub—inside and out—to stifle any trouble with the Ku Klux Klan and other haters.

New York columnists and critics (holidaying in Miami Beach) were among the capacity opening audience. All of them panned the hell out of her act.

Minty Danton Walker of the New York *Daily News* dismissed her as a "clotheshorse." The others were disappointed in her offerings—songs rendered in Harlem French.

At the première a drunk yelled: "Awww, sing an American song!" I asked the management to escort him out.

She apologized and said she had been in France for twenty-seven years, but if the orchestra would play the one number she remembered best, she would sing it.

The song was "Peg O' My Heart."

The audience applause was polite. Mine was the minority vote. I liked her act.

After her proformance I went backstage to tell her how good she was.

She thanked me for my assistance and compliments and then went into her real "act."

"I am dedicating the rest of my life to fighting for my people," she intoned.

"Why don't you entertain the public," I suggested, "and let people like me fight for your people? I've been fighting for your people and all minorities long before it was fashionable." I told her to ask Negro showman Larry Steele and many other colored people where I stood. In the column next morning I flung this orchid at her: "Josephine Baker—a Real Star!" I also said it on my coast-to-coast broadcast.

246

It won her an immediate booking—two weeks—at New York's Strand Roof. At ten thousand dollars per week.

Her manager sent me photos of the big way she was billed on Broadway. Her name was in the marquee lights. Bunting draped all around the marquee read: " 'A Real Star!' says Winchell." They were advertising my name as large as hers.

The new generation, it appears, wasn't buying her unfamiliar name. They bought my recommendation.

She made Broadway history when the Roxy Theater (a few streets north at Fiftieth—the Strand was at Forty-seventh) booked her at twenty thousand per. The Roxy never before "played" an act that appeared that close—at the Strand.

I mentioned her act at the Roxy almost daily—sugary notices. A colored "writer" was in her Roxy dressing room at the time. "Yeah," he critic'd, "that Winchell ain't so hot. He once gave a book of mine a plug, but it didn't sell more than a few dozen copies." He didn't say how many copies his flop would have sold without my orchid. It was during this booking that the "Stork Club incident" was manufactured—an incident in which I played no part. But you'd never know it from the atomic attacks in the national Negro press and in the New York *Post*. I was the chief target, Number One whipping goat. In fact, I wasn't in the Stork Club when Josephony charged discrimination. I had left two hours before it "didn't" happen.

My witnesses were Yvonne O'Brian and her husband, Jack. Discrimination? Well, you decide that.

When I arrived at the Stork Club, Mr. Billingsley reported, "A friend of yours is coming in after the theater tonight—Josephine Baker with a party."

"How do you know?"

"One of her party, a woman, phoned for the reservation. When it was okayed the lady said, 'Josephine Baker, a Negro, is in our party. Is that all right?'

"Yes, of course." And so the reservation (including Miss Baker) was accepted.

When the group arrived, shortly before midnight, the "Gold Chain" at the entrance to the club proper was dropped and they sashayed in. That was Hurdle Number Two.

The velvet rope at the Cub Room was unfastened for them—Hurdle Number Three.

247

Miss Baker's friends proceeded to their table. She paused at Table 50, near the doorway, to greet the movie star Ann Sheridan and her fiancé, Steve Hannaghan. I was seated opposite the O'Brians. Miss Baker didn't see me. I waited a bit for her to stop chatting with Ann and Steve. But she was too busy to be interrupted.

I told the O'Brians that I had promised Darryl Zanuck, the Twentieth Century-Fox giant, I would go to the Globe Theater on Broadway to catch a "sneak preview" of his new flop, *Rommel*.

"Let's go," I said to my companions, "we'll be late."

We hastened to the theater, where the glorification of the Nazi general infuriated me. I panned Zanuck for filming it. "The least you could have done," I complained in print, "was wait until we get back our war dead!"

A press agent had just returned from soldiering in the war. He was so broke he still wore his unpressed khaki. When Baker's manager asked me to suggest a press agent for her I recommended him. They put him on at two hundred and fifty dollars per.

He was on the job about a week when he chucked it. "I just couldn't take money from a woman like her," he said. "She told Poston, the reporter, a lot of lies about what happened in the Stork."

A Negro reporter for the *Post* named Ted Poston inflamed readers with maniacal charges against the Stork owner and this Innocent Bystander.

The New York *Post* series on Miss Baker's fraudulent story was edited by its top editor, James Wechsler. But in fairness to her, she vigorously objected when Poston said: "Where was the great liberal and friend of the underdog sitting when this insult happened to you?"

"Oh," Baker complained, "don't drag Mr. Winchell into this. He wasn't even there at the time!"

Mr. Poston dismissed her with, "let me write this my way. I will destroy him." That was the big idea. The blatt needed circulation at the time.

So here we are—being charged with "failure" to stop Miss Baker from being "discriminated against" in my friend's supper club—while I was fighting a friend named Zanuck for glorifying a Nazi. Never a dull moment.

The Negro press, which had reported (with high praise) my many wars against racists in New York, California, etcetera, all published the same canned editorial—furnished by the NAACP. The idiotorial was headlined: THE DESPICABLE MR. WINCHELL. The late Walter

248

White, then leader of the NAACP, phoned me how miffed he was to learn that I had "failed" his people.

"Listen, you sonofabitch!" I exploded. "I fought for the rights of your people long before there was any NAACP!"

"I am warning you," he shouted, "that I will order lightning to strike you down!"

"Oh, drop dead, you phony bastard!" I yelled—and hung up.

An obliging man. He dropped dead shortly after.

Then Josephine Baker sued the *Mirror* over my comments about her spurious charges in the Stork Club—for four hundred thousand dollars.

A hairdresser in a top department store on Fifth Avenue read about her lawsuit and phoned our legal department. He furnished an affidavit which stated in part: "I asked her why she was getting so prettified and dandified."

"I am going to the Stork Club tonight," the affidavit alleged.

"Oh, really? I didn't know Negroes were welcome there."

"That's why I'm going," he swore she chuckled. "I am going to put on the finest performance of my career there tonight!" Fakery at its phoniest! By a has-been I helped climb the heights again.

When the Hearst barristers submitted the hairdresser's affidavit to Baker's counsel at the pretrial examination, he threw his arms in the air in surrender. He told his client he would not continue as her lawyer if she didn't forget the whole thing.

That was the End of That One.

On her brief tour of the nation the public prints reported how often she complained of "discrimination" and caused scenes. The Negro press did not, so far as I know, print Miss Baker's public statements that she was a supporter and fan of admitted Communist Fidel Castro.

The wire services covering her tour of South America also disclosed some of her alleged outbursts there. One quoted her as claiming that "she actually saw lynchings of Negroes everywhere in the U.S." Princess Charming.

When I tangled with Josephine, Sullivan rushed over to a radioaf's microphone and said he wanted to defend Miss Baker—anything to get into the same headlines.

His opening statement (which I didn't hear, but which others did) was, "I despise Walter Winchell for what he has done to Josephine Baker." When I exposed the fact that Miss Baker was pro-Commy and (when it was fashionable) pro-Mussolini and Hitler, Sullivan said, "How can she be both?"

I rebutted with documented proof: her own quotes as reported by the Associated Press, United Press, and International News Service.

This is to debunk some of Miss Baker's alibis—that she was never anti-American, anti-Semitic, or pro-Communist and pro-Fascist. Miss Baker, it appears, allied herself with whatever team was winning. "Anti-Semitic?" she was once quoted as saying, "Why, I married a Jew!"

The following news clippings were collected by James E. Bowden of the Hearst Corporation legal department to combat her lawsuit against me and the papers that printed my charges.

From the New York *Post,* October 1, 1935: "Le Vesinet, France, Oct. 1 (AP): Josephine Baker announced today she will campaign to get Negro help for Premier Mussolini against Ethiopia. She charged Haile Selassie maintains slavery and that Mussolini will free the slaves. She will recruit an army of Negroes to aid Italy."

An article from *The New York Times,* May 10, 1943, datelined Fez French, Morocco quotes Miss Baker as saying she will never return to the United States.

From the book, *Les Mémoires de Josephine Baker:* In this book, noted the Hearst barristers, on which she admitted having collaborated with the author, she is quoted as having said, "The Jews exploited the Negroes in America. . . . In Harlem the Jews reduce the Negroes to slavery."

The House Un-American Activities Committee Report for January 1950, reveals that "witnesses testifying before that body identified Baker's agent, Robert Wachsman, as a member of the Communist Party."

From the Hearst legal department: "On Easter Sunday, 1950, while Miss Baker was playing at the Politeama Theater in Bari, Italy, she induced a member of the audience to sing 'Giovinezza,' the official song of Fascism—causing a riot and police intervention."

A clipping from *Bohemia,* a Cuban publication, dated December 10, 1950 (printed in Spanish), reports Miss Baker said over the air from Radio Station CMQ, "I do not want anything to do with the United States."

The New York Times for April 24, 1950, ran an article reporting her appearance in Bari, Italy, when she invited members of audience to sing 'Old Giovinezza,' the official Fascist song—one singer was arrested."

The New York *World-Telegram and Sun* for May 27, 1951, ran an article reporting that Communists had a field day in Harlem distributing literature during the Josephine Baker celebration in that community.

The New York *Daily News* for October 8, 1952, ran an article reporting that Baker had sung for Dictator Perón and said she was waging a campaign against the United States in six articles she had written for *Critica*—a Buenos Aires newspaper controlled by the Perón Government. In one of these articles she wrote, "In the United States they hunt Christ with a gun and hang Him from every tree." In another article for *Critica* she said the statements she was making were based on "personal observation in the United States."

The same *Daily News* report quoted Baker as saying in *Critica* that Negroes in the United States were treated like dogs.

The New York *Daily News* for October 17, 1952, ran an article quoting a statement by Miss Baker which had appeared in *Demoeraca*, another newspaper controlled by the Perón Government. Her alleged quote: "I have personally seen many lynchings in the U.S. and men, women and children killed like animals."

An article in the New York *Daily News,* November 6, 1952, deals with a lecture given in Buenos Aires at the Odeon Theater in which Miss Baker is reported to have said, "I shall count it an honor to be barred from the United States."

A Long Island *Press* article of November 7, 1952, states Miss Baker attacked President Eisenhower in one of her lectures in Buenos Aires and stated that she pitied the Americans who had elected him President.

The New York *Daily Mirror* on November 19, 1952, ran an article stating that Congressman Adam Clayton Powell had branded Baker a liar for statements that she made in her lectures about lynching in the United States.

From the Hearst Legal Department: "In Josephine Baker's examination before trial conducted in this office on June 14, 1954, she admitted that she was arrested in Havana, Cuba, about a year ago, charged with Communism. She said she beat this charge."

From *The New York Times,* reporting Baker's visit to Havana, Cuba, to help Castro celebrate the anniversary of his revolution: "Havana, July 25th. Josephine Baker, the Broadway star who became the idol of French music halls, arrived here to celebrate the 13th anniversary of the start of the Cuban Revolution. Premier Fidel Castro personally extended the invitation when she was here earlier this year."

So there you are, you stupids of the press and other news media, who breast-beated: "Winchell is ridiculous when he says she was once pro-Red, then pro-Fascist. How can you be both?" Ask Miss Baker, you bastards.

☆

Then another fraud named Father Divine, who said he was God (and his followers believed it), read that my mother died. I heard him declare in his holiest tones in one of his radio talks (and he printed it in his rag): "Something had to be done to hurt this man, and so I ruled that his mother should die." The bum eventually was exposed as a rapist of young Negro girls and an all-around crook.

I therefore ordered "lightning" to strike him dead, which it did.

☆

From the New York *Enquirer,* April 21, 1952: "As far as Negro prejudice goes, it is doubtful that any man in America can offer as good a record as Winchell's. We were with him when he invited Sugar Ray Robinson to Gulfstream racetrack near Miami Beach. At the track Robinson said to WW, 'Well. I'll see you later.'

" 'Where you going?' asked Winchell.

" 'Down to the enclosure for colored people.'

" 'The hell you are,' WW exploded. 'You're going where I go!'

"They spent the day in the clubhouse restaurant."

★

SENATOR McCARTHY'S BOY ROY

The first time I ever saw Roy M. Cohn, brilliant young barrister and son of a devoted mother and daddy (a Justice of the New York Appellate Division) was when Roy patronized the Stork Club for the first time. He was then about twenty-three. Cohn was a very plump lad—too plump—and he was no fashion plate then. He also was cursed with facial blemishes: pimples, blackheads, acne.

He violated owner Billingsley's cardinal law: "no table-hopping." The youngster kept Sammy Glicking from table to table, greeting friends of his family and people he knew—lawyers, judges, politicians, *et al.*

"Who the heck is that sloppy-looking guy?" Billingsley demanded of his waiters and captains. They did not know. He had come in with others.

I overheard Mr. B. signal "Oxo!"—his code word for "Bar him."

"Hey, Sherman, don't do that!" I interrupted. "His father is a very important judge!"

"Heavens to Betsy!" replied Sherman. "I didn't know that—thanks."

Sherman then proceeded to give Roy the full treatment that celebs, stars, politicians, editors, publishers, and columnists (with wide syndication) got: no check, plus "Sortilège" perfume, cravats, and other gifts.

Roy Cohn had Columbus'd a new world! He came in every night almost—and brought other freeloaders. After we met and sat together at the Number One table in the Cub Room, Table 50, a chumship began.

One of his father's intimates told me that when Roy was a tot of five, Papa never brought home the papers with the funnies. Papa's pet paper was *The Law Journal.* The Cohn family friend revealed that Roy grew up to be a good lawyer "because the poor kid's only reading matter, besides fairy tales and other children's books, was the deadly dull *Law Journal!"*

Good vignette for the col'm. I made it public many times—in the paper, on the air, in interviews. The story was echo'd often by others in mags, books, columns, etc. Roy was getting a quick national rep. People introduced themselves to him in the other places about midtown. He rewarded me with juicy items about lawsuits, legalities, and so forth.

Now I have a terrible confession to make public for the first time: I was indirectly responsible for Roy M. Cohn landing on the McCarthy Committee as chief counsel.

One night in the Stork Cub Room I introduced Roy to my Big Boss, Richard E. Berlin, the man W. R. Hearst, Sr., in his will had made top man of the Hearst Empire. Before I introduced them I briefed Mr. Berlin on Roy Cohn. "This kid's a real genius, Dick. Everybody who knows him down at the U.S. courthouse says so. Very clever—rarely loses a case. You ought to give him some of the Hearst cases. He's a winner." Mr. Berlin was impressed—very.

Shortly after that, Berlin supped at the Stork with Senator Joe McCarthy. I had never met the Senator before.

Berlin invited me to sit with them. "Senator McCarthy," said Boss Berlin, "is another great Commy-fighter. He will soon have an investigating committee go after them all."

Roy came in looking for me. I introduced Cohn to McCarthy. They became what they became.

When the McCarthy Red Probe was the top-rated radio and teevee program, no newspaperman got more "firsts" than I. Saturday nights (about 1 or 2:00 A.M.) I could always depend on Roy meeting me in the Cub Room. He never failed to bring a batch of memos—written in my style: brief, concise, punchy scoops. Then he would jot down a lot more at the table.

After a snack Roy would go home. I would hasten to the New York

253

Mirror and my typewriter to finish getting my Sunday night coast-to-coaster ready.

The news about Washington—what the McCarthy Committee would do on the following day, names they would subpoena, who would testify, what McCarthy would charge—was made public via my newscast. The late Monday (and early Tuesday editions) invariably confirmed the beats.

What a source! The opposition papers in New York and elsewhere called me a "McCarthy stooge," a McCarthyite," Roy Cohn's "Svengali."

Roy also gave inside info to other Hearst writers like George Sokolsky, liberal in other years, later a conservative and bitter Commy-warrior for Hearst and other papers.

Pegler had been a long-ago defender of Jews when Hitler was on the way up. (You didn't know that one, did you? I didn't either, until I found some old columns of Mr. P's in my files, but my eyebrows haven't come down yet)—Pegler was also fed anti-Red material, via Roy—right out of McCarthy's dossiers.

But Pegler was now a Fuehrer. His anti-Semitism, anti-Blackism, and all his other maniacal anti-isms did not stop him from accepting Jewish Roy Cohn's tips. What a Phonus-Bolonus!

Pegler and Winchell—at the time, and for many years—were not speaking to each other except in our columns.

Not even Hearst monarch Richard E. Berlin or Roy Cohn could get me to shake hands with him. In fact, whenever Pegler came into the Stork Club I took a walk—to some other late-spot. This made the owner of the Stork Club glum. Pegler didn't plug Mr. Billingsley's place the way I had for decades. Pegler rarely mentioned it.

One night Bill Corum, a star sportswriter for Hearst, asked me to forget the feud with Peg; saying that Peg was miserably bored sitting in his Park Avenue apartment. He missed coming to the Stork Club, but he knew that if he did, I would exit or wouldn't come in. "Why don't you forget it?" Corum said. "Peg's really a good guy."

Billingsley sat there listening. He didn't make the same request, but I knew he wished that I would not continue the feud—considering all the Hearst executives who patronized the Stork.

I had stayed away for many weeks once—another time for three years, because Mr. Berlin permitted his editors to kill my rebuttal to a George Sokolsky rap at me in Hearst papers and then I tried to fight back at Pegler's pokes.

Berlin never stopped them from knocking the hell outta me. When I exposed Reds (by name!) for full columns, and Lefties on news mags and other New York and Washington rags, Mr. Berlin thought that was Just Peachy. But when I "took on" some Fascist or pro-Nazi publishers, editors, and columnists, it never got in print.

They couldn't stop me from doing it over the air, however. Oh, you wonderful sponsor, Andrew Jergens!

Joe McCarthy soon found out where I stood. He found out that I was a newspaper reporter; that when he came up with anything that stood up—like evidence of the Alger Hiss plants in government high places—or when former Reds (turned government witnesses) took the stand—I credited madman McCarthy with the disclosures. But when McCarthy waved a paper in the air at the hearings and declared, "I have here a list—a list of seventy-six names of Communists working in top-security jobs!" I went to his office at noon recess to request that list—figuring that if he gave it to any newsman, I'd be Mr. Lucky.

But he was very busy gabbing with his staff and reporters on Far Right papers. They were so busy talking and giving him suggestions and "stuff" on whom to accuse next that I had no trouble stealing a carbon of his "list" that was on a stack of other papers on the desk. I didn't have to reach for it. It was right there near my pickpocket fingers.

He saw me make my exit and yelled, "Mr. Winchell! What do you think of the President [Eisenhower] *now*?"

I came back—relieved that no one had witnessed my burglary. With a finger pointed at him I said: "Senator, I am *devoted* to the President —let's get that straight, okay?"

He faked a smile and sourcasmed, "Every man to his own taste." His staffers and the right-wingers on the papers gave me a glare. I never went to his office again.

Now we are back in the Senate Caucus Room for the afternoon session of the Army Hearing. Peress, Coleman, Harry Dexter White, and others were being accused of being "subversive." At the press table I studied the list of "seventy-six names," reading it as I held the list under the table.

The slip of paper did not have seventy-six names at all. It listed seven. Every name on it had been mentioned in the papers and over the air weeks earlier.

"What a faker," I thought. What a faker.

Nudging newsmen and women on both sides of me, I whispered,

"Looka what I gotta!" I folded the paper to hide the "list"—showing them only the head over it and a memo line to remind him to say, "I have here a list of seventy-six names!"

The newspaper people were amazed. "How in hell did you get it?" some asked.

I turned on my cat-ate-the-canary grin and cooed, "Military secret."

I exposed the McCarthy fakery the following broadcast. I knew the Hearst paper I worked for in New York wouldn't publish it.

I also told Roy M. Cohn what I had done—and what a phony the list was, considering every name on it was stale news.

Roy's scoops about the McCarthy probe became fewer, and then none. But he continued donating trivia about other Washington and New York matters and cases involving divorces of famed folks, criminal cases, etc.

In short, I was marked lousy by Senator Joe and his staffers. They had the Hearst papers in their hip pockets—but not Walter.

Some McCarthyite!

Washington's Drew Pearson started covering Capitol Hill with Robert Allen in the long ago. My columns and broadcasts often pattycaked their reporting and skewps. We became allies.

Pearson, in a note wrote: "Thanks for the many boosts. We are merely trying to do in Washington what you have done in New York."

After Pearson and Allen "divorced," Drew won a prime-time fifteen-minute spot on the same network I was on. "I don't care where you put me," he reportedly told radio execs, "just so long as it is the same night Walter goes on. Before or after his broadcast will be okay with me."

Both of us despised the same frauds and we demolished many of them. When a bigot or member of Congress or any politico attacked me (or they him) we went to each other's "rescue." "The Katzenjammer Kids of Journalism," I label'd our Act.

Then Came Der Tag. We splituated over Senator Joe McCarthy's furious assault on Pearson in a Washington hotel washroom.

Pearson was relieving himself when in came McCarthy, who beat him up. Pearson's columns and broadcasts had "beat up" McCarthy for months. Now it was the atomic-tempered Senator's "Getting Even Time."

The incident must have taken place the day before I went on the air. Pearson phoned me Sunday afternoon and said: "What are you going to do about that sonofabitch?"

"Not a thing," I said. "It's not my table."

"Where am I going to put it? In the Hearst papers? Over King Features Syndicate—Hearst-owned? They are on McCarthy's team! The network lawyers are killing a lot of my stuff about lawmakers."

Pearson hung up. His newscast went on at 6:00 P.M. Mine at 9.

On came Pearson's program. I listened to his reports to make sure I didn't use anything he had first. Some of our sources often carelessly gave us both the same "exclusive."

His fifth item sourcasm'd: "New York City: Many people are wondering about Walter Winchell's peculiar palship with gang chief Frank Costello!"

Drew immediately went on my Ingrate List. The End of a Beautiful False Friendship.

As another of my favorite quotes goes: "Too many people remember the Bumps and forget the Caresses." Old Pal Pearson forgot the many plugs I gave him when he started his column. Story of My Life.

Now it is 1968 as I jot this down. Both of us are older if not wiser. And mellower—until the next round.

When my personal world began collapsing—grave illness in the family, the first hospitalization in my long life, my paper, *The Mirror,* dead, and then my next paper dead—I wanted to quit and take it easy in my sunset years. The word got around town that I was on "the way out" as a Hearst headliner, that a TV columnist was quietly being groomed to take my place—which he eventually did, on the ill-fated *World Journal Tribune,* which folded fast: in about eight months.

Press agents, other newspaper people, actors and actresses I had helped "make it to the top" treated me like a Has-Been, A Once-Was. A "Dead Duck," one column-imitator gloated. The hell with them all, I shrugged. I've seen it happen to other byliners for nearly fifty years, in and out of the news biz.

The very first to disown me was—one guess: R.M.C.

He never found time to answer my calls, or to sit in the Stork with me and let Mr. Billingsley pick up the check. Roy romanced other columnists instead. I could spot almost every item he gave them for their daily stint.

Then came the time when Mr. Cohn was in deep trouble with the law. He had been indicted and, if found guilty, would have gone to the can or been disbarred—disgraced.

257

One of his close pals phoned me in Hollywood. "Now listen carefully, Walter," he began, "if ever a guy needed a friend, it is Roy. I want you to take the first jet out of there and come to New York, take the stand, and be a character witness!"

"Character witness?" I groaned. "I couldn't be that phony!"

"Roy's in big trouble—he needs help from his friends!"

"He stopped being my friend long ago. I never stopped being his. Anyway, I am not going to risk my life in any plane to save his. I also have trouble with my roots. I'm going to have dental surgery. I won't do it. I'll write the judge a letter instead."

I sent His Honor a letter (Special Delivery, air mail) testifying that I had known Roy M. Cohn for many years; that I had never heard anything about him that was "illicit, illegal, or sinful," and so on.

I not only wrote the judge that letter, I featured it at the top of my column two days after the judge received it.

Mr. Cohn, former friend, was acquitted.

★

MARILYN AND JOE

When Joe DiMaggio was King of the New York Yankees (and the National Pastime), and Marilyn Monroe was on her Way Up to become Queen of Girlywood, she had never heard of him.

They finally met—and ignited on their first date. A blind date, of all things.

It happened like this: The scene was the Villanova, a popular-with-celebs Italo pastafahzool spot on the Strip between Hollywood and Los Angeles.

At the bar near the door were Vince Edwards (not yet famous as "Ben Casey") and a press agent. Mr. DiMaggio came in alone.

DiMaggio without a Doll? "He must be waiting for some Babe," one of the chaps assumed. "Hey, Joe!" called one.

DiMaj came over and traded baseball and girl-talk with the pair.

"Doesn't look right, Joe, seeing you without a chick."

"Just got in," he reported with a chuckle. "I know a few in this town."

"Would you like to meet a real doll?"

"I always like to make new friends."

One of the men went to a phone booth and called Marilyn. "What's a nice girl like you doing home alone—or aren't you?"

"Just got in. I had one of those days. It's so hot. Gonna take a bath."

"Then wotcha gonna do?"

"Do my hair, make a sandwich, and read a book."

"I'm over at the Villanova with one of my idols, Joe DiMaggio. I'd like you to meet him. Swell guy."

"What's he do?" cross-examined Monroe. "An actor?"

"What's he doooo? Ha! He's the most famous baseball player in the world, Marilyn: the Number One Home Run Hitter. C'mon over."

She came over in about half an hour looking like "Marilyn Monroe" without all that studio gook. No false eyelashes, no counterfeit anything. Just a touch of mascara on her orbs and Just Enough lipstick on That Mouth!

"Marilyn, honey," announced her friend, "meet my pal Joe of the New York Yanks."

"Hi, Joe," she cooed.

Then her date-getter had her meet the other lad. They all had a drink. Marilyn was then a Coke fiend. Never hooch.

The familiar small talk was exchanged. Then the man who introduced them said he had to leave with his pal and to "Have fun, you two."

Joe and Marilyn sat at a booth, ordered another round, and tcht-chatted. Their he-and-shelectricity lit up the dimly illuminated ristorante.

"You like spaghetti?" Marilyn asked Joe.

It broke him up. When he stopped laughing, he told her he was from San Francisco, where his family owned an Italian-American restaurant on Fisherman's Wharf.

"I've been eating spaghetti, macaroni, and all the other pasta since I was a baby!"

"Well then, that's fine," said the very happy Marilyn. "That's the only thing I can cook. Let's go to my place and have some."

At her kitchen in a mini-apartment on Doheny (not far from the Villanova) DiMaj let her toy with the cooking for a while, and then gave her a lesson in How It Should Be Done.

It was such a happy time. As Mitchell Parish's poetry goes in Hoagy Carmichael's "Star Dust": "When our love was new and each kiss an inspiration . . ."

They dated for two years.

In Hollywood, New York, at the Yankee's Florida training camp, in San Francisco, and when she had a day or two off from the studio—she wing'd to wherever he was.

Or Joe jetted to Girltown and his Girl. The papers kept them on page one a lot of the time.

It was Romeo and Juliet, Garbo and Gilbert, Hepburn and Tracy, Liz

Taylor and Mike Todd, Taylor and Fisher, Taylor and Burton, Frankeee and Johneee . . . Frankeee and Anybodeee.

There was the time in New York when a famed ham wouldn't quit sending her wires, flowers, gifts, and phone calls for a date. Joe heard about it from one of Marilyn's gal-pals, who feared he'd hear it wrong.

He told his closest friend, "Gentleman George" Solotaire, the most lovable man and Broadway theater-ticket broker in town, about the pest bothering MM. Solotaire, a short fellow (with a heart condition) decided to take on the nuisance.

"You butt out of it," he cautioned DiMaj, "you might get your name in the papers."

"Gentleman George" phoned the girl-botherer. "Look, pal," he said in his always–polite tone, "Miss Monroe is keeping company with Joe DiMaggio. It's been in all the papers for a long time. Why don't you get smart and forget about it? Because if you don't, Joe might get sore and hit you for a triple!"

During Joe's last World Series with the Yankees, I heard that he was breaking the rules and doing the Greenwich Village joynts with Marilyn. I kept phoning his hotel until he came in around 5:00 A.M.

"You know I'm not going to print it, Joe, but the leak is all over Lindy's, the Stage Deli, the Copa, El Morocco, at Jack Dempsey's— everywhere along The Street. Some column will pounce on it. If the Yanks lose, you'll be The Goat."

"Don't worry about it," Joe said sleepily, "I'll be there on time."

And he was—as usual.

The next day he homer'd.

This tender scene unfolded in Hollywood at Marilyn's apartment. Joe was looking at television. Marilyn was sewing. And Thinking.

DiMaggio was not the source for the next scene. He never discusses the women in and out of his life. This is to let him know why I know it happened. The source was his pal, Solotaire, whom I promised I'd forget it—unless I reminisced when I "did" a book.

Tennyrate, Marilyn was sewing—and thinking—when she suddenly removed her specs, put down the needle and thread, walked over to Joe and, getting down on her knees, with her elbows on his and chin cupped in her hands, plaintively said: "Guisseppe, darling, I want you should marry me, please?" And so they were wed and didn't live happily ever after.

Their flaming romance lasted two years. The marriage—nine months. They never stopped adoring each other, mind you. Even when they separated, they dated often, driving the columnists nutz—guessing wrong.

She made her first trip to Japan (with him), where the fans went mad about him every time he played against Japanese teams after baseball season in the United States. This time, the Japanese movie public went daffy about his wife. They had never seen their favorite American actress in person before.

They didn't give Joe less adoration. But ah, so! "So prett-teee Ma-wah-win Mon-woe!" No getting away from the fact. Marilyn stole that show!

Then came the press conference to announce her divorce plans. The movie, baseball, and general public were saddened. "First the laughter, then the tears," as they say when a Lover becomes a Loser.

One of New York's great psychiatrists won renown and wealth healing the minds of the sick-sick-sick-in-the-head-rich, many of them with marriage problems. His counsel to men and women suffering the Mister-and-Miseries reconciled several famed couples on the Verge-of-a-Dirge.

One evening he invited me to dine at his home.

"Whatzamatta, Doctor, you got the downs or something?"

This specialist in the art of healing heads and hearts sighed: "You are a worldly man. You have written about people like me. Could you help me solve an agonizing problem?"

"That's your department, Doctor," I said, "not mine. What's wrong?"

Breaking into tears, he sobbed, "My wife left me. What can I do to get her back?"

Movie star Errol Flynn (many times wed) described the ideal wife: "I don't care if she doesn't know how to cook—so long as she doesn't know a good lawyer."

FIGHTING CANCER WITH CLASS

It was Richard Rodgers, Oscar Hammerstein, and Leland Hayward who dreamed up the Damon Runyon Cancer Fund's most unusual annual gift.

When Rodgers and Hammerstein's *King and I, Oklahoma, Carousel,*

Pipe Dream, and *South Pacific* were Broadway standouts, Dick phoned me at Miami Beach: "The fund will get all of our house seats. Should bring you about a hundred and twenty-five thousand dollars more or less a year."

Every producer in New York followed suit. The Runyon Fund peddles the best down-front, on-the-aisle pews. We sell them for the regular box office tariff plus "a donation." That could be from twenty-five dollars a ticket and up. The donation is tax-deductible.

Thanks to all ticket brokers who, when they have no seats left, suggest that the playgoer phone the Fund. The late "Gentleman George" Solotaire was the first to do that.

The Runyon Fund to date has been enriched (via these house seats) by $1,450,000. So thankxxxxx again, Richard, Oscar, and Leland. (You, too, Dorothy Rodgers!)

In 1955, when Rodgers and Hammerstein were prospering with five musical clicks on Broadway at the same time, I suggested to Sherman Billingsley, the owner of the Stork Club, "Why don't you invite all the casts of their hits and give a night honoring Rodgers and Hammerstein?"

I emceed the event.

Next day in the *Daily Mirror* I devoted the column to it. The title (from one of their top ditties) heading that col'm: "SOME EN-CHANTED EVENING!"

A few weeks later Sullivan devoted his teevee show to honoring R & H. He called it: "Some Enchanted Evening."

I tell you, Eddie hated me but loved my Word-Weddings, Three Dotz, and ideas. How can you "hate and despise" a fellow who makes you rich?

Two other women in my frenetic and frantic career who have made my various jobs easier to juggle are Suzanne Statler and Dorothy Moore. Dorothy is vice-prez and manager of both the Runyon and WW Foundation funds.

Susie started as a file clerk at the Runyon Cancer Fund. One day, when Rose was indisposed (merely an agonizing toothache and various other aches in her busy fingers) she phoned Miss Moore to send a girl over to answer the phones, etc. Susie got demoted and was sent over. On her first day! She quit soon after, for a job in a Beverly Hills bank. Her beau was on the Los Angeles *Times* staff.

I started narrating and appearing in Desilu's *Untouchables* and *WW File* TV shows. I persuaded Susie to quit the bank and work for me. She now wears two pieces of millinery. Weekends (Sats and Sundays—

Rose's two days off) proofreading, then recopying the revisions in the column, and the rest of the week dittoing the newscast copy.

Her favorite fellers include Sammy Fain, composer of hundreds of delightful songs ("I'll Be Seeing You"; "Love Is A Many Splendored Thing") and movie/stage star Franchot Tone, who adored her via the mail and cables—when he wasn't adoring the field.

Dorothy Moore, my right arm at the Runyon Cancer Fund, is this kind of a gal. When I named her executive director (following the death of the man who hired her) I told Dorothy she would get the same high wage he had received. She wouldn't think of it.

Her salary was then about a hundred and twenty-five per week, paid by the Winchell Foundation—not by monies from donors to fight cancer. All expenses for fourteen years were paid by the WWF.

Miss Moore, Canadian-born, another very efficient and attractive woman, refused to accept a yearly salary of twenty-five thousand dollars.

The Runyon Board of Directors persuaded her finally to name her "raise." She agreed to accept half.

Marlene Dietrich was the only distaff director of the Runyon Cancer Fund for many years. She would, at her own expense, go to various places where some group like the Fraternal Order of Eagles wanted a celebrity to come and not make a speech but accept their donation. The Eagles gave a minimum of a hundred thousand dollars a year over ten years after they pledged to give us a million, which they did. And they haven't stopped.

Marlene got on a plane to Rochester. When it got out onto the strip something went wrong. It was a very hot summer day. The air conditioning went out of business, and the people were sweltering. There they were out on the strip waiting for mechanics to fix whatever had happened.

After about a half an hour of being miserable, Marlene took off the jacket of her suit and sat with no bra. Nobody could get off the plane. The doors were still locked, and you can imagine the free show they got. When she wanted to light a cigarette she dropped her hands from her little old titty-tittys (incidentally I saw them, and they are kinda cute) and enjoyed her cigarette.

The plane finally took off and arrived in a torrential downpour. The plane couldn't get anywhere near the airport to deposit the passengers, and it was a long walk through slush—not only slush but mud. Marlene told me later, "Up to the tops of my legs and I am valking," with her charming, sexy accent, and oy gevalt what a figure!

Incidentally, the first time I ever used the word "sotcha" was when she knocked them on their behinds at the Lunt-Fontanne, where she was a smash. I said, "You are a sotcha." And she said, "Sotcha, What's a sotcha?" I said, "Don't you know what a sotcha is? Sotcha as in sotcha girl." That got a chuckle. Now she walked, muddy and dirty, and nobody met her. Finally she got to the dinner and made a little speech thanking the Eagles from the Runyon Fund Committee and from me, the treasurer, and from the people of the United States who have been so generous in making the Runyon Fund the trustee of their more than $30 million, never a penny ever deducted for expenses of any kind.

Then Marlene took the next plane back, after going to a hotel and taking a bath—but still in the same dirty clothes. She didn't take anything with her, as she had planned to take the very next plane back with the 100Gs. So hurray for Marlene Dietrich, a beautiful, beautiful girl. A sotcha.

The women in my life, you see, are all High-class Broadz.

MAGIC WAND

Song star Roberta Sherwood was my biggest show biz skewp.

She tried for nearly twenty-five years to "make" the Big Town. The nearest she got to New York was Elizabeth, New Jersey. She married Don Lanning, a Broadway musical comedy star, and they raised three sons and once owned the largest restaurant on Biscayne Boulevard, Miami.

Then several sour breaks—including Mr. Lanning's grave illness—put them out of business. Roberta had to take whatever bar and grill owners could afford—to feed her family.

"Sometimes," she said, "I got as low as ten dollars a night."

"Oh, Roberta," I said, "who works for ten dollars a night?"

"Hungry people," was the reply.

On January 15, 1956, I found her in a café at Miami Beach. She was singing love songs, torch songs, sittin' on the porch songs—"You're Nobody Til Somebody Loves You"; "Cry Me A River"; "Take Your Shoes Off Baby And Start Runnin' Thru My Mind"—and so many other greats.

A few columns later I reported: "Att'n Networks, Recording Execs, *et al:* Take the fastest plane, train, or bus and go to Murray Franklin's place opposite the Roney Plaza, Miami Beach, and find yourself a gold mine named Roberta Sherwood!"

The Copacabana landlord, J. Podell, booked her "blind" at five thousand dollars per week. She jammed his Copa every night. Top spots around the nation booked her for as high as ten thousand per. Her records and albums made her wealthier.

When I was at ringside at her première nights, she never looked at me until she got to "You're Nobody Til Somebody Loves You." The line that made my heart smile, however, is when she grinned at me and tenderly sang, "Just in time. *You* found me just in time . . ."

From WW column February 22, 1956:

"The colyum's newest enthusiasm: Rowan and Martin, a corking team of hilarious comedians, who never resort to the cross-eyed bit or the knock-kneed routine, etc., to milk a howl. We caught them for the first time at the Lucerne Hotel, Miami Beach, where they fractured the spectators. They have been buried in the hick town spots for two years but they will go far in show business once the Broadway Rip Van Winkles wake up. Both are good-looking guys . . . Personable people . . . Refreshing talent. They belong in a Broadway musical but will settle for the Copa or Latin Q. to help pay their taxes."

P.S. In 1969 the Rowan and Martin *Laugh-In* television program led the ratings a lot of the time.

★

HOWARD HUGHES

The one beat I had that I lost—because I tried to check it with the people involved—is the story that still bugs me—the secret and never confirmed 1957 marriage of Billionaire Howard Hughes and movie star Jean Peters. They admitted the merger via cards to friends signed "Howard and Jean Hughes."

For many years, reporters have searched the marriage records in every state in the union without success. Where were they wed? Abroad, maybe?

"Mr. Hughes," someone suggested, "may have married himself to Miss Peters on one of his own planes. He was the Captain. Perhaps as the skipper of his own ship in Bimini waters?" Perhaps. Very likely, too.

Anyway, Mr. Hughes was my radio sponsor at one time: TWA airline commercials.

In Hollywood one night I asked one of his aides, Walter Kane, to check a story with Hughes. "If someone told it to me," I said, "they will tell it to others. People will gossip. That's nearly everybody's second favorite indoor sport. Tell Hughes it's around that he and Jean are secretly wed."

"Oh," poof-pooft Mr. Kane, "I doubt that very much. If anyone would know, I think I'd be the one."

"I am not going to hold it another day," I told Kane. "These things leak!"

Kane pledged he would contact Mr. Hughes about it. Next day I was told, "Nothing to it!" That same afternoon, the Los Angeles *Herald-Express* published it under the byline of Louella O. Parsons, the Number One Movietown gossipist.

Hughes and the Hearst boys are close friends. But the story appeared on the inside pages—buried, as they say—because the editors apparently did not want to risk responsibility. They headlined it "HUGHES SECRETLY WED, SAYS LOUELLA." "Says Louella"—if it proved wrong, she'd be the goat, not her editor. See?

When I yelled my head off at Hughes executives about losing the beat, one bluntly said: "Look, we have to live out here with the people who cover Hollywood. Take it easy, relax. Louella would be very angry with Howard if a story about him appeared under any but her signature."

I've relaxed ever since when it came to checking news about Mr. Hughes—never bothered to check anything about him with his staffers since. When they scream over the phone about something I've reported, I give them the same reply they gave me. "Take it easy, relax." And I hang up.

The latest "news" is that the Hugheses have a grown son. Can't imagine why it hasn't been noted anywhere, considering that the rumor or untrumor has been echo'd a lot among the Hollywood elite.

Why not confirm or deny? If it is true, it will eventually be made public, when their wills come up for probate.

I don't think I will be around to know. If the heir is an heiress, kindly Forget-The-Whole-Theeennng.

★

LUCILLE BALL AND DESI ARNAZ

Back in 1938 in Miami Beach I walked into a floor-show spot at 2:00 A.M. near the Roney Plaza Hotel. The legend was that its real owners were remnants of the Capone mob.

266

I took a table in the rear. Nobody, I thought, recognized me. I ordered a drink, relaxed, and was soon captivated by the eyefuls in the chorus.

The star was a young Cuban, Desi Arnaz, whose specialty was the bongo drum. Arnaz belted out his songs in a professional style (in fractured American and Español) and had the almost capacity crowd in his hip pocket. But his Big Finish gave evidence that Arnaz was going places in show business. This was the first time I had witnessed the "Conga Line."

Onstage he led the line of dolls who held on to each other's shapely hips as they played Follow the Leader. Every bit of footwork that Desi extemporized, the girls aped.

One-Two-Three-Kick! One-Two-Three-KICK! The audience loved it. The encores were abundant. These were done off the stage in the audience, where Desi would select patrons from every table until nearly everyone was one-two-three-kicking and making happy fools of themselves. One of the merriest audience participations I ever saw.

After the show Arnaz came to my table. "Are you Meesta Wullta Weeonshawll of New York?"

"Yes."

"You like me?"

"I like your act. Good show."

"Mebbe plizz you put my name in the paper in New York and mebbe I get a job there?"

"I will write about you and the show in tomorrow's New York *Mirror.*"

That was in 1938. In 1958 I was working for him!

He and his wife (at the time) Lucille Ball had become the nation's Number One television pets with their *I Love Lucy* series. They started on the CBS payroll at five thousand dollars per week, and in five years they were the proprietors of their own Desilu Studios—one of the speediest success sagas in showbiz.

One New Year's Eve at their annual party in their Palm Springs home, after everyone had gone Lucille dropped exhausted on a divan and slept. Desi asked me to stay awhile. He was pretty blotto.

"You are very weary, Dez, why don't you go to bed?"

"No, no," he hiccuped. "You remember when you took me and Lucy in your police car in New Yurq?"

"Yes, I do. It was an exciting night. Go to bed."

Desi asked: "What was the most exciting thing you ever saw on one of those rides?"

"I'll tell you some other time. You are slightly dead. Sleep it off."

"You say I am dronk, no?"

"You can't keep your eyes open. You are falling asleep on me."

"What was the most exciting thing you ever saw in your car? I have a reason."

I unfolded a thrilling episode revolving around the Park Lane gang—three white hoodlums who terrorized shopkeepers and others for months. They got their name following a holdup of a laundry named The Park Lane. They shotgunned the owner to death.

One of the killers, a tall, slender man of twenty-three, had a large scar on his face the result of a knife fight. Every cop and detective in New York was looking for anyone with that facial advertisement.

Months after that murder I was cruising in the 24th Precinct. My companion was Damon Runyon. The hour was about 2:15 A.M.

It was one of the coldest nights. A blizzard came hours later. So did the most exciting police call I ever responded to—and it involved the Park Lane Gang.

"Signal Thirty! Signal Thirty!" signal'd Police Central. "Twenty-fourth Precinct. Twenty-fourth! Three white men in a white cab last seen speeding South on Manhattan Avenue from One hundred and twenty-first Street. Proceed quietly. Use caution! They are armed!"

Runyon and I were then turning into Manhattan Avenue near 115th Street. "This is it, Damon! This is why I do this every night. The action! No show or movie can match the real thing."

Our car stopped at 116th Street and Manhattan for the lights. The southbound traffic contained several white cabs!

"Oh, brother," I said, "this is too close! Look at all those white cabs alongside us!" When the lamps turned green I decided to get the hell away from there. I turned east and then south to wait for other calls regarding the escaping trio.

The police box kept busy reporting more clues. "That Signal Thirty in Twenty-fourth," breathlessly reported the police voice," that white cab's last three numbers are zero-three-zero—zero-three-zero—white cab—three white men wanted for a holdup in the twenty-fourth. Proceed *quietly!* No sirens, no red light. They are armed!"

Runyon and I were now at 106th Street and Central Park West, then a two-way street. On 101st Street—five blocks south—the melodrama was reaching its climax.

A 24th Precinct police car goofed by turning into a one-way street.

But that goof paid off big for the police. The driver of the car said to his partner, "What were those three license numbers, Charlie?" Charlie replied: "Zero-three-zero—that's the cab right there—right there!"

Charlie got out with gun drawn as his partner excitedly asked Police Central to rush cars to the scene—on 101st Street between Manhattan Avenue and Central Park West.

The cab driver was busy jotting down the address and amount he had gotten from his fares when Charlie pushed the gun in his face. "Where did those three guys pick you up?" he demanded.

"What three guys?" the cabbie deadpanned.

"You know what three guys!" boomed the cop impatiently. "You picked them up around One hundred and twenty-first Street and Manhattan, didn't you?"

The frightened hackie pointed to the building where he had stopped. "They went in there. They all had guns. One had a shotgun."

Police cars from several precincts in the West Side of upper Manhattan converged on 101st Street near Manhattan. All had their sirens wide open—disregarding the warning to proceed quietly. Cars from the 24th, the 20th, the 28th, and from the 22nd—the 22nd Precinct covers all of Central Park. Six cars in each precinct, two cops in a car—each with a gat in his hand. They surrounded the area from 101st Street to 103rd, between Manhattan Avenue and Central Park West.

The detectives sped to the scene. So did the police crews carrying klieg lights that turned the area into daylight. The wanted men could not possibly escape.

They heard screeching sirens. Two elected to make a dash to the roof. The third apparently decided it was too cold to make his last stand in the bitter freeze. He got lucky—for about fifteen minutes.

He tried the doors of his neighbors, hopeful of finding one that was unlocked or opened into an empty flat. He found one that the occupant had neglected to lock. He snapped the lock, undressed, and placed his shoes under the bed. The legit occupant of the room slept soundly.

Chief of Detectives Mullrane of the 24th and his men went from floor to floor in the six-story building, knocking on doors, waking one and all, looking for the desperadoes.

Suddenly from the roof came sounds of shooting. The janitor of the place, who had guided the cops, was shot in the groin.

The police klieg lights revealed the hiding place of two of the men—behind a large chimney.

"Come out of there with your hands high," yelled a detective with a carbine, "by the count of three or we'll shoot that chimney down!"

The pair surrendered. One had the telltale big scar on his cheek. The Park Lane gang!

Now Mr. Mullrane and his men had reached the hiding place of Number Three—but they didn't know it yet.

Mullrane knocked hard and persistently on the door. It was opened by a man in his underwear—long drawers. Feigning yawns, he patted his mouth to stifle them, and muttered, "What's the matter?"

Mullrane pushed the door open wide and with his flashlight found the light switch. The real tenant of the one-room didn't budge, sleeping like a baby that had been drugged.

The detectives awakened him. "What's wrong, what's wrong?" he asked sleepily. "What the hell's all this?"

"What's your name? What do you do for a living?" shouted Mullrane.

He gave his name and said he worked as a counterman at a drugstore in the theatrical sector.

"Who's this guy?" demanded Mullrane, pointing to the fugitive.

"I never saw him in my life!"

"Where are your shoes?" asked Mullrane of the sleepy man.

"Under the bed, aren't they?"

Mullrane picked up the shoes, and stuck a hand in both. They were ice-cold.

Mullrane picked up the other pair of shoes on the other side of the bed and felt the insides—which were very warm.

"Oh, you darling!" said Mullrane gleefully as he ordered the owner handcuffed.

The Park Lane gang are still languishing in prison.

"That," I told Desi, "was the most exciting police call of all."

But he was giving off a few lusty snores. I started to leave.

"Wait a minnit," said Desi. "How many more like that one you got?"

"Many more."

"Make a helluva series," he said, getting up and showing me out.

Next noon I got a phone call from Desilu's executive director, Bert Granet. "Mr. Arnaz," he said, "would like you to join him for lunch. Will you be able to come in half an hour?"

"Okay, yes."

"Before you see Mr. Arnaz," said Granet, "stop and see me. I want to ask you something."

In Granet's office he went over a tall pile of memos. "The one thing that eludes me," he said, "is why did they say they'd shoot down the chimney?"

I looked over Granet's shoulder at the memos and saw that Desi Arnaz, who was so sleepy and so very spifflicated, had remembered almost every detail of my 3:00 A.M. recital. "Total recall!" I astonished. "I thought he was so drunk!"

Desi signed me to star in *The Walter Winchell Show*. It ran thirty-nine weeks over ABC-TV. I see it now and then on the reruns—the fore-runner of Desliu's smash click *The Untouchables,* which I narrated for four years.

The newcomer Cuban who in 1938 asked me to give him a good notice in my column—which he deserved—twenty years later was, with his wife, reported worth $20 million. As the old saying doesn't go: "Cast your bread upon the waters and sometimes you get Angel Food Cake in return." The residuals from *The Untouchables* kept coming in for a long time. But I never got a penny in residuals from *The Winchell File,* because I was a greenhorn about such teevee matters.

Desi was generous, however. "How much did you get last time on the air?" he inquired during the negotiations.

"I was paid seventy-five hundred from Old Gold to do a variety show for them."

"I'll give you that," said Dez. "I will also give you half-ownership."

"That's fine," I chuckled. "The government needs the taxes."

The Winchell File, which did come out of my files most of the time, perished after one year, but it was peddled to another firm which ran it for several years under its original title and then under the name of *Crime Report.* I didn't rate residuals, I was later informed, because I was half-owner. Most of the seventy-five-hundred-dollar salary went to taxes, and people I never met wound up with some easy loot. Show biz.

Lucille and Desi, once one of the happiest marrieds in Hollywood history, began having the Apartache. Their public suffered, too, when the rumors of their decision to divorce were confirmed.

Lucille tried hard to save their merger. Nobody knew that so well as I knew it. I tried hard, too, to keep them together.

Desi and I went to Las Vegas to appear at the Tournament of Champions golf event, a Desert Inn promotion. Desi went as a player. I was there representing the Runyon Cancer Fund, which received thirty-five thousand dollars annually for a long time from the Desert Inn's Wilbur Clark and his partners. The first night I paused to watch Desi at a dice table. He seemed to own every hundred-dollar chip in the place: mountains of them in front of him.

Next day I learned that he had stayed too long and wound up losing a bundle. Rumors said he lost almost fifty thousand dollars. Lucille phoned me. "What's new?" she said mournfully.

"Have you a cold?" I asked her. "You sound very down."

"No, I haven't any cold. Just the blues."

"What's with Desi?" she continued. "Has he lost our studio yet?"

"When I watched him for a while," I reported, "he seemed to be owning the Desert Inn."

"He lost sixty-five thousand dollars!" she informed. "Walter, we haven't that kind of money to lose!"

"Only last week," I reminded her, "the newspapers said you both were worth twenty million!"

"On paper!" she intoned. "On paper!"

They were put asunder that same year. That $20 million talk was just that—talk. When Desi quit Desilu, he settled for $3 million—not 10.

Authors of books, plays, and television shows about the underworld may appreciate this editing: When a Mafia chief gives one of his men the "Kiss of Death," it does not mean that the recipient is to be killed. It means that the one who is kissed is to do the assassinating.

The kiss on the mouth translates: "Our lips are sealed forever."

Many of us made the same boner. The first teevee show to feature the inaccuracy was *The Untouchables,* of which I was the narrator.

In 1969 Mobfia executives enjoyed telling me how they laughed when they saw us all "get it so wrong."

☆

Oh, I don't believe it! From the Independent Editorial Services News Letter of February 11, 1959: "Winchell's Sunday night broadcast is now required listening for the foreign affairs committees of both branches of congress. His information on Latin American doings is two weeks ahead of official reports."

★

PAPA

The first time I met Ernest Hemingway was at the Stork Club. Drama critic George Jean Nathan introduced us. Both got so drunk and double-talky, I left an hour later without a single anecdote or something clever I could quote.

Mr. Hemingway became a warm friend shortly after that meeting. He kept all of us in the New York colyuming racket supplied with jokes and stories about his career.

When he was almost killed in two accidents—once while hunting in Africa and again later in a plane crack-up—he wrote me several letters while convalescing. One letter bawled me out for feuding with a mutual friend, another columnist he liked.

"I want you," Hemingway scolded in large print, "to make up with him. I like you both. You punks are such little kids! If you do not reconcile with him, when I get back I will go straight to the Stork Club and flatten you!"

His brother, who wrote a book about Hemingway (after the Great Guy died), quoted Ernest as having said: "Winchell is the greatest newspaperman that ever lived."

I wrote Leicester Hemingway my appreciation, adding: "You'd be amazed at the great number of people who don't think so!"

My pet quote of Mr. H's: "Life is very simple. It's work or it's bull-shit!"

How veddy true.

When I was ill in 1960 (staph infection) and was forced to quit broad-casting, Roy Alexander, then a top editor at *Time,* phoned Mrs. Winchell.

"*Time,*" said Mr. Alexander, "has many inquiries about Walter from newspapers all over the country. Rumors say he is thinking of retirement. Is that true?"

"News to me," she replied.

"Have you any idea when he will resume?"

"Maybe never!" she exploded, hanging up.

When I asked her why she'd said it, my wife (who rarely raises her voice) said she had read *Time*'s many heckles and could not be pleasant to people who tried to Blow-The-Man-Down.

The next issue of *Time* carried her quote, "Maybe never!" It cost me over fifty papers that week.

Mickey Mantle's quote: "There's one good thing about having a bad year. Nobody wants you for banquets."

When I recovered I got on the phone and wooed them back.

WHITE HOUSE PRESS PLANE

United Press International star Merriman Smith, the dean of White House correspondents, and some of the others who covered the White House and Washington, invited me to come along when President Eisenhower was campaigning for reelection. Ike made three speeches in the Deep South, last stop Miami.

My first trip with the presidential press people! I loved it. Nearly all of the reporters gave me trivia they couldn't use.

When Eisenhower flew to the Orient in 1960 I was invited to make that hop, too.

In Manila, as we readied to jet to Tokyo, I phoned my editor at the Manila *Evening News* to thank him and his staff for their hospitality.

"You all are not going to Japan," said Ye Ed.

"We aren't? How come?"

"Maybe the President doesn't know it yet, but he won't be allowed to land there."

"How the hell do you know that?"

"I just got off the phone with our man in Tokyo. Because of the rioters and demonstrators. Very anti-Yankee Doodle!"

"You sure?" I asked him.

"Positive. No Japan. The head of a foreign state is not allowed to set foot on Japanese soil unless Hirohito agrees to receive him. And the Emperor will not risk big trouble with the anti-Yankee mobs!"

I hung up and hurried to the lobby, where the press corps was waiting for the bus to take us to the Carrier *Yorktown* and the China Sea.

I had the top newsbreak of that day—and didn't know it! I did not see Ike's press chief, James Hagerty, standing nearby. Breathlessly I told Hearst star Bob Considine and Charles Mohr, covering Ike for *Time* mag, "We are not going to Japan!"

"We're not what?" both exclaimed.

"We are not going to Tokyo. I just—"

"Where the hell did you get *that* crap?" Mr. Hagerty growled. "I'm running this show. You're not."

"Oh, Jim," I oh'jimmed, "I didn't see you standing there or I would have told you what I just learned. I phoned my editor here to say byebye, and he told me he got that news a few minutes ago from his Tokyo man—a UPI guy."

Hagerty walked away, sizzling still.

An hour or so later, as I was doing my copy for the New York *Mirror* and other papers, I saw the press bunch rushing by me. "What goes?" I asked one.

"Hagerty just called an emergency press conference."

Oh-oh. Here it came. Hagerty must hate me by now. It must be about what he called my crap. I didn't gloat about it. I felt sorry for him and his embarrassment when we next met. By the time I got to the big room for the conference all chairs were occupied. I joined those squatting on the floor. The only space left for me was right under Jim's microphone and nose.

"I have a statement," he began. "We are not going to Japan. The *Yorktown*," he continued "will take us to a harbor near Seoul, where choppers will take us from there." And so on. As Hagerty intoned confirmation of my skewpee, he gave me a look that could kill.

I turned from his glare. Bob Considine and others recorded the incident in front of the Manila hotel. They reported: "Walter Winchell, making his first overseas hop with a President, enjoyed every cub-reporter's dream. He knew we were not going to Japan before anyone knew it, including White House press chief Hagerty."

They did not mention that my Manila editor had told me the scoop. For which a very tight embrace to Considine, Charles "Chuck" Roberts of *Newsweek*, and Charles Mohr.

Dammit, I thought, I'll never be invited to go on a press plane with the President again.

But I was—often. Jim Hagerty got over it and we continued friends.

As the late star reporter Bob Casey used to say: "It's wonderful to be a newspaperman. You meet so many interesting and wonderful newspaper people!"

★
JFK

A sensational story starring John Fitzgerald Kennedy happened in Los Angeles minutes after his nomination for the presidency.

The story was a dandy for front pages. But the editors of the New York *Mirror* shuddered when I phoned them about it. "Oh, for Christ's sake!" one ed thundered. "He's a married man! I thought you never touched that kind of story!" He hung up.

I have never touched that sort of story—willfully or intentionally. But he didn't stay on the horn long enough for me to explain *how* I knew it.

The story: When Mr. Kennedy won the 1960 nomination in Los Angeles only one of his intimates knew where he was. No others on JFK's staff or in the news media could locate him for pictures or ask how he felt about being a winner, and so on. They couldn't find him because he was stashed away in a top-floor apartment of a swank sector apartment building owned by one of his close friends, multimillionaire Jack Haley, former song-and-dance-man and movie star.

JFK, I assume, had gotten away from us all, to enjoy a matinee nap (to launder it). At any rate, the photographers and reporters traced him to that building and were in front of it clamoring for admittance. The Democratic candidate was informed by phone (by the one man who knew) that the press had discovered his hideaway—and to let them in.

For a reason that always eluded me, sophisticated, grown-up Jack Kennedy decided not to take the elevator down. He climbed out the window to the fire escape, and was almost down when a third-floor tenant, hearing somebody outside his apartment window, recognized him.

The man was a longtime pal, a very ill film star. "Jack!" he greeted the distressed Kennedy, "wot the hell are you doing out there?"

"Jeezuzz," panicked the next President, "don't let this get in the papers!" JFK climbed into the star's home and took the elevator down from that floor. His pal, the ex-star, phoned his favorite newspaperman, Jim Bacon of the Associated Press. Bacon resigned months after for a tall-wage P.R. job. Mr. Bacon was later demoted (by himself) to gossip columnist. He sure knows juicy gossip when he meets it. The story decorated page one of my flagship paper in the Far West, the Los Angeles *Herald-Examiner*.

It must have gone out over the AP wire. But I was told days later that no other paper printed any part of it.

Is a Puzzlement, no?

More of a riddle to me was why Hearst's tabloid New York *Mirror* (my alma mater for nearly forty years) wouldn't use it. Prob'ly because the *Mirror* was Hearst-owned and the Hearst papyri was "for" the Democrats' election—and for J.F.K.

But so is the Los Angeles *Herald-Examiner* pro-Demo. It is now Hearst's Number One paper. The *Her-Exam* enjoys the top circulation in the evening field—one of Hearst's most prosperous blatts—because Don Goodenow, the managing editor, and city ed (at the time) Agness Underwood Print the news!

Strange, too, that Mr. Kennedy's competitors for the White House (Nixon and Co.) either didn't know about his fire escapade—or as gentlemen, wouldn't touch it.

When very rich John F. Kennedy ran for the presidency, an interviewer asked him, "Why do you want to live at the White House?"

"For the seat of power," said JFK. "What else could I do, go into business and make money?"

When Kennedy politics is the subject, I remind my audience of JFK's "victory" over Nixon in 1960—how the Nixon people kept the press and TV-radio people waiting until after midnight (California time)— 3:00 A.M. on the East Coast, before the "defeated" Nixon conceded. He had just won California among many other states.

Mr. Kennedy just made it with the slim margin of about 119,000 popular votes.

Said knowledgeable insiders, if the vote-tally people in several states had counted all—or any—of Nixon's votes, he would have won. The states, they said, were Illinois (especially Cook County) and two Southern border states. Nixon lost Illinois by 8,858 votes.

The Nixons finally came to the microphones for the grim concession.

You'd think that the reporters, interviewers, and others would have had their melodramatic punch line, but no. One greedy television man had one more question, which he addressed to the very lovely and very sad Mrs. Nixon, alongside her demolished mate.

"Pat!" the TV man called to Mrs. Nixon. "Have you a statement?"

Trying to keep the tears from drowning her, Mrs. Nixon lost her composure, poise, and dignity. Getting closer to the mike Pat yelled: *"They stole it!"*

In 1967, after a long spell of oblivion, Nikita Khrushchev ("voting" in some Moscow "election") put in a plug for Bobby Kennedy by lying that it was he (Nikita) who had helped defeat Nixon with the famed "kitchen" confrontation at an American-sponsored "Made in U.S.A." know-how show in Russia.

The famed photo showing Nixon waving a finger under Mr. K's nose won Nixon a lot of votes. But Nikita in 1967 claimed that it was he who helped JFK win.

The fact is that three men were sentenced to seven and a half to fifteen years at Joliet Prison for confessing (after they were trapped with the evidence) that they did not count all Nixon votes in Cook County, Illinois. If they had tally'd them, and the other two small-state vote counters had given Nixon an honest count, JFK would not have become President—and would probably be alive today.

★

FS AND JPK

He was a cub sportswriter for a New Jersey newspaper when he was eighteen. His ambition was to become a newspaperman with a by-line. But his editors denied him that honor. So he resigned and tried the Major Bowes Amateur Hour. He won first prize. Radio, movies, records, nightclubs, and other show biz branches bombarded him with offers. He was on his way.

The Jersey newspaper that had failed to encourage him phoned him for a feature interview. "We want you to encourage youngsters who are ambitious," the voice said.

Frank Sinatra obliged.

Glenn Neville, the managing editor of the New York *Mirror,* started my day off pleasantly with this memo: "Walter: The most beautiful short story I ever read.—Glenn."

Attached was the following vignette:

Frank Sinatra toured the world delighting underprivileged children (and tots in orphanages) at his own expense. "Because," he said, "as one of the privileged I want to do something for the underprivileged."

Intimates report that at one institution for blind children, a darling

278

honey-haired girl of about seven told Frank: "Mr. Sinatra, we all love you and your pretty songs. Please come outside so I can show you our lovely flowers" . . . The star took her hand, went outside with her, and exclaimed: "Oh, you are so very right. The flowers are beautiful."

The wind toyed with the child's curls. Sinatra said: "Oh, that silly old wind upsetting your very beautiful hair."

To which the sightless youngster responded: "Mr. Sinatra, what color is the wind?"

One of his aides walked into Frank Sinatra's dressing room the other day and announced: "Someone waiting to see you. He's very important."

"How important," chuckled Frank, "can a *he* be?"

Long before former U.S. Ambassador to the Court of St. James Joseph P. Kennedy was stricken, his favorite refuge was a lavishly appointed inn at Lake Tahoe, Nevada. The landlord was Frank Sinatra, then the top recording troubadour and movie/television star.

Joseph P. was always close to people in show business. He backed plays, film firms, long-ago movie pet Gloria Swanson (one of Hollywood's top ticket sellers), and other theatrical ventures—not always for the profit in it, just for the fun of assisting people he liked who needed money.

The Lake Tahoe joynt was where many of Hollywood's stars (both sexes), starlets, and young people who hoped to be stars and starlets were invited. Marilyn Monroe, frinstance. She was no longer Mrs. J. DiMaggio.

Peter Lawford (then wed to Kennedy's daughter Pat) was often a guest. His wife, too. The champagne and other booze flowed like a mini-Niagara Falls.

Anyway, it was always Drunc-Time at Lake Tahoe, according to people who talk too much to newspapermen. Many of the alleged Sodom and Gomorrah carryings-on made the columns from coast to coast—sometimes with the initials of celebrity participants. Besides the alleged orgies and "circuses" (in which men and women made like Adam and Evil for sex-starved watchers) and other whoopdee-doo-hoo-hah, some of the "in" set went in for common ordinary necking, petting, and—deleted by the author. Sinatra, we learned, was so embarrassed by the conduct of some of his guests that he barred them. (End of Yock.)

One mad midnight (the story goes) he was very upset about Marilyn being so sick from too much Laughing Soup and Wyoming Ketchup. She had never taken a drink before she met DiMaggio—nor when she was his wife. Now she couldn't stand. He ordered her carried into a limousine and instructed the driver to hasten to her home in Hollywood, hours away. Marilyn slept it off in the limo.

Another wild fun-night Sinatra did the same thing to kin of powerful Washington people. They, too, were reportedly carried by Sinatra flunkies—to his private jet—and sent back to Los Angeles before local reporters enjoyed a "leak."

When JFK was campaigning for the presidency (and the nomination) Sinatra gathered his intimates (Dean Martin, Sammy Davis, Jr., Joey Bishop, *et al.*) and jetted all over the nation staging shows to get funds for the campaign.

Others in the Rat Pack, as the Sinatra Set was labeled by writers and columnists (I didn't mean that to sound offensive, it just came out that way—to quote the oldie) started flinging around their "weight" when they were romanced by JFK's team of money-for-the-campaign men.

One of the "pack" told off U.S. Customs people at an airport when they held up his departure to inspect the luggage. "I'm a pal of the Kennedy family," he growled, "are *you?*"

The customs people ignored the insult, as Mr. Ham fumed.

Sinatra and Friends also were invited to the Inaugural Ball.

But something happened after that.

The Kennedy clan omitted his name from family parties. The gossip flew that Jackie barred him from being invited to the White House after the JFKs moved in.

Many of us on the papers believed that Jackie, no dope, had heard about her husband's Hollywood chums arranging parties where the most gorgeous hookers and actresses "entertained." When JFK was at the Beverly Hilton (Beverly Hills, California), the pushovers of the round-heel set didn't have to show any pass to get to JFK's floor. No federal agents halted them for identification.

One of the loveliest ladies in movietown was rated VSP: Very Special Person, Number One Girl—once deep in Sinatra's heart.

If Jackie ever heard about these parties—and people *dooo* talk—it might explain why Sinatra and Co. were on her deadrop-list.

Frankeee was a disillusioned fellow. "Man," he reportedly told chums, "they sure fall out of love with you fast."

In 1962, not long after Marilyn had to be taken home, she died from an accidental overdose of barbiturates. The-Man-In-Her-Life at the time failed her when she phoned him to hurry-hurry-hurry: "I think I took too many sleeping pills! I can't remember!"

To which (goes the persistent legend) he panicked and shrieked, "My

God, I'm a married man. I can't get involved!" DiMaggio, to whom Marilyn always flew when she was blue, barred that heel (and several other persons in the group) from the funeral.

I took on the army of press people for Joe.

One photogger fooled me good. "Hey, Winchell!" he yelled, when I came to the door of the funeral director's office, "I'm from the *Herald-Examiner!*" (My paper in Los Angeles.)

I appointed him "pool man"—so that every cameraman got pix.

"Don't forget to rush copies of Joe down to my city desk!" I yelled.

"Oh, Walter," one said, speaking for them all, "that guy is a free-lancer. He'll peddle those exclusive shots to *Life, Time,* or some mag!"

When I got back to the *Herald-Examiner* to check if the pix had come, I realized that he was The City Slicker (not I) and that I was The Big Hick. I phoned *Time-Life* in Beverly Hills and told them about it.

"Yes," I was informed, "we bought some."

I exploded. "The other guys will think I double-crossed them. Will you please rush down at least one photo of DiMaj to the *H-E?*" He kept his word.

Thanks to whomever it was I spoke with at *Time-Life,* Beverly Hills.

DiMaggio and Sinatra, longtime close friends, became former friends.

Joe, who had never stopped loving Marilyn, ordered roses placed at her vault in the Westwood Village resting place—twice weekly. Westwood is a suburb of Los Angeles not far from Hollywood, where Joe and Marilyn first met.

☆

Now back to the "ranch" and Joseph P. Kennedy and his final flings. Overheards: "He may be old, but he's still in there pinching."

Maurice Chevalier's wistful comment on When To Quit Playing The Lover: "It is simple. One day you compare your face in the mirror with your passport photo. If you are honest, you know it is time to stop."

Not long after one of the wild parties at Tahoe, Mr. Money was stricken with the stroke that almost ended his life several times.

Whether his stroke had anything to do with what happened to Sinatra and his Tahoe asylum, I do not know. Perhaps the sour luck that Sinatra suffered was coincidence. You decide that. (FS rooted for HHH, not RFK.)

But Sinatra's troubles with Nevada lawmen atomic'd. He lost his sexotic harem at Tahoe. I believe he gave it up when the license was canceled. Anyway, Frank had haddittt. His long run and prosperity in Las Vegas at the Sands Hotel (he owned several points—making him very rich) and his front-paged fight with a man thrice his size (Sand's gaming casino chief Cohen who spoke for the management—not necessarily new owner Howard Hughes, but very likely) resulted in a long "exile."

Israel, days before, had defeated Nasser and his eunuchs in a war that lasted six days. Following that brawl, in which Frank lost two front teeth, the gag that swept show biz was: "Sinatra shoulda known better than to fight a Jew on a desert."

★

NO TEARS

Following *The WW File*—real cops-and-robbers melodramas that I had witnessed—and four years of narrating Desilu's *The Untouchables,* I was signed by Bob Enders at a four-figure wage plus a hunk of the profits. Enders was then a struggling TV showman-producer, now an exec at one of the Hollywood studios.

Mr. Enders had acquired Washington correspondent Andrew Tully's sequel to *The Untouchables*—one of Tully's many books about Feds and crime. The title: *Treasury Agent.*

Richard Arlen, a longtime film favorite, had the lead as the U.S. Treasury's Number One criminal-catcher. I narrated.

It was a Big-Timer. I persuaded the New York chiefs of ABC-TV, then in Movietown inspecting new pilots for the upcoming season, to view it in one of the Desilu projection rooms.

The ABC-TV giants were Ollie Treyz and Tom Moore, who eventually inherited Mr. Treyz' top ABC-TV job. I sat between them. Desi was busy sampling some 100-proof Laughing Soup.

Treasury Agent came on screen. It opened with the seal of the U.S. Treasury, to convince the viewer that the story was not make-believe. The seal dissolved into me in a half-shot—meaning down to my waistline. "My name," I began, "is Walter Winchell. I'm a reporter. Here is a story I never made public before."

Hot damb! What an Entrance!

I could not imagine it not being as big a click as "Elliot Ness" star Robert Stack and the *Untouchables* sagas.

After only about three minutes, Mr. Treyz—who could make you and break you with his verdicts—whispered, "I don't want you associated with any other series except *The Untouchables*. I'm not buying it."

Gahdamb! Just like that! I thawt I'd die.

Out-of-business and The Big Money again—because one man reaches a decision after seeing only a few minutes of a pilot.

Mr. Enders lost a mini-mint producing it. It was a long time before he connected with a studio again. In the meantime, Mr. Treyz (who lost his job at ABC-TV) chief'd one of the biggest flop-fiascos in television, costing Texas backers and others many millions when they starred Bill Dana (a very funny fellow) in a TV series of Old-Hat late-night "shows" from Vegas.

Not long after, Tom Moore's luck curdled, too. The board at ABC-TV changed chiefs. Mr. Moore, according to the TV pages, was not happy about being "kicked upstairs." I knew that miserable feeling of being On Top—and then not being anywhere near it. It took me months to get over the shock of being a Loser.

I never let Ollie and Tom know that I knew (when Desi was negotiating to produce *The Untouchables*) that the Messrs. Treyz and Moore had blackballed me as narrator. It was producer Quinn Martin and Desi Arnaz who insisted that I get the job. Treyz and Moore agreed reluctantly.

And now, as they looked at a bit of the thrilling *Treasury Agent,* they blackballed it—and me—again! Charming chaps. "That's show biz!" and all-that-other apcray.

ABC-TV (and radio)—which once wrote me a letter signed by chief Robert F. Kintner that said in part: "Thanks for your long service and loyalty of 27 years in not leaving us for other network offers"—suffered several setbacks.

Too bad. But No Tears.

In Las Vegas several years ago I was the Tropicana's headliner following the run of Desilu's *The Winchell File*. Gordon Jenkins, composer of the glistenable "Manhattan Tower," composed the music to the next bit of doggerel. I read the verse over the backstage microphone as Nat Brandwynne's large orchestra backgrounded Professor Jenkins' delightful melody and the chorusirens did the Old Soft-Shoe.

No music firm liked it well enough to publish it. But the fact that Jenkins was the composer was glory enough for me.

Darling

I know you miss me when you're at a bar,
  And when Roberta Sherwood is the Star;
Or Ella's rendering her lar-dee-dar,
  I know you miss me.

I know you miss me when you're One of Three,
  And two go dancing to a rhapsody . . .
And leave you staring at your daiquiri,
  I know you miss me.

I know you miss me when Sinatra sings,
  Or when they're playing any song of Bing's;
And when they're zinging "Holiday For Strings"
  I know you miss me.

But when the endless-friendless night is due,
  I miss you, too.

★

JACK PAAR *vs.* GOSSIP COLUMNISTS

I never met Jack Paar except via the Boob-Tube.

I missed his initial program, so busy was I at the time in Hollywood, appearing in films or narrating *The Winchell File* for Desilu Studios. The 6:00 A.M. calls meant that I had to get some sleep before Paar went on.

The publicity and the warm reception many reviews embraced him with put my pencil to a memo pad: "Catch Paar's show." The time would have been his second or third week on the air.

Paar's professionalism, stage presence, and wit resulted in this two-line column salute: "Jack Paar's delightful nonsense is always welcome over at this typewriter."

Some time later, enjoying his midnighter—I could stay up late that night because my teevee assignments permitted—I heard him proclaim his aversion to the gossip columns.

His Number One target was the late Dorothy Kilgallen. Besides her appearances on the *What's My Line?* show, she did a three-Dot bitchy column for the New York *Journal-American* and King Features Syndicate. Dorothy also starred on the front pages when she was assigned to report murder and other sensational trials. If she ever wrote anything about Mr. Paar that offended him, I do not recall. But she very likely did. Anyway, he disliked her intensely and once poked ridicule at her "non-chin"—but so had Frank Sinatra and some other entertainers whose acts and conduct she knocked.

One *Tonight* stanza I heard Paar say, "Winchell is another who doesn't like me or my show. He has never mentioned me or it—never had a good word to say about me." Apparently my first orchid for his talent had eluded him. Perhaps aides neglected to call his attention to it.

I even started a "fight" with a fellow on *Daily Variety* in Hollywood who had "a thing" about Paar. Jack Hellman, a fair, ferocious critic, kept yapping away at newcomer Paar. I did a paragraph about Mr. Hellman's thumbs-down notices about Mr. P.

Apparently Paar never read that column—nor did anyone tell him I had "taken on" a *Variety* critic because of him. I submit the above to show how wrong Paar was when he childishly informed his teevee audience, "Winchell has never said a good word about me!"

At any rate, Paar was clicking large coast to coast and feuding with his network censors and other network executives, with the Hearst papers and various columnists, with one of his top boosters, *New York Times* TV oracle Jack Gould (who shrugged it off and forgave him for his opinions), and anyone else Big Enough to duel with—for the publicity it ignited.

One of Paar's most amusing programs was the first time he had Elsa Maxwell as his co-star.

Elsa was one of my aversions. Her social-climbing racket ("Want to meet society? Let me throw a big party and invite you") was her chief way of making ends meet for many years. She was very good at dreaming up novel parties. The socially registered hookers (and others who were not debutramps) adored Elsa.

Cole Porter helped support her for decades—as did many others in Cafake Society, Cafooey Society, and Caphony-Souseity. New Yorker Harry Evans once sent out a letter to people who wanted to become a member of Cafooey Society. Some of the queries were: How many times has Elsa Maxwell spoken to you voluntarily? Do you think Lucius Beebe is here to stay? How many names of socialites can you read in a row without throwing up?

The Waldorf Astoria management (at the time) gave her a swank suite on the house for the "prestige" she brought with her hifalutin' friends. Then one day the new landlord decided the Waldorf didn't need freeloaders. She moved to another swank hotel. They also wearied of Elsa's dreary doings—her outbursts at bellmen, maids, and other employees, her public denunciations of the Duke of Windsor and his wife—and her attacks on other well-knowns in print and on the air.

A few columns before La Maxwell went on with Paar, I ran a bit of nonsense—a cheap gag in which she was Heroine. (If I'd respected her, of course, I would not have printed it.) It went this way: "And then there's the one about Elsa Maxwell colliding with a Mack truck. The truck lost."

Prett-tee Baaaad, wot? Elsa's feelings were hurt. Making fun of her tonnage that way! I was a cad.

Now along comes Mr. Paar and makes a brand-new life and career for Elsa, who'd publicly announced that she had "never had a man in her life."

The Lez said about it, the better.

Paar, who made a racket out of rapping gossip columns, was one of the best gossips himself. He often disclosed on the air that folks were having a baby, getting a divorce, or doing the hanky-panky bit.

Mr. Paar, who publicly ridiculed Dorothy Kilgallen's "chinless" chin, and gossip columnist Lee Mortimer's Oriental wives (two, maybe more), told Elsa before going onstage that she could say whatever she liked about people she detested—especially WW.

Paar and Elsa sat on chairs and chatted away on that hilarious show. He adored the way she panned the beejeezuzz out of people, the way she gossiped about them all. He loved egging her on to tell more, etc.

Relentless Elsa Maxwell became a television "star" that night.

The viewers screamed and howled at her irreverent opinions.

Paar kept feeding fuel to the blaze she started. Then she got around to Walter.

"That terrible, terrible man," she said for openers, "and what a phony American! He keeps telling his readers and listeners to be sure and register so they can vote and *I can prove* that Walter Winchell never registered or voted in his life!"

I did not hear that, but my chiefs at the New York *Mirror* were told about it and editor Glenn Neville contacted the NBC network's legal department. "Paar and Miss Maxwell," he told the NBC lawyers, "made a big boo-boo when Paar permitted Miss Maxwell to make a misstatement of fact. We consider it damaging over at the *Mirror*. I am rushing over a news photo of Winchell in a booth before casting his vote at the last presidential election."

NBC legalites ordered Paar to display the enlarged photo of me, voting

286

at a hotel on West Fifty-eighth Street, Manhattan, on the next performance. That show I caught.

Paar, grim and miserable (having been caught with his fly open that way), reluctantly displayed the picture—if you blinked, you missed it—and announced halfheartedly that Elsa had "made a mistake" and was "misinformed about Winchell never registering or voting in his life." So furious was he about having to do it, he added: "Well, I did something about correcting an inaccuracy, which is more than I can say about Mr. Winchell. He once had an item implying that my wife and I were on the verge of a divorce—a lie, a lie! When I asked his secretary to tell him to correct and retract it, he refused. His Girl Friday told me: 'Jack, I am sure the boss will make it up to you some other way.' "

Miss Bigman doesn't call strangers "Jack." She never said it or had a message from him. An aide he probably instructed to get a correction apparently didn't—but told Paar that he did.

When you do a column, one of the first things you do is make the correction soonest. In that way, in case of a lawsuit, you can tell the judge and jury that you did correct or retract. Because if you did, they cannot make you pay punitive damages for malice or being misinformed, etc.

I asked Rose Bigman to look up the files and find the item Paar says I printed about him and his wife. Paar, it appears, never gave my girl the date, the year—no clue to when. But when she could spare the time from her busy grind, Miss Bigman searched and searched the files from the time Paar made the Big-Time, and could not locate the item that had aggrieved him.

She wrote asking him to be more explicit. No reply.

An incident I prob'ly will never forget. Wish I could. A Roosevelt Hospital nurse, a grandma-type, carelessly brought my wife a newspaper. The banner headline shouted: "JACK PAAR ATTACKS WINCHELL!"

"Look, Mrs. Winchell!" ejaculated nursie. "Your husband's name!"

The shock gave my gravely ill wife her third heart attack.

Paar has never forgiven me for making him look like a jurq—and as innacurate as "those awful gossip columnists!"

In 1968 Paar confessed on the air that *he* "never registered to vote

287

until Bobby Kennedy convinced him he should do so." Elsa Maxwell had never voted either! The feud was on.

I have heard Paar on some of his programs use gags and lines from the column. Perhaps his "writers" didn't tell him they were stale; that they saved my columns and borrowed from them freely. One of Paar's "witty" cracks—when someone threatened a lawsuit—was, "Ho, hum. They can sue. But I am warning them, they will simply have to take their turn in line!" Syllable for syllable from Winchelliana. I used it on the air more than twice. In the column, too.

But I enjoyed hearing Paar use stuff I had created or quoted. In a column snapping back at him, I shin-kicked: "Jack doesn't like me. He just likes my Act!"

One evening at the Stork Club, owner Sherman Billingsley said: "You just missed Jack Paar and his family. I never saw him here before to-night. He asked for me to come to his table. I think he came here, really, to see you."

"Looking for a fight?" I chuckled. "I'm not in condition, Sherm."

"No," said Mr. B. "He was very nice. Lovely wife and daughter. They came early because he goes to sleep early for the next day's run-through with his staff and writers. He asked: 'Is Mr. Winchell in the place?' and when were you expected. I told him eight P.M. was too early for you—that you usually did not come in until after midnight. "He seemed very sincere about meeting you," Billingsley informed. "He even paid you a compliment. He said he'd like to meet and shake hands —that he'd never realized, until you went on a month's vacation, how dull your imitators were."

"You are making this up, Sherm!"

"No, honest. That's what the man said. No kidding."

And so that is some of the inside stuff about our war with Paar.

He is now a wealthy man—and a happy one—since deserting the Rate Race. I miss his "act" on the air. The man is good. I trust he never becomes a gossip columnist. If he ever did a gossip column—and they left him alone—I fear he'd run us all out of business.

I may be a sonofabitch, but I'm not sonofabitchy. I mean—I wasn't. If I were, I would have printed the following long ago.

The front pages of *Variety* and the blatts coast to coast were appalled by the disclosures that many people on the air were "on the take." The dirty word for it was payola. This followed the revelations about some quiz shows in which some people were illicit—"in on the racket."

Some of Paar's foes sent affidavits about certain persons on the show who had allegedly demanded kickbacks or loot to get them on it.

I flung the rough guessip or gossip into the nearest wastebasket. Nh-nh! That would be a real shortcut to a lawsuit. Perhaps criminal libel.

The same people who sent me that info apparently sent it to government probers then investigating payola on the air. One of the sleuths for that committee saw me on a Washington interview show. He asked me to come see him that night after the program. He told me he had learned that some Paar people might be guilty of using "muscle," like gangsters do. Did I know anything about it?

"No, sir," I told him, "never heard such a thing!"

"Paar," I added, "isn't that kind of a guy, I feel sure. If it is happening, it is a safe bet he doesn't suspect it."

"Well," was the government detective's answer, "this, I hope, is off the record. We think we have a case. It involves inserting plugs for firms who do not buy commercials."

"News to me, mister," I said. He thanked me and I did not see him again until about a month later when I met him in a New York café.

"How goes the payola thing?" I asked him.

"I resigned a week ago," was his startler. "I'm returning to my law practice."

"Why did you quit?"

"I was visited by Robert F. Kennedy," said the ex-prober. "He came into my offices, shook a menacing finger under my nose, and loudly cautioned me to lay off investigating people on the Paar show. His punch line was: 'Don't forget! My brother *may* be the *next* President of the United States!' "

Bobby and Paar became a steady-date until June 5, 1968.

☆

I was defeated only once in a court in my forty-seven years in the papers and on the air. Ooops, begya pod'n. A guy who sued for twenty-five thousand dollars settled for a hundred. I quoted him as calling himself a "rat."

Many of the aggrieved people who sued me were either criminals, Commies, Nazis, or other scum who won headlines that shouted: SO-ANDSO SUES WW FOR LIBEL!" And then dropped the subject.

Frigzample: In 1946 E. P. Dutton published a book titled *The Plotters*. I quoted from it often on the air and in the column. The "Reverend" Gerald L. K. Smith sued me and Station WXYZ, Detroit radio depot, for slander, etc. But the Holy Man didn't show up in court. His Honor threw out the case.

I do not recall ever being sued over an item reporting a romance or a divorce. It was usually some Red, Red-fronter, Nazi, Fascist, Bundist, criminal, or cancer racketeer.

The very few cases I "lost" were mini-settlements (out of court) by the network or paper's insurance company lawyers, who told me: "It's cheaper than filing a brief, and anyway, you need the sleep instead of having to be in a court at nine-thirty A.M."

The insurance people for ABC (over which I did newscasts most of my adult life) paid off plaintiffs with small sums like fifteen hundred dollars and less, which they said, too, "were a lot cheaper than pre-paring briefs."

Then the American Cancer Society asked me to help expose two racketeer-rats who were bilking people in the forty-eight states with a phony cancer-cure racket!

"We have no microphone or TV cameras or syndication the way you have, Walter," they said. "We will give you the documentation about them and a letter holding you blameless for any damages. Please say you will do it."

So I did it. On the day the two frauds went to the Leavenworth Fed-eral clink for two to five years, they started a lawsuit—not for libel, slander, or hurting their feelings: they sued me for "conspiracy"!

I had little sleep for six weeks, sitting in the dock like a prisoner. After the jury said "Not guilty" I went home for some slumber.

That evening, about 9'ish, I was breaking my fast in the Stork Club's Cub Room when in walked the Federal judge who had presided. "Are you nutz?" he yelled at me in front of all the people.

"I don't think so, Your Honor, why?"

He was livid with rage. "I fixed it so those bums could never appeal, and you gave them five thousand dollars in the corridor not to appeal!" First I heard of it.

The insurance people for ABC had paid the two cancer-racketeers five thousand dollars after I had won the case! In a fury, (Oh, Man, have I got a bunch of furies!) I yelled at President Robert F. Kintner over the phone, "ACS asked me to help them expose those guys!"

Mr. Kintner sighed and said: "We can't stop insurance people from making settlements," so I demanded my release from the juiciest con-tract I ever had. My weekly network salary was sixteen thousand dollars.

☆

Another time, I reminded my readers: "James Wechsler, the editor of the New York *Post,* was formerly the national secretary of the Young Communist League." He eventually was forced to confirm it before a congressional investigating committee. His explanation for his former association with the Young Communist League was that he was "so young" at the time (twenty-two) "when college students joined something."

When John Edgar Hoover was twenty-one he didn't join a scummy outfit. He became a clerk in the Department of Justice. When Lindbergh was a big kid he wrote history by making the first solo flight over the Atlantic to Paris. When I was twenty-one I enlisted in the Naval Reserve as an apprentice seaman. But Mr. Wechsler joined a group whose fathers in Russia were for the overthrow of governments by force and violence. Now here was Mr. Wechsler, the American-born "fighter" for minorities, in charge of the editorial department of a New York newspaper—molding opinions for readers who had not yet been informed of his youthful "mistake."

This man liked the way I dealt with solons in Washington and elsewhere who were Fascist-minded. He patty-caked me in print. Then he tried his darndest to demolish me for my attacks on Communists, Reds, Pinks, and Gliberals.

His publisher, Dorothy Schiff, once offered me a job on that paper. She made the offer in front of two of her three-dot imitators. "Why don't you come over with us," she romanced. "Why work for those Hearst Fascists?"

"I have a seven-year contract," I told her. "You wouldn't pay what I'm overpaid. They give me twelve hundred dollars a week for five columns. And fifty percent of the syndication gross."

"But I will!" she said.

When her paper tried to "expose" me, I retaliated.

The counterattack stung them. They were all so brave when they thought they had me on the canvas. But when I fought back, they screamed: "Help! Police! Murder!" They sued my paper, the New York *Mirror.*

My Hearst employers told me to stop: "We are now in litigation. Cut it out."

The case was dropped years later when Mrs. Schiff told Hearst brass that she didn't want to sue another newspaper and that she knew my contract held me blameless for damages of any kind. "If Walter will just say he is sorry, we'll forget it."

I refused to say I was sorry for anything. They knew damb'd well I wasn't sorry.

Months later I was visited by the Hearst Number One legalite, my publisher on the New York *Mirror*, Charles McCabe, and my editor, the late Glenn Neville, the man I knew shuddered at being any part of that double-cross cast.

"The *Post* people," said the lawyer, "will drop the lawsuit if you sign this. I am instructed by the Hearst Corporation to tell you that if you don't sign it, the *Post* will drop the suit against us and start one against you—and we will not be responsible for any damages!"

I signed it to keep my contract and bankroll intact. I knew then I would never again sign another deal with Hearst.

William R. Hearst (the founder of the once-great Hearst chain) was a pioneer in fighting Reds, Pinks, and Leftists. He must have spun in his tomb at the surrender by his heirs and trustees to an editor who admitted he was once the national secretary of the Young Communist League.

Wechsler's chums on a few newspapers in which my column appeared dropped me. Almost every paper that fired me saw my column immediately taken up by a paper in the same town.

★

THE END OF WESTBROOK PEGLER

Westbrook Pegler called me (among other things) "Gent's room journalist." I pinned a label on him that stuck: "Westbrook Pegler, the Presstitute."

I survived the Heel professionally. He destroyed himself.

Pegler was a brilliant writer, no argument about that. He was best, they say, when he was on the sports pages.

His father, Arthur, was a better newspaperman, veteran scribes told me. But papa went into the journalistic history books for counterfeiting a front-pager that opposition papers exposed as a fake. It dealt with a "mysterious" ship off the three-mile limit of New York waters, "where gangsters and high-society people gambled for high stakes and played strip-poker with Broadway chorines. Orgies Galore!" It Never Happened.

But son Westbrook, the self-ordained high priest of what is decent and ethical journalism, never exposed his pater—or ever mentioned his own false "flashes" that he peddled to Roy Howard's blatts.

He specialized in indicting other newsmen for "not checking and getting the facts straight." Look who's talking! Pegler, working in London for United Press during the war, suddenly was recalled for alleged fakery of news.

Pegler's first wife (a newspaper gal named Julia Harpman) was Jewish, he said. None of us in the news biz could figure out why he became the Number One anti-Semite in and out of the paper, considering how much he adored and loved Julia.

Long after she died in 1955 Pegler shouted anti-Semitic profanity in the Stork Club and on the pavement outside, where he had fallen blind drunk, "starched," "stiff," "fried," "blotto," and "woofled." Leonard Lyons, a columnist born on Manhattan's Lower East Side and a devout fellow, went to Pegler's aid. Lyons leaned down to help Pegler get up. "This is Leonard Lyons," he said. "Let me help you, Peg."

"Get away from me, you Jew bastard!" was the two-legged rodent's reply.

Pegler married two other women after his beloved Julia passed on. Both mergers made him poorer: settlements out of court, alimony, etcetera.

There is this paragraph to add. It was Topic A in New York's night-life circles when it happened. The scene was the Stork Club gent's room. A man twice Peg's weight (and in condition to handle himself with his fists) came in and stood alongside Pegler.

"Ahhhh!" flipcracked the wag, "Westbrook Prickler!"

Nobody, it appears, could stand him except his Julia.

Pegler also attacked W. R. Hearst in his syndicated pillar—called "The Chief" insulting names. "I would rather starve," he wrote, "before I would work for Fascist Hearst!" A few months after he wrote that thunder, he went to work for Mr. Hearst. Presstitute was the right word, see?

Pegler's column for the Scripps-Howard papers (and later in the Hearst chain) attacked President Franklin Delano Roosevelt, his wife, Eleanor, and their four sons' flawless war records. It was quite a brawl while it lasted. Pegler and his allies were far to the Fascist Right. They stood for the scummy things Hitler and Mussolini went to war for. The FDR–New Dealers were against Germany's Number One phaggitt (Hitler) and Mussolini's murderers.

Westbrook Pegler was livid when he learned how much Hearst paid me. But what drove him daffy with envy, jealousy, and frustration, was not being able to "Blow The Man Down." And how he tried.

293

For a long time he never mentioned my name when he downgraded me—until I returned the compliment by belting back. He tried his damndest to destroy me as a newspaperman, and when I was a U. S. Naval Intelligence Officer during World War II, he sent a letter to the Navy Department alleging things that would have given me an out-and-out reason to sue him for criminal libel. His letter stated that he could prove many things about me that "should get Winchell stripped of his uniform."

This was great stuff for the many isolationist—anti-FDR-New Deal solons in both houses of Congress. Some of them reprinted his crap-aganda in the *Congressional Record*.

A lot of his charges belonged in a court where they try cases for criminal libel, but the Navy executives told me they didn't believe a word of his allegations. They said to forget it. When *they* tell you to forget it —that's an order.

But thanks to Pegler's wild attacks, U.S. Senator Warren G. Magnuson of the Senate Naval Affairs Committee inserted my naval history in the *Congressional Record*. The Navy debunked Pegler's potshotting paragraph by paragraph. Newspapers carrying my column reprinted it.

That was the end of Pegler's drive to have me cashiered out of the Naval Reserve. But his attacks didn't stop. They were echoed by the hundreds of Eleanor- and FDR-haters in their pamphlets and publications. Some still reprint Pegler's libel—I mean those who are still breathing. Nearly all of them are dead and forgotten.

When I said that Pegler "destroyed" himself, this is how the destruction should accurately be recorded. His vicious attack on war correspondent Quentin Reynolds (Pegler called him a coward, among other slanderous, dirty names in print) started Peg's toboggan drive.

Colleague Reynolds, a reputable newsman for decades, had suffered many ordeals back in New York, losing his lovely wife to a rich man and losing a radio and TV sponsor. And now Peg's malicious lies. Reynolds proved in court that he had been no coward when the Allies invaded Normandy (as Pegler constantly reported) and that Pegler's never-documented charge that Reynolds had proposed a sex frolic to Heywood Broun's widow, a darling woman, while riding with her in the funeral limousine was a lie. Mr. Reynolds' brilliant barrister, Louis Nizer, also proved to the jury that Reynolds had never romped around the Broun estate pool in his Birthday Suit.

The case against Westbrook Pegler, former Good Guy gone goofy with hate against almost everyone, was won by plaintiff Reynolds. The verdict: $175,000 punitive damages and $1 compensatory damages. Of the $175,000, $25,000 was to be paid by Hearst Consolidated Publications, Inc., $50,000 by the Hearst Corporation, and $100,000 by Pegler.

The newspapers said that "it was the largest libel judgment" in many years. Pegler hysterically demanded that the Hearst brass "give me the same thing you give Winchell!"—meaning indemnification against damages of any and all kinds, court and legal fees, et&cet.

Pegler, in short, was still bugged by me. Nobody drove him so screwy.

Lawyer Nizer's reward was sugary. His best seller, *My Life in Court,* still sells big, and the case took place many sensational trials ago.

So that was the start of Pegler's plunge to Nowhere.

The following is my idea of Poetic Justice, alias "Sweet Revenge." One of my California editors, who treats me like one of the family instead of one of the staff, was discussing underpaid newspaper people.

"Well," I confessed, "you are looking at the most overrated and overpaid reporter in newspaper history. How about a raise?"

He didn't answer.

"When do you people give raises around here, anyway?" I teased. "This paper pays me a lousy ten bux a week. I don't need the money. The govvinmint needs the taxes!"

He left his desk and returned minutes later with the billings from King Features Syndicate. "Look," he said, pointing to a line marked "Winchell Package."

"What's a package?" I asked him. "A package of my columns?"

"No," he explained, "the Winchell Package forces us to buy four stupid comic strips, a horoscope bore, a dull hints-to-beauty column, and Pegler's hokum—just to get your column! Imagine finding out that Mr. Pegler (who tried for decades to get me flung out of the Navy and the newspaper biz) couldn't get that famed West Coast newspaper to buy his bigotry and libels—unless it bought my column. In short, Presstitute Westbrook Pegler, the Pulitzer Prize winner, winds up as a Piggy-Back-Rider on the back of his favorite Gentzroom Journalist.

"But I never see his stuff in your paper," I told Ye Ed.

"We never use it," he informed. "We fling his and the other bunk into the nearest wastebasket. But the price for the Winchell Package is a hundred and forty dollars a week!"

"And King gives me only ten?" I boomed. "I never heard of a Winchell Package. I'm going to tell the Senate committee investigating syndicates about this gimmick."

"Oh, gahd!" the source exclaimed. "Don't get us into trouble!"

Justamunit, W," a voice from the gallery just interrupted. "What has all of that got to do with Pegler's last ride as a Hearst writer?"

Okay, let's get back to This-Little-Peggy-Went-to-Market.

Bitter over his defeat by Reynolds and Nizer, and at having his once-popular punditry chopped by Hearst lawyers and editors, Pegler and Hearst were on the Verge-of-a-Dirge. At that time, I had a spot of my own with Hearst and King Features—which I made public over the San Diego airwaves.

Pegler decided to lean on me for his last brawl with the Hearst hangmen. He phoned me from his Tucson "prison." "Walter" (he prefaced warmly), "what in hell is this feud about between you and the syndicate? I am having the same trouble with the sunzabidges!"

I told him.

Pegler, still sizzling over the Hearst choppage of his monotonous Hate and his many other defeats, was impressed. He must've thought he had a new ally in me. He jetted down to San Diego and asked the TV depots to show him the film tapes of my bombardment against Hearst. He adored every word of it, they told me.

Pegler proceeded to a small burg in Texas where his audience included many anti-Catholics, anti-Jews, and anti-Negroes; Birchers, Klansmen, Nazis, and other dung. His ferocious speech there made the wire services.

The Hearst brass had had Enough. He was paid off and assigned to Oblivion. The joint announcement of his Big Finish with Hearst did not include the real reason for their divorce.

And here comes the Delicious Irony again. The Pegler oration in Texas that ended his newspaper career was practically word for word what he enjoyed hearing me say over the San Diego and Los Angeles mikes and TV cameras. Pegler, the Pulitzer Prize winner, winds up being another Winchell-copycat.

A few years ago Pegler suffered humiliating defeat when Robert Welch's mag for Birchers dropped his maniacal wild-with-hate outbursts—which he was giving them for free. Then he phoned me from his Tucson retreat to ask me to help him in his Hour of Peril. "Walter?" he began, "this is Peg. I wish you would find out anything you can or have in your files about a woman who is trying to take my last cent. I've given her almost everything because the courts ordered me to. You have ways of finding out things. Will you do it for me, you rascal you?"

"Yeah, shoor, shoor," I conned him. "I'll get to work on it today. I'll call or write you what I dig up. Take it easy—don't let women throw you. They're all shortcuts to the electric chair or gas chamber. Okay?"

That was the last he ever heard from me. The phoniest enemy a guy could ever despise.

Then he was stricken. One of the New York columns reported that Pegler had lost an eye and was doomed with The Big C.

Yes, Mr. and Mrs. Reader, I certainly did relish putting all of it down. Believe me, I was being kind. They won't print what I wanted to put into the record about Mr. Pegler's terrible indictments and incitements against many helpless people here and abroad.

"Too rough," one editor told me. "Why make the reader sick to his stomach?"

☆

From page one of the New York *Journal-American,* July 21, 1962: "This newspaper called the FBI in Washington early today, seeking details on Mr. Winchell's part in breaking the Bache & Co. stock thefts. Inspector E. G. Kemper said Mr. Winchell supplied information which led to the arrest of two men in Newark yesterday, and also worked with agents in San Francisco. But he declined to elaborate further on Mr. Winchell's role in the case."

The exclusive story (with my by-line) was one of the most exciting in a lucky career. I was invited by one of the gang's chiefs to hasten back to New York from Hollywood to arrange "a deal" for the return of millions of dollars in stolen stocks and bonds.

This man owned part of a Manhattan demolition company. He told me he was the "brains department" of the huge theft and that he was being double-crossed. That is why he wanted me to expose them all.

"I must see you at once," said Mr. Smith, which is not his name. "My story is bigger than the Brink's case in Boston. I will tell you where to dig up many other stolen bonds—not only from Bache and Company but from other Wall Street brokerages."

This frantic man wanted me to get him a guarantee from the insurance people involved that there would be no reprisals. He also said I must get him one hundred and fifty thousand dollars in tax-free money plus a passport "so I can start all over again somewhere in Europe."

"I cannot promise any deals," I told him over the long-distance phone. "The FBI makes no deals, and I can't come to New York. I am going through considerable dental work out here."

I talked the man into flying to San Francisco to tell me his tale and instructed Rose Bigman to arrange a plane ticket for him via my editor at the New York *Mirror*. She was told that the legal department advised against it. "It may be a hoax," they said, "and the paper might be sued."

His ticket was arranged by the FBI. The chap who sold the ticket also took "Mr. Smith's" picture with a tiny camera in his lapel.

When I was informed that "Smith" was on his way to the West Coast and would arrive at 4:30 A.M., the G-men (about twenty of them) turned my presidential suite apartment in the Mark Hopkins Hotel into a shortwave radio and bugging apparatus.

Frank Price, special agent in charge of the San Francisco FBI, and an aide took me to the airport. When the plane's landing lights were spotted, Mr. Price tapped me on the shoulder and said, "You are now on your own. Good luck." The agents hurried away.

"Smith," whom I had never seen before, recognized me as I waited at Gate 30. In the hotel suite he unfolded highlights of the robbery and called the G-men "a bunch of jerks," which, of course, was eavesdropped on by the J. Edgar sleuths.

"At the racetracks," he said, "we would spot nice-looking young kids losing tens and twenties. We'd approach them and say, 'You got a nice face, you look like you come from a good family. How'd you like to work in a Wall Street brokerage for sixty-five dollars a week?' They always accepted. Then, when they were in hock to us at the tracks, we'd tell them how to smuggle out the bonds. We've been doing this for six months. It's the greatest racket since prohibition."

He agreed to surrender to the FBI after I reminded him that "Specs" O'Keefe, in the cast of the Brink's burglary, was out of prison and happily married because he had cooperated with the Boston FBI.

Several hours later the very weary "Smith" agreed to surrender to the G-men in their offices nearby. He repeated most of his story to them —filling in the holes. "Smith" also said the sum reported missing ($1,300,000) was not accurate. "It's more between six and seven million smackers," he insisted.

The result: About fifteen of his confederates (most were called respectable business people) are still behind bars.

My source was rewarded by the lawmen. He was not charged with anything.

★

"WHITE HOUSE CALLING!"

When Senator Barry Goldwater was competing for the Presidential primaries in 1964, I ran a newspaper poll: GOLDWATER OR JOHNSON? Readers were invited to mail in a postcard with the name of the candidate they wanted to win.

The cards came in bundles, most of them from Southern California Republicans and from the six states that Goldwater later won for President. Very few cards mentioned LBJ. As the poll indicated, Goldwater won the primary in California.

When Johnson and Goldwater were nominated, I repeated the poll. Goldwater's crowd sent cards, many with the same handwriting—but different names. One afternoon the cashier in the barbershop at J. Myer Schine's Hotel Ambassador (Los Angeles) announced, "You have a call from the White House." Landlord Schine, getting a shave, was impressed.

I took the call. The caller said, "My name is Busby, White House. Please hold—a friend wants to talk with you."

"Hello, Walter," said another voice.

"Who you?" I asked.

"Lyndon Johnson."

"Hi, Mister Pressadint!" I ejaculated. "What have I done now?"

"How'm ah doin'?" he asked softly.

"How do you mean, Mr. President?"

"How'm ah doin' with your silly poll?"

"I'm cutting it out at once. I found out they were stacking the cards. They contact Republican Clubs and suggest members shower me with postcard votes for Goldwater. Stupid. Tomorrow I'm printing the reason I am stopping it."

"How do you think I will come out?" the President asked.

"I wish I knew. May I suggest you contact your leaders and—"

"My Whaaaatttt?" LBJ interrupted.

"Your leaders!"

"My leaders?" he shouted, "Ahm the leadahhhh!

The patrons in the barbershop, who could hear him, rocked with laughter, too.

I was among the more than two hundred newsmen at the Century Plaza Hotel (Beverly Hills) when LBJ was the honored guest at a Democratic rally. Secret Service people ordered we all be confined to a spacious lobby room. We could see the demonstrators across the way. But they could not restrain the President. LBJ suddenly dashed from his guardians to shake hands with some friend—a politician, a child, or a newsman. The large foyer crowd surrounded him, losing the Feds about a dozen feet away.

When I got too close to the President in the lobby, a secret service agent almost flung me to the floor. I had just done a full column praising the U.S. Secret Service. Guy Spaman, special agent in charge of the Secret Service in Los Angeles, saw me manhandled. He shook his head as though to say "Oh, Brother."

Next morn at about seven-thirty I was in the rear of a small group to see the President's Air Force One take off for Washington.

LBJ suddenly deserted the cordon of Secret Service men to greet friends—one of whom could have been an assassin.

At the Los Angeles Hotel Ambassador when Southern California Democrats hosted a fund-raising affair, newspaper people were not permitted near the entrance to the same Embassy Room where Senator Kennedy was later shot. I had been invited by Demo chiefs to join them at a table close to where LBJ would make a speech. I elected to remain with my colleagues but refused to be confined in the Colonial Room nearby. "I live here," I told a Secret Service man.

He apparently was ordered to stand in front of me—belly to belly. Frank Sinatra came out to go to the washroom. I started over to speak with Frank but was surrounded by agents who barred the way. Along came Gov. Pat Brown with LBJ's then press chief, George Reedy. I told them "at least one reporter and news photographer" should be permitted in the big ballroom "in case something happens." No dice.

That's the way to *protect* a President.

I made the Veterans' Day weekend trip with the White House press corps when the President flew to eight states—coast to coast. The first stop was Fort Benning, Georgia. I stood near Secret Service people about twenty-five yards from where LBJ spoke. I saw two agents usher a good-looking man, dressed impeccably, away from the microphones. They escorted him to a field gate and told him to keep going.

"What was that all about?" I asked.

"He had no press or other credentials," one said.

"Then how could he get that close to the President?"

"We have only two eyes," one said.

"Why," I persisted, "wasn't he held until you all found out his name and address and why he got that close?"

The protection for Barry Goldwater by San Francisco lawmen was so tight that when I tried to get through the crowd waiting to see the candidate and his wife get into their limousine his top aides said, "Nobody! Nobody!" Top GOPeople came along and okayed it.

Earlier that week in Los Angeles, as Mr. Goldwater and aides (one was L.A. Sheriff Peter Pitchess) got into the Hotel Ambassador elevator to go up to Goldwater's suites on the fifth floor, I was stopped by a hotel security officer when I pushed my way in with them.

Sheriff Pitchess okayed me. He introduced me to Mr. Goldwater.

When we got out on the fifth floor the Sheriff (a former G-man) said: "Why don't you two get to know each other?"

Goldwater said: "Why don't you like me?"

"I don't dislike you, Senator, I'm a Democrat."

The newspaper postcard poll I conducted (before the California primary) was confirmed. He was the choice. He thanked me for it.

MR. STORK CLUB

The Stork Club continued to prosper.

Another persistent fable was that I was a sotto voce co-owner.

The Billingsley family knows I was not—and never was. His tax accountants ditto—so did Internal Revenue. The ownership was in the name of Mrs. Billingsley and, I suspect, in the names of their three daughters, Jacqueline, Barbara, and Shermane.

When Billingsley bought the U.S. rights to a French firm's perfume he invited me to be a partner. He said Morton Downey, Arthur Godfrey, and Steve Hannagan, all his close friends, would also be invited "to get in on the deal."

"No thanks, Sherman," I said.

"Why not?" he challenged. "If the business fails it would be deductible, and if it is successful, you'll wind up with money you can keep— seventy-five percent of it!"

"I appreciate all that, Sherman," he was told, "but if I become a partner with you or anybody, I would no longer be free."

"I don't understand what you mean by free."

"I could never write and publish a story about you or them," said I.

"You would write a story about *me*?" Sherman inquired, astonished.

"I don't say I would. I mean I don't want to be in a spot where something involving you or some patron became big headlines—and my editors assigned me to cover it. Anyway, no thanks."

There was the time Sherman was being given a hard time by a married socialite he had befriended when she was in large trouble. She never let go of her clutch. She supplied newspaper foes and others with "inside" stuff about his private goings-on—a good deal of it the fury of a woman scorned.

One night in his Cub Room (which I had christened at his request) when business was slow and that annex (for celebrities) was not half populated, Sherman was in a sullen mood. He kept talking about what an ingrate the lady was.

"I wish," he sighed, "you would print what a tramp she is."

"Now look, Sherman," I objected, "don't involve me in this. You know I don't operate that way."

He suddenly turned on me! "Oh," he groaned, "you, too!" His voice hit a hysterical high.

I just looked at him, astonished no little myself. He had never talked to me that way before in all the four decades of our friendship.

"Just forget it," he said caustically, "I can get all the other guys [meaning columnists and newspaper execs] to do it for me. I can buy them all for a dime a dozen!"

"Gee, Sherman," I rebutted, "thanks for not including me in that dozen." So saying, I got up and left. I stayed away from the Stork Club for almost three years.

Nobody ever got the story right. His detractors and mine kept reporting various reasons—all of them wild and stupid. I never stopped mentioning the Stork Club, however. If a quip or a news item came out of the Stork, I so reported. This added to the knockers' confusion. They couldn't figure it out.

One evening about 9'ish I was strolling along East Fifty-third Street, where the Stork was then (now Paley Park). Like a homing pigeon I walked in, flung my Cavanagh at the girls in the checkroom, and proceeded to my usual pew (Table 50) in the Cub Room. His loyal staff spread the word quickly: "Walter is back!" They phoned Sherman at his upstairs office.

I was inspecting the menu, and was happy to note that a dish bearing my name was still on it, when Sherman sidled alongside. He embraced me with a tight hug and then wept.

I kidded him out of it. Neither of us ever mentioned the long absence. We went into the usual gab about this person and that one, as though there had never been a rift. We never had a difference of opinion of any import again.

In the almost forty years that I knew Sherman he included me among the many newspaper people and others who could never get a tab (a check—a bill); his gifts were many—rare liqueurs, Napoleon brandy by the cases. He gave many of us costly suits, via gift certifs to buy a three-hundred-and-fifty-dollar suit at Knize, a swank haberdashery on East Fifty-sixth Street, New York City.

I learned recently the fee for a suit there is five hundred dollars, so I guess Knize has lost me. I cannot forget the days when I was a young song-and-dance-man or a cub reporter on *The Vaudeville News* and couldn't even afford a suit at some cheap Broadway store unless I borrowed the eighteen bux.

Knize's chief fitter once told me: "It's not the higher cost of the material, it's the higher cost of labor." Izzatzo? I never made any of those phony Best Dressed lists anyway. People who know me well will tell you that I look like a Doll in my set-of-threads. Always in blue: navy blue suits, pale blue shirts, navy blue cravats, blue sox, and Baby-Boo eyes!

Billingsley gave away more costly gifts, souvenirs (sometimes motor cars) and gems purchased at Tiffany's and Cartier's.

Mutual intimates informed me of Sherman's "putting the bite on" some of his longtime wealthy patrons and alleged pals. Many came through for him. But many of those who accepted his gratuities failed him when he needed financial assistance.

I was in Hollywood at the time, narrating teevee pilots or my own cops-and-robber series, and *The Untouchables*.

A chum phoned: "Has Sherman touched you yet?"

"Meaning what?"

"He's dead broke," said the caller. "The Hearst brass gladly gave him money to pay bills like the rent, etcetera. Bill, Jr., I hear, gave fifty dollars when Sherm told him he was penniless."

"I just cannot believe Sherman is broke," I said. "But he hasn't phoned or wired me for financial help—his pride, perhaps."

In 1966 I became a patient in a hospital for the first time in my life (since being run over when I was young). They didn't tell me that a longtime pal was in a room across the hall from mine—dying. Sherman Billingsley.

When Sherman's youngest daughter Shermane told newspaper friends she was readying a book about her father, I phoned her. "If," I told Shermane, "you do not invite me to write the foreword, it will make me very sad."

She said: "Oh, if you only would!"

I suggested she change her planned title to *Mr. Stork Club*. She said that she was not a writer—that she had simply put down many things her parents had told her over the years. "I was recommended to Whitney Bolton of the *Morning Telegraph*," Shermane said, "to help me put it in order."

"He's just the right man to do it," I told her. "He's been around as long as most of us who have written some of Broadway's history."

Weeks later at a First Night, Bolton told me: "She can write! She needs no help from any of us." She planned to reveal something in her book I had never heard before; that Sherman had been kidnapped and brutally beaten by Vincent "Mad Dog" Coll months before Coll snatched gang chief Big Frenchy, who was held for a thirty-five-thousand-dollar ransom. Shermane disclosed that her father had been Coll's prisoner in a Bronx garage for three days and nights. He was freed when Mrs. Billingsley ransomed her husband for twenty-five Big Ones.

"Oh, Shermane," I exclaimed. "He never told me that. And he told me almost everything!"

She permitted me to make it public in the column. Not one newspaper or wire service picked it up.

She told me several other never-before-published bits of lowdown about people he liked and people he didn't—and vice versa. Not in a gossipy manner. She revealed some of the stories to check them.

"Is it true," she queried, "that my father did this or that?" I debunked a good many of the legends.

Shermane also made my day when she said: "My father always told Mother and the rest of us that if we ever needed counsel or help, we could always trust the only man he trusted—you."

Weeks after that visit I asked Shermane if there was anything I could do for her and the family. Did Sherm really die broke?

"Yes," she confirmed. "He told Mother that he went through seven million dollars."

"But you're all living at a pretty fancy apartment house. He must have left something to your mother. Talk has it that Sherman put a good deal of money in your mother's name for the well-known rainy day."

"We live there," reported Shermane frankly, "to keep up the front Daddy kept up as long as he could." Shermane then punctuated that statement with this Punctuation Mark: "Walter," she said sadly, "Mother is going blind. Unless she has an operation on her eyes, according to specialists, she will be sightless."

"Oh, no!" I said. "Find out what retainer the doctors want for the operation."

"I think," she said, "the whole fee is twenty-five hundred dollars."

"You will get a check for that amount tomorrow."

Next day Shermane phoned: "Mother said thanks very much, but her heart doctor told her not to undergo eye surgery at this time. The shock might kill her."

When we discussed it days later, Shermane said: "If we need your check, I promise you'll get it back from my first royalties, if any, on my book."

Another revelation from Shermane was the "real reason" Dorothy Kilgallen, the *What's My Line?* and newspaper star, died.

Myrtle Verne, Girl Friday and column-helper for Dorothy Kilgallen, reportedly told the following to mutual friends. Miss Verne was later chief aide to society columniss Doris Lilly of the New York *Post*.

"Dorothy stopped off with friends after the *What's My Line?* show and got home about midnight. She did her column and probably went to bed around four A.M. Everybody in the household was told not to disturb her.

"She had an appointment with her hairdresser for noon the next day, Monday. The hairdresser appeared at Dorothy's home on time and waited for her to summon him. When she didn't call or come down, I went to her room to awaken her and tell her the hairdresser was there.

"I thought she was sleeping. She had been reading Bob Ruark's latest book. It was in her hand. Her head was to one side. She appeared to have fallen asleep while reading, a longtime habit. Afterwards, I recalled that she looked just like an angel in her fluffy, white nightwear.

"It wasn't until I spoke to her twice and touched her that I realized she had passed away. I just couldn't believe it. I nearly passed out before I ran from the room to inform the family and call a doctor."

The title of Ruark's book that Dorothy was reading was *The Honey Badger*.

"She died," I reminded Shermane, "from a combination of barbiturates and liquor, according to the coroner."

"Yes, I know, but that's only a part of it."

"I hope you're not going to tell me that the bunk spread by a gook in Texas is true—that Dorothy was poisoned because she knew too much about Jack Ruby and Oswald!"

"No," said Shermane. "One night, after Dorothy died, Daddy told us that not even her parents, who often sat with her at Table Fifty, ever knew how much Dorothy drank. At the table she usually had one or two drinks. But many times she excused herself to go to the ladies' room, where she said that she could phone the city desk with a story instead of using a phone at the table where people might overhear her. In the ladies' room," Shermane continued, "Dorothy would take a mini-bottle from her purse and enjoy another two drinks—sometimes more."

"How would Sherman know that?" I asked.

"The woman in charge of the ladies' room told him!"

The irony of it! I recall many of Dorothy's columns in which she warned readers: "Never mix booze with sleeping pills. It can kill you!"

So there's the believable cause for Dorothy's sudden passing. It would have "killed" her, I suspect, if she had lived long enough to see *What's My Line?* die after her seventeen years as a feature on it, and to agonize when her paper perished—the New York *Journal-American*, on which she apprenticed as an excellent reporter and later a syndicated paragrapher.

If Dorothy had lived she would have inherited the newspapers I appeared in before I decided to change syndicates. She enjoyed a wide syndication, anyway, but her successor replaced me in several papers when I quit Hearst after thirty-eight years.

Long before any of the other three-dotters publicly stated "WW made it possible" for them to prosper as columnists, Miss Kilgallen said it in an article she wrote for *Cosmopolitan*.

The Texan who stupidly "made" the gullible wire services with his concoction that "she was one of fifteen persons who mysteriously died" (following Jack Ruby's death from The Big C) is probably shrugging off the above. But he had his moment in the limelight which has killed more men than bullets.

☆

306

I like *Philadelphia Inquirer* publisher Walter Annenberg. And not just because of his first name. His father was the first outoftown publisher to run my stuff—in a Miami Beach paper. The start of my initial syndication—years before I went over to Hearst's *Mirror* and Hearst syndicate, King Features. The *Miami Herald* took me on when that Beach blatt died.

The column ran in the Philly *Public Ledger* about 40 years ago. Then the *Ledger* folded, and Walter Annenberg bought the *Ledger*'s name and goodwill, etcetera. And my col'm. The *Philadelphia Inquirer* overpaid me $200 weekly for five columns (the highest fee for me from any newspaper). Apparently it kept me on for decades to keep the column from appearing in the opposition papers. But I always wondered why Mr. Annenberg's *Inquirer* seldom published the various New York gossip columns it acquired. When it did print us all, the *Inquirer* used only excerpts bunched in a mini-box. If it weren't for that $200 per, I'd have requested the editors to release me, so I could try my luck, even at a lot less money, with other Philly papers.

I found out only in the late 60's why the *Inquirer* was anti-gossip-column—after it suddenly expelled all of them. It was because of a long-drawn-out libel suit by Stork Club owner Sherman Billingsley, who sued the *Inquirer* and its New York guessipist for millions.

The columnist, whose imitation of my format was better than all the other carboncats, made a bubu that cost him his job. Not only with Mr. Annenberg's Philly paper, but Annenberg's outlet in Gotham—the *Morning Telegraph*.

That paper often front-paged the col'm once weekly (on Saturdays) when its readers patronize the racetracks. You can buy it at all tracks.

Mr. Clunk put us all out of business in Philadelphia—because he fell for an oft-repeated hunk of bunk.

Billingsley, who never sued anybody (certainly not newspapers or newspaper people, many of which and whom helped him prosper) decided to stop the "rumor" that his Stork Club tables were bugged.

The columnist's "expozay" said he could "prove" it was true. At examination-before-trial, however, when Billingsley's lawyers challenged him to submit his "proof," he couldn't do so. The case never reached a courtroom.

Both Annenberg and Billingsley each squandered over a million arguing about it. That is why Mr. Annenberg fired us all.

He fired gossipists from his *Inquirer,* but not from his other prosperous paper in Philly, the *Daily News.* (Is a puzzlement, no?)

When I asked *Inquirer* editors to put the column in Mr. Annenberg's
Philly *Daily News,* they said they had too many gossip columns. "Sorry."

Most of the Philly *Daily News* chatter-columns are 3-dotters 2-column
measure—Winchell-format style colums. The story of my life.

I died in Philly, but the ghouls survived.

(End of long, deep sigh.)

SIXTIES VIGNETTES

John P. Lewis, an editor, knows a four-year-old named Johnny who arrived at his nursery school sporting an overseas ribbon a soldier friend
had given him. Two other tots were very impressed. "Is it a real overseas
ribbon?" one queried. "What did you get it for?"

"Because," was the reply, "I shot a lot of Viet Cong soldiers and cut
off their heads and killed them all dead and I shot down their planes,
too."

"What else?"

"That's all. Then my mommy gave me my milk and I took a nap."

"What an impolite dress. It stares right at you!"

Capsule Criticism of Gina Lollobrigida's vocaling on teevee: "Don't
Listen—Look!"

Sarcasm by an anti-inflationist: "You got two nickels for a dollar?"

The only Winchell with two *l*'s I could find in the New York City
phone tome in 1918 was Ben Winchell of the Remington Typewriter
Company. No kin. But in 1967 there were many Winchells—among
them David Winchell, a Canadian mining man, and Paul Winchell, the
ventriloquist who won a Major Bowes Amateur Contest on radio in the
long ago. Paul, now renowned, told interviewers who queried "Any re-
lation to Walter?," "No, I got my name from Major Bowes." The Major

couldn't remember Paul's last name of Wilchek, and so he announced: "The winner is Paul *Winchell!*" Of course, as the winner of a nationally networked contest, he had to use the name Major Bowes had accidentally bestowed.

And the irony of it! When ABC-TV chief Robert Kintner offered me TV, I stalled for years. Paul Winchell beat me to television and cashed in. Little children asking for an autograph (whose mothers were confused, too) invariably looked up at me and wistfully inquired: "But where's your dummy?"

Fame! I had been on the air since 1929 (and in the papers since 1920) and now the kids shrugged. So did their parents. Paul was the "Winchell" who got into their homes five times a week.

The latest Winchell I heard on the air is Bill Winchell, a news reporter in the Midwest. He lands on the coast-to-coasters when there is a riot or some other big story. Very expert newsman.

Joan Winchell (her father is Ed Winchell, a Beverly Hills Realtor) had a by-line in the Los Angeles *Times* for several years over a column about cafés, restaurants, etc. Most of the time the *Times* had other by-liners in seven or eight point type. But the title of her column was in large type. No "Joan"—just the last name, "WINCHELL."

My col'm appeared in the opposition, Hearst's Los Angeles *Herald-Express,* later called the *Herald-Examiner* after a merger—meaning the death of another Hearst paper. The *H-E* editors and staff enjoyed seeing their mighty opposition play up the name of a newcomer to journalism (Joan) when most people on the papers can't get a by-line until they prove they "sell papers."

Joan Winchell often told me that she enjoyed having readers ask: "Is Walter your daddy?" Many mutual readers gushed, "I love your daughter's column."

But I knew Joan had reportorial talent when I first met her—during a Republican convention (Eisenhower goddit) in San Francisco. We met in front of Jack's, a popular restaurant where philanthropist-financier Lou Lurie (former newsboy in Chicago) held court daily. Jack's is Lou's "Stork Club"—same table every noon, where celebrated people and friends are his guests.

On the sidewalk I was introduced to pretty Joan Winchell. We traded quippage and kidding. I was no little surprised when I read her piece next day. It was headed: *"Winchell Interviews Winchell."* It was crowded with good reporting and writing—anecdotes I had told her and flip crax she had ad-libbed. Alas, Joan lost her column one day and returned to public relations for swank places in Palm Springs and other Southern California inns.

That's the trouble with being a columnist. When you lose your col'm you often wind up with the press agents you considered pests. Often it is some pluglicity agent you failed who gives you a job. I hope that never happens to me. I'd rather go back to stealing stamps than fawn over some newspaper byliner—like a mendicánt begging for a break.

When you lose a column (and they think you're washed up) you find out how many friends never really were.

Years before, I caught the carbon of a memo to King Features Syndicate chief Joseph V. Connolly from Richard E. Berlin, the very top man in the Hearst Empire:

"Dear Joe: I ran into Walter Winchell last evening. He was quite irritated about the way his column was being cut. Said it was becoming increasingly difficult to work for the *Mirror* and, accordingly, he was losing all interest in his work and thought he had better leave."

Now I was in the city room of the *Herald-Examiner* in Los Angeles, talking shop with the guys, when in walked Stan Progar, features editor. He was showing assistant managing editor Aggie Underwood (my favorite female in the news biz) a column that had just come in from King Features.

The *Herald-Examiner* received my stuff by wire same day it was ready for the *Mirror*'s composing room. King Features airmailed proofs to the newspapers (in fifty states) that didn't want the expense of Western Union or Hearst Headline Service tolls.

"How in hell," Progar asked Aggie, "do you get a column out of three paragraphs?"

Miss Underwood, an Angel-of-a-guy, called out across the city room, "Walter, come over here!"

"That's my column," I groaned. "What's this bit?"

There had been eleven paragraphs—about 980 words. A thick black pencil, more like a crayon, had X'd out eight paras.

"This is ridiculous!" I said. "This stuff has already appeared in the New York *Mirror,* every word of it okayed by the lawyers and editors. The bum who butchered this column must be nutz!"

"Jeezuzz!" I profaned. "That fourth paragraph was okayed by Richard E. Berlin, the Number One man at Hearst Corp! It was handed to my Girl Friday by *Mirror* publisher Charles McCabe and Glenn Neville, my wonderful editor."

It was a blast at the New York *Post,* with which I tangled often, and it with me. It "exposed" the *Post*'s alleged "fakery" in page ads reporting their latest circulation numbers. "Eighth Avenue" brass had attached a copy of the latest ABC (Audit Bureau of Circulation) figures—showing that the *Post*'s circulation was about a hundred thousand less than their ads announced.

"Rose read it to me via phone at my house. She said it came from Eighth Avenue"—(meaning the Hearst Building on Eighth between 58th and 59th streets)—"and that Mr. Berlin had sent it, saying: 'Walter will like this—tell him it's all documented and not to worry about it.' "

And here's this stupid syndicate editor deleting what Mr. Berlin had written for my column. His sending it—the first time in almost forty years that Mr. Berlin had contributed a line to me—was tantamount to an "order."

This upset me so much that I couldn't wait to get to every microphone and teevee camera in Los Angeles so I could pop off.

"Imagine," I said to Paul Coates, the TV interviewer (a columnist for the Los Angeles *Times*) "my chief boss at Hearst Corporation, Dick Berlin, sends this paragraph to me, and a dope at King Features kills it!"

"This isn't the first time, either," I growled. "Someone at King has been murdering or deleting almost every anti-Commy line I write. The irony of it! W. R. Hearst, who hired me in June 1929, practically invented exposure of Reds in the United States.

"Mr. Hearst dies and one of his reporters, me, picks up the torch he had to drop, and continues fighting Krushchev and Company every day almost. But a King Features wotzit throws my anti-Scummy stuff on the floor! No wonder the Hearst Empire is crumbling!

"When I started on the New York *Mirror* in 1929, Mr. Hearst owned twenty-three papers coast to coast. That list is now down to seven papers. I want the hell out of there. I don't want to resign from the *Mirror*, I love the *Mirror* and every staffer and copyboy on it. I no longer want to have any connection with King Features."

In San Diego I repeated most of that outburst over some of the radio and television stations. *Time* mag and AP and UPI interviewed me about the blasts.

"Yes," I told them all, "put it in the paper. I'm through with King Features!"

When the stories ran in New York, an intimate of Mr. Berlin and the Hearst heirs told a mutual friend to phone me at once.

The intimate of Mr. Berlin was Morton Downey. Jack O'Brian was the mutual friend who phoned.

311

"Morton asked me to call you. Morton said 'I never knew Walter to ever kick a man when he was down. Walter thinks Dick is ducking his phone calls from the Coast. Walter doesn't believe Dick is at his retreat in Murray Bay, Canada. The truth is that Dick likes Walter very much. But he has a heartache and has gone away—never even contacts his office about anything.'

"Morton," continued Jack, "told me to tell you to revoke your resignation edict—calm down. You've been through these things before. I also ask you to stop that big mouth of yours. Don't be a fool, you fool!"

I promised O'Brian I would revoke the resignation, and I did so that hour.

Then the New York *Post* sued over that "deleted" paragraph—which had run in the New York blatts, of course. At the examination before trial the *Post* lawyers asked: "Do you subscribe to the Audit Bureau of Circulation?"

"No, I do not."

"Somebody told you about the circulation numbers?"

"Yes."

"Who told you?"

I looked at the Hearst lawyer and said: "I'm going to tell the truth."

"Go right ahead," he nodded.

"I got what I printed from my publisher and editor."

The exam was over. The *Post* then named as codefendants the Hearst Corporation; Richard E. Berlin; William Randolph Hearst, Jr.; Mr. Mc-Cabe (the *Mirror* publisher); editor Glenn Neville; and the whole cast of Hearst chiefs.

The *Post* lawyers, I learned later, had caught them all with their pants unzippered. The Hearst brass, they documented, had sent me ABC circ figures that were six months stale. Mr. Berlin and Company were, according to the *Post* people, pretty lousy reporters.

But there was no trial. The Hearst chiefs decided to write it off as a tax loss. I was told they presented the New York *Post* with seventy thousand dollars. I suppose the Hearst record books show that "Winchell lost seventy thousand dollars for us."

But my statements about the Hearst brass started my own exit as a Hearst man. They didn't fire me, which I wish they had. They simply "waited" (the way I said I wait to return a "compliment") and about five years later—when the *World Journal Tribune* was the graveyard for both the New York *Mirror* and New York *Journal-American*— one Hearst chief evened things.

312

The very first edition of the "Widjit" (as the knockers nicknamed the new paper, the *WJT*) announced in a good-sized ad, "Broadway's New Number One Gossip." It was purveyed in the WW style (three-dot stuff) by a prolific writer who has publicly stated that he is "another graduate of Winchell U." When he was conductor of the New York *Journal-American*'s teevee col'm, I flung orchids at his talent. "He is," I patty-caked, "the H. L. Mencken of TV criticism." Now he, too, was used to do the Winchell-bit by W.R.H., Jr., who ordered that my column was to be edited to the bone until I "surrendered and resigned."

My name rarely appeared in the paper's Index on page 1. My column appeared only once a week, on Saturdays (I wrote five). It was cut, sometimes, to one-third.

★

WHAT AND WHO KILLS A NEWSPAPER?

Three newspapers for which I colyum'd also went out of business in three years (1963–1966) chiefly because of long strikes—which means stupid union chiefs and ditto editors and publishers. But the last one died because it was the dull bastard child of old parents who were forced to marry each other to stay alive.

Every since the *World Journal Tribune* folded after eight months there have been many theories on what caused its quick demise.

Co-owner Jock Whitney pulled out his hefty backing, hastening its end. Men and women who were on that flop blamed its death on the newspaper unions, bad management, poor distribution, and amateurish judgment in assessing the reading desires of the public—such as dropping several longtime features dealing with Broadway and nightlife. *Editor & Publisher* and many other authorities on newspapers revealed that Scripps-Howard publisher Matt Meyers had said: "We tried to give it to anybody free. We couldn't give it away!"

One *WJT* editor, in an article for a mag, disclosed that the unions were not the reason the new paper was "assassinated." He certified that the paper perished because of "gross mismanagement."

Actually, each one had its part. But there is one essential factor nobody has assessed. Fundamentally, a newspaper exists to furnish news—and news that affects the community is handled by the city desk. An editor on the *WJT* (more than thirty years in the news craft) told me the *WJT* city desk "was the worst in newspaper history."

When the troika (three publishers of as many former papers) split up the various departments, the *World-Telegram* and *Sun* people took over the city desk. Sylvan Fox was appointed city editor. He asked for a raise, a perfectly normal request, considering the fact that he was stepping up into one of the most important posts at the new whatzit. Mr. Fox was turned down. He quit and got a job with Mayor Lindsay's administration and then went on to *The New York Times*.

Two young men were assigned to his chair. Both (according to ex-staffers) "were completely unequipped for the job." It became a standing gag among the rewrite men that the *WJT* never carried a story that hadn't appeared the night before in the early editions of the *Times*.

It must be remembered that both of the young geniuses (running the city desk) came very cheap. An example of their efficiency: One day a bulletin came in datelined Hawthorne, New Jersey, about a dozen miles from New York City. It told of an explosion in a manufacturing plant that killed two men.

One of the new city desk chiefs showed it to his colleague—then edited the copy. Handling it as a local story, he knocked out the dateline and inserted "Hawthorne, New York" (which is about thirty-five miles from New York City) as the locale of the accident. He sent it along as a "short" for page one.

When the news editor called over and asked if they were covering it, he was informed, "It's out of our territory and only worth a short."

The next edition of the New York *Post* (Manhattan's only other P.M. blatt) came up to the city room—and gahd knows the *Post* was never noted for speed on a story—the *Journal-American* used to beat the girdle off of it on every yarn. The *Post* "played" the accident in banner headlines on page one. By this time, of course, the Associated Press had been sending in a story, and the *WJT* city deskers finally became aware of their oops.

But the damage was done, and the *Post* had two editions on the streets before the *WJT* decided to come in last with the story.

Ironically enough, the *WJT* then sent a team of reporters and photographers to Hawthorne, New *Jersey*—and the next day (twenty-four hours late) its first edition was full of all sorts of human interest stories and pix of the tragedy.

The above is just one instance of the many times the *WJT* city desk took a beating from the opposition. The sad part of it (adds the source) "was that nobody could tell the two young men who replaced Sylvan

Fox anything! They knew it all and everything they knew was worthless."

Following the foldo, one of the duet was hired by another local paper, but he lasted a couple of thousand minutes. The other chap has a minor job in a network newsroom. He was luckier than the more than six thousand newspaper people who are still looking for employment because the *WJT* (and two Hearst papers) were governed and edited by oafs.

Rose found out that what her boss had written—many times—was mercilessly true:

"On Broadway, first they shake your hand. Then they shake their heads."

"There's nothing so dead as an ex-critic, columnist, or newspaper publisher. Ex-Anything!"

"When they want you, they kiss your ass. When they don't, they kick it!"

"I like Walter, but 1938?" one editor was quoted in *Newsweek*.

Many of my outlets around the nation went out of business for other reasons—high cost of production, strikes, etcetera.

Several publishers replaced me with style-burglars who worked for peanuts. When I asked an editor of a small Midwest paper why he had dropped me, he replied, "You cost us twenty dollars a week. We are cutting down—your replacement gets five!"

So this lady (whose husband is another imitator I introduced to my best sources around Broadway) said—within earshot of people waiting for their hats and coats—"Don't look so sad, Walter. Cheer up. My sweedee now has many of the papers you used to have!"

Rosie hasn't an enemy in the world (so Pussycat is she). When we both were on the New York *Mirror,* and later, the New York *Journal-American,* nobody ever said an unkind thing to her or about her. So I couldn't believe it when, during my temporary loss of a New York outlet, I learned that anyone would say or do anything to wound her. But a louse—using my format—won the distinction of being the only one to make her mizzable.

In a restaurant one 6'ish she greeted him with her friendly "Hi!" as she had always greeted the Big Prig.

"Screw!" he said (between hiccups). "You're a has-been. So's your washed-up boss!"

It wrecked Rose's night. "You're not a has-been," she consoled me.

"You are just going through a storm. You'll be back on a paper one day soon. I read it in your horoscope, honest!"

One of my imitators once said to a radio interviewer in Chicago (I was also a guest): "I never told Walter this before. But when I was breaking into the newspaper business in a small town, they put me in charge of the syndicated columns. My job was to cut them down to fit them all in. Winchell's word-weddings confounded me. I couldn't understand his 'Phffft!' or 'Infanticipating' or 'The Soandsos are posting the Renotice.' So I chucked his columns on the floor and they often didn't get in the paper."

"And now" (I couldn't resist the gentle stiletto) "you're one of my rich copycats."

All of them were helped by Grandpa when they first started colyuming. I gave them items and quips I picked up while I was on vacation— my vacations were usually at the Stork Club or Lindy's and the other spots we all covered. I gave Dorothy Kilgallen (a Hearst coluMiss) a lot of the trivia and news breaks I picked up while "resting." I couldn't stand not seeing a good news tip or gag in print.

I've told gags and stories on myself to my friends and false-friends for years. "Anything for a laugh!" as the line goes. I'm the one who "breaks himself up" when the gag about me is hilarious.

I introduced many of my "competitors" to celebrities—terrific news sources: G-man J. Edgar Hoover, for instance. But most of these befriended newcomers were my worst boosters.

None of them ever thought of sending the Damon Runyon Cancer Fund a dime donation (or penny or dollar) for "inside stuff" they peddled—that I told them. Even the worst criminals send a few bucks to what they call "the Conscience Fund." When a mag or newspaper did a job on me in a series of "exposés" this rat-pack supplied most of the exaggerations and bunk.

A ghost writer for a former editor I hated thinks I do not know that he authored more lies and knocks about me than other punks. The shmuck finally lost his column when his paper perished.

I just read a few pages of a book by Stanley Walker, written in the 1930's. Mr. Walker was a country boy from Texas who made his mark in New York as a top city editor for the *Herald Tribune*. I often introduced him to the gayer night spots and people when he first came to town. I played up his talent in the column. He gave me the best of it in his book. But one story he pinned on me never happened.

I had told Mr. Walker that story. It was about Otto H. Kahn, a lead-

316

ing banker. It was a famous story that made Kahn a boob. Walker pinned it on me.

Perhaps Walker forgot I told it to him. Anyway, he got it all screwed up.

Poor man. A victim of incurable cancer, he later took his life with a shotgun blast on the porch of his Texas home.

Oh, don't go. You must meet another heel on my long list of Ingrates.

He was getting sixty dollars per on a now-dead sheet. I heard he was to be fired.

I told my boss, Joseph Connolly, at King Features and Int'l News Service, "I know a helluva good writer who should be with Hearst! Dick Berlin suggested long ago that Hearst people should be on the lookout for 'comers'—that we all should bring in new blood."

Without asking me the man's name, Mr. Connolly said, "Will he go to Washington? We need a man down there."

"Yes, he will," I said. "May I tell him to see you?"

"I can pay him only a hundred and twenty-five a week!" said my boss. (Twice the lad's soon-to-end wage.)

"Oh, I'm sure he'll be glad to start for that, Joe!"

The man shook my hand as a phony would—and then couldn't wait for the next day's edition of a paper that was belting me around. He then hastened into Toots Shor's place, where many newspaper people dined. Waving the front page before all eyes, he hysterically shrieked: "Look what they did to the bum today! Wow! This'll surely wreck him!" Charming chap. Make that read "Prince Charming!"

That fellow became one of the top byliners. Writes like a writer.

When he was with another paper, I was its target for a series (the 164th article, book, or series meant to canvas me).

He supplied some of the hokum. This Prince Charming not only became my Second Favorite Falz-Friend and Judas, but he had the gall to swipe column formats that I had swiped before he was born! I went along with our mutual deception, never letting him know that I knew of articles he wrote—under a phony by-line. What-the-Hell? Dog Bites Man.

Why am I jotting this down without naming him? I mentioned him dozens of times when he needed a syndicated plug—in the long ago, before I taught him how to walk on water. The people I hope will read this chapter are those who know us both. They'll know the name of El Ratto.

"Blind" reportage like this usually starts "insiders" clucking and telling each other, "You know who he's rapping, don'tchu?"

317

He'll know. I'm just returning the salute he gave me when he thought I was down for the count.

The reader may wonder why I have goosed some of the above-mentioned ingrates.

Before I go to hell—which can't be too far off—I want them all to know that I've wearied of the mutual deception. I have forgiven, but I don't have to forget. I'm not a fighter, I'm a "waiter." I wait until I catch an ingrate with his fly open, and then I take a picture of it.

When some heel does me dirt (after I've helped him or her) I return the compliment some day. In the paper, on the air, or with a bottle of ketchup on the skull. I don't make up nasty things to write about them. I wait until they get locked up for taking dope or pimping, and then I make it Public. Vindictive? You're gahdamb'd right! You Botcha Me, I Botcha You!

When you reach seventy you shrug at everything. So what? Most of them tried to run me out of the business. My reward is knowing that I've "carried" the ingrates for nearly fifty years.

Rosie's prediction came through sooner than I expected. I wound up on six New York papers. The *Morning Telegraph* (front page on Saturdays, the day racing fans pack the tracks)—thank you, Walter Annenberg, publisher, Stewart Hooker, and managing editor Saul Rosen. They took me on after five newspapers in New York went out of business (when a Feller needs a Friend). The *Morning Telegraph* overpays me, too. For once a week, the loot is fifty bux. *Variety* ("The Show Biz Bible") gives the column a swelegant play Wednesdays on the "Literati" page read by the indullectuals in and out of show biz. Ditto the Newark *Evening News,* which then circulated in New York. The *Washington Examiner* (I'm also associated, by heck!) also bought it. Then its landlord, O. Roy Chalk, bought the col'm for his *El Diario-La Prensa* (in Espanol!) read by Spanish-speaking people in the fifty states and throughout Puerto Rico.

My sixth New York City outlet was the New York *Daily Column:* over sixty well-known columnists and editorial page cartoonists for New Yorkers who missed the wide diversity of opinion of men and women journalists whose wordage disappeared when five Manhattan papyri perished, thanks to some greedy newspaper union leaders and "dated" publishers who got rich brain-picking their feature-writers. End of Thumb-In-Eye.

Then I took on the biggest load I ever lifted—in 1968, when I was seventy-one: Newscasting on teevee five days a week with United Press

318

International News Films; also five columns a week for McNaught Syndicate plus another UPI series of documentaries—as narrator. Back in The Tall Brackets again. So was Rose Bigman.

Humorist Ed Howe's shin-kick: "When a man tells you what people are saying about you, tell him what people are saying about him. That will immediately take his mind off your troubles." The drunk girl-hurter —who got lucky because I was born—doesn't know how close he came to losing his job to the Has-Been.

Until 1967 I was without a paper in the capital of the nation—only in a breezy little paper named *Roll Call* (at no wages) distributed to solons in both houses, the Department of State, the White House, and other government people and—I believe—at the National Press Club, of which I have long been a member. But in 1967 I landed in O. Roy Chalk's snappy and novel newspaper the Washington *Examiner,* which circulates in cities between Washington and Boston. I was also named associate editor. Associate editor?

When Mr. Chalk and his editor, Jack Limpert, told me I was now an editor, the first thing I asked was: "Now that I'm an editor, tell me something, you Butchers! How do I make syndicated columnists miserable?"

So much for Cissy's ex-editor whose book buried me (in Washington) with his: "Winchell never got another newspaper in Washington."

That was then. Now all of the copycats who got lucky because I got lucky, and who were in Washington, D.C., blatts when I wasn't, have been dropped. Except Grandpa.

Ed Sullivision said it best in a frank interview with the *Ladies' Home Journal* in 1967: "Walter invented the Broadway column and wrote it better than anybody. His sources of information were fantastic. You must remember that there was a time when he could move governments. Any columnist had to run in his shadow. Me included." He admitted: "Wherever I went and wanted to get—Winchell was always there ahead of me!"

That statement (and much more—all warm) started scads of my "illegitimate newspaper children" admitting the same thing.

Television's longtime star and this former foe reconciled one supper time in September 1967 in Dinty Moore's restaurant, after a thirty-five-year cat&dawg fight. Earlier in these memoirs I quoted the reason: his warm words and salute in a magazine article to this Old Enemy.

Mr. Sullivan's twentieth anniversary on TV was celebrated at The Friars Club. I was invited to sit on the dais. I wanted to make a short

319

speech. It was not delivered because my newspaper boss phoned, wanting to see me at once.

This is what I wanted to say:

> Jack Dempsey and Gene Tunney are now the best of friends. They met in the boxing ring. After forty rounds and forty years, fighters and newspaper people get to know each other better. The more I knew Ed, the easier it was to like him. He is the best competitor to like that any columnist ever had.
>
> As we both grew older, we found that we were citizens of a kingdom more beautiful than Camelot. Not a never-never-land, but a very real and magic place called Broadway. Ed Sullivan is as much a part of Broadway as Times Square, Dinty Moore's, Toots Shor's, Lindy's, Max's Stage Deli, *Variety*—and The Friars. When you all honor him tonight for his record-breaking run of over twenty-one years on the air, you also honor the newspaper craft, for which, thank you.

They call it mellowing. As I put this down, I am en route to seventy-two. Eddie will next be sixty-six. He has survived many a feud in and out of the newspaper and show biz and a decade of ulcer trouble, plus a motor car crash that almost killed him. He has also reconciled with other teevee headliners with whom he had warred—and they with him.

When we shook hands, he said, "Walter, don't ever let thirty-five years separate us again."

★

MR. AND MRS. UNITED STATES!

There was a time when Americans, looking at the horrors of Nazi Germany were alarmed. They alerted each other against fascism with the phrase "It *can* Happen Here!!" And now in 1968 it *is* happening here —with military groups . . . not militant, mind you, but armed and military gangs claiming the protection of the Bill of Rights.

Hitler did the same thing on his way to power. He used the concepts of Free Speech and Free Assembly to destroy the Democratic Republic of Germany in a shudderingly close parallel.

When the German Republic suppressed his Storm Troopers, Hitler declared that it was destroying the right of assembly. When the Nazis elected a minority to the Reichstag, that minority refused to let the

Reichstag carry on its business. They stomped, shouted, and withdrew at will—paralyzing the chamber. At the same time, they opened their real offensive—disorder in the streets, copycatting the methods used by the Kremlin.

Meanwhile, the German Communists took the same tack. The German people—who, at that time, wanted neither—were trapped between the two extremist minorities. Both the Nazis and the Reds were highly organized. The majority were not. Neither the Nazis nor the Communists stopped at murder and arson . . . in fact, both deliberately provoked riots. The unorganized majority were helpless. The German capitalists—promised protection by Hitler—poured money into the Nazi coffers.

The Nazis, calling their movement a "public political party," turned it into a highly disciplined private army. They refused to permit the Republic to function. The German Republic in desperation, though the Nazis were a minority, admitted them to a coalition government. That was the end of the Republic. The Nazis simply forced democracy at gunpoint to work itself to death.

There was a bitter joke at the time. The joke was that the peaceful majority would have stopped Hitler's Nazis but they couldn't get a police permit!

The inescapable conclusion is that the only protection of an unorganized majority is in the fearless enforcement of the law. Like the Nazis and the Communists, the Ku Klux Klan (and its like) are slugging at this Republic. Like the Communists, the Black Muslims (and their like) are doing the same act. Negro leaders (who should know better) are playing right into the paws of American Fascists. Thirty-four major American cities were subjected to rioting and fires by arsonofabitches last year.

There is no use mincing words. The streets of our cities are no longer safe. And who offers to make them safe? . . . The White Supremists. They offer the vast frightened majority of Americans "safety"—the same kind of safety offered the German people by Hitler.

For their criminal purposes one Adam Clayton Powell and one Reverend Abernathy are just what they need. Why? Because if the late Reverend King's successor, Reverend Abernathy, is allowed to stage a sit-in in Congress, why can't the Kluxers?

If Abernathy's legions can block the Capitol in the name of free assembly, why not the Klansmen? If rioters and looters of major cities are described as "a social movement," why aren't the Klan's night rides of terror the same thing?

There was another phrase used in the 1930's: "It's later than you think." It is much later in the 1960's than it was in the 1930's. The United States in the 1960's is beginning to bear an agonizingly close resemblance to the German Republic of the late 1920's. What is the answer? The answer is this simple: It is a matter of life and death to a Republic to enforce its laws.

That means the KKK leaders, the Black Muslimau-maufia, the White Minutemen, and the others attempting to divide and conquer have a common place in this Republic. And that common place is behind prison bars.

As with Germany in the 1920's, the United States in the 1960's must face the facts—and the facts are that the first line of defense of the Republic are the civilian police forces. They are defending not only their lives, and the lives of the peaceful American majority, but the life of the nation itself. In the days of the Weimar Republic there was a great sign over the Law Palace: "Justice Will Be Done, Though The Heavens Fall." Justice is not being done in the United States. The roof and the heavens are falling in.

The last poll showed that 65 percent of the American people believed that the courts were not enforcing the law. If the Gentlemen of the Bench will take their noses out of their law books long enough to look out the window and see what is happening on the streets, they will find something which should cause them some concern.

Their black robes are considered by many as the garb of undertakers —of our beautiful and wonderful country.

☆

Echo Dept. In 1968 President Nixon made headlines with "Let Us Go Forward Together!"

Franklin Delano Roosevelt said it in 1933 this way: "Together We Cannot Fail!"

☆

When you get up in years, son, you sort of stray. Memories, you know. My intimates kid me about it often. When they remind me to get back to what I was saying, I chuckle, "How's that for neat retrieving?"

Yes, you do meet many interesting people when you're a newspaperman. My many, many very lucky breaks, one after the other since I became a reporter in 1920, helped me stay around for Three Score and Ten Years.

The newspaperman enjoys a ringside pew every day and night of the week, month, and year. The newspaperman can sit at his window and

322

review the Passing Parade below. He sees everyone he likes and doesn't. He sees everyone who likes him and doesn't. Eventually they all come within his view. That's why he has the most enviable job.

He can either drop a flower. Or a flowerpot.

A GLOZZERY OF WWORD WWEDDINGS

Adam-and-Eveing it . . . going places together
Ankled up an altar . . . were married
Bologny Boulevard . . . Times Square
Bundle from Heaven . . . baby
Bundle of threads . . . girl
Chicagorilla . . . a Chicago gunman
Chewsday . . . Tuesday
Chune . . . tune
Crudd . . . a person as unimportant as the phlug you find in the corner of
    your pockets
Cupiding . . . in love
Curdled . . . ended a romance
Debutramp . . . instead of debutante
Fun Milk . . . liquor
Giggle Water . . . liquor
Go-Ghetto District . . . the Ghetto
Hard-Times Square . . . Times Square
Hardened Artery . . . Broadway
He's phluggy . . . a little silly, screwy, dumb
Imaging . . . going to have a Blessed Event
Infanticipating . . . going to have a Blessed Event
Increasing the Mom-and-Population . . . anticipating a Blessed Event
Is my face red! . . . embarrassed

324

Joining the Renobility . . . divorced in Reno
Joy Juice . . . liquor
Laughing Soup . . . liquor
Lohengrin it . . . to marry
Main Stem Femmes . . . Broadway girls
Melted . . . divorced
Merge . . . to marry
Merry Magdalens . . . chorus girls
Middle-Aisle it . . . to wed
Old Foofff . . . a pest
On Fire . . . in love
On the Merge . . . engaged
On the Verge . . . about to be divorced
Panz . . . a pansy or sissy
Parenticipating . . . anticipating a Blessed Event
Park Rowgues . . . newspapermen
Phffft . . . separated
Phlicker . . . movie
Profanuage . . . profane language
Renovated . . . divorced in Reno
Revusical . . . a revue
Rumorogues . . . gossips
Satdee . . . Saturday
Shafts . . . legs
Sealed . . . wed
Sin Den . . . nightclub
Swelegant . . . even more than elegant
A Swifty . . . a swift wisecrack
Telling It to a Judge . . . getting a divorce
Terpsichorines . . . chorus girls
That way . . . in love
The Grandest Canyon . . . Broadway
This-and-That-Way . . . on the verge of parting
Times Squareguy . . . a Broadway habitué who is on the level
Times Square . . . Broadway
Two-Times Square . . . Times Square
Uh-huh . . . plenty in love
Wildeman . . . a pansy or sissy
Wyoming Ketchup . . . liquor
Yurrop . . . Europe

INDEX

Abbandando, Dasher (Abbadabba), 198-99
Abernathy, Rev. Ralph D., 321
Adams, Franklin Pierce (F.P.A.), 42-43, 45, 61, 62
Adams, Samuel Hopkins, 168
Adler, Polly, 116
Albee, E. F., 24, 33
Alexander, Roy, 172-73, 273
Allen, Jay, 173
Allen, Robert, 256
Amberg, Pretty Boy, 115
Anastasia, Albert, 117, 183, 225
Ander, Dr., 195
Annenberg, Walter, 307-8, 318
Apfel, Gussie (Lila Lee), 12
Aristotle, 67
Arlen, Richard, 282
Arnaz, Desi, 229, 266-67, 270-72, 283
Arno, Peter, 57-58, 159
Asbury, Herbert, 85
Aster, June, see Winchell, June
Atkinson, Brooks, 174
Austin, Warren, 151

Bacon, Jim, 276
Baer, Bugs, 39, 67, 69, 102, 205
Baerwitz, Samuel, 19-20, 22
Baker, Josephine, 245-51
Baker, Phil, 48
Ball, Lucille, 57, 266-67, 272
Bankhead, Tallulah, 158, 224
Barkley, Alben, 130
Barrow, Mark, 46
Barrymore, John, 29
Barth, Belle, 157
Becker, Lt., 9
Becker, Mrs. (Lt. Becker's wife), 9
Beehler (theatrical agent), 22
Benchley, Robert C., 59-60
Benny, Jack, 88
Berger, Meyer, 117
Bergman, Ingrid, 221-24
Berkson, Seymour, 231
Berle, A. A., Jr., 126, 151, 212
Berle, Milton, 29, 234-35
Berlin, Irving, 164
Berlin, Richard E., 71, 253-54, 310, 312
Bernie, Ben, 21, 81, 164-65
Bernstein, Sholem, 198
Biederman, Lester, 60

"Big Frenchy" see De la Mange, George
Big Gus, 49
Bigman, Rose, 24, 91-92, 195, 215, 262-63, 287, 298, 315
Bilbo, Theodore G., 94, 154
Billingsley, Barbara, 301
Billingsley, Jacqueline, 301
Billingsley, Sherman, 17, 48, 72, 93, 131, 136-37, 171, 237, 247, 252, 254, 257, 262, 288, 301-2, 304, 307
Billingsley, Shermane, 301, 304-5
Bishop, Joey, 280
Bitner, Harry, 71
Blondell, Joan, 166
Boadman, Lillian, 11
Bolitho, William, 1-4
Bolton, Whitney, 304
Borah, William E., 94, 154
Borden, Lizzie, 180
Bowden, James E., 250
Breckinridge, Henry, 105
Brisbane, Arthur, 43, 78, 91, 110
Broun, Heywood, 42-45, 294
Brown, H. Rap, 243
Buchalter, Betty, 147
Buchalter, Louis "Lepke," see Lepke
Buchanan, Jack, 48
Bullitt, William C., 152
Burrows, Abe, 33, 37
Byrnes, James F., 209, 211

Caesar, Arthur, 43-44
Calloway, Cab, 245
Cambridge, Ruth, 46, 65, 82, 91
Campbell, Jeremy, 218-19
Cannon, Jimmy, 100
Cannon, John S., 236
Cantor, Eddie, 11, 69, 81
Capone, Al, 74-77
Capote, Truman, 44
Carmichael, Hoagy, 3, 259
Carmichael, Stokely, 243
Casey, Bob, 275
Castro, Fidel, 249, 251
Cermak, Anton J., 97
Chalk, O. Roy, 218, 318-19
Chamberlain, Neville, 128
Chambers, Whittaker, 149-53
Chandler, Happy, 133-34, 174-75
Chaplin, Charlie, 45
Chapman, John, 65

326

330

Quarters, Tot, 50

Rand, Sally, 101
Rankin, John E., 94, 133, 154, 160
Rapf, Harry, 18
Rascoe, Burton, 59, 61
Reagan, Ronald, 94
Reedy, George, 300
Reilly, Michael F., 179
Reiser, Dr. Sidney, 105
Reles, Abe, 183-84
Reneger, Marie, 197
Reynolds, Quentin, 174, 294
Richman, Harry, 81
Rickenbacker, Capt. Eddie, 195
Riggs, Jerry, 197
Ripley, Robert, 52-53
Roberts, Charles, 275
Roberts, Chip, 98
Roberts, Mrs. Evie, 98
Robinson, Sugar Ray, 246, 252
Rodgers, Dorothy, 262
Rodgers, Richard, 11, 181-82, 261-62
Rogers, Will, 4
Roosevelt, Anna, 186
Roosevelt, Mrs. Eleanor, 186, 215-16, 293
Roosevelt, Gen. Elliott, 178, 186-87
Roosevelt, Frank, 186-87
Roosevelt, Franklin Delano, 54, 94-98, 125-27, 151-55, 161, 164-65, 169, 178, 185-89, 192, 212-16, 293-94, 322
Roosevelt, Jimmy, 186
Roosevelt, John, 186
Rosenberg, Ruthie, 10
Rosenbloom, Jake, 183
Rosenthal, Herman, 9
Ross, Harold, 168, 170-72
Rossellini, Roberto, 221
Rosten, Leo C., 78-79
Roth, Lillian, 81
Rothstein, Arnold, 225
Rowan, Dan, 265
Ruark, Bob, 305
Rubinoff (comedian), 81
Rubinstein, Serge, 129
Ruby, Harry, 18
Ruby, Jack, 306
Runyon, Damon, 31-33, 36, 39-40, 109, 192-93, 220, 245, 261-62, 268
Runyon, Mrs. Patrice, 39

Schiff, Dorothy, 291
Schinasi, Bubbles, 134

Schine, J. Myer, 299
Schmeling, Max, 124
Schnibbe, Harry C., 162
Schoenfeld, Dr. Dudley D., 104-6, 109-10, 113
Schultheiss, Lt. Arthur, 226
Schultz, Dutch, 116-17, 122
Seed, Dave, 15
Seneca, 223
Shapiro (member, Murder, Inc.), 117
Sharpe, Violet, 109, 110
Sheen, Fulton J., 156
Sheridan, Ann, 248
Sherwood, Robert E., 97, 178
Sherwood, Roberta, 264
Shirer, William, 174
Shubert, Jake, 63
Siegel, Bugsy, 50, 117, 184, 197-98
Silverman, Sime, 71
Silvers, Lou, 11
Simon, Simone, 81
Simmons, Mr., 97
Simpson, Wally, 119
Sinatra, Frank, 278-82, 285, 300
Skolsky, Sidney, 80
Slocum, William J., 178
Smith, Al, 54
Smith, Frederick James, 123
Smith, Gerald L. K., 161, 289
Smith, Howard K., 174
Smith, Merriman, 97, 240
Snyder, Ruth, 64
Sobol, Louis, 64, 80
Sokolsky, George, 254
Solotaire, "Gentleman George," 262
Somerset, Mrs. Pat (Irene Martin) 12-13, 166
Spaatz, Carl "Toohey," 214
Spaman, Guy, 300
Stack, Philip (Don Wahn), 205-7
Stack, Robert, 282
Stalin, Joseph, 125, 150, 178, 202-4, 208-10, 212, 215-16
Stallings, Laurence, 45
Stassen, Harold, 209
Statler, Suzanne, 262
Steele, Larry, 246
Stettinius, Edward, 209, 227
Stewart, Margie, 6, 8-9
Stiles, Hinson, 145
Stowe, Leland, 124-25
Stratton, Robert, 189
Stripling, Robert, 152
Strong, William R., 107
Sullivan, Ed, 20, 39, 41, 63, 78, 80-81, 83, 90, 101-2, 262, 319-20

331